# MODI'S FOREIGN POLICY
*Challenges and Opportunities*

# MODI'S FOREIGN POLICY

## *Challenges and Opportunities*

*Editors*

N.N. Jha

Sudhir Singh

in association with

SOCIETY FOR SOCIAL EMPOWERMENT, NEW DELHI

INDIAN COUNCIL OF WORLD AFFAIRS

PENTAGON PRESS

**Modi's Foreign Policy: Challenges and Opportunities**

*N.N. Jha and Sudhir Singh (Editors)*

ISBN 978-81-8274-873-6

First Published in 2016



*Published by*
PENTAGON PRESS
206, Peacock Lane, Shahpur Jat,
New Delhi-110049
Phones: 011-64706243, 26491568
Telefax: 011-26490600
email: rajan@pentagonpress.in
website: www.pentagonpress.in

*Branch*
Flat No.213, Athena-2,
Clover Acropolis,
Viman Nagar,
Pune-411014
Email: pentagonpresspune@gmail.com

Printed at Aegean Offset Printers, Greater Noida

# Contents

# Preface

India came into being after a long struggle against one of the most powerful colonial powers of the contemporary world in 1947. The first Prime Minister of India, Jawaharlal Nehru, had two options in the immediate aftermath of independence: first, to enter into an alliance with either of the two existing blocs namely Capitalist block led by the United States and the Communist bloc led by the USSR; second, to maintain neutrality. Mr. Nehru opted for neutrality. The then international scenario had presented an extremely complex situation in the wake of cold war that was in its initial phase. Nehru's embrace of neutrality led to the emergence of Non-Aligned Movement (NAM). This decision has been under consistent attack and has been criticized on various counts about its failure towards not serving the purpose at several fronts. Nehru was abided by the Wilsonian idealism and kept the egalitarian agenda of national interests under the carpet.

Tibet issue was taken up firstly in the United Nations by Pakistan because Nehru was apprehensive if India will raise it at international platforms then China will be angry. In the 1950s Tibet was boiling and needed India's support but Nehru was optimistic that goodwill and justice will prevail to Chinese leaders and justice will be delivered to Tibetans. This was a Himalayan blunder that converted India as a weak nation for decades to come. Nehru avoided Patel's Kautilyan advice on Tibet. Few years before 1954 treaty in which Nehru surrendered Tibet to China, Sardar Patel advised Nehru not to believe China. Writing to Nehru on 7$^{th}$ November 1950, Patel warned Nehru that "China is no longer divided. It is united and strong. Recent and bitter history also tells us that communism is no shield against imperialism and that the Communism are as good or as bad imperialists as any other. Chinese ambitions in this respect not only cover the Himalayan slopes on our side but also include parts of Assam.

...Chinese irredentism or imperialism are different from the expansionism or imperialism of the western powers. The former has a cloak of ideology which makes it ten times more dangerous. In the guise of ideological expansion lie concealed radical, national or historical claims."[1]

The Chinese attack of 1962 was an ample proof of the adverse impact of that policy, when India was face to face with the situation akin to the theory of Prison Dilemma in international politics; i.e. either to seek the support of USA or should it align with USSR.

India could not have a strong international personality despite the strong legacy of promoter of peace, non-violence, and international brotherhood at the global level. The collapse of the USSR provided the possibility to India to acquire a strong international personality. Consequently, since P.V. Narsimha Rao to Modi government every successive regime has kept the agenda of national interest above the egalitarian agenda of idealism in the realm of foreign policy. The process of globalization has also been a push factor in this regard in international politics. The Pokhran-II (May 1998) further emboldened the Indian might in the realm of international politics. The whole world was compelled to concede Indian might but not as the promoter of peace but also as a power to be reckoned with, which could assert itself if necessary for protecting national interest and sustainable development.

However, the erstwhile dynamics of the international politics has taken a new turn after 11 September 2001 terrorist attack on US World trade centre. This attack has changed the whole gamut of international politics and also proved that even the US is not safe vis-à-vis terrorist attacks. This also challenged the US claim to unipolarity in the world. The advent of multi-polarity in international politics has provided a new impetus to the emergence of India as one of the dominant pole. At the same time it has left many challenges for the formulators of foreign policy to cope and respond adequately to the changing circumstances.

Since its inception Indian foreign policy has been obsessed with Pakistan and China. We have fought three and half wars with Pakistan by now and one war with our northern neighbour China. It is also true that Pakistan has been partially successful towards making India bleed at thousand places since the defeat of 1971 war. Not only in Punjab, Kashmir but also throughout India they have been creating troubles. In the backdrop of NATO withdrawal from Afghanistan, the threat of terror has increased. Consequently, in contemporary world Indian policy-makers have to achieve many important goals to transform India into a dominant power in the international system. All these development makes it imperative for Indian policy-makers to reformulate the contours of foreign policy. The first challenge before the policy-makers is to decentralize the focus (Pakistan and China) of erstwhile foreign policy and articulate the national interest in broader perspectives of changing international scenario. There are many arenas in the globe which has remained away from the radar of our foreign policy. Prime Minister Modi visited Australia, Fiji, Sri Lanka and Canada within first year of his rule and the important fact is that since the last three decades not a single Prime Ministerial visit has taken place in these countries despite their enormous importance in the pursuance of our national interests. Right from its inception in 1991 not a single PM has visited all 5 countries of Central Asia which PM Modi has visited within a week together in July 2015. Central Asia is extremely important for the promotion of our national interests. Energy security is of utmost importance. Kazakhstan, Turkmenistan and Uzbekistan are endowed with enormous hydrocarbon reserves. Two of these countries Kazakhstan and Turkmenistan are in the Caspian littorals, thereby promising to open the door to other energy rich Caspian states. Connectivity through the North-South Transport Corridor featured in Modi's speeches in both countries as much as the impending implementation of the two gas pipelines. These are implementable but hinges on the political situation in Pakistan and Afghanistan.[2.] After nuclear deal Iran could be an important facilitator of our interests in Central Asia. PM has visited entire Central Asia and pledged a lot, now it is the time to implement possible assurances to promote our national interests.

India had organised Africa Summit at New Delhi in October 2015; perhaps it was maiden larger gathering of African leaders in 21st century after March 1947 Afro-Asia summit at New Delhi. In the backdrop of growing importance of Africa due to abundance of natural resources and engagements of important global powers, it is a Himalayan step to engage Africa in a massive way. It is an open secret that energy security remains core of the saga of our growth and needless to say that Africa could be a good source of energy security in coming decades.

Till the end of the cold war, our foreign policy formulators have been obsessed with Pakistan and later on China. These countries have importance for us but we must realize that we have already emerged as an important Asian power and contesting hard as a global power. For the realization of our global power status we must decentralize our focal attention towards all regions of the globe. Modi government has understood this reality and acting with this vision. Till August 2015, just within 13 months in power, Prime Minister has already visited over 21 countries covering four continents. Senior and Junior foreign ministers have visited countries of all continents.

Since the days of Kautilaya maximization of national interest has remained the sole concern of bilateral relationship. There are no permanent friends or foes in international politics and the only permanent thing is commonality of interests.

Narasimha Rao government initiated "Look East Policy". India is well connected with its immediate neighbour Southeast Asia on various counts.

Buddhism is one of the prominent religions of this region that has its origin in India. There are enough commonalities in the field of culture too. However, there still remains a tremendous scope for more economic, technological and cultural cooperation between India and nation-states of Southeast Asia. Our relationship with ASEAN countries has a huge imprint on our overall foreign policy. Modi government has converted 'Look East Policy' into 'Act East Policy' and extended it to East Asia as well.

China is concerned of India's look east policy and calls it as being borne out of a misguided "fear of China", reflecting "a lack of understanding of the (Peoples Liberation Army's) PLA's strategic ambitions."[3]

Compliance of the norms of international law has remained core concern of ASEAN and East Asian countries in South and East China Sea. China has declared both Seas as their backyard lakes and unwilling to obey the norms on UNCLOS (1982). Despite high profile trade relations with China, ASEAN and East Asian countries are concerned very much for the compliance of international laws in this dispute. The Philippines is also a disputant country against China over South China Sea. Its President's concern about it is worth mentioning here.

"The Philippines is one of the disputant countries against China over South China Sea. Philippines President Benigno S. Aquino III called for nations around the world to do more to support the Philippines in resisting China's assertive claims to the seas near his country, drawing a comparison to the West's failure to support Czechoslovakia against Hitler's demands for Czech land in 1938.

Like Czechoslovakia, the Philippines face demands to surrender territory piecemeal to a much stronger foreign power and needs more robust foreign support for the rule of international law if it is to resist.

If we say yes to something we believe is wrong now, what guarantee is there that the wrong will not be further exacerbated down the line?" he said. "At what point do you say, 'Enough is enough'? Well, the world has to say it—remember that the Sudetenland was given in an attempt to appease Hitler to prevent World War II.[4] Tokyo and Manila are even more expressive about their willingness to uphold territorial claims, no matter the cost. On many occasions, Abe has vowed publicly that he will 'never make concessions' over the sovereignty of the Diaoyus/Sankakus and will defend 'Japanese territory at all costs."[5]

South China Sea has become a bone of contention between China and the disputant countries of ASEAN. It has emerged as potential global flashpoints. The Nation of Bangkok warns in an editorial that:

> "If the current tension continues in South China Sea, especially between the Philippines and China, it could lead to an all-out war. This is not

> an alarmist's warning but a real concern. With poisonous rhetoric and growing tension, there is a possibility that conflicting parties would cross the line. This could be a result of miscalculation".[6]

Chinese behaviour in the backdrop of their acquisition of economic power has become unruly which is bound to create conflicts. China wanted to dominate Asia as America is dominating the globe but wanted multiple power structures at the global level. For Mearsheimer, rising powers tend to seek regional hegemony and China is heading in this direction.[7] The Chinese have refused to be adhered by international law to resolve South China Sea and East China Sea dispute with ASEAN and Japan respectively. In case of Tibet too, China has violated all norms of the international standards to respect human rights. To vindicate the prevailing situation in the Asia-Pacific the following statement of the Philippines President is self-explanatory

> "If we say yes to something we believe is wrong now, what guarantee is there that the wrong will not be further exacerbated down the line?" he said. "At what point do you say, 'Enough is enough'? Well, the world has to say it—remember that the Sudetenland was given in an attempt to appease Hitler to prevent World War II."[8] In the backdrop of changing security architecture in Asia, deepening Indo-Japan bonhomie is interesting. India-Japan relations have grown phenomenally since Pokhran-2 (1998) and due to convergences of interests have emerged as an asset for India particularly in East Asia and rest of Asia in general. Modi government has upgraded zero sum game policy with China. For that purpose Japan has emerged as a golden asset for India. In his August-September 2014 Japan visit, PM Modi and Japanese PM Shinzo Abe proved that they have immense convergences and are bound to cooperate. Chinese are extremely jealous from this deepening relationship. The growing bonhomie between United States and India has created a situation akin of 'Prisoner's Dilemma' for China. During the Cold War era India-United States relations were termed as 'Estranged Democracies' that has been again expressed as "Engaged Democracies' in the 21st century. President George W. Bush (2000–8) contributed immensely to cement these ties.

President Bush and his Indian interlocutors were careful not to define their relations in terms of opposition to China. Bush's surprising warmth to India, his willingness to invest huge political capital in transforming the bilateral relationship, and his courageous decision to facilitate nuclear energy trade with India were widely interpreted as driven by a desire to make India a counterweight to a rising China. While there were no official proclamations to this effect, a key architect of Bush's India policy, Robert Blackwill, would later reveal the centrality of the China factor. "President George W. Bush based his transformation of US-India Relations on the core strategic principle of democratic India as a key factor in balancing the rise of Chinese power," he noted. He made it clear that this was not based on the concept of 'containing' China. Nonetheless, Blackwill added, without this China factor at the fore 'the Bush Administration would not have negotiated the Civil Nuclear Agreement and the Congress would not have approved it.'[9]

During President Barrack Obama's tenure (2009–16) the Bush era's warmth has declined a bit but again it is improving in the second half of his tenure. The warmth President Obama has shown during PM Modi's visit in September 2014 is self-explanatory. China has been extremely jealous of this cooperation among democracies. President Obama became maiden U.S. president to visit India twice and also first to become chief guest for Republic Day functions in January 2015. The Chinese became jealous of Obama's New Delhi visit.

Democracy has become an instrument of fear for the Chinese especially after 1989 student movement in Beijing. Chinese have adopted Globalization in 1978 but forgotten that it has two components and without freedom it will not be sustainable for a longer period of time. Chinese think otherwise and always apprehensive that success of democracy near their border may facilitate the wind of democracy in China as well. Coincidently majority of ASEAN countries, United States, Japan, Australia and India all have adopted democracy as a way of governance.

Global Times, the mouth piece of Chinese regime had expressed this frustration in December 2010. "'The title of "the biggest democratic nation" looks like a glass of red wine enjoyed together by India and the West. But it doesn't generate anything substantial that is of India's national interests. With a huge population and much work left to be done in developing the economy, perhaps India won't get too drunk to act superior in front of China, because such superiority will delight India much less than it delights the West.' See who wins the Dragon-elephant contention".[10]

Australia is also close to this region and the relations between India and Australia has been smooth thus far, but scope is there for further deepening. PM Modi visited Australia in November 2014 after a gap of 28 years and this visit has further deepened the relationship.

China has emerged a critical foreign policy challenges for India. Despite high profile trade, trust deficit is prevailing between India and China. China has blocked UN move to corner Mumbai terror attack (2008) fountainhead Lakhvi in July 2015. During BRICS & SCO summit in Ufa, Russia (July 2015) PM

Modi had expressed his concern to Chinese President. In recent years China has clubbed its Pakistan policy with India policy. Since 2006 every South Asia visiting Chinese leader compulsorily visits Islamabad.[11] India demanded that China respect India's 'core national interests' in relation to its territorial integrity, in much the same way that Delhi defers to Beijing on Tibet and Taiwan. This new equivalence between Tibet and Kashmir marks a new moment in the long-running territorial disputes between India and China.[12] Weeks before September 2014 Chinese President's India visit, foreign minister Sushma Swaraj demanded that Beijing must respect Indian sensitiveness if it wishes that New Delhi will reciprocate.

Despite the fact that Pakistan is the China's best weather friend, Chinese policy towards India and Pakistan is quite interesting. China has understood that growing Indian profile at the global level has provided new phillip to their calibre of diplomacy. China is concerned that India should not be part and parcel of western block led by the United States. In July 2015, SCO Ufa meeting therefore China has not blocked India's full membership. But weeks before helped Pakistan at the UN on Lakhvi issue to just keep it in a good mood. We have to understand this duality of 'Prisoner's Dilemma' in Chinese behaviour. This is all set to be sustainable in a foreseeable future.

General Zia-ul-Haq started to use militancy as an instrument of Pakistan's foreign policy and till date it has been remained sustainable. Right from the commencement of 'Operation Enduring Freedom' Pakistan has remained the recipient of largest largesse from the United States due to its participation in 'global war against terror'. Despite that it gave safe havens to Osama Bin Laden and Mullah Omar. More importantly, as the senior most US military officer in 2011, Admiral Mike Mullen, told the US Congress, the Haqqani network is a "veritable arm of the Pakistan's Inter-Services Intelligence Agency."[13] Pakistani military has sustained the unique Afghan policy since 1979 not to stabilize Afghanistan and use it as rear base. In December 2014, NATO forces have withdrawn from Afghanistan. New Afghan President, Ashraf Ghani has taken some conciliatory steps to garner Pakistani support for peace but since 2009 every year more than 2500 innocent people have killed and Pakistani invisible hands are responsible for these deadly attacks. Combined right from 2009 till July 2015, 16,874 people have been killed in terror related violence.[14] Right from January 2015 to July 2015 4, 921 people have been killed which is self-explanatory. President Ghani showed his will to cooperate with Pakistan but increasing number of casualties has forced him to change his mind. Afghan President Ashraf Ghani lambasted Pakistan on Monday over a recent wave of insurgent attacks in the capital Kabul that killed at least 56 people. "The last few days have shown that suicide bomber training camps and bomb-producing factories which are killing our people are as active as before in Pakistan," Ghani told a news conference.

"We hoped for peace but we are receiving messages of war from Pakistan.[15] President Ghani is now aware about the core motives of Pakistan. Now India along with likeminded countries like Iran, Russia, United States, Central Asian Republics, China must take every steps to stabilize Afghanistan.

Pakistan has always been a non-entity for India on almost all counts. Despite consistent Pakistani cross-border support to all shades of anti-social activities in India through ISI nurtured non-state actors, India has revealed tremendous courage, patience and success towards managing the same and this vindicates the fact that Indian capability has enormously increased. Under Modi government it is the need of the hour to keep Pakistan engaged even when it is an open secret that no tangible results are awaited. It will help Indian expansion as responsible global power.

With China, which has remained India's second obsession, in spite of border problems both the countries have been converging towards building positive relations and they are now engaged constructively in economic exchange. Despite the legacy of hatred the Chinese have understood the basic fact that in post-9/11 world system the US is hell bent to encircle China and for that purpose India could be of immense importance. Given this reality in the changing parameters of the international system, the Chinese are quite intelligent to understand that they are required to keep India into good humour. During Kargil conflict both Prime Minister and Chief of Army Staff of Pakistan visited Beijing to garner Chinese support which they not only declined but even suggested Pakistan that they could enter into dialogue with India for an ultimate solution of all outstanding issues including Kashmir. In addition, China has already conceded that Sikkim is an integral part of India and established trade links with historic silk route passing through the Nathu La Pass and connecting Tibet. Mansarover yatra has also started from 2015 through Nathula in the backdrop of Prime Minister Modi's May 2015 Beijing visit. India-China had around $5 billion bilateral trade in the mid-1990s but by the fiscal year of 2014-15 it has around $ 70 billion. Although huge trade balance in favour of China has remained unpleasant for India. The Sino-Indian border problem still remains unresolved but dialogue is going on to find a solution to the same. During PM Vajpayee's June 2003 Beijing visit it was agreed that national security adviser from both sides will lead their respective delegations to resolve the border dispute. But till August 2015, despite 18 rounds of high-voltage meetings, no progress has been made.

The evolution of post-9/11 world order has brought about tremendous changes in the international system which has necessitated an overhauling and reformulation of foreign policy of almost all important countries of the world so that they can respond to emerging new challenges. In this rapidly changing international scenario, traditional geo-politics has given way to the logic of geo-economics. Every important nation is keen to improve upon their economic profile in spite of bickering in relations at the bilateral level. The US–China, China-Japan, ASEAN-China and Sino-Indian relations are classic examples of this argument. Both the US and China have variety of differences but their economic relations are surging ahead. In recent years despite border disputes, India and China are also engaging and courting each other to enhance their geo-economic relations. There are some other important areas in this changing international scenario, which has led to certain changes in traditional contents of India's foreign policy.

First is the energy security. Currently India is the 5$^{th}$ largest consumer of energy. It has been estimated that India would be among top three developed countries of the World in 2030 and would be at number three in terms of energy consumer superseding Russia and Japan. This expanding economy needs more energy and therefore it is needless to say that it needs to reformulate the whole energy policy keeping this reality in mind. We are geographically closer to the major sources of energy. Traditional means of transporting energy has given way to technology driven energy transfer where local, regional and international politics plays a greater role in the energy market. India requires rethinking in next 5 decades how it could ensure energy security for itself. Of course, India could develop its domestic means of energy but it need to exploit external sources of energy and that requires fundamental reformulation into policies towards energy rich countries of the world.

Another important sector is Diaspora, which emerges as an important factor into post-cold war international politics. We have around 35-40 million Diaspora across the globe. Majority among them are settled into the powerhouse of the international system (western world) and emerged as an important determinant factor into the formulation of their respective countries foreign policies. The post-9/11 scenario has provided a new opportunity for India to exploit the situation. In last financial year (2014–5) our Diaspora has sent $70 billion as remittances pushing China into third place. At the same time it is an open secret that we have not been adequately successful to safeguard the basic interest of our Diaspora, which we need to focus with our increasing profile into international system. Diaspora is not only contributing enormously into our sustainable sound financial health but additionally they are brilliant unpaid Ambassadors of our interest situated at the powerhouse of the international system. We need to strengthen this component of our foreign policy.

Maritime security has emerged as an important field of study in the emerging paradigm of foreign policy. Indian Ocean is an important ocean where over 80 per cent global trade is traversing. Our economy is expanding and this sustainability needs more energy consumption and for that purpose we have to ensure maritime security. It has been said that whosoever has dominated Indian Ocean has dominated Asia therefore we must take every possible steps for the strengthening of our maritime security. China has announced $40 billion 'maritime silk route' policy. The basic intent of this policy has been to contain India in the Indian Ocean region. It is also following 'string of parleys' policy within South Asia against India. We have to reformulate our policies to cope up these situations.

Science and technology sector is an important sector in which India has done marvellous progress. It has provided us scope to engage more and more countries. Right from newly emerged Central Asian Republics to poverty-ridden African countries, India has tremendous scope to support their developmental work especially in the field of science and technology.

India has immense soft power leverage in Asia-Pacific in particular and rest of globe in general. Earlier we had only soft power, now we have adequate hard power at our disposal. With the combination of soft and hard power India could achieve unique position in Asia-Pacific which is all set to replace as the custodian of global power in coming decades.

Since inception Indian foreign policy has been obsessed with idealism which into the realm of international politics is bound to fail. India needs to reformulate the whole contours of its foreign policy. We must not get obsessed with Pakistan and China and must decentralize our attention across the globe and every region of the planet must be under our focus. There is no permanence in international relations; the only thing which is permanent is commonality of interests. Nearly 2300 years back, the brilliant Indian scholar, Kautilaya insisted on this point in an excellent manner in his seminal book 'Arthshastra'. It is pertinent and relevant even today than his lifetime and we need to incorporate it as the main determinant of our foreign policy.

Indian democracy has developed remarkably in comparison with democracies which came into being after the end of the Second World War. We have made tremendous progress at domestic level. But at the political level India has not made much progress as still for the electoral benefit political parties keep opposing or supporting foreign policy issues as per their electoral interests. This is not a healthy trend. Political parties need to reformulate their behaviour with the view that they have no difference on basic features of foreign policy and of course successive government needs to keep political parties more engaged in the process of the formulation of foreign policy. We must take some lesson from western democracies, where changing of governments has very minimal impact on the priorities of their foreign policy.

In western world, the academic community has been part and parcel of the formulation of foreign policy and that needs to replicate into our case too. The increasing profile of India at global level has also put us into delicate situation and to cope with the situation we need to engage this class into the decision making process. The intellectual communities are aware about the nitty gritty of the foreign policy than the carrier diplomats and there is a strong need of their synergy for the protection and promotion of our national interests.

Since independence Indian foreign policy has been guided by certain cardinal principles. Prime among them is 'third world unity'. This was one of the basic determinants of our foreign policy. Although in post-cold war scenario, India has acquired enormous prestige at the international level. But with this ratio Indian engagement has not increased with the third world countries. We have been under various colonial regimes for centuries and they have exploited us blatantly and so is the case of the third world countries. Without empowering the suffering of humanities of those countries, we could not establish justice based international system. Fortunately, we have acquired tremendous development in science and technology sector. We need to develop those hapless countries with our technological expertise and thus cement the basic unity among third world countries. This would be an important contribution towards the establishment of justice based international system and in the restoration of multi-polar international system as well.

Another important determinant of Indian foreign policy has been decentralization of power structure into the international bodies including the United Nations. In 1945 when the UN came into being, permanent membership was extended to only to five countries. At the outset of 21$^{st}$ century the power dynamics of the international system has changed in a dramatic manner. There is an urgent need to decentralize the UN system and the incorporation of five or ten more permanent members into the Security Council to ensure democracy within its structure. India's candidature to the Security Council as the permanent member is the strongest one. India needs to shape its UN policies to cope up these challenges.

The contemporary world is confronting many turbulent issues, which has posed severe challenges for the survival of humanity. Climate Change is one of the most serious among them. The developed countries have damaged the environment through their industrial waste and excessive material life style but they have not done adequate arrangements for the safeguards. Now the whole humanity is confronting the challenges posed by the climate change. It is estimated that if corrective measures are not taken with immediate effect, sea level will enhance and all low lands will submerge. Additionally this change will create many problems and could escalate conflicts therefore there is strong need to explore the matter seriously. Our foreign policy must take it as one of the immediate priorities because our neighbourhood is going to be submerged. The developed countries that have contributed enormously to create this situation must contribute generously into the corrective measures. Likewise eradication of poverty, removal of illiteracy and prevention of drug abuse and trafficking and HIV/AIDS are working as the push factor of conflicts throughout the world therefore international community must take it as serious challenges.

These are the broader issues that have been widely covered through different articles included in this book. The book is intended to provide an intellectual input to the formulators of the foreign policy to cope with the changing international system. We hope that this book will be of some use to all stake holders of the foreign policy, and at least to offer a wider spectrum to the students of foreign policy.

**Nagendra Nath Jha**

**Sudhir Singh**

## NOTES

1. Guha, Ramchandra, *India After Gandhi: The History of the World's Largest Democracy*, Macmillan, London, 2007, p.169.
2. P.L. Dash, "When Central Asia Calls", *The Indian Express*, New Delhi, July 27, 2015.
3. Dai Bing, "India and China s great game in full swing", China Internet Information Center, October 22, 2010. Stable URL:- http://www.china.org.cn/opinion/2010-10/22/content_21181802.htm Accessed on January 8, 2011.
4. Keith Bradsher, Philippine Leader Sounds Alarm on China, *New York Times*, New York, February 5, 2014.
5. Teddy Ng,' Shinzo Abe Slams Beijing "Provocations" on Island Tour *South China Morning Post*, Hong Kong, 18 July 2013.
6. "Temperatures rising in the South China Sea", *The Nation*, Bangkok, 28 May 2012.
7. Mearsheimer, John J. China's Unpeaceful Rise, *Current History*, 2006, 105 (690), p. 161.
8. Keith Bradsher, Philippine Leader Sounds Alarm on China, *New York Times*, New York, February 5, 2014.
9. Robert Blackwill, The Future of US-India Relations, Address to the Confederation of Indian Industry, New Delhi, May 5, 2009, available at http://www.stratpost.com/the-future-of-us-indiarelations- blackwill accessed on January 9, 2011.
10. Global Times, December 16, 2010, available at http://opinion. globaltimes.cn/editorial/2010-12/602061.html accessed on January 10, 2011.
11. Xinjiang has been boiling since last few years and emerged as bleeding grounds of China. It is an open secret that all Non State Actors of Pakistan has extended its support to this movement. Despite this serous factor since 2006 every Chinese leaders (President, PM) while

visiting India visiting Pakistan also. In September 2014, Chinese President could not visit Islamabad due to ongoing unrest in Islamabad.

12. Pranab Dhal Samanta, India equates Jammu & Kashmir with Tibet, *The Indian Express*, November 15, 2010, available at http://www.indianexpress.com/news/india-equates-jammu-&-kashmir-withtibet/ 711151/ accessed on January 11, 2011.
13. C. Raja Mohan, "After Mullah Omar", *The Indian Express*, New Delhi, August 4, 2015
14. "2014 among deadliest years in AF with 10k civilian casualties", *The Times of India*, New Delhi, August 9, 2015.
15. "Ashraf Ghani slams Pakistan over recent Kabul attacks", *Dawn*, Karachi, August 10, 2015.

# Acknowledgements

The Balance of Power at the global level has changed in a dramatic manner since the end of the cold war. This situation has provided a unique opportunity for India to garner maximum benefits out of this situation. Since the end of the cold war, successive Indian governments have changed their policies to cope with the emerging situations. The Narendra Modi led NDA-2 government has adopted a proactive foreign policy. The Society for Social Empowerment had organized a national seminar about this theme in the University of Kerala in December 2014.

We are extremely grateful to the Indian Council of World Affairs, New Delhi, for their kind support to our efforts. Countless number of people contributed to this process and we are grateful for them as well. At the same time, we are grateful to the contributors, three among them are from abroad.

We would again like to express our appreciation to all the people who have contributed in this endeavour. Finally, we are also thankful to the Pentagon Press for their hard work and dedication to bring out this volume within time.

**N.N. Jha**

**Sudhir Singh**

# About the Contributors

Dr. Alok Gupta is Associate Professor, Central University of Bihar, Gaya, Bihar.

Dr. Alokka Dutta is Associate Professor, Bhagini Nivedita College , University of Delhi.

Dr. Amulya Kr. Tripathi is Associate Professor, Behrampur University, Orrisa.

Prof. A.P.S. Chouhan is Dean, School of Politics, Jiwaji Univeristy, Gwalior.

Dr. Bibhuti Bhusan Biswas is Assistant Professor, Central University of Jharkhand, Ranchi.

Dr. Chandra Mohan Upadhaya is Associate Professor, Kisan P.G. College, Bahraich, Uttar Pradesh.

Dr. Deepak Yadav is Assistant Professor, Kalindi College, University of Delhi, New Delhi.

Prof. D. Gopal is Dean, School of Social Sciences, IGNOU, New Delhi.

Dr Geetha Govindasamy, Senior Lecturer, Department of East Asian Studies, University of Malaya, Malaysia.

Jayshree Tandekar, Research Scholar, Centre for International Politics, Organization and Disarmament , School of International Studies, Jawaharlal Nehru University, New Delhi.

Dr. K. Jayaprasad is Associate Professor, Department of International Relations, Central University of Kerala, Kasaragod.

Dr. Koushiki Dasgupta is Assistant Professor, University of Gour Banga, West Bengal.

Dr. Mohar Chakravorty is Assistant Professor in Political Science in South Calcutta Girls' College, Calcutta University, Kolkata.

Nazmul Arifeen is Research Officer at Bangladesh Institute of International and Strategic Studies (BIISS), Dhaka, Bagladesh.

Dr. Pranav Kumar is Assistant Professor, Central University of South Bihar, Gaya.

Dr. Pramod Kumar Sharma is ICSSR Post Doctorate Fellow, School of International Studies, Jawaharlal Nehru University, New Delhi.

Rakhee Viswambharan, Assistant Professor & Head, Department of Political Science, Sree Narayana College, Chempazhanthy, Thiruvananthapuram, Kerala.

Rayeesunisa, Research Scholar – (FDP), Centre for South and Southeast Asian Studies, University of Madras, Chennai.

Prof. R.F.I. Smith, Adjunct Professor, School of Management, RMIT University, Melbourne, Australia.

Dr. Roshini Kujur is Assistant Professor, Behrampur University, Orrisa.

Dr. Sabu Thomas is Assistant Professor, Post Graduate Department of Political Science Government College Madappally, Calicut, Kerala.

Salu D'Souza is associated with Diaspora Center, Central University of Gujarat, Ahmedabad.

Sayna, V.V. is Research Scholar, Pondicherrey Central University.

Dr. Sumit Kumar is ICSSR Doctoral Fellow, UGC Centre for Southern Asia Studies, Pondicherrey Central University.

Dr. Suresh R is Associate Professor & Hon. Director, V K Krishna Menon Study Centre for International Relations, Department of Political Science, University of Kerala, Kariavattom, Thiruvananthapuram, Kerala.

Dr. Sudhir Singh is Assistant Professor, Dyal Singh College, University of Delhi, New Delhi.

Prof. S. Manivasakan is the Director, Centre for the South and Southeast Asian Studies, University of Madras, Chennai.

Prof. Tridib Chakraborti , Department of International Relations, Jadavpur University, Kolkata and former ICCR Chair Professor, Dublin City University, Dublin, Ireland.

Unnikrishnan G. is Research Scholar, Department of Political Science, University of Kerala, Trivandrum

Prof. Y. Yagama Reddy (Retd.), Centre for Southeast Asian & Pacific Studies, Sri Venkateswara University, Tirupati.

Commodore R.S. Vasan Indian Navy (Retd), Director Chennai Centre for China Studies and Head Strategy and Security Studies, Center for Asia Studies, Chennai.

# 1

# India's Foreign Policy towards Nepal: NDA-II Accomplishments and Opportunities

*Alok Kumar Gupta*

Prime Minister Narendra Modi spelled out his vision for India in his Independence Day address on August 15, 2014, from the ramparts of Red Fort. Since then he has made a visit to Nepal, Bhutan, Bangladesh and Sri Lanka in the neighbourhood alongside other countries of the world. Nepal is the only country where the PM has made two visits. His pro-activeness is suggestive enough of making a concerted effort at improving relations with the neighbours and undercut the entrenching Chinese influence in the region before it is too late. However, such visits have attracted mixed reactions from across the political spectrum.

India's foreign policy stands during the UPA regime raised many pertinent issues. Prima facie it seems that it was gross miscalculations on part of India's diplomatic community in many cases while conducting its relations with other countries and especially with its neighbours. India has always been cautious of her international personality among the comity of nations and has been craving for a role to be reckon with in different parts of the world so that it has its own say as well as a strong personality in the emerging world order; more so when she is aspiring for a permanent birth at the Security Council. India also realizes that it has to carve out a space for itself both in the neighbourhood as well as in other parts of the world to maximize its national economic interests.

However, India's aspirations have not been matching her actions and stands, on issues which may have a great bearing upon international relations and the emerging world order. Accordingly, it makes it imperative to explore as to why India is failing on most occasions to make necessary and befitting interventions to maximise upon its national interests. Whether in its neighbourhood or in other regions of the world, India seems to have been lacking an apt response to the political development and maximise upon its national interests.

India cannot afford to miscalculate especially in case of small nation-states, which are right under its belly and a potent turf for Chinese strategic game plan. The Chinese growing their presence within the courtyard of the Indian sub-continent is a matter of serious strategic concern. India requires adopting a neo-realist understanding of regional political development as well as a neo-liberal approach of larger and broader engagement of her South Asian neighbours to keep the Chinese at bay. It is in this backdrop that this paper intends to explore the accomplishments and opportunities of NDA-II Government in Nepal. Nepal undoubtedly is a potent economic investment destination for India. Therefore, its strategic importance both from the viewpoint of political and economic security as well as opportunity cannot be turned a Nelson's eye.

There is hardly any doubt that when Prime Minister Modi assumed the office he had little experience in the arena of Foreign Policy. However, he revealed his determination to take charge and steer the course of India's foreign policy from the day he took oath. He did not come out with any doctrine in foreign policy, rather he chose to become pro-active, which came to define his nimble foreign policy approach.[1]

## The Backdrop

India's policy towards its small neighbours has not been altogether a successful one, which could be said to be in tune with India's national interest. Several reasons are responsible for the same. Pakistan and its continued disturbance in Kashmir take away most of India's energy. On the Tamil issue India almost intervened in the internal matters of Sri Lanka. The 1990 economic blockade against Nepal brought untold sorrows to the erstwhile kingdom in addition to their uneasiness over several unequal bilateral treaties with India. The landlocked Bhutan's excessive dependence on India and its sovereignty question, and Bangladesh's unhappiness over the construction of Farakka Barrage on the river Ganga, sharing of Teesta waters and the failure of the long pending Land Boundary Agreement (LBA) were the stumbling blocks in the road of India's bilateral relationship and understanding.[2] Therefore, despite India's growing clout in the region, it has always been challenging to keep immediate neighbours in good humour. This is the situation in spite of the fact that India has always made efforts at having close cooperative ties with these neighbours. According to some scholars this is due to India's overestimation; whereas others attribute this to extraneous factors, i.e. growing Chinese influence in the region. Undoubtedly, China has been quite successful towards befriending these immediate neighbours of India. However, there is also the counterview that it is the smartness of these small neighbours that they are benefitting from both the powers by pitting one against the other. Therefore, the prevailing situation of India's relationships with neighbours in general, and Nepal in particular, presents a backdrop that is quite challenging and hence NDA-II has to strategize India's foreign policy in a manner that it is able to keep its neighbours in good humour undercutting China and also managing good and healthy relations with China. Prima facie it may seem a herculean task, but is achievable given the quantitative and qualitative superiority of diplomatic community in India.

## Neighbourhood First

This is a phrase which was coined by the Modi-led NDA-II government. It was explained by Minister for External Affairs Sushma Swaraj as 'forging good relations with neighbouring countries' and hailed it as Modi's 'fast-track' diplomacy. As stated above, Narendra Modi even before becoming Prime Minister had revealed that his foreign policy will actively focus on improving ties with India's immediate neighbours. Accordingly, he commenced his innings by inviting all heads of the State/Government of South Asian countries in his Oath Taking Ceremony. He also held bilateral talks with those leaders on the successive day in his office, which was described in Indian media as "mini SAARC Summit". During the launch event at ISRO he asked Indian scientists to take the endeavour to develop a dedicated SAARC satellite to share the fruits of the technology like tele-medicine, e-learning, etc., with the people across South Asia to complement the currently operating Indian Technical and Economic Cooperation Programme in the region.[3]

Accordingly, in consonance with his promise, immediately after assuming the office Modi made a visit to Bhutan, Nepal, Sri Lanka, Bangladesh and many other countries of the world. The commencement of his visit with Bhutan and other neighbours speaks volumes about his intent as to the kind of value accorded by his government to India's smaller neighbours. Pursuant to his visit the way Modi signed agreements and reached understandings with the leadership in Nepal and Bhutan on different contentious bilateral issues showed his sense of urgency in dealing with India's small but important neighbours. Sushma Swaraj too visited 11 countries within a span of 100 days (including Bangladesh, Nepal, and Bhutan) to improve upon India's relations with these countries.

Modi further held bilateral meetings with his counterparts from Bangladesh, Nepal and Sri Lankan President on the side-lines of the Session of General Assembly of the United Nations in September 2014. He made emphatic efforts at strengthening SAARC as a strong regional block and also to improve bilateral ties.

## NDA-II towards Nepal

The biggest challenge before Nepal has been to carefully calibrate its relations with its giant neighbours and not rush headlong into confronting or provoking either China or India. However, both China and India compete with each other to wean away Nepal. Every new government immediately become conscious of the prevailing geopolitical reality the moment it gets into office. Modi, thus became the first Indian Prime Minister in the last 17 years to visit Nepal, on August 3-4, 2014, to commence a new beginning. His visit was termed as 'historic' for focussing on 4Cs—cooperation, connectivity, culture and constitution—to enhance bilateral ties. Indian media was quite euphoric about his visit and claimed that Modi had won hearts and minds of Nepal's people. He met not only with the ruling political leadership but also string of Opposition leaders from Maoists to Royalists. Mr. Modi met Unified Communist Party of Nepal (Maoist) Chairman Prachanda and Pro-Monarchy Rashtriya Prajatantra Party (Nepal) leader Kamal Thapa.[4]

Modi in his speech to Nepal's Parliament made efforts to efface the existing image of India that it is good at committing but slow at keeping the commitment. There were concerns regarding delays in project execution and Modi affirmed them that the present dispensation in India will be different from the past. India also promised Rs. 25 crore for the renovation and restoration of the 17$^{th}$ century structure of Pashupatinath Temple. He tried to forge a new relation with a 'new chapter' in bilateral relations, which was to serve as a model and catalyst for regional partnership in future.

Modi also flagged off the Kathmandu–Delhi Passenger Bus Service 'Pashupatinath Express'. Necessary modalities were then being worked out to operate the bus service on either daily or on alternate day basis. Kathmandu–Varanashi and Pokhara–Lucknow bus services are also on the anvil. India also signed an MoU and agreed to fund the cost of about INR 550 Crores towards construction of the National Police Academy at Panauti, located approximately 32 km South East of Kathmandu.[5] India extended at a concessional rate of interest of one percent a Line of Credit (LoC) of USD 1 billion to Government of Nepal from EXIM Bank which will be utilized for hydropower, irrigation and infrastructural development projects. India also signed MoU seeking to strengthen, promote and develop cooperation in the field of traditional systems of medicine and medical plants between the two countries on the basis of equality and mutual benefit.[6]

India being the largest source of tourists coming to Nepal both countries sought to enhance cooperation in the tourism and hospitality industry and also entered into detailed MoU and agreed to establish a Joint Working Group to implement the same. Both the countries also entered into an MoU on twinning arrangements between Kathmandu-Varanashi, Janakpur-Ayodhya and Lumbini-Bodhgaya as sister cities. It shall help in promoting cultural exchange, sharing of knowledge and expertise as well as develop stronger people-to-people relations among them. The Ministry of Youth Affairs and Sports, GoI, and Ministry of Sports and Youth Affairs, GoN, aims to facilitate youth exchanges between India and Nepal, such as young politicians, entrepreneurs, doctors, journalists, and teachers, sportspersons, and youth festivals. The objective is exchange of programmes, experiences, skills, techniques, information and knowledge in the areas of youth affairs. PM was also a witness to the signing of the Project Development Agreement (PDA) for the 900 MW Arun-III by SJVN and GoN. During PM's visit Nepal Bharat Maitrigency and Trauma Centre in Kathmandu was also inaugurated which has been estimated to be built at a cost of Rs 100 crores. PM handed over one Dhruv Advanced Light Helicopter (ALH) Mark-III to the Nepal Army, which had been a long-standing request of Nepal Army.[7]

India in the established traditions of peace and prosperity demonstrated its shared values, civilizational and cultural heritage by gifting a sapling from the Bodhi Tree at the Mahabodhi temple in Bodh Gaya to be planted near the Ashoka Pillar at the Maya Devi Temple complex at Lumbini.[8] Thus the PM's visit showed all signs of India's keen collaboration with Nepal with a lot of promises for the future. Nepal also shared its expectations with the Prime Minister of India of all that it requires from India in future at an expedited rate.

## Power Trade Agreement

India and Nepal inked the Power Trade Agreement (PTA) in September 2014 and the same was mentioned as the most significant achievement of the 18th SAARC summit. It has the potentials to address the increasing power demand in India and Nepal and enhance the economy of the two neighbours. Both the governments termed the deal as historic. The agreement authorises the two governments to develop transmission interconnections, grid connectivity, power exchange and trading through governmental, public and private enterprises on mutually acceptable terms. It also allows licensed electricity producers, buyers and traders from both countries to engage in cross-border electricity trading, including via power exchanges, and to seek cross-border transmission access as per the laws of the respective countries.[9] The agreement needs a meticulous scrutiny as the onus of effective management and balancing of both the investors and buyers will with Nepal. Internal political state-of-affairs remains a cause of concern for the success of the PTA. A clear implementation strategy thereby specifying Nepal's role as well as the degree of ownership of the project must be carried out for forward movement in this regard.

## Operation Maitri: India's Role as a Friend in Need

Nepal was hit by a high-intensity earthquake on April 25, 2015, i.e. magnitude 7.9, thereby causing tremendous loss of life and property. India demonstrated the role of a true friend and neighbour articulating a quick response and rushed with food and rescue to help the calamity-struck country by launching 'Operation Maitri'. Union Minister for State for Home Kiren Rijiju mentioned that the suffering that Nepal is going through is also felt by India as both the countries share cultural ties.[10] There is no doubt that India fulfilled its duty as a neighbour and responsibility as a friend through the said Operation. It was aptly remarked by the Minster for External Affairs, "Nepal is not only a friendly country, but also our neighbour. In any emergency, first help always comes from a neighbour and then comes the relatives."[11] India's response was started within 15 minutes of the quake.[12] According to other sources within six hours of the devastating earthquake, India was the first nation to send its search and rescue teams to Nepal with the first Indian Air Force (IAF) aircraft, carrying relief material, reaching Kathmandu along with ten National Disaster Relief Force (NDRF) teams, one Army Engineering Task Force and 18 army medical units.[13] Soon it became the biggest post-disaster operation ever launched by India outside its territory.

The Indian response to the crisis in its neighbourhood was based on a multi-pronged strategy sending army personnel and helicopters for search and rescue operations. NDR contributed in various quake-hit areas while the Indian Army and Indian Air Force provided support to the Nepali government's efforts. Several Indian state governments also made generous contributions in relief distribution, including the Indian Red Cross, and provided hundreds of tonnes of relief materials. Prime Minister Narendra Modi himself took interest and monitored the entire efforts of the government during the humanitarian crisis. Cabinet secretary regularly met the National Crisis Management Committee for updates and plans of action.[14]

India not only made a prompt response to the humanitarian crisis but the scale of the intervention was enormous. Nepali Prime Minister Sushil Koiralamade remarked, "I have no words to express appreciation for the Indian assistance."[15] The humanitarian intervention made by India was well in accordance with its strategic interests and in line with its response to growing regional responsibilities. Many policy analysts took critical view of India's response saying that India did to pat its own back. However, all such quick interventions are subject to criticisms like administrative decisions. Fact remains that India may need to intervene militarily in its neighbourhood when national interests are threatened and people in its proximity are in great need. While India may prefer to do so with a clear mandate from the United Nations Security Council and under the UN flag, it may not be averse to joining 'coalitions of the willing' when national interests that are threatened are 'vital' in nature and consensus in the UNSC proves hard to achieve or the time lag may lead to loss of life and liberty of the people, thereby causing considerable loss. The aim of such operations must be to further India's national security and foreign policy objectives. Thus, Indian interventions in Nepal were highly commendable and the task of reconstruction and rehabilitation is not yet over. Hence, prospects of future cooperation in this regard are still there and India is more than willing to cooperate in this direction.

## Impending Issues: Bottlenecks between Neighbours

There are a number of impending issues between India and Nepal that require to be addressed and negotiated in consonance with the national interests of both the countries as such issues are of strategic importance for India. One such issue is related to partnership in fuel between India and Nepal. Nepal is completely dependent on India for the supply of all kinds of fuel such as petrol, diesel, domestic LPG and jet fuel. This issue of energy dependency goes beyond traditional trade and economic relations. Indian Prime Minister Narendra Modi agreed to the construction of a new oil pipeline between the two countries thereby raising hopes in Nepal for improvement not only in the existing trade relationship but also in the overall bilateral relationship.[16]

The oil pipeline construction is in the agenda since last 15 years and the ball has always been in Nepal's sphere. The 41-kilometer long pipeline from Raxaul in Bihar, India to Amlekhjung in Nepal has been planned with the investment of Rs. 200 crores with an extension of the pipeline to Kathmandu in the second phase.[17] The pipeline shall be of great advantage to Nepal as it would reduce cost of petroleum products and would enhance regulated supply and reduction of adulteration and wastage that are caused during transportation via roads. Modi's Nepal visit has brought serious momentum and a task-force has been formed to decide the operational model of this agreement. The pending problem is related to the time duration of purchase agreement where India wants that Nepal must commit for a 15-year purchase and Nepal wants status quo as it has been importing fuel from the Indian Oil Corporation under a broad five-year supply pact that is renewed on the basis of mutual understanding.[18] Other bottlenecks for India are the land-locked geographical status of Nepal and its small market size. However, this may also be taken as leverage for India as it negates entry of a third country including China in near future in this trade with Nepal. Therefore, India requires resolving the issue and proceeding further as it shall have tremendous scope for India to enhance its influence over Nepal where it has always been wary of a Chinese scoop.

Another impending issue between India and Nepal is related to contention of river water sharing. The fact of the matter is that both the countries have multiple water sharing treaties that have been signed from the 1950s to the 1990s; and they were lauded and considered as path-breaking. However, in the long run these treaties have proven to become major bones of contention between India and Nepal. For instance in case of Koshi Treaty (1954) and Mahakali Treaty (1996), there still remains contention regarding two principal issues: water rights, and the question of the management, control and operation of the barrages.[19] Information sharing and cooperation on water issues has remained crucial. Therefore, the two countries need to arrive at a common framework of perspectives on the subject. Inclusive approach for water management and control would forge trust and accountability on both partners. Both the countries must aim at a sustainable water relation in view of tremendous potentials of producing hydroelectricity and sharing the same on payment basis. Bangladesh has already made demand on India that it must be allowed to share the electricity being produced in Nepal and Bhutan.

## Conclusion

The hallmark of NDA-II foreign policy is that well understood the nature of neighbours. This government has revealed pro-activeness, intent to mean business, and strong will and urge to strengthen friendly ties with other smaller neighbours. Therefore, as envisaged this shall help India to expand its soft power within the region. The soft power penetration achieved by China cannot be undone under any circumstances; therefore the way out could be to curve out a space for itself in the immediate neighbourhood, which NDA-II has deftly pursued and is on the march. The real challenge is not to check China's advance in the region, rather to allow China to continue but at the same time give a tough, continuous, consistent and meaningful competition to China on the turfs of these small neighbours. Eventually, earn the trust and faith of these neighbours that they come to realize that their future lies with India and is more in tune with Indian culture, traditions and historical past.

India will always have to face the ghost of China within the South Asian region. Therefore, it shall have to learn to live within the shadow of China and as an arch competitor in the region. India's alignment with United States may have potentials of realignment within South Asia in favour of China and to the detriment of India. Accordingly, India shall have to be extremely careful about the same and continue to deliver and rise to the expectations of its neighbour.

Modi's government must encourage public-private partnerships and government-to-government investments in India's neighbourhood, beyond concerns about China. According to World Bank and Asian Development Bank, South Asia is one of the least integrated regions in the world. Therefore, by investing in maritime, road, railway, dams like infrastructure and enhancing regional connectivity, India stands to gain in terms of both military and economic security. Therefore, there is hardly any doubt that under the present political dispensation India has made great strides in recent years to expand its political and military weight in the Indian Ocean. It now requires building and strengthening the economic dimensions of maritime power. A careful note of warning could be that whatever promises have been made to Nepal during the visit and otherwise also must be delivered on ground at a faster pace to further strengthen the faith and trust of both the Governments and the people of the two traditional friends in the intention, capacity, and ability of India. Another caveat could be that India should not only demonstrate a flexible approach to the several deals that it has been envisaging but also be watchful that signing immature deals in the past has not served any purpose. Therefore, to create a conducive atmosphere India must address Nepal's genuine concerns.

## NOTES

1. Modi's first foreign policy outlook were revealed during the run up for the Prime Ministerial candidature in his party in 2013 when he in a Network 18 program called 'Think India, dialogue forum' and outlined the following points: (i) Improving relations with immediate neighbours would be his priority as peace and tranquillity in South Asia is essential for realizing his development agenda; (ii) Significantly he pledged to introduce the concept of para diplomacy in India where each states and cities would have liberty to forge special relations with countries or federal states or even cities of their interest; (iii) bilateral trade going to dominate the relations with most countries except few important global powers with which India shares a strategic partnership. Anil Kamboj, "Modi's Foreign Policy—A Positive Approach", *World Focus*, December 2014, p.9.
2. Anil Kumar Mohapatra, "The Neighbourhood Diplomacy of Modi Government", *World Focus*, December 2014, p. 76. However, the LBA with Bangladesh has been resolved and implemented towards the end of July 2015.
3. Ibid., no.1, p.10.
4. Suhasini Haider and Damakant Jayshi, "Modi concludes historic visit to Nepal", *IST Kathmandu*, August, 5, 2014.
5. The Academy will cater to training of 410 Napalese police officers annually. See "Outcomes during the visit of Prime Minister to Nepal" (November 25-27, 2014)., www.narendramodi.in
6. "Outcomes during the visit of Prime Minister to Nepal" (November 25-27, 2014)., www.narendramodi.in
7. Ibid., no.6.
8. Ibid., no.6.
9. Kalpana Jha, "India-Nepal Power Trade Agreement: Challenges before Opportunities", Article No. 4854, March 24, 2015, *Institute of Peace and Conflict Studies*, www.ipcs.org Retrieved on August 20, 2015.

10. "Operation Maitri": India fulfilled its Duty as Neighbour, Says Swaraj", *The Hindu*, May 15, 2015.
11. Ibid., no.10.
12. "Nepal Quake: India started 'Operation maitri', airlifts many", *The Hindustan Times*, April 26, 2015. Retrieved on April 27,2 015 from www.hindustantimes.com
13. Anil Giri, "India Winds up Operation Maitri in Nepal", *IANS India Private Limited/Yahoo India News*, June 4, 2015, https://in.news.yahoo.com/india-winds-operation-maitri-nepal-135003192.html retrieved on August 26, 2015.Operation Maitri consisting of Indian Combined Armed Forces Task Force was finally de-inducted on June 4, 2015. According to the Indian embassy in Kathmandu, one IAF C-17 aircraft took off from Tribhuvan International Airport at 2.30 p.m. on Thursday taking the remaining relief team along with two ALH and three MI-13 helicopters.
14. Ibid., no.4. According to Indian Embassy in Kathmandu, 16 NDRF teams (over 700 personnel) were deployed in various parts of Kathmandu where hundreds of houses were damaged and stayed over five-week. It set-up medical camps at six places and treated 992 affected people and established communication link with the crisis management machinery in India. A task force of about 300 Indian Army officers and men led by a major general was deployed in Nepal. Similarly, an air vice marshal of the Indian Air Force was deputed to Nepal to lead and coordinate air support by about 150 officers and men of IAF for rescue and relief.C-17, C-130, Il-76 and AN-32 aircraft of IAF conducted a total of 37 sorties to bring over 570 tonnes of relief material (food, tents, blankets, water, tarpaulins, baby food, medicine, etc.), rescue and heavy earth moving equipment, engineering and communications equipment, ambulances, RO plants, oxygen generators, two army field hospitals with 18 medical teams, 18 army engineering teams and 16 NDRF teams. A brigadier of the Indian Army was deputed to Pokhara where the Indian Army's Pension Paying Office was involved in seamless coordination with Nepal Army and local authorities to reach rescue and relief to the areas closest to the epicentre. Mi-17 and Advanced Light Helicopters of the Indian Army and crew were put at the disposal of the Nepal Army for rescue and relief. They performed over 1,679 sorties, evacuated over 993 people—mostly Nepalese and foreigners, inducted over 1,689 Nepal Army troops, carried over 4,963 passengers—out of which about 500 were Indians, and airlifted close to 770 tonnes of stores. The Indian Army helped foreign military and other teams to induct, de-induct and evacuate, including those of the US, China, France, Singapore, and UN Disaster Assessment and Coordination (UNDAC). The Indian Army deployed 18 medical teams. Its two field hospitals in Lagankhel (45-bedded) and Sinamangal, two medical teams at Barpak, one team each at Sinamangal, Gorkha and later Dhading attended to 4,174 patients in OPD, performed over 300 surgeries, attended to 214 admit cases and discharged over 115 patients. It also stated that over 14,000 tonnes of relief material were received from India by 2,000 trucks.
15. Ibid., no.15.
16. Kalpana Jha, "India-Nepal: Disparate Partners in Fuel Diplomacy", 29 January 2015, Article No. 4821, *Institute of Peace and Conflict Studies*, www.ipcs.org Retrieved on August 26, 2015.
17. Ibid., no.16.
18. Ibid., no.16.
19. Ibid., no.9.

# 2

# Transition from 'Look East' to 'Act East': India's Constructive Engagement with Myanmar

*Alok Kumar Gupta*

Indian Prime Minister Narendra Modi's visit to Myanmar to attend the East Asia Summit (November 2014) provided a great spurt to ailing Indian 'Look East Policy' (LEP). The visit was though for a different purpose, but it was occasioned to materialize the clarion call of Modi 'Act East Policy' (AEP), which means a more nuanced position of acknowledging the need to 'act' or to 'get one's act together' to move ahead on the implementation of projects and proposals that have been initiated in principle but are lagging in practice. Just a few months back when in May 2014 Narendra Modi was taking oath as Prime Minister of India amidst an impressive guest list, an invitation was not extended to the head of this "close neighbour"—Myanmar—in his swearing-in ceremony. Questions were raised for the same in the Indian media, where some said it was a slip, others were of the opinion that since the invitation was extended to the South Asian countries, Myanmar technically did not fit into this category, and yet few also claimed that invitation was extended only to full democracies in the region and there is currently a democratic intermission in the country.

After five months the perceptions were tremendously changed with Modi's three-day visit to Myanmar. The visit justified Modi's call of 'AEP' and envisaged the zeal to drive policy into the action-oriented phase. This also defied the democracy related question, else it would be considered as a shift in India's stand from idealism to realism. The visit highlighted the three Cs: culture, commerce and connectivity. India's cultural ties with Southeast Asia are being considered as a significant one that will help push critical ties forward. However, the spurt that the visit has brought requires to be visualized in the larger milieu of past and present engagement of India and Myanmar as well as evolving a paradigm of India's Foreign Policy in the neighbourhood under the present political dispensation in India.

There is a 'strategic shift' in Indian Foreign Policy over the last couple of decades, which is often portrayed as 'paradigm shift' by many observers of India's Foreign Policy. The strategic shift could be spelt out in terms of India's change in policy from 'isolation', 'silence', and 'sanctions', on the basis of its cherished national values of democracy and avowed principles of 'Panchsheel' to a pragmatic approach of 'constructive engagement' and 'enhancing connectivity' to better facilitate its 'influence' over the other states, especially those political regimes which are considered to be untouchables by many. India has also embarked on a 'strategic partnership' and 'special strategic partnership' from erstwhile simple strategic relations with nation-states of the world. This pragmatic shift is of course motivated by available investment opportunities wherever they are sighted, so that it keeps on maximizing its economic interests.

*Panchsheel* itself has undergone a considerable change from Nehru to Gujral and to Manmohan Singh. The principles which were oriented towards 'peace' through 'non-aggression' and 'non-interference' in the idealism of Nehru, got oriented towards 'peace' through 'materialization of economic concerns' in the foreign policy response of Manmohan Singh. Thus, India's vision of the world has been changing to keep pace with the changes in the world. Dynamics of India's relation with Myanmar too requires to be understood in the same light of changing global scenario. Since 1992 India has been crafting strategy to have a long-range connectivity and engagement with Myanmar. However, wishes require to be matched with actions. Therefore, this article explores India's foreign policy response towards Myanmar with changing political and strategic scenario.

## Changing Contexts: Past to Present

British annexed Burma in the nineteenth century and today's Myanmar was ruled as a province of British India but was separated and made an independent colony in 1937, largely at the demand of Burmese nationalists who did not identify with the nationalist India independence movement.[1] India and Myanmar share a long 1,624 kilometer (1009 miles) border.[2] They also share a maritime boundary in the Bay of Bengal. A large population of Indian origin (according to some estimates about 2.5 million) lives in Myanmar. Myanmar is a country where Indian and Chinese influences intersect. Myanmar is not only a gateway to the ASEAN, but is critical to the furtherance of India's Look East Policy. Accordingly, it determines the strategic concerns of India.

Since attaining independence from the British rule Indo–Myanmar relationships have seen many ups and downs. During 1948–62, their relation was friendly and cordial in the days of Prime Minister Jawaharlal Nehru and Prime Minister U Nu. However, during 1962-–88 relations virtually froze with the military rule under Ne Win adopting an isolationist policy. Domestic policies including the expulsion of ethnic Indians soured the relations. From 1988 as a result of the sympathy of the Indian government to the pro-democracy movement which started in 1988, the relations were completely strained.[3] Earlier, India and Myanmar signed a Treaty of Friendship in 1951. The visit of the Prime Minister Rajiv Gandhi in 1987 laid the foundation for a stronger relationship between the two countries.[4]

India adopted a pragmatic and realistic approach towards the military regime and engaged in an open dialogue in 1993. Bonhomie continued since then except for a minor hiccup in 1995 when Aung San Suu Kyi was awarded the Nehru Peace Prize for International Understanding.[5] The visit of Maung Aye, Vice Chairman SPDC, the second most powerful military junta leader in November 2000, changed the entire scenario. There has been all-round progress in political, economic, and military relations as well as cooperation in technology, Human Resource Development, infrastructure, education, space, health and other fields.

## *Trade Relations between India and Myanmar*

The first Border Trade Agreement was signed in Delhi in January 1994 and was implemented in April 1995 with the opening of a cross border point between Moreh (India) and Tamu (Myanmar). The border trade which had a spurt in the beginning with export of Indian goods worth Rupees 31 crore and imports from Myanmar worth Rs. 15 crore in 1996–7 had declined to a level of Rs 5 crore in export and import by 2004–5 according to official statistics. As of today the trade value is a dismal 1 crore only.[6] Trans-border trade has failed to provide any benefit to local people and there are procedural hiccups for obtaining licenses as well apart from the failure of law and order and absence of proper infrastructures.

India turned to the largest buyer of Burmese exports by the year 2000, purchasing around $220 million USD worth of goods.[7] The economic ties were further strengthened with the formation of Mekong-Ganga Cooperation. In 2001, India–Myanmar Friendship Road was completed, facilitating India's efforts to open up trade routes with South East Asia. Since, then there has been considerable growth of trade as well as negotiations and agreement for further deals.[8]

Myanmar is on a forward march, where a number of countries have located their tremendous interests and have thus started courting for furthering their business opportunities. McKinsey and Co. reported in June 2013 that Myanmar's economy grew 27% between 2010 and 2011, which will likely be maintained through 2018. The Global Consultancy firm contended that a growth rate of 18% could be maintained through the rest of the period to 2030, which might radically increase Myanmar's Gross Domestic Product (GDP).[9] Therefore it has provided enhanced prospects for trade between the two countries.

## *The Infrastructure Projects*

The 160 km India–Myanmar Friendship Road on Burmese territory, from Tamu to Kalemyo, was built by the Border Roads Organization and completed in 2001. India is involved in the India-Myanmar-Thailand Trilateral Highway Project. Further, Indian companies are involved with the business of oil exploration and hydropower projects, such as Tamanthi Dam in Sagaing division in Myanmar. The Kaladan Multi-Model Transport project will link India's landlocked northeast region by road and waterway, utilizing the Kaladan River which runs through Arakan State.[10] The construction of port facilities and jetties at Site-tway, Paletwa and Kaletwa will be financed by the Indian government, with Essar Projects Ltd., while the highway linking Paletwa and Myeikwa on the India border isto be constructed by the Myanmar Ministry of Construction and to be completed in 2015.[11] During Myanmar's President visit in October 2011, a Memorandum of Understanding (MoU) was signed for the upgradation of the Yangon Children's Hospital and Sittwe General Hospital. Also, an Agreement on programme of Cooperation in Science and Technology for the period of 2012–15 was made that renewed the earlier agreement signed in 2010.[12]

## *Political Transition in Myanmar: Changing Dynamics*

Myanmar took a nascent step towards democratization in 2011, and most emphatically with Suu Kyi's party contesting the by-elections held in April 2012 and winning convincingly. Thus, the previous path of realpolitik and engagement with military regime in Myanmar out of geo-strategic and security considerations, the changing dynamics of political scenario provided a real thrust to India's 'Look East Policy'. Therefore, it must have been used to reinvigorate the policy and further its national interests by increasing its investment in the country that reportedly has huge gas reserves in the western province of Arakan and adjoining seaboard, estimated at more than 30 trillion cubic feet or more.[13]

With the former military leader U Thein Sein assuming civilian leadership, the changing political equations in the country lead to consequent convergence of India and Myanmar. Thein Sein is largely seen as pragmatic and reform-minded, keen that Myanmar becomes part of the globalised economic grid, not a pariah state shunned by major economies. Myanmar wants to open doors for several economic players, as it has managed to build relations with India and is now focussing on USA, thus not putting all eggs in one basket.[14]

Undoubtedly, India had to face international criticism for re-orienting its priorities and entering into relations with the military-ruled Myanmar on account of its own notions of vital national security and geo-strategy. Myanmar like most other South Asian countries has fast become a strategic chessboard in view of: first, United States' growing influence in the South Asian region to counter China; second, China's growing economic and political influence in Myanmar; third, India's envisioned policy of an elevated engagement across a broad spectrum before it is too late and Myanmar is lost to China. Therefore, it poses a great challenge to Indian policymakers towards enhancing their stakes in Myanmar. Moreover, Myanmar became a member of the ASEAN in 1997. It is the only ASEAN country which shares a land boundary with India; therefore it is the gateway to ASEAN, which India must be interested to exploit and engage with.

## China's Engagement of Myanmar

China and Myanmar have been close allies since the time People's Republic of China (PRC) came into being. China's substantial economic, military and political support is vital in view of the sanctions imposed by the West and the mounting pressure by the regional and international forum. The Chinese have built an all-weather road from Kunming in Southern China to Mandalay in Central Myanmar and volume of trade has increased hundredfold.[15] It has thus been proved beyond doubt that economic sanctions have not deterred the military regime pursuing its agenda. China has had a three-fold objective in pursuing and cementing its ties with Myanmar.[16]

First, it set its eyes on Myanmar's natural resources of oil, gas and timber, needed to meet their huge domestic demand. Second, China aimed to better its security capabilities by expanding its access to the Bay of Bengal and the Andaman Sea and thereby allowing for greater protection of its 'southwest silk road' trade routes and the development of a modern maritime reconnaissance system. Third, China has been bent on pushing policies to deny India strategic space in the South Asian Region. While China has long maintained a friendly relationship with Myanmar, India appears to have changed its position on the regime much later.

## India's Leverage vis-à-vis Myanmar

Of late, Myanmar has been realising that it is being stifled by China. Therefore, Myanmar must have been looking for an ally as an alternative to China which could stand by it in the hours of need. India may emerge as a viable and trustworthy alternative ally for Myanmar. India's rising economic potential necessitates such engagements with Myanmar. Mutual strategic and security interests also make it imperative for India to cultivate Myanmar to enhance interconnectivity and increase the points of contact between the two countries. India no doubt has been improving its ties with China, therefore, given China's interface with Myanmar may have an impact on India's relations with Myanmar; however, it is in Myanmar's interests as well.

China was more in tandem with the previous authoritarian government and propped it in exchange for commercial concessions. The new quasi-civilian administration has given precedence to democratic administrative practices of state-building. Therefore, the shift has brought Myanmar closer to India and poses a considerable threat to China's future influence in Myanmar, witnessed in part by the government's suspension of US$3.6 billion Myitsone dam project commissioned to Chinese investors by the previous military junta but vigorously protested against by local communities.[17]

Today, with the public opposition in Myanmar towards Chinese-built or Chinese-funded projects, particularly in the Kachin region, there is definitely a space India can try and fill in.

## India's Concerns vis-à-vis Myanmar

India's concerns is two-fold: on the one hand India is over-conscious of its image in the larger comity of nations that it is a peace-loving democratic country, which works for the cause of promoting and strengthening democracy in different parts of the world, therefore, how can it build progressive relationship with a country where military is in power and is working contrary to the ethos of democracy; on the other hand its strategic and security considerations outweigh the concerns for democracy in Myanmar.

India wishes to exploit Myanmar's natural resources. However, it has not been smooth for India as, between 2004 and 2007, there were protracted negotiations for the construction of a pipeline to India to transport natural gas from the Shwe gas fields in Arakan State. Negotiations failed and the direction of the pipeline moved to China.[18] Such failures again become a serious concern for India.

India is to solicit Myanmar's role towards combating insurgency in the northeast. In April 2007 it was reported that Indian and Myanmar security forces were conducting joint military operations along the Indo-Myanmar border to neutralize insurgent groups. In July 2010, Shwe and Manmohan Singh agreed upon a strategy of increased security cooperation and a strengthened collective effort to fight the insurgents and combat terrorism along the border of the two countries. There are serious concerns that weapons and other military equipment, such as helicopters, sold or donated by India for combating insurgents could be used by its military against ethnic civilians. India is not among those countries which support a global arms embargo on Myanmar.[19]

Myanmar refugees are nearly 70,000 in numbers residing within India are another important concern of India. Most of them are in north-eastern India, and they often accuse India of harassing them by arresting and deporting. Not being a signatory to 1951 UN Refugee Convention and those who enter India without authorization are considered illegal immigrants. Therefore, India will have to find a way out with the cooperation of Myanmar to settle the issue of refugees.

India needs to push ahead its Look East Policy that was initiated in 1992 and was a strategic shift in India's vision of the world and India's place in the evolving global economy. It can do so by opening and putting in place workable channels of communication by roads and railways, the India-Myanmar region must be free of violent insurgencies. Several Northeast Indian insurgent groups have bases in Myanmar. The United Liberation Front of Asom (ULFA), the National Socialist Council of Nagaland (Khaplang), and several Manipuri rebel outfits have well-entrenched camps in the country's Sagaing Division, bordering North-eastern India.[20]

India has called for a bus route from Imphal in North-eastern India to Mandalay in Myanmar. Potentially more important is Myanmar's location between India and China. As reported in one of the conversation with the present Prime Minster Narendra Modi, Chinese Premier Li Kequing warmly suggested the construction of a Bangladesh-China-India-Myanmar (BCIM) economic corridor that would connect Kunming in China to India's Northeast through Myanmar.[21] It would seriously help India tighten-up its lukewarm relations with China. It shall also provide a boost to India's much neglected Northeast region.

Northeast India is significantly different from the rest of India in terms of languages, religion, culture, and even race and is in many ways more Southeast Asian than South Asian. Surrounded by Myanmar, China, and Bangladesh on almost all four sides and connected to the rest of India via only a narrow corridor, greater interconnectivity with international neighbours could bring this region much needed economic development and stem the rise in insurgency that plagues the area for the past 60 years.

## Changing Strategic Scenario: Challenges and Prospects

When Myanmar witnessed the takeover of power by the military junta, economic sanctions were imposed by the Western power in view of the atrocities committed on the democratic movement in that country. India too adopted a close-door policy to Myanmar and neglected any engagement with the same. However, when India learnt that China has been working on massive expansion of its economy in Southeast Asia and Myanmar, India gradually has been adopting an open-door policy.

Consequently, today India's Myanmar policy cannot be comprehended without factoring China in. So far India's Myanmar policy has been a response to rein China in and not leaving the field open to it—instead of a concerted bid at building a good neighbourly relationship for a solid hold in the region. India also needs to take note of the fact that China is an 'all-weather friend' of Pakistan and in the recent past the linkages between Myanmar and Pakistan have also grown, and thus India will have to devise a diplomacy to prevail in an atmosphere where China-Myanmar-Pakistan converge.

Narendra Modi has appointed a seasoned former general, Vijay Kumar Singh to the federal Ministry of Development of North East Region (MDONER). Only time will say how much of dynamism has been infused into the region. Therefore, Modi government needs to be abreast of the following challenges in its relations with Myanmar:

First, The Indo–Burma treaty of 1952 on Border Affairs was designed to ensure free movement of the local ethnic tribal for meeting their daily socio-economic needs with a tacit understanding that population on both sides of the international border, from the same ethnic group, will be allowed free passage within 40 km on both sides for the purpose of carrying on local trade and social visits. The treaty has been modified from time to time to meet the changing needs. However, in its implementation it has experienced stumbling blocks and even with the best intention to overcome the same, Indian traders find little attraction in continuing legal trade relation with Myanmar. The major constraints towards the growth of border trade are poor state of infrastructure, such as road connectivity, telecommunication facilities, banking and other financial network; dual currency exchange rate system of Myanmar, i.e. official and non-official rate of exchange; and absence of currency exchange counters. Besides these the absence of law and order in Manipur as a whole with frequent closures, strikes and blockades by different organizations and presence of militant groups has led to illegal collection of taxes.[22] Therefore, lack of peace, security and safety in business premises has been demotivating and a cause of grave concern towards enhancing the border trade between the two countries.

Second, Myanmar's transition from authoritarianism to democracy presents immense challenges as well as opportunities for neighbouring India. India being the largest democracy and one of the closest neighbour of Myanmar, it requires to keep pace with the rising expectations of Myanmar's pro-democracy forces, which India supported in the 1990s but later moved closer to military government driven by commercial interests and to develop diplomatic ties. It is a welcome diplomatic shift from 'idealism' to 'realism'. The present government must further build on the same.

Third, there is a border dispute as well between the two countries.[23] The diplomatic row over 'Pillar Number 76' in the north-eastern Indian state of Manipur on the Indo-Myanmar border in Holenphai village near Moreh has added to long-running border problems.[24] Although the two sides have agreed to negotiate the issue peacefully, past misunderstandings and alleged intrusions have raised alarm bells on both sides of the border. This too requires to be settled at the earliest for smoothening the relations.

Fourth, Myanmar has been facing clashes between Muslims and Buddhists in Rakhine state and central regions. It has developed serious regional ramifications with cross border dimensions in which its spill-over into India is a great cause of concern. Radical groups have been threatening to target Buddhist installations in India. The outburst of Buddhist nationalism in Myanmar is thus no longer an internal affair as it has long-term implications for security in wider South and Southeast Asia, including the Indian subcontinent.[25] As reported the pogroms led by Buddhist monks have radicalized Muslims outside Myanmar, resulting in retaliatory attacks against Buddhists in other regional countries. India must tighten its security networks to prevent the spill-over into its religiously mixed region including northeast.

Fifthly, Myanmar in its urge to ease its relations with the West and derive economic benefit from them initiated a move towards democracy. However, it has not yet achieved the goal of democracy yet. Nobel laureate Aung San Suu Kyi who spent about 15 years under house arrest raised her expectations from India when she said, "Myanmar has not yet achieved the goal of democracy…we hope that through this difficult last stage, the people of India will stand by us and walk with us as we proceed along the path which they had taken many years before." Thus, India requires rising up to the occasion and her expectations without sacrificing its ideals in the course of becoming a realist.

Sixthly, the political reforms initiated in Myanmar and consequent easing of Western economic and financial sanctions as a reward has opened new gates to India in Myanmar.[26] India needs to be increasingly proactive and give priority to securing its own economic and financial interests. There are areas like oil and gas exploration, which shall attract major and minor powers of the world as well as the region. Early bird catches the worm; therefore, India must make its move as early as possible.

Seventhly, India's economic interests in Myanmar at present are largely through the public sector. With the growth of Western business interests India must devise means and mechanism to promote and engage its private sector at a larger scale to fill the gaps.

Eighthly, given the nature of investment in Myanmar namely public sector, bureaucratic hurdles and procedural delays at times frustrates the cause of furthering better and improved relations. Therefore, it makes it imperative that more and more private sector involvement be encouraged to consolidate the ties. The challenges will be the absence of a fully democratic culture within Myanmar to carry out the effective negotiations for transition from public to private sector.

Last but not the least, Myanmar now understands it well that India views it as its gateway to ASEAN and east Asia, therefore, the quasi civil regime of Myanmar has found itself in a key geo-strategic position, and is bent on using it as a strong hand in negotiations with India. Therefore, onus lies on the Indian diplomatic community as to how they are going to neutralize this leverage in the bargaining process and turn the relations in a positive-sum-game for India.

## NOTES

1. Akhilesh Pillalamarri, "Why was Myanmar's President Not Invited to Modi's Swearing-in Ceremony?", *The Diplomat*, June 03, 2014.
2. Ibid., no.1.
3. T. Haokip, "Indo Myanmar Relationship on bilateral and economic cooperation", *E-pao* (Now the World Knows), www.e-pao-net July 18, 2014. The Article was originally written for *The Sangai Express* and posted on March 11, 2013.
4. Rajiv Gandhi was the first head of State to visit Myanmar in 1987. The high point in the bilateral relations was the visit of Senior General Than Shwe, Chairman, State Peace and Development Council (SPDC) in October 2004. To reciprocate, the Indian President Dr. A P J Abdul Kalam visited Myanmar in March 2006. A number of agreements and Memorandums of Understanding were signed during this visit.
5. Ibid., no.3.
6. Ibid., no.3.
7. "India-Burma Relations", www.arakanrivers.net, Retrieved on July 28, 2014.
8. Ibid., no.7.
9. Anup Roy and Remya Nair, "Indian banks make inroads into Myanmar", *Livemint*, June 20, 2014, http:www.livemint.com/industry/ttkm8D3Bts5r99m8qXyj4K/India-banks-make-inroads-into-Myanmar.html (Retrieved on July 11, 2014).
10. Non-government actors in Myanmar are increasingly opposing projects in parts of the country being sought to be implemented with Chinese finding. A case in point is the cancellation of a $20 billion railway line connecting Kyaukpyu in Myanmar and Kunming in China due to public opposition. The construction was to be carried out by the China Railway Engineering Corporation. See Wasbir Hussain, "India's Myanmar Mission", www.ipcs.org Article No.4583, July 29, 2014.
11. Ibid., no.7.
12. Dr Monish Tourangbam and Ms. Ramya, P. S., "India-Myanmar Relations: Assessing New Dynamics", *World Focus*, September 2014, No. 417.
13. Ibid., no.12.
14. Ibid., no.12.
15. Ibid., no.3.
16. Wasbir Hussain, "India's Myanmar Mission", www.ipcs.org; Article No. 4583, July 29, 2014.

17. Sonu Trivedi, "New Role for India in Myanmar", *Asia Times*, September 16, 2013, www.atimes.com
18. Ibid., no.3. Retrieved on July 28, 2014. India is seriously interested and pursuing for Myanmar's oil and gas reserves. In 2005 Essar Oil signed contracts with the military regime to make onshore and offshore explorations for oil and gas in Arakan state.
19. Ibid., no.3..
20. Ibid., no.17.
21. Ibid., no.1.
22. Ibid., no.3.
23. India and Myanmar signed a Memorandum of Understanding (MoU) on May 8, 2014, on Border Cooperation. This MoU provides a framework for security cooperation and exchange of information between Indian and Myanmarese security agencies. See Wasbir Hussain, "India's Myanmar Mission", www.ipcs.org; Article No. 4583, July 29, 2014.
24. Ibid., no.17.
25. Ibid., no.17.
26. Australia and the European Union have lifted travel and financial sanctions against Myanmar, while the United States has taken what US officials have referred to as a more 'calibrated' approach. While Washington has suspended most restrictions on investment and financial services, it still maintains a list of targeted sanctions against certain individuals from travelling to the US and blocks imports of specific products such as jade and rubies of which trade is still dominated by state and military interests. See for detail Sonu Trivedi, "New Role for India in Myanmar", *Asia Times*, September 16, 2013, www.atimes.com

# 3

# A New Foreign Policy Agenda for Modi: "Look West"

*Alokka Dutta*

India has seen West Asia almost entirely through the prism of commercial interests, namely imports of energy and exports of migrant labour. This is understandable given these two factors have supported poverty reduction, a central policy priority. Now, however, geopolitical winds are shifting as West Asia is rapidly becoming more strategically important to India. This is due in part to the anticipated decline, relative to other powers, of Washington's interest and influence in the region, creating room for newcomers. China's growing involvement further increases the stakes, as does India's ambitions for a sphere of influence encompassing the Western Indian Ocean. In responding to opportunities and threats, Delhi should adopt a long-term vision, targeting states and actors most important for India's strategic ascendance and increasing engagement commensurately. A 'Look West Policy' (LWP) like India's famed 'Look East Policy' (LEP) has often been spoken about, but there has not been a formal institutionalisation of the same. This will need a concentrated focus—like the LEP—for the region, to formulate effective policies. While trade is a significant component of this relationship, the essence of the LWP will be the multi-dimensionality of its character. As much as India trades with the region, also important are the issues of security, culture, people linkages and those of wider geopolitical and geostrategic linkages.

It is also true that India has always been supportive of Arab cause, especially Palestinians since India's independence. The great leaders like Mahatma Gandhi and Pandit Jawaharlal Nehru strongly supported the rights of Arabs. They felt that the socio-economic and political problems of West Asian people were not different from those of Indians. Both the leaders had a similar view on the issue of Palestine and other West Asian countries in the same sense that England belongs to the English or France to the French.[1] India had in fact, supported the cause of Palestine in every UN and other international forums. She extended all possible material and moral support to Palestinian people.

It is, however, witnessed since the early 90s that India's West Asian policy began to shift from its earlier policy. The proactive policy towards West Asia has continued under the new government of Prime Minister Narendra Modi who has given India's Foreign policy the much needed boost. It is now debated whether India's changing West Asian policy is in favour of India's national interest or not? This could be understood by considering some factors which are vital in explaining India's interest in West Asian countries.

## Economic Factors

No doubt political and diplomatic factors based on national interest are important. But at the same time, economic interest is one of the most crucial factors that should be given priority, while formulating foreign policy. Taking this factor in to consideration, India has a good relation with the West Asian countries since ancient times. The trade relation between the two can be traced back to the early part of the 20th century. Geographical proximity and economic interdependence are perhaps two factors responsible for having greater interaction between the two regions, which lead to mutual beneûts. There have been substantial commitments of investments by way of joint ventures from both sides. Many agreements were signed between India and these countries in order to promote trade and investment in their countries. It is noted that Indian imports from the region were estimated at more than $3 billion, while exports were estimated at less than $2 billion in 1991. These values increased to more than $8 billion of imports and less than $4.5 billion of exports to this region in 2000.[2] It is thus observed that bilateral trade got impetus on account of economic liberalisation taking place in India and the West Asian countries. The total value of trade with this region was more than $5 billion in 1991, then $12 billion in 2000. This would be expected to go up to $130 billion by 2013–14 which was around $100 billion in 2009–10.

It we look in terms of other countries, Saudi Arabia is one of the most important trading partners in the Gulf region. It is the 14th largest market for India and accounts for 7 percent of India total exports.[3] On the other hand, India is the fifth largest market for Saudi Arabia contributing about 4.5 percent of its total exports. Thus on the trade front, India has to explore opportunities to add more items to its export basket. Currently, India's export to Saudi Arabia mainly constitutes cereals, manmade filament, apparels and clothing, iron and steel.[4] The country has to focus more and more on value added industrial products and services. It is moving steadily towards a free market economy with gradual decontrolling of many important sectors of the economy. The service sector that offers potential of greater employment opportunities has been identified as one of the major focal areas. This offers an excellent opportunity to Indian industries to forge partnership with its counterparts in the Kingdom to build strong and vibrant economic relations between the two countries.

UAE is another major trading partner of India in the Gulf region. It is in fact India's biggest market in this region. India's exports to the UAE are diversified and contain a large basket of goods. Thus, the significance of the UAE is that for India it is not only important for imports but also for exports. This is so because UAE has emerged as the topmost trading partner in the region. The UAE alone represents 70 per cent of India's exports to the GCC Countries.[5] Exports to the UAE comprise 6 percent of India's global exports. The major items of exports from India are gems and jewellery, textiles, manufactures of metals, machinery and instruments, plastic and linoleum, tea, Basmati rice, drugs, pharmaceuticals and chemicals primary and semi-finished iron and steel. Besides, exports are also emerging as a prospective area. On the other hand, India's main imports from the UAE are petroleum crude and products, pearls, precious and semi-precious stones, gold, metalliferous ores and scrap, fertilisers and organic and inorganic chemicals.

There are many advantages to have good trading relations with the UAE. One being that it is nearby, and Dubai has emerged as the major trade centre and a gateway to entire Arab world. Almost 95 percent of trade to the GCC and 85 percent to the WANA region transits through Dubai. It is noted that many Indian companies are setting up their centre in Dubai and Sharjah and bidding for many ventures into the world market. Thus we can say that UAE is an important trading partner in this exports.[7] Narendra Modi became the first Prime minister to visit UAE after 34 years. After a successful two-day visit to the UAE in August 2015 both states came down heavily on countries sponsoring terrorism against other states. The two sides decided to elevate India–UAE relationship to a comprehensive strategic partnership and chart out a new course for cooperation in key areas like trade and investment, defence, security, maritime security and intelligence sharing.

There is substantial trade to Qatar via Dubai. A number of consumer goods from India are available and popular in Qatar. There are good prospects for diversification and expansion due to the low level of customs duties in Qatar

(4%), which is close to the proposed common GCC external tariff of 5%. India's export basket is fairly diversified and includes foodstuffs, spices, tea, coffee, textiles, ready-made-garments, jewellery, light engineering goods, basic chemicals, steel pipes, and consumer electronics. As the Qatari market is competitive and highly quality conscious, there is room for expanding our exports further in areas where we are globally competitive.

India's imports from Qatar consist largely of urea, ammonia, sulphur, ethylene and polyethylene. India has substantial dealings with the Qatar Fertiliser Company (QAFCO) and the Qatar Petrochemical Company (QAPCO). India has not been a major customer for Qatari crude oil/products. However, it is set to emerge as one of Qatar's most important customers for LNG. With the third largest gas reserves in the world, Qatar is poised to emerge as a significant international supplier of energy for many decades to come. The Government of Qatar has made large investments in the development of its two LNG projects and port at Ras Laifan. With its large, expanding and long-term requirements of natural gas, India is naturally keen to take advantage of the existence of a reliable and virtually inexhaustible source of natural gas situated so close to its own consuming centres. This is the biggest agreement of this type in the world and will significantly raise the economic and commercial profile of India in Qatar, and of Qatar in India. This will also make India the biggest buyer of natural gas from Qatar. Within a week of Prime Minister Modi assuming office, South Block hosted two important events: the foreign minister of Oman visited the new Indian minister of external affairs, and a ministerial delegation from Qatar followed shortly after, to hold foreign office consultations with their Indian counterparts. The timing of these visits is significant. It signifies that the Indian leadership is earnestly working towards deepening New Delhi's engagement with West Asia.

India and Bahrain enjoys a trouble free and close political relationship. They also have a mutually beneficial bilateral economic cooperation. Bahrain is a small country but important one. Both these countries are very close to each other in many respects. India also exports a comparatively large amount of goods and services to Bahrain. Since most of Bahrain's needs are met through imports. There exists a good potential for enhanced exports from India. The Indian private sector could play a more active role in this area—participation in exhibitions, bilateral business visits and consistency in quality and supply schedules can go a long way in promoting Indian exports. The policy of Bahrain Government joint ventures especially in the small and medium industries.[8] India can take a lead in this field in order to enhance exports to Bahrain.

There are mainly five items of exports from India to Bahrain. These are textile, wood, vegetables, meat and rice. Moreover, there are good prospects for export of Indian products, particularly agricultural products, sanitary fixtures, drugs pharmaceuticals, plywood, ceramic tiles, power generation and transmission equipment, light engineering goods, leather products, textiles and related products. Information technology is the new emerging field of India's efforts. There are large number of NRI business communities in Bahrain, which is engaged primarily in trading activity. They have invested in their business establishment in Bahrain. These establishments include agencies for Titan and IHMT watches, India televisions, etc.

Our relations with Oman are historical There is evidence of people-to-people contacts dating back to the seventh century. In olden days, there was constant sea trade between the two countries. An Indo-Oman Treaty of Friendship, Navigation and Commerce was signed by Sultan Said and the President of India in 1953.[9] It was probably one of the first agreements to be signed between India and any Arab country. The umbrella agreement for cooperation in the hydrocarbon field was a breakthrough in exploiting the potential for economic competition with Gulf States. The economic content was further concretized with the signature of the Agreement on Economic, Trade and Technical Cooperation which aimed at strengthening cooperation in the economic, commercial, industrial, tourist and technical fields. There was also the setting up of a Joint Commission to meet annually to follow up and to review developments.

The recognition of Oman's strategic significance was further highlighted by the demonstration of a new political will and new economic initiatives. India's need for energy sources particularly for the Southern Grid and the possibility of supply of gas through a submarine pipeline heightened the awareness on both sides of the existence of common strategic interests. This has become explicit in Oman's proposal to develop a 'Strategic Trade Alliance'. It is interesting to note that Oman is the only country in the region where India has the surplus balance of trade.[10]

The cooperation between India and Kuwait has increased in the field of science and technology. A number of visits have taken place between the two countries especially between the two apex bodies in the field of science and technology Kuwait Institute of Scientific Research (KISR) and Council of Scientific and Industrial Research (CSIR). A number of Indian Scientists/ Researchers are with KISR and other such organizations to develop cooperation for mutual beneûts.

The trade relations between India and Iran continued to register growth. The new economic policies followed both by India and Iran provided new opportunities for economic cooperation. This is of course in the field of energy sector oil and gas. The other fields where cooperation is required are in the field of textile machinery, bio-technology, power generation, agro-processing. Apart from this, Iran could play a very important role in providing India and commercial linkages with the central Asian countries. They are emerging as big markets for Indian goods.

India and Iraq have traditionally been very close to each other. Iraq was one of the major sources of India's oil imports and also was good markets for Indian goods. But after the Gulf crisis in 1990-91 and in 2001, its economic activities were badly disturbed. Iraq is fighting its own battle to get rid of foreign powers such as the US and the UK. They have undemocratically invaded Iraq and are still occupying it, taking the pretext of bringing democracy there. As far as the relation with Israel is concerned, it must be taken into consideration of the national interest in mind. Israel cannot be more important than these Gulf countries from any point of view. The previous NDA government was misled and adopted the policy which favoured Israel rather than Gulf countries. It is noted that as soon as this current regime came to power, it is realised by the government and there is a correction in its foreign policy towards the Gulf. India accords high priority to its relations with Iran, Prime Minister Narendra Modi told visiting Iranian Foreign Minister Javad Zarif when the latter visited him in August 2015. Prime Minister Modi's upcoming visit to Iran will be a milestone in bilateral relations of the two countries.

We further see that India's economic relations with Yemen have been positive. After the first meeting of Indo–Yemen joint committee, cooperation on trade and investment, small scale industry, telecommunication, hydrocarbons, civil aviation, construction, science and technology, health and education, etc., was decided.

Then there is a relative importance of the Gulf in comparison to Israel. It is noted that India has a flourishing mutually beneficial economic connection with the Gulf region. India's crude oil import from the Gulf is worth $17 to $18 billion annually, India's annual trade with Arab countries is about $10 billion. Whereas, Israel's annual trade with India is only about $1.2 billion. Thus we can argue that the Gulf countries are a vital destination not only for trade and investment but also for energy supply to India.

## Energy Factor

The energy factor must be taken into account, while deciding West Asian policy. This is so because the Gulf's energy capacity is not only important to the Indian economy but also to the world economy. It is considered to be the integral part of the global economy because of its one third share of world oil production.

The Gulf has well over half of the world's proven oil reserves. Most of the supply required to meet growing world demand is expected to come from OPEC especially from the region. It is expected that production would rise to 60 mbd by 2020 from 28 mbd in 1998. Virtually all this increase will come from this region.[11] Thus, the Persian Gulf region remains the largest depository of oil reserves and the major source of hydrocarbons. OPEC estimates are that oil reserves are over one trillion barrels, which can meet the requirement for more than 40 years. This was all due to the new discoveries, which added the net 415 billion barrels to the World reserves.

The global proven natural gas reserves are put around 15.9 trillion cubic meters which is 38% increase over the 1988 estimates. Despite all this, the pace of energy consumption which is so high that it cannot be ignored; it can upset current supply of energy. It is also obvious that hydrocarbons are non-renewable source of energy. So, their life span is bound to be limited. But this is also true that threat is not so imminent as far as physical reserves are concerned. Definitely, it is going to continue a longer period of time. It is also possible that by that time, there may be more new discovery of oil and gas in this region.

Thus, the Gulf holds an indispensable position in terms of energy stock for most of the countries like India. The region holds 63 percent of total world oil reserves and 34 percent of the world proven natural gas.

Additional advantage to the Gulf. Thus it is now clear that the Gulf is enormously important to India simply because it meets the bulk of our energy needs and there are a large number of Indians in the Gulf. India must adopt a policy that can promote mutual understanding of the economic cooperation. India has to play a proactive role in order to maintain its interest in the region. if it wants to maintain its growth of 7-8 percent in GDP. It is also clear that Gulf is strategically e most important to India mainly due to its proximity geographically. Hence, importing oil from this region is economically most viable.[12] Thus, having a cordial, strong and good relation with West Asian is crucial for India.

According to the Vision Document, the share of oil and gas in the total energy will be 45 percent by the year 2025. India's oil consumption has exceeded 100 million tonnes of which 33 million tonnes are indigenous. While remaining 77 million tonnes comes from other countries. The demand for crude oil and petroleum products is expected to grow to 190 million tonnes in 2012, and 364 million tonnes in 2025. On the other hand, it is noted that domestic production has been declining. Indian oil reserves would dry up even if only 30 percent of its demand were met from domestic production. The demand is growing at the rate of 5.77 percent to meet this growing demand. There are five countries that provide bulk of it. These countries are Saudi Arabia, UAE, Kuwait, Iran and Nigeria accounting for more than 75% of oil. This clearly indicates the importance of these countries as far as the case of India's imports is concerned.

It is also observed that Saudi Arabia is the leading country that accounts for nearly 20% of total imports. The GCC countries such as Saudi Arabia, UAE, Kuwait, Qatar and Bahrain account for more than fifty percent. The Persian Gulf, which includes Iraq and Iran constitutes around 60 percent of import.[13] Thus, India is presently importing 70 percent of hydrocarbon which is expected to grow in future, since the consumption of energy is rapidly increasing in India owing to development taking place in different sectors of the economy. It is evident that there is a dominance of the GCC countries in terms of oil supply to India.

Just like food and defence, energy security challenges is one of the most important concerns for India in the age of globalization and liberalization. So, it has been realized that it now is strategically important for India to have strong economic linkage with the Gulf countries in order to meet energy security challenges. This is so because India still imports more than 60 percent of its oil from the Gulf countries and this percentage is expected to rise further. Presently India ranks sixth in the world in terms of energy consumption, the US, China, Russia, Japan and Germany come before India in this respect. India is amongst those countries which imports over 70 percent of petroleum requirements from outside the country. Moreover, it is important to note that out of the total petroleum imports, more than 60 percent comes from the Gulf which constitutes six Gulf Cooperation Council countries such as Bahrain, Kuwait, Qatar, Saudi Arabia, United Arab Emirates and two more countries, Iran and Iraq. These countries are crucial countries for oil importer like India and China which has also recently become a net importer of oil. Hence, we can say that Gulf has immense significance for India not only for trade and energy but also for employment opportunities available in this region and remittances sending home.

## Employment Factor

The Gulf countries are not only important from trade and investment, oil and natural gas point of view, but they are equally crucial for India in terms of employment to Indians in their respective countries. It is reported that at least 5 million Indians are employed in this region. These expatriate Indians remit more than $10 billion dollars to India every year.[14] Prior to the mid-70s, there were mainly Arabs such as Egyptians, Yemenis, Palestinians, Lebanese and Sudanese in this region. It was noted that the Gulf monarchies grew increasingly worried about the possible political repercussions in the 1970s. Palestinians were viewed as politically subversive. Yemenis were involved in various anti regime activities.

As a result, the Gulf countries started to opt for workers from South and South East Asia who were seen as less likely to get involved in host countries politics.

After the oil boom of 1973, the Gulf countries recruited foreign workers from both Arab and Asian countries for construction and industrialization. Indians also benefited from it. These were about 2.5 lakh Indian expatriates in 1975. This number rose to over 1.5 million in 1991. In the year 1999, there were 3 million Indian nationals gainfully employed in the Gulf. The number of Indian workers in the Gulf reached over 3.6 million in 2004. Of this, Saudi Arabia alone had 1.5 million Indians and UAE had 1 million Indians. Qatar and Bahrain had more than 1,00,000 Indian each. There were about 4.5 lakh Indian expatriates each in Kuwait and Oman.

It is also true that Saudi Arabia and the United Arab Emirates import the maximum number of Indian labour in their respective countries followed by other GCC countries. This is evident that there is a shortage of manpower in these countries which is supplied by surplus manpower countries like India. The Indian government is now changing its migration policy in order to promote manpower employment in these countries. This is important because the manpower contributes significantly in the development of the country where they are employed as well as to the country where they come from. Hence, we can say that this expatriate Indian labour force is the real asset to India and to the host countries as well. This is so because both India and host countries are beneficiaries on accounts of the contribution made by these-expatriates.

Moreover, it also noted that all the Gulf States have launched many developmental programmes and schemes for overall "development of their countries. They need highly qualified and trained personnel who can work in their developmental-project. Hence, they will have to rely on skilled expatriate workers. It is 'here suggested that Indian government must act in this direction in order to enhance the prospect of Indian workers in this region. Since India has a vast reservoir of well-trained technical manpower in all disciplines such as Engineering, Medical, Management, Computer Sciences, etc., it is desirable that a large number of Indians may be able to find lucrative job abroad, especially in the Gulf. This can be made possible if we have strong and friendly relations with West Asian countries as we have had in the past.

## Remittance Factor

It is proved beyond, doubt that Gulf remittances brought by the Indian expatriates help in the foreign exchange earnings to a great extent. It was fully realized by the Indian government at the time of the Gulf crisis which took place in 1990. Before the Gulf war, the annual remittances were more than $2 billion. By 1994–

5, it amounted to $6.2 billion. At the turn of the century, this amount went up to 12 billion in 2000–1. By 2003–4, it amounted approximately $14 "billion a year which was a major asset to the country. In 2005, India's remittances reached $ 21.7 billion that replaced China whose remittances were $21.3 billion. Of India's $21.7 billion, $16 billion came from the Gulf countries.[15] In 2010, the World Bank reported that India had received $55 billion from abroad. It was estimated that during the last 5 years the remittances have been more than double and India continues to retain its position in the world. It is interesting to note that the major chunk of remittance is still coming from the Gulf. Thus the Gulf region is very important for India in this respect. This huge amount definitely strengthens India's balance of payment. Kerala is one of the Indian states whose economy is largely based on the Gulf remittances. There are many other such states like Andhra Pradesh, Tamil Nadu; Punjab, Bihar, etc., where a huge amount of remittances are coming. These remittances are used for economic development by migrants' household in India. PM Modi from his recent visit to UAE is looking to lift bilateral trade that currently stands at $59 billion, attract investment into infrastructure projects at home and connect with the large Indian community that makes up nearly 30% of U.A.E.'s population and sends millions of dollars back in remittances each year.

## Social and Cultural Factor

Education and health, which are in fact the crucial factors for human resource development, is identified as a major sector for future cooperation between India and the Gulf countries. Many agreements were signed between the two sides to promote cooperation in the field of education and arts. Two important languages Arabic and Persian of this region have been taught in India for a long time. In the same way, "Urdu and Hindustani are spoken and understood by the people in the Gulf region. Bollywood films and stars are very popular in the Gulf. They frequently visit Dubai, Muscat and many other Gulf cities for various promotions and performances on popular demand by people. This all clearly indicates the significance of common culture prevailing in the Gulf and India. Not only this, there are over 60 Indian schools which have been established in the Gulf countries. All these schools follow CBSE pattern, except one which is affiliated to the KSB (Kerala State Board)." Indian Ambassador is the patron of all the Indian schools in the country. The control of the Indian schools is under the Board of Directors who is appointed by the Ambassador from among permanent members of the Indian community. The Board coordinates the functioning of management committees of all Indian schools.

There are more than 30 Indian schools in the UAE. They are doing well and the CBSE curriculum is fulfilling the needs of Indian children and Emiratis.

There are several such schools in Kuwait too that are all well established and are serving the needs of the large Indian community residing in Kuwait and the Kuwaitis alike. It is noted that there are four major Indian schools, such as Indian school, Muscat: Indian schools, Al Ghubia Indian school, Wadi Kabir and Indian school, Dar Sait that are located in Muscat (Oman). Recently an Indian school of Seeb an adjacent township has started functioning. The oldest school is Indian school Muscat initially known as Arya Kelavani Mandal which was founded in 2nd July 1939. Hindu Maliajan Association took the responsibility of managing the school. Thus, the presence of 15 Indian schools in various pans of Oman indicates that Indian community attaches a great deal of importance to education for its coming generation. For higher and technical education generally India is the preferred choice.

There is educational prospect on both sides. Indian IT companies have been actively involved in setting up an IT park in Muscat & Knowledge Oasis in Muscat (KOM). Both the IT colleges have an Indian connection. One is in affiliation with Manipal Academy of Higher Education while other is a joint venture with Birla Institute of Technology Ranchi.[18] They have received a good response.

Omani companies also have several joint ventures in India. Oman Computer Services International develops Computer Software at Bangalore. Shantha Bio-techniques, Hyderabad, is one of India's most well known bio-technology companies. Nisma Airocon International, Chennai manufactures heat pump air conditioners. The Zubair group has set up a furniture manufacturing unit in Tamil Nadu in collaboration with Balaji group of Chennai. Bahwan Cybertec has an IT training company in Chennai and regularly sends trainees from Oman to India. These trainees go back to Oman with great satisfaction.

Sultan Qaboos University in Muscat is the only university which is well reputed and most important institution of higher learning in Oman. It was found that many Omanis have studied in India and they still keep coming in large numbers to Indian universities and institutions of higher education especially in technical subject such as engineering, IT and medicine. Bangalore, Pune, and Chennai are the major cities where they prefer to come for education. It is presently estimated that there are over 1500 Omanis who pursue higher education. It was also found that every year a number of Omani officials come to India to acquire training in different fields under the ITEC programme of the government or India. There were about 53 Omani officials will come to India in 2004 for number of training courses in different fields such as IT, audit, pharmaceuticals, Entrepreneurship, language Agriculture and rural development Accounts and Finance, Educational Planning and Administration, etc. This sector in fact needs to be focussed on more seriously for mutual benefits. More and more Gulf students should be attracted to pursue their higher education in India.

As far as the socio-cultural factor is concerned, it is witnessed that a large number of Indian Muslims go to two holy places (Mecca and Madinah) for pilgrimage every year on the occasion of Eid-al-Adha. This pilgrimage provides enough opportunities for cultural interaction between Indians and West Asian people. This cultural interaction strengthens our overall relations for our mutual benefit.

## Conclusion

While there was a general consensus among the scholars on the need for greater Indian involvement as our interest are manifold in this region, the actualization of this involvement remains a significant challenge. That West Asia is currently in turmoil is an understatement. There are a number of challenges that plague the region and have caused significant upheaval in recent years. First is the horrific rise of the Islamic State (IS) and the spread of its extremist ideology in Iraq and Syria. The spill-over effects of IS to other countries in the region and the spread of extremism to other parts of the world are also grave concerns. Second, the repercussions of the Arab Spring are still being felt in the region with Syria and Yemen on the brink of civil war. Military intervention by other Arab states in these conflicts and the rapidly intensifying humanitarian crises that these conflicts have created are serious causes of concern for the region. Third, the Arab states are greatly wary of Iran's nuclear aspirations and its increasing involvement in the Arab world's conflicts. Finally, America's waning interest and involvement in the Middle East has created a future of uncertainty for regional security.

India has traditionally followed a 'hands-off' approach toward West Asian countries and consequently enjoyed good relations with them... West Asia has always been of strategic importance to India with roughly seven million Indians residing in the region and the Gulf supplying nearly two-thirds of India's oil and gas. A pro-active Indian approach to West Asia and its problems would also ensure greater visibility for India vis-à-vis the rising influence of China. In recent years, China has signalled its geo-political and economic ambitions by signing multi-billion dollar investment deals and defence agreements with West Asian states. India on the other hand has shied away from pursuing stronger bilateral defence and security relationships for various ideological and geopolitical reasons, with the notable exception of Israel. It is argued that Prime Minister Modi's impending visit to Israel might raise concerns with the Arab states regarding Indian intentions in the region. However, India has long shared a close relationship with Israel, albeit a closeted one, and should not be a cause for any apparent concern now.

There is a sense that Israel and Arab states can both enjoy a stronger relationship with India based on mutual interests. Nevertheless, foreign policy has been prominent during the Modi government's first year in office. Even as West Asia is roiled by a range of conflicts, the government has successfully managed the mounting rescue missions for Indians living in trouble spots of this region. India needs to position itself as a force for stability in the region, which in turn will require enormous diplomatic engagement.

## REFERENCES

1. A K Ramakrishnan "Mahatma Gandhi Rejected Zionism" Released August 15, 2001 The Wisdom Fund, P.O. Box 2723, Arlington, VA 22202. http://www.twf.org
2. Bansidhar Pradhan, "Changing Dynamics of India's West Asian Policy", *International Studies*, Vol. 40, no. 1, 2004: p. 4.
3. Anisur Rahman, "Indo-Saudi Relations: A Need for Coming Closer", *Strategic Bulletin*, Vol. IV, no. 2&3, May-Sep 1999: p. 20.
4. Jaideep Singh and Tersest Schaffer, "Overview South Asia Monitor", *CSIS*, Vol. 9, no. 2, Thursday 29, 2004 (accessed through Internet)
5. Shivaji Sarkar, "Tapping Alternative Market", *Special Gulf News*, (accessed through internet) published on 14/8/2004
6. Ibid.
7. Govt. of India, Annual Report, 2000-2001, *The Gulf, West Asia & North Africa*, p. 38 (accessed through Internet)
8. Indian Embassy (Bahrain) Indo-Bahrain Relations, http://indianembassy-bah.com
9. Embassy of India (Muscat), Indo-Oman Relations, http://www.indemb-oman.org/india-oman-relation.html
10. Muhammad Azhar, *Gulf Economies and Indo-Gulf Relations*, Delhi: New Horizon Publishers, 1999.
11. Anisur Rahman, "Gulf a Crucial Factor in India's Energy Requirements for Development", in S.N. Malakar (ed.) *Book on India's Energy Security and the Gulf.* New Delhi: Academic Excellence, 2006, p. 28.
12. Ibid
13. Girijest Pant, India's Energy Security: The Gulf Factor, Occasional Paper Series: CWAAS/SIS, JNU, GSP 2002.
14. Anisur Rahman, *Indian Labour Migration to the Gulf: A Socio-Economic Analysis*. New Delhi: Rajat Publications, 2001, p. 34.
15. *The Times of India*, New Delhi, Friday, November 18, 2005
16. Ministry of Overseas Indian Affairs, Government of India, Annual Report 2010-11.
17. P.C. Jain, Indian in Oman, GSP Occasional paper, Series (CWAAS/SIS/JNU New Delhi).
18. Embassy of India, Muscat. Into-Oman Relations, (accessed through internet) http://indemb.oman.org/commercial-services-eco relations.html

# 4

# Modi's Foreign Policy: A Changing Scenario on Indo-US Relations

*Amulya K. Tripathy and Roshni Kujur*

## Introduction

### U.S.-India Relations from Cold War to Post-Cold War

After India achieved independence in 1947, in this period the US viewed South Asia as a region largely peripheral to its central strategic needs. Though the decade of 50s was endorsed in poverty and underdevelopment, as a weak and a divided nation was staggeringly picking up its broken bits, the policy of Non-Alignment, had polarized into two blocs. The decision of the US to sell arms to Pakistan further distanced the two countries and India felt alienated from America. India's strong socialist leanings and growing closeness with the Soviet Union further strained the relations further. The reign of John F Kennedy (1961-1963), saw India as a partner against the rising power of communist China. During the 1962 Sino-Indian war, the US publicly supported India's interpretation of its border with China in the eastern Himalayas and even ferried military equipment to India.[1] (Neville 146).

However, despite its potential importance and occasional periods of Indo-U.S. cooperation, India refused to serve US as an active ally in the battle against global communism. For its part, India refused to join either the American or the Soviet side in the Cold War conflict and instead charted its own "non-aligned" policy.

The collapse of Communism, American interests and outlook towards the international order gradually changed. Meanwhile its continued help to Pakistan kept India estranged from it. However, the 80s saw some sunshine and the bilateral relations began to improve due to numerous high level visits and inking of several economic, military and cultural agreements.

"The key of American perspective vis-à-vis India during the Cold War had been the strategic importance of its military ally namely, Pakistan, to whom it had funnelled some $650 million under Military Assistance Programme (MAP) alone between 1950 and 1980. In fact, Pakistan had become the second largest recipient of MAP aid (after Iran) and that this assistance had been provided as part of a general "Northern Tier" strategy to limit Soviet expansion into the middle East, South Asia and the Indian ocean".[2]

Indira Gandhi's visit to the US in 1982 resulted in the latter agreeing to supply fuel and spare parts for the nuclear power plant at Tarapur. Rajiv Gandhi's visit to the US in 1985 was a great success on a bilateral agreement on scientific and technological exchanges which followed with the Indo-Us Bilateral tax treaty in 1988.

## U.S.–India Perceptions in post-9/11

The 9/11 attack on America in 2001 became a new parameter that began to influence politics world over including the Indo-US relations. Stephen P. Cohen said, no part of the world has more been affected by the terrorists' attack of September 11, 2001, than South Asia.[3] Terrorism, nuclear proliferation, rise of China and economic and environmental concerns became major factors determining the ties between the two states at the dawn of the new millennium. While the terror attack on Pentagon and World Trade Centre created suspicions against Pakistan, China's rapid rise became a major cause of concern for the US as it turned towards India as the safety valve in South Asia. Bill Clinton's love for India catapulted the position of a 'strategic partner'. There were a number of factors which made South Asia a central point in US war against terrorism. Also, American foreign policy began to develop a feeling of threat from the Islamic revivalism after the end of the Cold War as Afghanistan and Pakistan shared the regime of Taliban. As the United State prepared to launch its global war it put a tough choice before the states that "Either you are with us or against us". This indicated a decisive message with regard to the future course of relationship between US and Pakistan? Thereby in 2000, India and the USA agreed to establish a Joint Working Group on Counter-Terrorism. In the same year Bill Clinton's visit to India changed the equations between the top leaderships of the two countries. In 2001, Bush lifted post-Pokharan II sanctions imposed on India. In 2002, the Indo-US High Technology Cooperation Group came into being. In

2005 an Open Skies Agreement was signed between the two countries. In the same year Manmohan Singh visited America and many agreements, including the civil nuclear deal, were inked. In the 21st century, the US has become India`s largest investment partner with American direct investment of $9 billion accounting for 9% of total foreign investment into India. The end of the Cold War freed India-US relations from the constraints of global bipolarity, but interactions continued for a decade to be affected by the burden of history, most notably the longstanding India–Pakistan rivalry and nuclear weapons proliferation in the region. Recent years, however, have witnessed a sea change in bilateral relations, with more positive interactions, as President Bush calls India a "natural partner" of the United States and his Administration seeks to assist India's rise as a major power in the new century.

What factors will create certain challenges for the United States and India under Modi? As the United States and India built a new relationship over the past 15 years, one of the claims for the relationship concerns the shared values of the two multi-ethnic, multi-religious, secular democracies. While he has been legally cleared in India, Modi has never formally apologized for the riots. Many Indians and some Americans worry that his background in the RSS and his views of India as a homeland for Hindus may portend a Hindu-first approach—creating a chilling effect for India's minorities, and moving India away from the celebration of diversity.

## NDA II: Modi's Foreign Policy

After a historic election victory, Narendra Modi was sworn in as India's 15th prime minister on Monday, May 26, ending two terms of rule by the Nehru–Gandhi dynasty. Modi's political vehicle, the Bharatiya Janata Party (BJP), advocates a strong India that can resist pressure from world powers or regional rivals. Indeed, when in power previously, it was a BJP-led government under Atal Bihari Vajpayee that made India into a nuclear power and underlined its independence by refusing to sign the Nuclear Non-Profileration Treaty.

But Modi—equipped with the strongest mandate to rule in a generation—is not expected to pursue a Hindu nationalist policy. Modi "may have started his career on the extreme right, but he's coming more toward the centre now. And he will have to," says Sreeram Chaulia, a political analyst of the Jindal School of International Affairs in Delhi. This also applies to foreign policy where Modi has little experience, says Professor C.S.R. Murthy of Jawaharlal Nehru University in the Indian capital: "In my assessment he is not sophisticated enough to understand the nuances of foreign policy and conduct the course of negotiations. It will take time. He will require some proper advice."

According to this school of thought, Modi will first have to deliver on his election pledge to get the country's faltering economy back on its feet. With an average growth rate of around 5per cent over the last two years, the economy has not been expanding fast enough to provide jobs for the 13 million young Indians flooding onto the job market every year. Moreover, the manufacturing sector only accounts for 15 per cent of the economy compared to 31 per cent in China. This is where Modi's expertise—on display for 12 years in Gujarat—in attracting domestic and foreign investment, creating jobs and a building a modern infrastructure could come into play.

After being sworn in as India's prime minister, speculation is mounting about what impact Narendra Modi's brand of Hindu nationalism will have on his country's foreign policy. India's foreign policy has long been determined by a triple bottom line—interests, values and public opinion. All three are relatively impervious to changes of government. Each BJP policy will adhere to at least one of those drivers, and the degree of change from previous policy will be determined by how the government interprets each driver and how readily changes can be pushed through a strong-willed foreign service. PM Narendra Modi began his tenure with a diplomatic coup of sorts, securing the attendance of all South Asian Association for Regional Cooperation (SAARC) heads of states and Mauritius at his swearing-in ceremony. One guest who stood apart from all was the Pakistani Prime Minister Nawaz Sharif.

The Indian PM inviting Pakistan for his big day was meant to be a chance to reset ties. But three months after this historic event, there was a definite freeze in the India-Pakistan relationship.

India decided to call off the Foreign Secretary level talks with Pakistan, that were to set the agenda for the two prime ministers after the Pakistani High Commissioner met Kashmiri separatist leaders in the capital. The Modi government dubbed the meeting as interference in its internal affairs, setting a new 'Lakshman Rekha' in Indo-Pak ties.

## Modi and Indo-US Relations: An Expectations Policy Agenda

Observing the Modi's US visit, a leading authority on Indo-US relations, Ashley J Tellis said, "It is important that both sides have an honest conversation about the kind of relationship they seek."

Prime Minister Narendra Modi's September 2015 visit to Washington has emboldened bilateral relationship. Bilateral relations have deteriorated in recent years because of poor policy choices in India on nuclear liability, taxation, and trade. Moreover, India's recent political paralysis and crumbling economic growth have suppressed the opportunities for more robust commercial ties. In these circumstances, the latter-day approach to India pursued by the administration of US President Barack Obama has not helped. By permitting sectoral interests to define the content of US engagement with India, Washington has allowed a pernicious transactionalism to gradually replace the strategic vision that previously guided the evolution of bilateral relations. This mistake was compounded by the obsessive complaints of senior US government officials about India's economic policies. If Modi's private remarks to visiting American officials recently are any indication, the Indian prime minister seeks to end this stagnation. But his approach, which seemingly centres on soliciting huge international investments for important, high-profile projects at home, offers poor prospects for any deep US involvement that would quickly resuscitate joint cooperation between the two countries.[4]

At the moment, these concerns remain speculative. Modi's national campaign focused on growth and governance. He has publicly denounced extreme anti-Muslim statements proffered by some of his supporters. And the last period of BJP governance at the federal level, from 1998–2004, offers an instructive precedent. Though the BJP established them as a national force in the early 1990s through appeals to religion—such as a truck kitted out like a chariot of a Hindu god for a campaign about temple-building—their term in government was marked by a different ethos. Under Prime Minister Atal Behari Vajpayee, the BJP moderated its most extreme wing, further liberalized the Indian economy, and transformed relations with the United States.

This may become Modi's legacy as well, should he rein in the religious nationalists and keep his own sights focused on his campaign promises of economic growth and surajya, or "good governance". And this is where Washington can best meet Modi—on the pragmatic common ground important to his Administration, and to the United States.

## Getting the Economics Right

Modi seeks to right the wrongs which have slowed India's growth and kept India near the bottom of the World Bank's Doing Business index in 2013, India ranked 134 out of 189, below Yemen. The BJP platform focuses on infrastructure, foreign direct investment, intellectual property rights, manufacturing, and restoring India to its pre-modern-era primacy as a centre of global trade. This trade-led political slate represents the best opening in some years to expand economic ties. New Delhi sees the United States developing trade deals across Asia and Europe, and wonders where it fits. Signalling these paths to broadened economic ties will restore confidence in India that the United States has a strategic goal in sight. Getting India on a path towards the hugely important TPP will underscore the priority Americans place on ties with India, on track to become the world's third-largest economy by 2025. It will also create a more constructive atmosphere in which both governments can continue working on current market-access frictions.

## Filling the void in Afghanistan

The US and NATO troop draw downs in late 2014 created great uncertainty for India. New Delhi fears that once the international presence departs from Afghanistan, the Taliban and related groups—like the Haqqani network or the Lashkar-e-Taiba, both designated terrorist organizations under UN and the US authorities—will refocus more forcefully on Indian targets. India has played a critical role providing development and humanitarian assistance to Afghanistan since the turn of the century, emerging as its fifth-largest bilateral donor. It is also the region's dominant economic power, with companies willing and able to explore opportunities in Afghanistan, and the business knowledge networks to provide trade linkages for a country that desperately needs to develop its own sustainable economy. India stands out as the country most capable of providing ongoing assistance, development partnership, technology transfer, education, and business connectivity appropriate for Afghanistan's greatest needs. It has also, in response to requests from Kabul, begun to provide security sector assistance such as training, and funding Afghan equipment purchases from Russia.

The United States should begin to consult much more intensively with New Delhi as the drawdown continues, pulling India into conversations akin to those of a close NATO partner. Washington should also focus urgently on the unresolved problem of Pakistan as a terrorist safe haven, including the egregious example of Lashkar-e-Taiba Chief Hafiz Saeed—on whom the United States in 2012 authorized an award of up to $10 million for information leading to his arrest—openly holding rallies across Pakistan.

## Visa Issue

Visas have emerged as a central friction in the US–India relationship, because New Delhi and the Indian IT services sector sees them as a market access barrier in the United States. This is a shame, because the growth in people-to-people contact has been one of the most successful aspects of the changed relationship between New Delhi and Washington. To keep up with the visa demand over the past decade, the United States has invested more than $100 million into building larger consulate facilities across India. Of all the H-1B visas (for highly skilled temporary workers) issued worldwide, 64 per cent go to Indian citizens; China is second, with a mere 8 per cent. From Washington's perspective, it's hard to see how Indians could perceive such a dominant position as constrained by barriers. But it's also true that the total number of H-1B visas available has shrunk since its high point at the end of the Clinton administration.

As the new Indian government settles into New Delhi, this pragmatic agenda, building on campaign promises critical to India and the United States will reinforce the larger strategic importance of a strong US-India relationship. While the jury may be out for some time on how Modi will govern India, the urgent need to regain a collaborative spirit on the economic front should be at the top of Washington's inbox. As US withdrawal from Afghanistan proceeds, India should be at the forefront of US consultation to ensure sustainable stability for the region.

Finally, given the difficulties advancing comprehensive immigration reform in Congress, there are some concrete steps the Obama administration can take to alleviate several frictions related to visa issues. Each of these would result in meaningful progress for both sides, and would advance US national interests.

## Modi's Mission in United States: A New Agenda

On the final day of Prime Minister Narendra Modi's visit to the US, Defence Cooperation Agreement was extended with India by another 10 years. The pact, which was to expire in June next year, will now be in force till 2025.

The development follows India's decision to increase the foreign direct investment (FDI) cap for the defence sector from 26 per cent to 49 per cent. The issue was taken up at Modi's extensive meeting with US Defense Secretary Chuck Hagel, before the prime minister's summit-level talks with President Obama at the Oval Room of the White House. The pact, New Framework for the US-India Defence Relationship, was signed in June 28, 2005, by then defence minister (now President) Pranab Mukherjee and his American counterpart Donald Rumsfeld.

The Indian Cabinet is yet to approve Rs 15,000 crore worth of US defence deals, including one for sale of 22 AH-64E Apache attack choppers, 15 Chinook heavylift helicopters and the Javelin anti-tank guided missiles. American defence equipment makers like General Electric and Boeing had met Modi a day earlier and expressed their desire to expand operations in India.

## Civil Nuclear Agreement

On the civil nuclear agreement between the two countries, an India-US group is to address all implementation issues for speeding up deployment of American nuclear reactors in India. The agreement on this had hit a roadblock in 2010, when India rolled out a nuclear liability law. For his summit talks with Obama, Modi drove straight from Blair House, where he was lodged, to the famous West Wing of the White House. The talks were first in a restrictive format and later at a delegation level.

At his joint media briefing with Obama after the meeting, Modi said both sides were "committed to taking forward the civil nuclear partnership agreement. We are serious about resolving at the earliest the issues related to civil nuclear energy cooperation. This is important for India to meet its energy security needs."

This was Modi's second meeting with the US President since taking charge as India's prime minister. On Monday, the two leaders had discussed bilateral issues over a private dinner in an informal setting. The body language of both leaders looked relaxed after delegation-level talks, with Obama sipping a drink occasionally and Modi wearing a constant wide grin. After this meeting, Modi took everyone by surprise by addressing the media, jointly with Obama, in Hindi. During his visit to the US, the prime minister had earlier addressed the United Nations General Assembly (UNGA) in Hindi. On economic ties, Modi hinted that the government was going for further economic and policy reforms that would help in "rapid growth" of bilateral trade and investment partnership. Both sides discussed the recent standoff over the World Trade Organization's (WTO's) trade facilitation agreement (TFA). Modi revealed he had frank discussions with Obama and expected US support in addressing India's concerns over public stockholding for food security. In a definitive step, Modi also sought easy access for Indian services firms in the American market. At the time of going to press, Modi and Obama were expected to issue a joint statement on strategic ties between their two countries. Later in the day, Modi was scheduled to address the US-India Business Council.

Obama's visit as Chief Guest for the Indian Republic Day (2015) showed a new venture of Modi's foreign policy with United States. It is beyond expectations, in spite of past embarrassed relations of Modi with the US. The same day after accepting India's invitation Obama administration informed it's old ally Pakistan that Obama will visit Pakistan too. It shows Obama administration's weakness with Pakistan.

## Obama Visit, a Sign of Progress

US President Barack Obama recently said that the United States could be India's "best partner", as he wrapped up a three-day visit to New Delhi by highlighting the shared values of the world's biggest democracies. Speaking to an audience of young people, the US president reiterated that the relationship between Washington and New Delhi "can be one of the defining partnerships of this century."[5] Relations between the two countries haven't always been smooth.

Another reason this visit was significant is that it symbolized a rapid improvement in the US-India ties, which were nearly undone at the end of 2013 over a row involving Devyani Khobragade, India's deputy consul general in New York. Accused of visa fraud and underpaying her house-keeper, she was arrested and strip-searched by the US law enforcement wing, sparking angry protests and diplomatic retaliations from India.

It appeared unlikely that Obama's visit would result in major policy breakthroughs on the issues that will dominate his agenda with Modi. But the mere fact that the talks were happening was being viewed as a sign of progress given the recent tensions that have marred relations between the US and India. The relationship hit rock bottom in 2013 when Indian Deputy Consul General Devyani Khobragade was arrested and strip-searched in New York over allegations that she lied on visa forms to bring her maid to the US while paying her a pittance. Her treatment caused outrage in New Delhi and India retaliated against US diplomats.

Ties between the US and India have been steadily improving since Modi took office last May. He and Obama met for the first time late last year in Washington, and officials from both countries say they quickly developed an easy chemistry. That came as something of a surprise to regional analysts given Modi's difficult history with the US. He was denied a visa to the US in 2005, three years after religious riots killed more than 1,000 Muslims in the Indian state where he was the top elected official.[6] On the White House Blog on Obama's visit it is said, The President and Prime Minister Modi pledged to enhance U.S.–Indian cooperation on our mutual climate and clean energy goals. From our highly successful US-India Partnership to Advance Clean Energy (PACE) umbrella program to technical work on emerging technologies, the US and India made important progress on combating climate change.

The agreements include:

- Enhancing bilateral climate change cooperation to achieve a successful and ambition agreement in Paris this year.
- Cooperating on Hydroflurocarbons to make concrete progress in the Montreal Protocol this year
- Expanding PACE-R, the US-India Joint Clean Energy Research and Development Center, to extend funding for research on solar energy, energy efficiency, and advanced biofuels.
- Launching air quality cooperation to help urban residents reduce their exposure to harmful levels of air pollution.

Further the US and India agreed on to combat climate change here.

## True Global Partners: Incentivizing Trade and Investment

Under President Obama, trade between the two countries has increased by about 60 per cent to nearly $100 billion a year—a record high. But that's still hundreds of billions less than the trade we do with China. "We've got to do better," the

President said, speaking at a US-India Business Council Summit in New Delhi. So, the US President announced a series of additional steps that will generate more than $4 billion in trade and investment with India while supporting thousands of jobs in both countries:

The Export-Import Bank will commit up to $1 billion in financing to support "Made-in-America" exports to India. OPIC will support lending to small and medium businesses across India that will result in more than $1 billion in loans in underserved rural and urban markets. The US Trade and Development Agency will aim to leverage nearly $2 billion investments in renewable energy in India.[7]

## The Obama Visit: A Sign of Development?

The US President Barack Obama's two-day visit to India can be summarised through meaningful issues that dampened trade, investment and strategic relations between the world's largest democracies. In this flash, we look beyond the much publicised 'bear-hug' to list four positive areas from the Obama visit and their economic implications for India.

## Civil Nuclear Deal: a 'break-through' but yet to workout

The two nations resolved a long-standing deadlock on the implementation of a 2008 civil nuclear deal, which was hamstrung by India's enactment of a liability law that exposed US nuclear plant vendors to excessive legal proceedings. Under the new arrangement, suppliers would be indemnified against unlimited liability through an insurance pool. If successfully implemented, renewed investments by US vendors would help in reducing India's widening energy deficit and aid infrastructure growth.

## Cooperation towards Strengthening India's Defence Capabilities

The two leaders endorsed efforts to enhance collaboration in defence technology transfer and co-development. India still imports an unreasonably high share (70%) of its defence equipment needs, a bulk of which (76%) comes from Russia followed by the US (7%). Thus, steps to upgrade India's domestic defence industry are imperative. In this context, policy efforts, including recent lifting of foreign investment limits in defence (49% from 26%) and deeper Indo-US defence ties bode well for India's domestic defence sector and the economy in general.

Commitment to invest USD 4 billion in India—a focus on renewable energy sector. The pledge includes:

(1) USD 1 billion in financing by the US Export-Import Bank to export 'Made in America' products.

(2) USD 1 bn to be lent by US Overseas Private Investment Corporation to small and medium enterprises in rural India, and
(3) USD 2 bn committed by US Trade and Development Agency for renewable energy. Meeting unmet demand for electricity in rural India, which constitutes 47% of 1.2 billion population, through renewable sources can greatly reduce India's kerosene subsidy bill and minimize resource intensity of the economy. Share of renewable energy in India's total installed power capacity has jumped from just 2% in 2002 to 13% currently. While greater foreign investments would help boost India's renewable energy sector further, it needs to be complemented by government efforts to tackle regulatory barriers, resolve land acquisition issues, ease infrastructure constraints and mitigate storage and distribution losses. India has other options beyond cooperation with China.

Diplomatic interpretations of Mr. Obama's visit centred on US efforts to make India its South Asian anchor and a strategic counter weight to China in its 'pivot Asia' strategy. This notwithstanding, we expect Stronger links with the US – the only bright spot in the developed world today—to help India improve its trade balance at least bilaterally. This would contrast with its rapidly deteriorating trade deficit with China, which recorded a huge USD 31 bn in 2013.

## Conclusion

US President's short visit to India certainly has long-term positive implications for India, especially so given that the Modi government has kept up the tempo on wide ranging reforms since its landslide victory in 2014. With that said, most reforms have been enacted through executive action while legislation remains a significant obstacle for the new Government given its lack of majority in the upper house of Indian parliament. This would weigh on India's ability to push through difficult structural reforms across land acquisition, labour, mining and taxation, which require legislative approval.

"I think Modi surprised everyone by, with very little hesitation, embracing the United States," said Milan Vaishnav, a South Asia expert at the Carnegie Endowment for International Peace. "To give credit where credit is due, the Obama administration stepped in very quickly after his election to signal that he was willing to do business."

Obama also had a good rapport with former Indian Prime Minister Manmohan Singh. However, US officials expressed some frustration that their personal warmth never translated into policy breakthroughs.

Though in NDA-II rule Modi has started the US policy in a new look, but all UPA policies are being followed. In spite of that, Modi is keen to progress on every aspect of Indo-US relations. From Obama's visit too it is evidenced a secular India can serve better in domestic as well international affairs.

This is also apparent from the visit of both leaders to each other's country and signed agreement for a steady progress in relations. Apart from international and regional compulsion, both leaders came in close ties leaving the past behind.

Recently Modi's approach towards South Asian countries has witnessed a new era. Where Ameria's role too evidenced. What constrained Modi is the Chinese's huge support to Pakistan on supply of military equipment and openly vetoed in UN against India, in support of Pakistan. Here India's role should be very cautious. Of course, it is to Chinese interest to be with India for its economic interest. Furthermore, Modi should seriously think over Obama's advice on secularism in India. India's secular foundation has been internationally known and it should be maintained.

## NOTES

1. Maxwell, Neville. *India's China War.* Dehra Dun: Natraj Publishers, 1970, pp. 146, 270–71, 364, 378, 385.
2. Tripathy, Amulya K and Tripathy, Rabi Narayan (2008),*US Policy Towards India A Post Cold War Study*, New Delhi, Reference Press, p. 2.
3. Cohen, Stephen P. *India Emerging Power*, Washington, DC: The Brooking Institute Press, 2002, p. 13.
4. Tellis, Ashley J. *What Modi must do in the US to reset the relationship*, Washington DC September 27, 2014 Last Updated at 00:24 IST
5. Obama, Barack, President, US and India Can be best Partner, Jan 27th, 2015
6. *Time Magazine*, 23 Jan 2015 Dr. Amulya K Tripathy, Head Department of Political Science, Science College (Autonomous) Hinjilicut (Affiliated College of Berhampur University) Odisha.

# 5

# Indo–Iran Relationship: Challenges and Opportunities in the Changing Context

*A.P.S. Chouhan*

The ties between India and Iran date to the Persian Empire of Cyrus the Great. The nations have long influenced each other in the fields of culture, art, architecture, and language, especially during 1526-1757 when the Mughals ruled India. India and Iran also shared a border until 1947. For many centuries, Persian remained the language of Indian judiciary. The first Persian newspaper was carried out not by any Iranian but Raja Ram Mohan Roy, an enlightened Indian social reformer of 19$^{th}$ century. However, after independence India's relation with Iran could not sustain the same warmth due to gamut of prevailing compulsions. Iran, along with Pakistan and Turkey, joined American-led capitalist block after Second World War and in contrast India adopted the dogma of non-alignment and tilted towards the Soviet Union-led socialist block. Pakistan has remained a factor between India and Iran. But after the end of the cold war many changes have taken place at the bilateral as well multilateral level and these changes have brought India and Iran closer than ever despite the fact that there are varied divergences of interests and opinions between the two countries. In the backdrop of July 2015 nuclear deal with Western world, Indo–Iran relationship is likely to become increasingly important to both countries in the days ahead, and within the ambit of this paper, this aspect will be analysed in detail.

It must be mentioned that the Indo–Iran divergences are manageable, therefore despite many odds India and Iran relations strengthened with the end of the cold war.

Long ago, Kautilya had opined that convergences of interests are the basic formulators of foreign policy. Growing India–Iran bonhomie has vindicated the fact. It has also rejected the traditional notion that religious similarity could be a common bond between co-religious countries. Saudi Arabia is the self-proclaimed harbinger of the global Islam and Iran also considers herself fit for the same role but both never had cordial relations at least after the end of the cold war. So is the case of Pakistan and Iran. The fact remains that there are more conflicts of interests between Saudi Arabia and Iran and between Iran and Pakistan. A major bone of contention between Saudi Arabia and Iran is treatment of Shia Muslims in Saudi Arabia and elsewhere. In the southern provinces of Saudi Arabia, Shias are in majority and additionally these areas are the important contributors of Saudi oil production. In the backdrop of Yemen crisis, sectarian angle is going to be significant within the Arabian world.

Besides, Saudi Arabia has propelled Wahabism, which perpetuates intolerant Islam and even considers Shias as non-Muslim. Being the richest country of the Muslim world, Saudi has propagated this ideology of Wahabism throughout the globe. Iran started protesting export of Wahabism by Saudi Arabia particularly after 1979 revolution and since then sustained its protest.

General Zia-ul-Haq had captured power after overthrowing an elected government in July 1977 led by Zulifikar Ali Bhutto (a Shia), therefore through implementation of Nizam-e-Mustafa in 1979 (Rule of the Prophet) Zia consolidated his position. Shias of Pakistan took this initiative as the beginning of their marginalization within Pakistani society as had been mooted to Ahmadis by declaring them as non-Islamic. Since then more than 10,000 Shias have been killed in Pakistan in sectarian violence. Pakistan is a Sunni majority country but Shias constitute around 20–25% of overall population, and they are educated, wealthy and possess big land holdings as well. There are ample evidences that Pakistani state and particularly army is nurturing Sunni sectarian groups to eliminate the sphere of influence of Shias.

Iran considers herself as the custodian of global Shias. Saudi Arabia considers herself in the same role, but for the Sunnis. The bitter enmity between both is accelerating violence within the countries where both sects are dominant by all counts. For the last three decades Pakistan has been converted into a battleground between Saudi Arabia and Iran to propagate their interests. We are aware of the connection between the Taliban and Al-Qaeda with Pakistan. The elimination of Osama Bin Laden in May 2011 at Abbotabad (Pakistan) has vindicated the fact that both have been working with tacit understanding. Interestingly, the Taliban and Al-Qaeda both are claiming themselves as the harbinger of global Islamic Ummah but they are killing Shias in Pakistan. Taliban ruled over Afghanistan from 1996 to 2001. During this period, they killed Shias in thousands and fiercely tried to divide the ethnic and sectarian mosaic of Afghanistan. In Mazar-e-Sharif many officers of the Iranian consulates have been killed during the Taliban period (1996–2001) and bring both Afghanistan and Iran at the brink of war. Due to mediation of Prime Minister (Pakistan) Nawaz Sharif (1997–99) the tension subsided. Even at this juncture Shias are under serious threat from the Taliban and its other outfits, and their sustainable elimination is on both in Pakistan and Afghanistan. We are aware that Saudi Arabia and Pakistan are two important countries out of three, who gave recognition to the Taliban government as required under the provisions of the international law. The third one was UAE.

Since March 2011, violence in Syria is taking place between the government and the opposition forces, and according to the United Nations till June 2015 around 2,25,000 people have been killed. The Tehrik-e-Taliban Pakistan had declared in July 2013 that they had dispatched their fighters to wage Jihad against the government forces in Syria. One of the most important motivating factors behind this decision of the TTP is that the President Assad is Shia. Saudi Arabia along with their supporters is with opposition forces and Iran along with China and Russia is supporting President Assad's government.

Afghanistan is a matter of utmost concern both for India and Iran. During the Taliban regime India and Iran along with Russia extended their support to Northern Alliance. By December 2014, NATO forces had already withdrawn from Afghanistan. Since last ten years, Karzai regime, an elected one was ruling in the country and tried to build the strength of Afghan National Army (ANA) but there are apprehensions that after the NATO withdrawal the ANA would not be able to properly contain Taliban. In this prevailing situation, Taliban may take over and given its previous governance record, it could be detrimental for the national interests of both India and Iran. In this situation they must forge a strong alliance to protect and promote their national interests in Afghanistan. Needless to say that Pakistan will not like this to happen, therefore India and Iran must formulate a combined strategy to cope with this situation. Saudi Arabia, traditional arch rival of Iran, will also support Pakistani position to export its narrow version of Islam as it had done during the previous Taliban regime. Needless to say that the Taliban has been the harbinger of the conservative version of Islam in Afghanistan.

Iran is traditionally a peaceful country. Iran established a national army only recently, under the Pahalavis. The country has no martial tradition unlike its western neighbour Turkey. After Iraq war, Tehran has avoided direct military conflict ever since, but its military expenditure is slight high compared to that of smaller Gulf countries.[1] India also never initiated any war but has only responded till date. In case of India and Iran there are less divergences and more convergences of interests therefore they must cooperate. The changing security architecture of

South and South West Asia has also pushed both countries on the same platform. There are many critical areas where national interests of the two countries are converging. Drug trafficking and terrorism is a major concern for both countries. Since last three decades more than 5,000 Iranian border guards have been killed while containing drug traffickers. Iran shares a large portion of her border with Afghanistan and Pakistan therefore drug traffickers find Iran a route convenient to export drugs to Europe. There are strong interlinkages between drug trafficking and terror network and India and Iran are the worst affected from this menace. Pakistan and Afghanistan are the dens of drug trafficking and terror network. For preventing this situation to spill over to India and Iran, it is must that they should do some concerted groundwork to cope with the future challenges.

Since independence Pakistan remains a mortal enemy of India. Iran extended its all round support to Pakistan during 1965 war. In 1979, the monarchy of Iran was thrown out by an Islamic revolution led by Ayatuallah Khomeini. He is considered as one of the leading Islamic ideologue along with Maulana Maududi of Pakistan and Md. Qutub of Egypt. Iran has been supportive to the rights to self-determination of Kashmir Muslims.

Cold war has changed many things within the system of international relations. Iran–India relationships have grown manifolds due to many compulsions brought by the end of the cold war. Many interests started to converge, which has been the real cementing force of foreign policy, as was aptly said by Kautilya. Three Indian Prime Ministers have visited Iran since the end of the cold war. In 1993, Prime Minister Narsimha Rao visited Tehran and opened new vistas of deepening relationship. In 2001, Prime Minister, Atal Bihari Vajpayee visited Tehran. This visit was unique because it initiated cooperation in many areas that were unexplored previously—Central Asia, energy and military matters, cooperation in Afghanistan that began along with strategic security. Iranian leaders had reciprocated these top visits. Many other dignitaries from both countries also visited each other. In 2003, Iranian president visited India and became Chief Guest for the Republic Day, a very special invitation only reserved for the closest Indian friends. In August 2012, Prime Minister Dr. Manmohan Singh visited Iran to participate in 16th Summit of the NAM. During this visit many rounds of negotiations were held with notable delegations. It was agreed that along with Afghanistan, India and Iran must work together on the areas of common benefits.

In April 2013, Foreign Minister Salman Khursheed visited Tehran and it was agreed that Chabahar port facility will be expanded. India and Iran have already connected Central Asia through this port while making Delaram-Jarnej road in western Afghanistan. It has also reduced Afghanistan's dependence over Karachi port for trade and other necessities. During this visit many bilateral agreements were inked ranging from energy supply to defense cooperation. India by all available calculations will become third energy consumer by 2015. In April 2015, surface transport minister Nitin Gadkari visited Tehran and pledged the connectivity of Central Asia and Afghanistan through newly developed Chabhar port jointly built by India and Iran. Iranian President Rouhani and Indian PM Modi met in Ufa (Russia) in July 2015 and had a 90 minutes bilateral talk. During this meeting it was pledged that India and Iran will accelerate their bilateral relations. In July 2015, Iran and Western world signed nuclear deal and now gradually decade long sanctions imposed against Iran will be lifted. In August 2015, Iranian Foreign Minister, Javad Zarif, had visited New Delhi and met PM and other ministers. Again it was pledged that cooperation on all fronts will be accelerated. During one day visit of Mr. Zarif issues related to Islamic State threat, energy investments, Afghanistan and development of Chabahar port were discussed. He also stated that India is an important player in West Asia and can play a leading role in the region. PM Modi conveyed India's commitment to work with Iran for development of the Chabahar port that would have far reaching benefit, not only for the people of India and Iran, but also for Afghanistan and the entire Central Asian region. Mr. Zarif acknowledged India's support during turbulent times. It is expected that PM Modi may visit Tehran by early 2016.[2] Iran has enormous energy reserves and India is today 5th global energy consumer and by 2020 will be 3rd energy consumer after pushing Japan and Russia. It is also opined by global economic pundits that India will be representing 23% of global GDP by 2043. For the sustainability of India's growth saga, sustainable and diverse supply of energy is must.

India has more than double Muslim population of Iran and one forth among them are Shias. They are peaceful, stay away from any anti-state activities and are contributing enormously in national developmental process. It is also a big state of satisfaction for Iran because almost all countries where Shias are under suppression are Islamic countries, but despite majority of Hindus, Shias are comfortable in India.

The United States and India have been in good relationship since last one decade. The atomic agreement inked in 2008 and deepening bonhomie is the testimony. Dr. Manmohan Singh visited Tehran despite huge protest by U.S.-led block. Tension still prevails between Iran and Western countries over the nuclear issue despite truce made by President Obama and President Rouhani after their telephonic conversation in latter part of 2013. In the backdrop of this tension, Dr. Singh's visit was path breaking. Many bilateral treaties were inked during the visit. This visit gave renewed hope to Iran and negated the notion that it has been isolated at the international level.

Afghanistan remains the top agenda between India and Iran because of convergences of interests. Iran never supported Taliban and forged Northern Alliance along with Russia and India. During its five years (1996–2001) of rule, the Taliban killed thousand of Shias in Afghanistan. Being the only Shia majority country of the globe and an immediate neighbour of Afghanistan, it was a matter of concern for Iran. Pakistan was among only three countries of the globe that recognized the Taliban according to the international law as the legitimate ruler of Afghanistan, Iran started to distance itself from Pakistan. Here it is of utmost importance to mention that in the post-cold war scenario the clash for the supremacy over Islamic world is prevailing between Iran and Saudi Arabia. In recent decades, Iran was compelled to understand that Saudi Arabia is getting closer to Pakistan therefore it has set a new tone for its relationship with Pakistan.

As Kautilya had said that an enemy's enemy is friend, therefore trust deficit between Iran and Pakistan has widened due to many prevailing factors and that has pushed India to cooperate with Iran on variety of issues. Iran has cooperated with several other regional countries, notably India and Russia, to gain influence in any post-American Afghanistan. During the Afghan civil war in the post-Soviet period, the three countries constituted the bloc that supported the Northern Alliance in opposition to the Pakistani and Saudi-supported Taliban forces.

## Strategic Imperatives for the Development of Chabahar for India and Iran

In order to address its need to secure energy routes, and to contain the growing Chinese influence in the Arabian Sea, Persian Gulf, and the Indian Ocean, India brought Iran into an economic and strategic alliance. India spent huge amounts on the Iranian Port of Chabahar. Iran was already working on Chabahar port in Sistan-Baluchistan, which will be easily accessible for Indian imports and exports through road and rail links to Afghanistan and Central Asia. The development of Gwadar in Pakistan by China just 70 km east to Chabahar, and Chabahar by India, resulted not only in open rivalry and competition between the two countries in the region, but also raised contention for the economic and natural resources of Central Asia.

Chabahar's geo-strategic location plays an important role in connecting India to Afghanistan and Central Asia both militarily and economically. India sees Central Asia, Iran, and Afghanistan situated at the crossroads of overland trading routes as a potential consumer market for Indian products. Similarly, Iran wants to get India's cost-effective source of high technology inputs.[3] India's ultimate objective is to bypass Pakistan, and also cooperate with Iran on a highway and rail system that leads from Chabahar port into Afghanistan and Central Asia.

Highway connecting Afghanistan and Central Asia has been in order since last many years. Rail system has to be restored.

On the other hand, there is active Chinese cooperation in the Port of Gwadar, since it is the only port which can serve the best interests of both China and Pakistan in the region. The Port will, therefore, enable China to keep a strict watch on India's growing influence in the Indian Ocean, the Arabian Sea, and Persian Gulf. Hence, the possibility of any future economic and military collaboration between India and the US in the region can be effectively dealt with. Another geographical advantage of the port is that it will reduce the distance for energy imports from Persian Gulf to China. Gwadar also holds a geo-strategic significance for China because of its proximity with the sea lane between West Asia and China. It is vital for oil trade. As a gateway to the Indian Ocean, Gwadar will provide Beijing with a listening base from where the Chinese may exert surveillance on hyper-strategic sea links. The military activities of the Indian and American navies in the region can also be closely watched. Gwadar port will also provide a strong base for Chinese ships and submarines. Since Gwadar Port can fulfil its political, security and commercial objectives vis-à-vis India, China has spent a huge amount on its construction. More significantly, Gwadar Port provides both Pakistan and China to strengthen its security vis-à-vis India. The port win also helps both China and Pakistan to promote trade with Gulf States possessing 63% of world's oil reserves.[4]

China has acknowledged the strategic significance of Gwadar no less than that of the Karakoram Highway.[5] This will further strengthen the relations between China and Pakistan. China is also interested to turn Gwadar into an energy-transport hub by building an oil pipeline from Gwadar into Chinese Province of Xinjiang. The proposed pipeline will carry crude oil from Arab and African states. Gwadar's strategic advantage to China is due to its close proximity with the Strait of Hormuz. The presence of the US forces in the region poses not only a threat to Chinese navy but, also to its commercial interest. Gwadar provides China with a strong base where it can monitor US naval activity in the Persian Gulf, India in the Arabian Sea. China has already set up electronic posts at Gwadar for monitoring maritime traffic through the Strait of Hormuz and the Arabian Sea.

Chabahar is a part of the Indian grand design to apparently develop transportation infrastructure. It is however viewed with suspicion to sabotage Pakistan's future strategy of expanding its influence in Central Asia and beyond. Chabahar provides India easy access to Afghanistan and Central Asia through Indian Ocean. India's ultimate desire is to connect Chabahar with Central Asian countries through roads and a network of railway system to bypass Pakistan, and to reduce the dependency of Central Asian countries on the Pakistani port of

Gwadar. Iran is already enjoying close socio-cultural and economic relations with the Central Asian countries. Iran is working on several projects in Tajikistan including the Anzob tunnel, and constructed a bridge over the Amu Darya that connects Chabahar with Khojent route. In addition, the construction of 218 km long Zaranj–Delaram highway that now links Afghanistan to the Iranian port of Chabahar also connects Herat and Kabul via Mazar-e-Sharif in the north and Kandhar in the south—thereby providing easier access to Afghanistan and possibly even further, to Central Asia via Iran.[6] Owing to the fact that Central Asian countries are land-locked, they depend on Iranian ports, especially on Chabahar for trade and commercial relations with the rest of the world. Moreover, Afghanistan is more friendly and close to India than Pakistan. In this regard, with its eco-strategic positioning in Iran, India gets opportunity to have an access to warm waters through this region. The creation of North–South Corridor is the best prospect for Iran to expand its transit corridor to India. The idea of North–South Corridor has multiple purposes and is, therefore, seen as an opening to bypass East–West Silk Road Project.[7]

Thus, India gains more security, political, economic and strategic advantages from Iran, Afghanistan and Central Asia as compared to China. Iran is more stable than Pakistan. It has better relations with Afghanistan and the Central Asian states, bordering Azerbaijan and Turkmenistan, Iran has a natural geographical advantage by providing access to Sea for the Central Asian States. However, intensifying competition between India and China in Arabian Sea and Central Asia, the growing US concerns about China's offensive capabilities, made the global and regional security environment more complex and sensitive.

If one has to be focused then it is crystal clear that stability of Afghanistan, containment of terrorism, containment of drug trafficking, integration of Central Asia with larger world, energy security, Pipeline issues and development of commerce and cooperation in energy sector are some of the important cementing points of bilateral relationship between India and Iran. The nuclear issue and Western sanctions on Iran and Kashmir issues are irritant factors between both countries.

There are range of divergences between India and Iran. These divergences need to be narrowed down. The first and most important among them is nuclear issue. Due to 2008 nuclear treaty, India and United States have been converted from being cold war era Estranged Allies to Engaged Allies in 21$^{st}$ century. This development maintains Kautilya's theory that convergences of interests play a decisive role in the realm of international relations. In the aftermath of July 2015 nuclear deal, several decade long sanctions imposed against Iran are going to be lifted. This seal has reduced the existing trust deficit between Iran and the United States. Islamic State has become a serious cause of concern for the countries of the Middle East. Iran is the only country within this region that has shown its willingness to contain Islamic State. The United States is also concerned to contain Islamic State. This is equally true to contain the resurgent Taliban in Afghanistan. The resurgent Taliban and the Islamic State is also a serious security threat for India, Russia and China. This prevailing security architecture in the Middle East and South West Asia has pushed India and Iran to deepen their relationship.

This cooperation will bring durable peace and cooperation in this most volatile part of the globe. India, today, is perhaps the only capable country to convince both of them on this issue. But instead of doing mediation with Iran and the United States, India has become party against Iran while voting on nuclear issue against Iran in the United Nations. Bringing closer to United States and Iran on the same page on diverse conflicting issues is in the larger national interests of India. It will also provide stability to the security of South West Asia. India must convey to the United States that Iran is mutually beneficial for us. India must also advice Iran that instead of confronting the US, it must cooperate with the Western world. Iran has been doing its efforts to free Shia places of worships in Iraq but it has yielded no adequate results till it was not vacated due to American military operation. After the elimination of Saddam Hussain in 2003, it was known that the one of the most pious places of Shia worship, Najaf and Karbala is in Iraq not in Iran. Iran must also shed its mindset of opposition for the sake of opposition to the United States. It is also equally applicable for the United States. India is better positioned today to mediate between two bitter rivals probably first time after the end of the Second World War.

Second most important irritant between India and Iran is Kashmir issue. Recently Iran has not extended its support to the cause but previously it had extended its support to Kashmir independence from India. Iran must understand with its experience in Iraq war that religion cannot be a promoter of national interests. Since many decades Iran is competing with Saudi Arabia on a range of issues. Both are harbingers of Islam so then a question arises that why are they fighting against each other? Only convergences of interests are cementing friendship in foreign policy. It is an open secret that in majority of the cases India and Iran's national interests converges therefore they must cooperate not only for the protection and promotion of their national interests but for peace and stability in the region.

Iran is yet another point of contention between India and the United States although recently India has been motivated by the US to participate in UN-led Western sanctions against Iran. Global concern over Iran's nuclear weapon development program, and the potential for subsequent proliferation, has driven US efforts to coordinate a coercive international sanctions regime. India, however, has a long historical and mutually beneficial relationship with Iran centred on trade, commerce, and cultural diffusion, with India currently importing significant amounts of oil from and facilitating the financing of Iranian energy companies—the targets of Western sanctions. India and Iran are two important old civilizations and have been connected to each other since millennia.

After the end of the cold war, there has been a shift in the global distribution of power: from the West to the East. While the political system globally can still be described as unipolar, Asia is characterized by multipolarity. The powers of Asia compete for power, influence and resources. Amongst the great powers on the rise is India. India is the seventh largest country in the world, the second most populous and the world's largest democracy.[8] It is one of the world's most powerful economies and has highly professional armed forces, which have made India emerge as an entity that can help shift the global balance of power. In this changing political environment, India has struggled to define itself and comprehend its power capabilities as well as the possibilities and limitations of that power. Indian global thinking is characterized by a lack of consensus on a strategic framework that can structure its foreign relations.[9] India could change the game while invoking real spirit of NAM in the context of Iran. Given the pressure of the United States on India in this context India must take the principle stand and advise both to settle their thorny issues through amicable means of settling disputes. Fortunately the situation is emerging to help India's ideal line on Iran.

## Concluding Observations

What complicates India's Iran policy is that the US and Iran are adversaries. The US wants to isolate Iran, partly through imposing strict sanctions on the country, and it wants other countries, including India, to follow suit. This forces India to engage in a delicate balancing act between, on the one hand, pursuing its regional goals and beneficial policies towards Iran, and on the other hand ensuring that the relationship with the US does not suffer. The question is how big a part the US has played in the Indian foreign policy decisions that concern Iran. Since President Rouhani's rule, Tehran has perhaps understood realist aspects of the delicacy of its diplomacy particularly towards the West led by the United States. The truce has been worked out. Still it is early to say that it will be certainly positive but the fact remains that after many decades window of opportunity has been visible. It is compulsion also of both the parties to resolve the crisis. Things are going on positively at least till date and one must hope that a win-win situation will be achieved by both the parties. At the outset of 21st century the contours of international system has changed radically. It has provided an opportunity to both countries. India is growing rapidly and all set to become third global energy consumer country by 2020. The sustainable growth of India could not be ensured till the ensuring of energy security. Iran is one of the top five energy producing countries and not far away from India physically too, therefore Iran could be an excellent energy security guarantor to India. In Central Asia too, Iran and India have several convergences. They wish to connect Central Asia with the Iranian port of Chahbahar. The road is ready and rail needs some more time to furnish. It will give an impetus not only to Central Asian Republics but to India and Iran also. Iran is an energy producing country and its growth depends on the sustainable sale of this precious resource. Due to growing requirements India is and will be an important buyer of Iranian energy products.

Eminent Indian security analyst, Raja Mohan has rightly stated in November 2013 "Any nuclear deal between Washington and Tehran will immediately bring down oil prices, relieve the current macroeconomic pressures on India, and improve Delhi's energy security calculus over the longer term. US–Iran rapprochement will help to strengthen Afghanistan against the Taliban and Pakistan and expand India's room for regional maneuver after 2014."[10] The deal between Washington and Tehran has already been concluded and it is time when Indian diplomacy must act and bring Iran and United States on the same page to ensure peace and stability in Afghanistan in particular and Southwest Asia in general. Iran is an important player and it had been part and parcel of Indian efforts along with Russia and Central Asian Republics to contain Taliban and formation of the Northern Alliance during Taliban rule over Afghanistan to contain the Taliban (1996-2001). In the backdrop of NATO withdrawal by the end of 2014 this proximity is utmost required and the US interest is also served. Containment of the Islamic State has remained a serious concern for the Western block, Iran, India, Russia and China. The way is executing the captives it reminds us about the medieval barbarism and through these heinous acts, IS has emerged as a threat to global humanity. Iran could be pivotal to contain IS because one of the undeclared objectives of the IS has been to weaken Iranian influence in the Middle East.

India will extremely benefit with its growing relationship with Iran and vice versa. Both countries have come together in several areas of interests—be it economic, strategic, or other matters, therefore they must minimize the divergences. In August 2013, Vice President of India was present in the swearing in ceremony of new Iranian President Rouhani. It was an excellent goodwill gesture. Both countries are availing good relationships but to cope up with the emerging challenges they urgently need to enhance it. Deepening India–Iran bonhomie is therefore must for peace and stability in Southwest Asia. The basic requirement for a country is to provide human security for its people. Both India and Iran could do it successfully through deepening of their relationship. It is of utmost need of the hour for both the countries to promote their bilateral relationship. Modi government is expected to forward its previous NDA government policies led by PM Vajpayee with timely modifications in the context of Indo–Iran relationship.

## NOTES

1. Shahram Chubin, "Is Iran a Military Threat", *Survival,* Vol. 56, No. 2, April-May 2014, 66.
2. "Can't forget support India gave us during difficult times, Iran", *The Times of India,* New Delhi, August 15, 2015.
3. Juli A. MacDonald, "Rethinking India and Pakistan's Regional Intend", *The National Bureau of Asian Research Analysis,* 14:4: 2009: 5-26.
4. Rajeev Ranja Chaturvedy, *Interpreting China Grand Strategy at Gwadar,* Institute of Peace and Conflict Studies, 14 February 2006.
5. *Dawn,* Karachi, July 4, 2006.
6. *Tehran Times (Tehran)* November 28, 2011.
7. Mohammad Arifeen, "Chahbahar Port: Its Importance for India", *The News International (Rawalpindi),* November 22, 2011.
8. Brzezinski, Zbigniew. 2012. *Strategic Vision.* New York: Basic Books, pp. 20, 162.
9. Pant, Harsh V., 2008. *Contemporary debates in Indian foreign and security policy: India negotiates its rise in the international system,* UK: Palgrave Macmillan, p. 1.
10. C. Raja Mohan, "The Great Game Folio", *The Indian Express,* New Delhi, 20 November 2013.

# 6

# India-Bangladesh Bilateral Agreements: A New Opportunity

*Bibhuti Bhusan Biswas*

## I

India-Bangladesh relations often highlight the importance of geographical realities in depicting Bangladesh's security dilemma vis-à-vis India. The problem of demarcation of the boundary has plagued Indo-Bangladesh relations in the past. Often termed as an India-locked country,[1] Bangladesh shares 4,094 kilometers of land border on three sides, and the fourth side opens towards the Bay of Bengal.[2] Sharing of common borders also creates a scope for generating a horde of disputed issues like illegal migration, cross-border criminal and terrorist activities, and so on. Several attempts have been made to arrive at a comprehensive settlement of the land boundaries between India and (then East Pakistan) Bangladesh since 1947. The Nehru-Noon Agreement of 1958 and the Agreement Concerning the Demarcation of the Land Boundary between India and Bangladesh and Related Matters of 1974 (referred to as 1974 LBA) sought to find a solution to the complex nature of the border demarcation involved. During Dr. Manmohan Singh's visit to Bangladesh, a Protocol was signed (referred to as the 2011 Protocol) to the 1974 LBA, on 6th September 2011, that paved the way for a settlement of the outstanding land boundary issues between the two countries.[3] But the two countries failed to sign an accord on sharing river water after objections from the Chief Minister of the Indian state of West Bengal. There was also no deal granting India overland access across Bangladesh to its land-locked north-eastern states. The two countries agreed to put in motion a deal that allows about 51 Bangladeshi enclaves inside India to be integrated within Bangladesh and about 111 Indian areas inside Bangladesh to become part of India. But due to change of guard in New Delhi the LBA was put on hold.

However, Prime Minister Narendra Modi very clearly stated that his Government policy is 'neighbourhood-first'. Mr. Modi's visit to Bangladesh in June 2015 shows the seriousness of the policy. His visit opened a new chapter in India-Bangladesh ties as they settled the 41-year-old boundary dispute which has been an irritant. Besides, he announced a fresh USD 2 billion line of credit for Bangladesh and promised quick implementation of the earlier line of credit of USD 800 million and full disbursement of USD 200 million. He also expressed confidence to have a fair solution to the Teesta and Feni river water sharing issues with Bangladesh with the support of state governments in India.[4] The principal opposition party Bangladesh Nationalist Party's (BNP) Chairperson, Khaleda Zia, described the passage of the Amendment "an important day in our national life." And also leaders of the two countries accepted the event as a new milestone in bilateral relations.

## II

Sheikh Hasina started her second term as Prime Minister of Bangladesh on January 6, 2009,[5] and paid an official visit to India on January 2010. As Awami League is known to be sympathetic towards India due to many historical as well as political reasons,[6] therefore it is quite natural that Indo-Bangladesh relations got a boost and both the countries have already initiated some important moves, despite evoking a strong reaction from the opposition-led Bangladesh National Party. Prime Minister Sheikh Hasina made a very pertinent observation in her press conference in New Delhi during her visit, "strong anti-Indian sentiments have always been there but if the common people benefited from India-Bangladesh relations, negative forces would be subsumed".[7]

The Modi Government followed the path of the previous Government, hence he took the issues between India and Bangladesh positively. The present NDA Government understood the significance and importance of resolving land boundary problems with Bangladesh, hence Mr. Modi successfully passed the Constitutional Bill through Rajya Sabha and Lok Sabha that was necessary to implement the Land Boundary Agreement with Bangladesh. Besides, Modi has shown his political dexterity by neutralizing opposition from his own party units in Assam and West Bengal. India and Bangladesh has signed 22 agreements including a significant one to settle the long-standing border dispute and also Prime Minister Narendra Modi and his Bangladeshi counterpart Sheikh Hasina inked a bilateral trade document after talks. Among the agreements LBA is one of the landmark achievements of Modi Government. India agreed to transfer 111 enclaves with a total area measuring of 17,160.63 acres to Bangladesh, while Bangladesh agreed to transfer 51 enclaves with an area measuring of 7,110.02 acres to India.[8] The implementation of the LBA helped in improving the quality of life of 51,549 people, who have been living in misery, lack of identity in the enclaves, and deprived of basic human rights. For all practical purposes, they have been stateless people, with a hand-to-mouth existence, denied access to schools and hospitals as well as other basic services. All the inhabitants can now look forward to a national identity and enjoy the same benefits and services as their neighbours living outside the enclaves.[9]

Apart from LBA, both countries have signed several bilateral agreements, such as Trade, Coastal Shipping, Inland Water Transit and Trade, Dhaka-Shillong-Guwahati bus service, Kolkata-Dhaka-Agartala bus service. Additionally, they have also signed a Memorandum of Understanding between Coast Guards, prevention of human-trafficking, prevention of smuggling and circulation of fake currency notes, extending a New Line of Credit (LoC) of $2 million by government of India to government of Bangladesh, Blue Economy and Maritime Cooperation in the Bay of Bengal and the Indian Ocean, use of Mongla and Chittagong Ports, Project under India Endowment for Climate Change of SAARC, Indian Economic Zone, Cultural Exchange Programmes, Education Cooperation, Submarine Cable Company Limited (BSCCL) and Bharat Sanchar Nagar Limited for leasing of international bandwidth for Internet at Akhaura, etc.[10]

## III

Bangladesh is occupying a strategic location in the eastern part of the sub-continent. Bangladesh has met many challenges and is now set on the path of economic development that has seen its GDP growth averaging around 6% annually.[11] Enhancing bilateral relations between India and Bangladesh promises to provide exponential benefits for both countries. For India, in particular, transit and transshipment across Bangladesh is important as it is expected to boost the economy of India's Northeast. Connectivity may provide the transmission channels through which development impulses can spread across the region and can add to the dynamism of economic and social progress of both India as well as its eastern and southeastern neighbours. For India, such developments promise to be harbingers of dramatic changes in its own eastern and northeastern states, including the city of Kolkata.[12]

Hence, to improve connectivity, the two sides signed a pact to allow Indian cargo ships to use Bangladesh's Mongla and Chittagong ports. The ships will now ferry cargo from Bangladesh to the Indian ports instead of routing it via

Singapore as they earlier did. Besides, India and Bangladesh signed another protocol on inland water transit and trade that will allow the use of rivers of the two countries to promote trade among India's northeastern states and adjoining parts of Bangladesh. India is hoping that the pact which has a five-year life will attract Indian companies to build ports and other infrastructure that will boost intra-regional trade. Bangladesh too stands to gain from this, with access to Nepal and Bhutan through Indian territory. The two countries also signed a pact to promote maritime cooperation in the Bay of Bengal and the Indian Ocean.

The Prime Ministers of India and Bangladesh Mr. Modi and Sheikh Hasina as well as West Bengal Chief Minister Mamata Banerjee flagged off the Dhaka-Shillong-Guwahati and Kolkata-Dhaka-Agartala buses. This will primarily benefit tourists and residents of India's landlocked northeastern states by cutting down travel time. The two countries will soon be part of a new regional arrangement among Bangladesh, Bhutan, India and Nepal that allows motor vehicle transit among the four countries. India will open two new consulates in Sylhet and Khulna in Bangladesh, while Guwahati will see a new Bangladesh consulate in the coming months. Hence the Modi Government is emphasizing its policy to Connect small countries like Bangladesh and Myanmar, to large countries like India and China, so that it can narrow down the existing development gaps. In addition, India's aspiration to connect to China and Southeast Asian economies through Myanmar and Bangladesh by creating cross-border transport-cum economic, energy and telecommunications corridors. This will ease India's national connectivity, particularly for its northeastern region.

## IV

Energy Security has always been a concern for India and Bangladesh, as with modernization, the use of energy has increased rapidly and people's lives and national economy have become dependent on the usage of energy. So, to maintain a secured future, different initiatives are being taken in the energy sector.[13] A look at the pacts signed and commitments laid out in the joint statement shows that India has positioned itself as a key partner in Bangladesh's energy sector. It is clear in the case of energy cooperation between India and Bangladesh that the challenges faced by stakeholders and advocates are not of a technical nature. The issues here are the lack of initiative, leadership and ownership of the issues. Mr. Modi very much award the complexity of the issue, hence agreed to partner Bangladesh in its goal of achieving an installed capacity of 24,000 megawatts (MW) by 2021 as he sought opportunities for Indian companies in power generation, transmission and distribution. Also India agreed to increase power export from existing 500 MW to 1,000 MW soon. Modi agreed in principle to consider Bangladesh's proposal to allow import from India to Bangladesh additional power in phased manner through construction of an additional grid interconnection in western Bangladesh. The two countries also agreed to evacuate power from northeastern India to Muzaffarnagar in India through Bangladesh by constructing 800 KV, 7000 MW HVDC multi-terminal bi-pole DC grid line.[14] Another pact was signed for the construction of a pipeline for the export of diesel from West Bengal to Bangladesh. Besides, Reliance Power signed a deal with the state-run Bangladesh Power Development Board to produce 3,000 MW of electricity at a cost of $3 billion. Adani Power Ltd will set up two coal-fired plants with a total capacity of 1,600 MW that will cost more than $1.5 billion. India and Bangladesh also agreed to hold an annual dialogue "to undertake comprehensive energy sector cooperation, including areas of coal, natural gas, LNG, supply of petroleum products in the sub-region, renewable energy, oil and gas pipelines.[15] As the policy makers and the people of Bangladesh always look towards India as a threat because of India's overwhelming political and economic power, but Mr. Modi is able to reduce mistrust and generate confidence among the policy makers and people of Bangladesh. Besides, he has given clear signal to the world community in general, and Bangladesh in particular, that India needs cooperation from all the neighbouring countries for overall growth of the region. Hence, the Prime Minister Sheikh Hasina's observation of in her press conference in New Delhi during her 2009 visit, "strong anti-Indian sentiments have always been there but if the common people benefited from India-Bangladesh relations, negative forces would be subsumed"[16] is proving to be right.

## IV

India and Bangladesh on several occasions had high delegation talk regarding combating terrorism, human trafficking, smuggling and circulation of fake currency notes as Bangladesh has been a major transit point for fake currency. Bangladesh is concerned about the home-grown extremism and terrorism, and therefore on 1 August 2013 the Bangladesh Supreme Court declared the registration of the Jamaat-e-Islami illegal, ruling that the party is unfit to contest national polls, which was the largest Islamist political party in Bangladesh. Furthermore, Hasina after taking office in December 2009 handed over four militants wanted by India for staging attacks in northeast India.[17] Therefore, the two Prime Ministers expressed satisfaction at the unparalleled level of cooperation between the two countries on security-related issues and reaffirmed their unequivocal and uncompromising position against extremism and terrorism as well as their commitment to cooperate with each other by sharing information about groups and persons indulging in terrorism. Apart from that both the Prime Ministers also reiterated their commitment that their respective territories would not be allowed to be used for any activity inimical to the other. As terrorism and extremism are always a big threat to national security as well as development, both countries are looking to extend all possible help to curtail such elements. Hence, the agenda of development and permanent settlement of problems took the front seat.

## V

Bangladesh is India's largest trading partner among SAARC countries.[18] The two countries are also looking to boost trade along the border. India announced a $2 billion new credit line to Bangladesh following a $1 billion assistance it provided in 2011 for infrastructure development. Aggregate trade between India and Bangladesh for the 2014-2015 fiscal year stood at $6.9 billion. However, trade is heavily in favour of India with its exports to Bangladesh at $6.2 billion. To reduce the huge trade deficit India and Bangladesh signed a pact to set up an economic zone that will allow Indian companies to set up companies to manufacture and export goods to India. India has always stood by Bangladesh during the need with aid and economic assistance to help it cope with natural disasters and floods. Previously India has also extended a line of credit of US$ 800 million and US$ 200 million grant to Bangladesh for a series of projects, including procurement of buses, railway infrastructure, supply of Broad Gauge microprocessor-based locomotives and passenger coaches and dredging projects.[19] Also opening of border "Haats" is providing trading opportunities for local people along the common border. Modi's visit to Bangladesh along with West Bengal Chief Minister Mamata Banerjee is a positive sign for the people to regain trust. Further, development of border infrastructure will be the first priority of both the Government to ease the trade, transportation of goods as well as connect Southeast Asian countries with SAARC. More particularly India's Northeast region will be benefited if India gets transit through Bangladesh. Besides, Bangladesh's economic as well as socio-cultural development is directly related to Northeast region of India. Hence, both the Governments are trying to address the trade imbalance and improvement of border infrastructure and reducing Non-Tariff Barriers. Modi Government policy is to engage Bangladesh in particular, and all other SAARC countries in general, to boost trade and people-to-people contact so that socio-cultural and economic development can move equally.

## VI

India has recognised the strategic significance of northeast with regard to its "Look East/Act East" policy. India is one of the fastest growing economies in the world and is working for peace and stability in the South Asian region largely, and to an extent in some other countries of the world too. Though Northeast region got huge natural resources this region was neglected for decades. The main uncertain block for economic development of the Northeastern region is the disadvantageous geographical location. Northeast region shared approximately 98 percent of its borders with Bangladesh, Nepal, China, Myanmar and Bhutan; hence, Northeast India seems to have a better scope for development and it can bring peace in the region.[20] The Narendra Modi Government seems focused on a new push to boost ties with Bangladesh with Northeast India as the key foothold from where to launch economic initiatives beneficial to both nations. The present Government in New Delhi is keen on cementing ties with all her neighbours as it is necessary to bring Northeast region to the mainstream, which is apparent from its decision to improve the quality of relationship with Bangladesh. It was for this reason that Gen. V.K Singh, Minister of State of External Affairs and Minister of state (independent charge) for North East Region, chaired a meeting with the Chief Ministers of the Northeastern states in Guwahati just prior to his Dhaka visit. The Northeast region is strategically very important for India and also for Bangladesh, as it reflects from the Gen. V.K. Singh's statement during his visit to Dhaka. He said India wants to further deepen trade ties with Bangladesh—"There is plenty of scope to expand Bangladesh's trade in India, particularly in the Northeastern region."[21] Modi Government's aim is to develop Northeast region in every aspect, so Bangladesh's cooperation is positively needed to achieve this goal. India-Bangladesh cooperation will curtail cross-border terrorism and will promote trade as well as reduce trade deficit. As Bangladesh market is slowly becoming an attractive investment destination for Indian companies, hence, Indian investors started looking towards investing in Bangladesh after the signing of the Bilateral Investment Protection and Promotion Agreement between India and Bangladesh in 2009[22] as well as signing of 22 agreements during Modi's visit to Bangladesh in June 2015. India needs cooperation of Dhaka to curtail Northeast Indian insurgent groups operating out of Bangladesh to normalise the situation. Hence, now the two governments need to remove the blockages in trade and connectivity. Whereas India can further improve the export and investment environment for Bangladesh, Dhaka can formalise its decision to let India use its Chittagong and Mongla ports for goods traffic to the Northeast.[23] Prime Minister Narendra Modi is taking all measures to connect Northeast region with the mainstream development and get transit through Bangladesh to rest of India. On November 29, 2014, during his visit to Northeast he promised that his Government will extend all possible help to develop the region.

## VII

India and Bangladesh are important to each other's progress and prosperity. By the smooth passage of the 119th Amendment all the political parties have conveyed to the people of Bangladesh that India is willing to work with them cooperatively as their preferred partner. Development of infrastructure and connectivity with Northeast region of India, Bangladeshi business and industry will gain investments. The linking of Nepal, Bhutan, and India's northeast to Bangladeshi ports will help make Bangladesh the natural bridge between South and Southeast Asia.[24] The events and issues discussed above illustrate that no foreign relations for Bangladesh attract the kind of attention and raise emotions among its peoples as ties with India do. This is very significant and makes it abundantly clear that the two countries are more than just close neighbours. It is now India's move to implement the agreements on the ground as soon as possible. Delay will only weaken the enthusiasm in Bangladesh, which is clearly in favour of India. In the larger context, it could create a South Asia development quadrangle when the land connections between Bangladesh, Nepal and Bhutan through India become operational. However, a single visit by Modi cannot achieve everything but a great beginning has been made.

## NOTES

1. Akmal Hussain, "Geo-politics and Bangladesh Foreign Policy," *CLIO*, June 1989, vol. 7, no. 2, pp. 99-100.
2. Of this 4,094 kilometres of border, West Bengal shares 2,216 km, Tripura shares 856 km, Meghalaya shares 443 km, Mizoram shares 318 km and Assam shares 262 km.
3. http://www.bbc.com/news/world-south-asia-14799350
4. *The Assam Tribune* (Guwahati), June 7, 2015
5. *Times of India* (New Delhi), January 7, 2010.
6. For details see, Nalini Kant Jha, "Pakistan, India and the Creation of Bangladesh," *International Studies* (New Delhi), vol.29, no.1, January-March 1992, pp.79-94.
7. *The Hindu* (New Delhi), January 13, 2010.
8. India and Bangladesh Land Boundary Agreement, available at http://mea.gov.in/Uploads/PublicationDocs/24529_LBA_MEA_Booklet_final.pdf
9. Ibid.
10. n. 5.
11. Pinak Ranjan Chakravarty, "PM Modi's Visit to Bangladesh Has Set the Tone for Future Cooperation to Bring Two Countries Even Closer" *Economic Times* (New Delhi), June 8, 2015.
12. Anasua Basu Ray Chaudhury and Pratnashree Basu, *India-Bangladesh Connectivity: Possibilities and Challenges*, Observer Research Foundation, Kolkata.
13. A. Ahmed, C.M. Shahariar and M.A. Rashid Sarkar, *Energy Cooperation in South Asia: Prospects and Challenges* http://bea-bd.org/site/images/pdf/4.pdf (cited on 25 August 2015).
14. What we learnt from Narendra Modi's Bangladesh visit http://www.livemint.com/Politics/JbGxtRjzQSjUDCgY7OLGQJ/What-we-learnt-from-Narendra-Modis-Bangladesh-visit.html (accessed on 25 August 2015).
15. *Times of India* ( New Delhi), 6-7 June 2015.
16. *The Hindu*, January 13, 2010.

17. n. 13.
18. http://www.mea.gov.in/Portal/ForeignRelation/Bangladesh_Dec2014_Eng.pdf
19. High Commission of India, Dhaka website: http://hcidhaka.gov.in/ (accessed on 25 August 2015).
20. Wasbir Hussain "India and Bangladesh: The Northeast Thrust" *Institute of Peace and Conflict Studies*, New Delhi
21. Ibid.
22. Amit Ranjan, "India-Bangladesh Border: The Post LBA Tensions," *Policy Brief*, Indian Council of World Affairs, New Delhi, 3 July 2015
23. Ibid.
24. Jayant Prasad, "Breakthrough in India-Bangladesh Ties," *The Hindu*, 11 May 2015.

## REFERENCES

Graham Lees, "Burma is the Key to India's 'Look East' Economic Strategy", July 19, 2007, available at http://www.worldpoliticsreview.com/article.aspx?id=941

Jairam Ramesh, "North-East India in a New Asia", Manipur Online, available at, http://www.manipuronline.com/NorthEast/January2006/northeastindia12

North-Eastern Region Vision 2020, Ministry of Development of the North-Eastern Region and North-Eastern Council, Agartala, May 13, 2008; also see, Namrata Goswami, "Looking 'East' Through India's North-East", IDSA Occasional Paper, No.2, June 2009.

Muchkund Dubey, India's Foreign Policy in Contemporary International Scenario (South Asian Publishers, New Delhi, 2009).

Sanjib Baruah, Durable Disorder: Understanding the Politics of Northeast India (New Delhi: Oxford University Press, 2006).

# 7

# Indo-African Relations: Changing Dimensions

*Chandra Mohan Uppadyaya*

Indo-African relations inform India's emotional, aspirational and a bit of nostalgic part of the foreign policy. This nostalgia is not confined to Africa only but quite evident in the third phase of our Look-East Policy, where economic and political affinities are expected to be cemented by our cultural legacy. Our convention of Asian Relation Conference way back in 1947, which ultimately culminated in the creation of NAM and our successful espousal of the causes of Afro-Asian countries, forms the aspirational part of our foreign policy. The non-alignment is the by-product of our idiosyncratic value system. As J Bandyopadhyaya has well said, "Although the cold war provided the necessary context for nomenclature and operational strategies of nonalignment, the nonalignment as such was an inevitable consequence of decolonization process rather than the cold war itself."[1]

Our aspirations are quite modest. India considers itself as a natural friend, philosopher and guide of Africa. We are emotionally attached with the continent because of the debt we owe to them. This was the place where one Mohandas Karamchand Gandhi went for one year to sort out some legal problems, and this was the land which returned to India a precious gift 'Mahatma Gandhi' within a short span of time.

A gradual shift in the global power structure is being discerned over the past few decades. In the famous words of Fareed Zakaria, "It is about great transformation taking place around the world...now we are living through third power shift of modern era. It could be called 'The Rise of the Rest'. Over past few decades the countries all over the world have been experiencing rates of the economic growth that were once unthinkable. For the first time ever, we are witnessing genuinely global growth. The share of people living a Dollar a day, or less, plummeted from 40% in 1981 to 18% in 2004 and is estimated to fall to 12% by 2015. This is creating an international system in which countries in all parts of the world are no longer objects or observers but players in their own right."[2]

## The Rising Africa and the Opportunities for India

Africa has decisively shed the stereotype of a "Hopeless Continent" since *The Economist* regrettably labeled Africa 'the hopeless continent' more than a decade ago. Africa has come a long way since then. This profound change has been acknowledged by the same magazine. At the end of year 2011 *The Economist* headlined 'the Africa Rising'. According to it the sun shines bright over Africa. On 24th November 2012 *Time* magazine published a report on Africa using the same caption as used by *The Economist* earlier. In a colorful article the *Time*'s journalist Alex Perry points out, "Despite Africa's rapid economic growth over the past decade, the continent still faces numerous challenges, especially converting growth into jobs. If Afro-pessimism is outdated, undiluted Afro-optimism is premature."[3] India and Africa have shared a close relationship in the past. The first India Africa forum summit held in New Delhi in 2008 marked the beginning of a robust partnership. The second Africa India Forum Summit, held in Addis Ababa in May 2011, emphasized the renewed focus of India to strengthen and enhance its partnership with countries in the African continent. Bilaterally, both India and Africa agree that strong cooperation between the two is necessary to take the relationship ahead.

The areas of cooperation are wide-ranging and include, among others, politics, trade and business, culture, etc. Greater economic engagement has been seen as crucial to boosting ties between Africa and India. India's trade with Africa amounts to $70 billion by the end of year 2012, and is expected to rise substantially in the near future. Mutual efforts to increase trade include initiatives such as Focus Africa. India's commitment to Africa was underlined at the highest level. The then President APJ Abdul Kalam (Late) affirmed, "Focus Africa program is one of the highest priority items for India."[4] The government has also announced 'Techno-Economic' approach for Africa-India Movement or Team-9 framework for cooperation, which has brought in a regional focus for its development projects and concessional loans; African countries in the region have been clamoring to be included. Shashi Tharoor succinctly puts it, "This co-equal multilateralism is an important feature of India's new model of engagement with Africa."[5] The New Partnership for Africa's Development (NEPAD), an economic development program launched by the African Union (AU) to accelerate economic growth of African countries and promote greater participation in the global economy, has attracted Indian investment. While a large proportion of Indian investment has been in the energy sector, significant investments have also been made in the infrastructure, engineering, chemicals, services, banking and finance, health, information technology and telecommunication sectors in Africa".[6]

Another significant link with continent is the presence of Indian Diaspora in African countries. The greater integration of this community can significantly bolster bilateral relations. This focus on Africa is not new. In the first few decades of our independence, Africa became the largest beneficiary of India's technical assistance and capacity-building programs writes former Union minister and renowned writer Shashi Tharoor. He rightly maintains, "These cooperation programs laid the foundation of the political and economic partnership between India and Africa in twentieth century".[7]

Our identification with issues affecting Africa was evident even during freedom struggle. India imposed sanctions against the apartheid regime in South Africa. The AFRICA fund further closely identified India with Africa's struggle against colonialism and apartheid as the acronym AFRICA stood for Action for Resisting Imperialism, Colonialism and Apartheid. This Fund, in fact, was crystallized in New Delhi in 1986.

Democracy, Development, and Demographic Dividend, Trade, Technology and Training are some of the buzz words now defining Indo–African relationship. The year 2015 promises to be a year when these narratives of a rising Indo-Afro-optimism, set to intersect, and impart a fresh resonance to the emerging vocabulary of the multi-faceted India-Africa engagement. The increasing convergence of interests, values and a burgeoning web of win-win opportunities will form a major part of our next summit expected to be held later this year itself.

This economic resurgence will be also reflected in other areas of engagement. Since the two sides launched an ambitious and multi-layered summit process in the summer of 2008, India has pledged over $5.4 billion in Lines of Credit for a wide array of development projects across the emerging continent. Over 65 per cent of this soft loan package has already been disbursed. Going by past record, the new Indian government is expected to announce an ambitious multi-billion dollar developmental package at the New Delhi summit in 2015. In a signature initiative, India is also in the process of delivering on its promise of setting up over 100 training institutes in different African countries, encompassing a wide array of areas ranging from agriculture, rural development and food processing to information technology, vocational training, English language centers, and entrepreneurial development institutes. Trade, Technology and Training remains the enduring tripod that frames the multifarious India-Africa relations and will remain so in the months to come.

Many countries may have higher bilateral trade with Africa, but what sets apart India's engagement with Africa is its focus on innovative capacity building programs and the deployment of ICT, the country's forte, to help build a knowledge economy in the African continent. No project illustrates this thrust on innovation and development-driven partnership better than the India-assisted Pan Pan-African 'e-network' that provides telemedicine and tele-education to Africans living thousands of miles away by linking them with top educational institutions and super-specialty hospitals in India. Over 1600 training institutes offering training under India's technical cooperation program to Africa; once they start functioning they could prove to be an asset in Africa's ongoing efforts to create a new generation of skilled and technology-empowered workers. The greatest challenge before Africa is to solve the continuing food scarcity. It is has been said that one of the most important impacts of climate change on human civilization will be an acute and permanent crisis of food supply. Reduction in crop yield could lead to higher prices of food and greater food insecurity; and increases in food prices globally could trigger regional food crises, causing political instability and further undermine the economic performance of weak and unstable states.

## Food Security

Food security is "a situation in which all people, at all times, have physical and economic access to sufficient, safe and nutritious food to meet their dietary needs and food preferences for an active healthy life".[8] Food security has three aspects: food availability, food access and food adequacy. The root cause of food insecurity in Africa is the inability of people to gain access to food due to poverty; hence the continent continues to lag behind in poverty alleviation. High prevalence of HIV/AIDS, civil wars, conflicts and poor governance, frequent drought and famine and agricultural dependence on the climate and environment have contributed to the problem of food insecurity. The challenges of food security in Africa include an under-developed agricultural sector, barriers to market access, effect of globalization which comes with liberalization of markets; disease and infection and government policies that emphasize structures and institutions rather than people. India with its experience of green revolution can help Africa solve the problem. Indian investment in agriculture and horticulture is mainly concentrated for export purposes.

African agriculture has the capacity to produce food and become a bread basket for India. India has started a multi-tiered cooperative partnership which involves engagement with pan-African institutions.

Indian investors are respected across Africa, "because they are reputed to be effective in the local environment, to ensure the highest employment generation...transfers technology and to be quite willing to live among Africans and employ African managers".[9] The Indian pharmaceutical industry has established such a good reputation for providing Africans with urgently needed healthcare, at affordable prices; this has forced Chinese firms to fake Indian packaging. Shashi Tharoor the honorable member of Parliament has paid the rich tributes to Indian companies when he says that if imitation is the best form of flattery, counterfeiting is the ultimate confirmation of the indispensible role India pharma is playing in Africa.

Like India, Africa is also afflicted by terrorism. But the similarity ends here. Unlike India, African land itself is used to produce the scourge of terrorism. The recent months have brought into focus the deadly spiral of terrorism ravaging a large swathe of the continent. The proliferation of terrorist and extremist groups in the continent like Al-Qaeda in the Maghreb, Nigeria-based Boko Haram, and Al-Shabaab and their suspected links with militants in other parts of the world entails a more proactive collaboration between India and Africa on the issue of terrorism. Looking ahead to the next stage in the India-Africa partnership, one can, therefore, expect a deepening of security cooperation across a spectrum of areas, including terrorism, piracy, and maritime security.

## The 'C' factor in Afro-Indian Relationship

India must draw right lessons from Chinese foreign policy. China is taking its role as a global superpower very seriously. Beijing has always liked to make its considerable presence felt in immediate neighborhood. Now China is looking to extend its sphere of influence in Africa. Leaders of 48 of 53 African nations were in Beijing for the three-day China–Africa forum. Unlike earlier Chinese regimes which aimed at propping up socialist governments in Africa, the main purpose of this summit was to ostensibly push trade and commerce. One of the primary reasons for Beijing wooing Africa is to secure a steady supply of oil to meet China's ever-growing energy demands. Already Angola has replaced Saudi Arabia as China s largest supplier of oil. Beijing also buys much of its copper, iron ore and cobalt from Africa. In 2012, the total volume of China-Africa trade reached $198-40 billion[10], a year-on-year growth of 19.3%. Of this, US$ 85.319 billion consisted of China's exports to Africa, up 16.7%, and US$ 113.171 billion was contributed by China's imports from Africa, up 21.4%. China has given generous aid packages to African countries to build road railways and schools.

The close ties between Beijing and Africa have important lessons for India. As an aspiring world power India needs to go beyond outdated Non-Aligned Movement-type rhetoric and engage seriously with Africa. New Delhi need not, of course, get into a race with Beijing. China which has nearly 1 trillion in foreign currency reserves can play much faster and harder than India. Besides, China as a permanent member of the UN Security Council can use its veto to great advantage in protecting rouge African states. Instead, New Delhi must look to revive its historic links with Africa and use the large Indian Diaspora, particularly in South Africa, to good effect for furthering trade. India must also be careful of formulating an African policy that avoids the pitfalls of China embracing regimes that have a poor human rights record. Both Beijing and New Delhi have been criticized for supporting the government in Sudan, which has been accused of grave human rights abuses, because of their investments in Sudanese oilfields. Trade with Africa must be uppermost on India agenda but it cannot be the only elements.

As India seeks to take its place in the high table of international politics, it must realize its responsibilities towards less developed nations. New Delhi's policy towards Africa will be a good indicator of whether India is ready to play the role of a great power in the future. On the personal account of former Diplomat and Parliamentarian Shashi Tharoor, it can be safely asserted that Africans look towards Indians not the way they look at West or China. They look towards India with admiration and gratitude. We need to increase our presence there. Our embassies are ill staffed and are unable to cope up with the needs of modern industries and entrepreneurship. Apart from rivalry with China, we can look for opportunities for cooperation and collaboration. India and China are jointly exploring and developing a Sudanese oil field, for instance. Chinese are known to adopt the deceptive ways of buying the foreign governments and offering easy loans which is nothing short of bribery. A democratic India can ill afford it. "There is a broader strategic dimension as well to the alleged rivalry in Africa—India's reported discomfort with the growing Chinese presence on African rim of Indian ocean (is one of them)...".[11] The other Chinese move of bringing South Africa under the BRICS umbrella is also a matter of concern for India, because this very move has reduced the IBSA to a virtual redundancy.

One interesting area of Chinese presence in Africa is that Chinese inroads have prompted something of an African backlash, with Zambia in 2011, electing a president who had campaigned on an openly anti-Chinese platform.

For India energy is the central motivational force to engage Africa in more than one way. With 70% of India's oil supply imported, mainly from West-Asia, we need to diversify our options. Africa obviously becomes our centre of attraction. ONGC and its foreign arm ONGC Videsh are already working in this direction. Nigeria is now supplying about 15% of the Indian requirement. Some other African countries, notably Sudan and Libya, are the destinations for our investments.

Besides bilateral issues, the Indo-Africa equations will also impact the contours of an emerging world order. As the UN celebrates its 70th anniversary, India and Africa should join hands to fructify the long-deferred dream of the reform and expansion of the UN Security Council, with seats for both New Delhi and the African continent in a reformed world body. In the intertwining of the Indian Dream and the African Dream, there is a lot at stake. As one prominent journal from Uganda, 'New Vision' wrote, which is worth mentioning, "Africa had a lot to gain from deeper links with India: 'there are lessons to learn from its strengths in agriculture, technology, financing and land tenure systems, and its development path offers a highly relevant example for Africa."

## NOTES

1. J bandyopadhyaya.
2. Zakaria Fareed, *The Post American World*, Penguin-Viking, 2008, pp. 3, 4.
3. www.howwemadeitinafrica.com
4. Shashank: "India-Africa Relations", *World Focus*, Vol. 25, Oct-Nov-Dec 2004, p. 50.
5. Tharoor Shashi: *Pax Indica*, Allen Lane-Penguin Books India, 2012, p. 261.
6. Shashank: "India-Africa Relations", *World-Focus*, Vol. 25, Oct-Nov-Dec 2004, p. 50.
7. Tharoor Shashi: *Pax Indica*, Allen Lane-Penguin Books India, 2012, p. 254.
8. Angel Mwaniki, "Achieving Food Security in Africa: Challenges and Issues" Cornell University, U.S. Plant, Soil & Nutrition Laboratory, p.1.
9. Tharoor Shashi: *Pax Indica*, Allen Lane-Penguin Books India, 2012, p. 260.
10. online available source.
11. Tharoor Shashi: *Pax Indica*, Allen Lane-Penguin Books India, 2012, p. 266.

# 8

# Russia in Asia-Pacific: A Power Balancer or Hegemon?

*Deepak Yadav*

The Asia-Pacific region has been identified as the world's new centre of gravity. The emerging new architecture revolving around Asian powers has given rise to questions about Russia's role in the region, given that the Eurasian giant has an Asian presence in the Far East. The mutual threat perceptions between Russia and other Asian nations have altered over the course of twenty years since the collapse of communism. Russia is now recognized as a non-threatening great power with global significance. The Asia-Pacific has always been a region of great importance for super powers throughout the Cold War and after, due to its unique geo-political and geo-economic importance. Both USA and USSR was engaged in a great ideological battle to get hold on this region and this is still continuing even after end of the Cold War. Russia has a long and varied history as a serious strategic player in Asia. It is only recently that it has been completely written off by the end of the Cold War and its attendant beliefs in the end of geopolitics. The mutual threat perceptions between Russia and other Asian nations have certainly altered over the course of 20 years since the collapse of communism, and Russia is now widely recognized as a non-threatening great power with global significance. However, regional analysts are still sceptical over the degree to which Russia's vested interests lie in Asia, and whether these interests are compatible with those of other regional players.

Russia is distinctly interested in Asia-Pacific affairs because more than two-thirds of its territory is situated in this region. Development of the rich natural resources of Siberia and the Far East will be of exceptional importance for the future progress of Russia and the many states of the Asia-Pacific. The population of these areas is small compared to the total population of Russia. This makes it even more important to ensure transparency, predictability, stability, and security along the vast perimeter of Russia's eastern boundaries. On the whole, inter-state relations in the Asia-Pacific region and the trajectories of their evolution are favourable and meet the fundamental interests of Russia. The developments in the Asia-Pacific deeply affect the political and economic climate worldwide. During recent decades, the economic centre of the world has been moving gradually towards the Asia-Pacific, and the international relations in the region are becoming more and more important in global affairs.

Russia consistently supports the establishment of a just and democratic world order based on strict observance of the international legal norms, goals, and principles of the UN Charter and on comprehensive security, sovereign equality, and mutual respect for the legitimate interests of all states. The fact that the vast majority of the Asia-Pacific states share this approach seems to explain why peace and stability prevail in the region. Since the Cold War ended, the political situation in the Asia-Pacific has been relatively stable and predictable. Many Asia-Pacific states have mutual territorial claims, and sometimes these contradictory claims can lead to drastic and even dangerous conflicts. However, these states have practical experience in solving such problems, which helps to avoid military action, material damage, and loss of human life. The agreements on the mutually acceptable demarcation of a huge part of the border between China, on the one hand, and Russia, Kazakhstan, Kyrgyzstan, and Tajikistan, on the other hand, is a good example of this problem-solving skill. India and China also have good prospects for settling their border claims.

Although the Southeast Asian countries and China have not agreed on the ownership of the Spratly and Paracel Islands, they have elaborated a Code of Conduct in the South China Sea and are looking forward to arrangements for joint exploitation of the areas in dispute. Russia welcomes the commitment of the countries participating in developing the Code of Conduct because it is an important step in resolving the territorial dispute. Rather than resuming their confrontation over two islands near the east coast of Kalimantan, Malaysia and Indonesia opted to settle their dispute through the International Court of Justice.[1] From time to time, the dispute over the Senkaku Islands ignites, but in words rather than military actions. Today, when inter-state relations in Asia have a five relatively low conflict potential, it is unlikely that territorial disputes could generate a serious challenge to regional security and stability.

The growing interest of Russian military-industrial and energy companies in Southeast Asia will give Russia cause to become increasingly interested in the security and stability of vital water corridors in the waters of East Asia. Despite protests from Beijing, Russia is intensifying its connections with Vietnam, arranging for joint oil and gas exploration and signing military contracts, including the sale of six submarines in 2009. Thailand, Indonesia, Laos and Malaysia are among other potential targets for Russia's armament deals. Most of those countries are America's partners in the "hub and spokes" cooperative security system and their close relations with Russia will only prove beneficial for the US, as Moscow would be more inclined to engage in conflict resolution that might erupt between China and them. Another area of joint interest is North Korea and nuclear non-proliferation. As stated in the Russian Foreign Policy Concept, political stability in Asia is crucial to Russia foreign policy priorities, especially on the question of non-proliferation. The readiness to participate in Korean talks and enforce a peaceful resolution is even more evident when placed in the context of Moscow's ambition to build a Trans-Korean railroad and a direct pipeline from the Russian Far East to the Korean market.[2]

The USSR was feared until the late-1980s for its bold force projection into the South Pacific and Indian Ocean. Some, such as Richard Herr, openly worried that the US and Australian policy of "strategic denial" vis-à-vis the USSR in the South Pacific had failed, and that regional governments had better acquaint themselves with this new reality. Canberra and Washington even worried that, in a nuclear war with the Soviet Union, the Naval Communications "North West Cape" facility would be a tempting first target—either by a nuclear strike or Special Forces raid—to prevent an American retaliation from the nuclear submarines, which the base commanded. In fact, the Soviets, according to one among their ranks, carried out some of their training in the deserts of Kazakhstan to mimic the arid conditions of the Australian desert in the event of a future raid. Since the 1990s, many have perceived Russia as a feeble giant with clay feet. This soundly demonstrates the current dismissive consensus around Russia's role in Asia. This default position made sense when Russia was indeed riddled by chronic internal ills, violent conflicts, economic misery, separatism, a public health collapse, and the largest peace-time depopulation in recorded history. But it no longer makes sense today.

## Russia–China Strategic Co-operation and the Geopolitics of Asia-Pacific

Russia being the largest country and China being the most populous country on the planet, both collectively are undoubtedly the two major powers of the international system. Russia being the successor of erstwhile Soviet Union wishes to regain the role once Soviet Union enjoyed, whereas China being a communist country is also showing signs of new ambitions based on her history, population and military power and also her emergence as an important international economic actor. Relations between Moscow and Beijing have gone full circle in the past half century, from alliance to containment and now to strategic partnership.

To understand the ebbs and flows in Moscow's China policy it is necessary to look into the Soviet history. History which is characterized as chronicle of the past provides the solid base for building up future relationships. In International Relations, there is no permanent 'friend or foe', today's bitter enemy can become tomorrow's staunchest ally. It is interest which runs supreme, and Russia and China are not exceptions to it. Despite being communist countries both Soviet Union and China counted each other as enemy number one and targeted each other with their nuclear weapons. But today Russia and China no longer consider each other as enemy and both countries have developed "very deep" relations in the strategic field.

China has the largest population in the world, while Russia is the largest nation in terms of territory. Both are permanent members of the United Nations Security Council. Obviously, the significance of Sino-Russian relations extends far beyond the interests of the two nations. It also affects the stability of Asia and the world at large.

Soviet-China relations before disintegration of USSR were characterized by a number of ups and downs. In February 1950, just four months after establishment of the PRC, the two countries signed the treaty of Friendship, Alliance and Mutual Cooperation. The first half of the 1950s was the honeymoon period. However, by the late 1950s differences in national interest and ideology emerged leading to serious disputes in early 1960s which developed in to acute conflict and border clashes in 1969. Hence in the late 1960s and 1970s the USSR regarded China as one of its main rivals and stationed approximately one million troops and one third of its SS-20 intermediate-range ballistic missile along the Sino-Soviet border, threatening to make a 'surgical' first strike on China', nuclear bases. Under serious threat, China had to prepare for a military intrusion from north. However, in 1980s two countries came to realization that these were not in the interests of either side and they made effort to alleviate the situation. These efforts resulted in the normalization of the relations during a state visit to Beijing by the then Soviet President Mikhail Gorbachev in May 1989. (Qimao 1999: 206–7)[3]. In the words of Gorbachev, 'New Thinking' stood for:

> "We need normal international conditions for our internal progress. But we want a world free of war, without arms races, nuclear weapons and violence, not only because this is an optimal condition for our internal development." (Gorbachev 1987: 10–2).[4]

On 15 September 1992, President Yeltsin signed the "Order of Russian Federation's Relations with China" and reaffirmed that:

(a) there is only one China;
(b) the PRC government is the sole legal representative of China;
(c) Taiwan is the part of China; and
(d) Russia will never establish official relation with Taiwan.[5]

Both Russia and China are opposed to US hegemonic policies and favour a multi-polar world order with different power centres. In April 1997 Chinese President, Zemin, paid another visit to Moscow on April 23 and the two countries issued a joint statement on the multipolarisation of the world and establishment of new international order. The statement rejected hegemony and power politics, and stated that 'Cold War' mentality must also be abandoned and bloc politics opposed. They called for preservation of the Anti Ballistic Missile (ABM) Treaty of 1972 between Soviet Union and USA and they supported lifting the UN Security Council sanctions against Saddam Hussain regime in Iraq.

On 24 November 1998, when Jiang Zemin paid another crucial visit to Russia, the Russian side reaffirmed its "four nos" position. The basic thrust of which was—no support for any conception of 'Taiwan's independence; no acceptance of the position of 'two Chinas' or 'one China and one Taiwan'; no support for Taiwan's participation in the UNO or other international organizations in which only sovereign states participated; and no sales of weapon to Taiwan.[6]

NATO bombing on Yugoslavia from March end to mid-June 1999 without getting any authorization from the UN Security Council sent shock waves in both Russia and China and tended to bring together the two in joint opposition of NATO action. NATO's intervention on 'humanitarian ground' was an ominous development. Being multi-ethnic and multi-religious states, both Russia and China have their own separatist movements, Russia in Chechnya and China in Taiwan, Tibet and Xinjiang province. Being a Slav country, Yugoslavia was traditionally friend of Russia and attack on it, aroused Russian sentiments in the form of massive protests in Moscow.[7]

Both Russia and China have greater common ground to chalk out their strategy to deal with the outside world compared to the issues on which they are at odds. Russo–Chinese link is built on a number of shared concerns which includes:

- The struggle against US led unipolar hegemonism;
- Unilateral humanitarian interventionism by passing UN;
- Islamic extremism and secessionism;

- Opposition to NATO enlargement and inter-reference in the internal matters;
- Opposition to NMD (National Missile Defence) and TMD (Theatre Missile Defence);
- Opposition to US withdrawal from ABM Treaty of 1972
- Restructuring of UN
- Opposition to US led NATO forces to stay longer in the Central Asian region;
- Near mutual acceptance of Russia's hegemony as a guarantor of order in Eurasia;
- Strengthening the SCO;
- Working together in the multilateral forums like WTO, etc.;
- Strengthening multilateralism by promoting BRICS

The declaration of 'New World Order in 21st Century' confirms that relations between two 'headed eagle' and 'dragon' have reached on its height. Both countries have gone very far and deep in their defence translations and no longer count each other as enemies. Their defence personnel, scientists, students are getting training in each other's establishments. Russia is building up nuclear reactors in China and has offered partnership in the state in the state-owned space agency GLONASS, which itself indicates the comfort level in their ever flourishing bilateral relations.

One of the prime reasons for developing close ties between Moscow and Beijing is the US factor, the common cause of concern for the both countries. US's continuous military and economic support to Taiwan and its huge military presence poses grave threat to the Chinese sovereignty. USA has also agreed to deploy TMD technology to Taiwan, which may virtually neutralize Chinese missile capabilities and would disturb the strategic balance in the region.

Russia is consistently under immense pressure from western human rights groups and media on the issue of human rights violations in the Chechnya war. These groups had virtually shut their eyes on Moscow Theatre tragedy and Beslan School crisis in which hundreds of Russian people lost their lives. It shows as if these human rights groups and media people are acting at the behest of their respective governments to settle their political goals with Moscow. When the issue of human rights violations by US forces comes from Iraq or Afghanistan, these groups keep their mouth shut.

To neutralize these double standards on terrorism, both Russia and China call for implementation of UN charter and International Laws globally without any fear or favour. The most frequent violator of international laws, Israel always go unpunished due to overt and covert support from the USA but a single incidence of Tianmen Square in China made her virtually untouchable in the international politics.

Initially there was some opposition within the Russian establishment to the entry of the US troops in Central Asia, an area of traditional Russian influence. However, subsequently, Moscow decided to allow air corridors, the use of its bases for the search and secure operations as well as sharing of intelligence regarding the terrorist networks operating in Afghanistan. Uzbekistan offered its airspace and bases to the US troops ahead of other CARs, whereas Moscow preferred to maintain the façade of coordinated stand of all the CIS states. Kyrgyzstan claimed that the granting of Manas air base was coordinated in advance with its partners in the CIS Collective Security Treaty.

Manas airbase of Kyrgyzstan is just 200 miles away from Chinese territory from where US troops can keep their eye on Chinese troop movements. Presence of US troops in such a close to Chinese border made security expert in Beijing uncomfortable. Beside military bases in Pakistan and Kyrgyzstan, US acquired military bases in Baghram and Kandahar in Afghanistan and bases of Khanabad in Uzbekistan.

Development of closer ties between Russia and US, especially after coming of Obama regime is causing concerns in Beijing. Before Obama regime, Bush administration worked closely with Russia especially after September 2001 terrorist attack.

After the September 11, 2001, attacks on New York and Washington and subsequent military action taken by US and NATO against Al-Queda and Talibans have radically altered the geopolitical situation in Central Asian Region. Russia and Central Asian republics acquired a prominence place in the US military strategy in Afghanistan military bases in Baghram and Kandahar in Afghanistan and the bases of Khanabad in Uzbekistan. It is believed that these facilities helped US military to quickly establish air superiority thought Central Asia and even to the Middle East. It is believed that in offering bases to the USA, the Central Asian States sought security against the threat of terrorist attacks as well as gain manoeuvering space vis-à-vis Russia and China. CARs hoped to gain financially from the US presence.

The impact of post-September 11 developments on China has been a mixed one. China gained in so far as combating international terrorism became the number one task of the US policy. Prior to it economically and militarily growing China was increasingly being projected as an emerging strategic rival of sole super power. China reluctantly, joined the international community in supporting the US war against terror but with certain conditions. China wanted UNSC to play central role in the war against terrorism as a guarantee against the US unilaterism.

In fact, China insisted that struggle against terrorism also includes the 'East Turkistan' terrorist forces or the Uighur separatist movement in Xinjiang province.[8]

There is no doubt that the prospects of a prolonged US military presence in Central Asian region are not welcome to either Russia or China. Post-September 11 developments in the region are seem as a set back to SCO, because SCO was created to forge Russia–China partnership in the Central Asia for jointly maintaining peace, stability and economic cooperation in the region and keep a check on the Western influence in the region.

Russian and Chinese interests also converge on the issue of eastward expansion of NATO. First time ever NATO crossed the border of a non-NATO member country, i.e. Afghanistan in the name of fight against terrorism. Both Russia and China opposed the bombing on Belgrade, the capital of Yugoslavia in 1999. Also the US B-2 bombers dropped bomb on Chinese embassy in Belgrade causing many casualties. These incidences proved beyond doubt that US led NATO forces are crossing their granted mandate in the name of fight against terrorism and in the name of humanitarian intervention. Russia and China have their own set of problems in Chechnya and Xinjiang respectively.

At the time when NATO bombing was on, the 50$^{th}$ anniversary celebrations of the founding of NATO took place in Washington in which all the former Soviet republics with exception of Russia participated. What aroused the further Russian and Chinese concern and even the concern in countries like India was the enunciation of new strategies doctrine of NATO that permitted use of force by it in regions beyond the areas of its traditional responsibility comprising the territories of its member states. So, now NATO forces could be used anywhere.

Against such unilateral hegemonism of the US and NATO, Russia-China wants a multipolar world with many power centres. The declaration between Yeltsin and Jiang Zemin in 1997 openly talked about establishment of multipolar world based on principles of Panchsheel. Both call for respect of State sovereignty, equality of states eschewing of pursuit of hegemony, non-interference in internal affairs of other states, an equitable and just economic order and the strengthening of UN. Both Russia and China also seeks to work closely with NAM and champion the cause of the Third World.

The major bone of contention in the smooth relation was border dispute which is now solved. China has not only settled in border dispute with Russia but also with the Central Asian Republics in a peaceful manner. With the border dispute gone, there are no any serious issues left between Russia and China to doubt each other's intention.

Peaceful solution of Korean Peninsula problem is also in the priority list of

Russia and China. The proposed NMD system of the USA is expressly aimed at providing defence against the 'rogue' states like Iran, Iraq and North Korea. The launch of Pyongyong's rocket over Japan in 1998 provided justification to US for such apprehensions. Russia and China therefore, have sought to minimize the perception of North-Korean threat. They favour a rapprochement between North and South Korea and one between US and North Korea.

To counter the eastward expansion of NATO and with drawl of US from ABM Treaty of 1972, President Putin made an overture to European Union and NATO to reach some compromise solution. He called upon to EU and NATO to join forces with Moscow and set up a joint anti-missile shield during his visit to Rome on 5th June, 2000. He said that such a system will avoid creating problems linked to an imbalance in the equilibrium of forces and ensures 100 per cent security to European countries.[9]

As far as economic ties between Russia and China are concerned, it lags behind political, diplomatic, strategic and military ties. It is apparent that the two countries are also to create economic interdependence. The economies of the two countries are mutually complementary. Russia is the major producer and supplier of energy while China is energy hungry and its needs are growing. Russia's main exports apart from defence equipment include fertilizer, steel, timber and machinery, while its main imports are consumer goods and food items.

There are some major pre-requisites for further growth in the scale and diversifications of Russo–Chinese economic collaboration. These are implementing joint programmes in the fuel and energy sector; stepping up cooperation in the field of investment; involving Russian companies in the strategy of accelerated development of China's western region; expanding cooperation between the two countries' border region and cooperation in the manufacturing sector and joint mastering of high technologies.

By strengthening trade with China, Russia will try to reduce its shortage of light industrial goods and electronics, create an economic infrastructure using cheap Chinese labour in the less developed areas of Russian Far East. Russia will also be able to reduce the financial crunch of its arms manufacturing units by selling weapons to China which includes more than $2 billion every year. Russia can also benefit by sending part of its well-educated labour force to China to help create high technology industries and reduce the chronic unemployment among highly educated youths.[10]

On the other hand China will get benefitted by sending a certain amount of its unskilled labour force to Russia to work in the unstaffed industries. The excess of labour force available in China is about 200 million. This arrangement will reduce some burden of unemployment among Chinese people. In addition, China will have a chance to participate in the economic opening of oil fields resources in Russian Far East and Siberia.[11]

## When the Dragon Embraces the Bear

Russian President Vladimir Putin had a fabulous APEC. After his country and China clinched a massive $400 billion natural gas deal in May—around the Power of Siberia pipeline, whose construction began this year—they added a second agreement worth $325 billion around the Altai pipeline originating in western Siberia.

These two mega-energy deals don't mean that Beijing will become Moscow-dependent when it comes to energy, though it's estimated that they will provide 17% of China's natural gas needs by 2020. (Gas, however, makes up only 10% per cent of China's energy mix at present.) But these deals signal where the wind is blowing in the heart of Eurasia. Though Chinese banks can't replace those affected by Washington and EU sanctions against Russia, they are offering a Moscow battered by recent plummeting oil prices some relief in the form of access to Chinese credit.

On the military front, Russia and China are now committed to large-scale joint military exercises, while Russia's advanced S-400 air defence missile system will soon enough be heading for Beijing. In addition, for the first time in the post-Cold War era, Putin recently raised the old Soviet-era doctrine of "collective security" in Asia as a possible pillar for a new Sino-Russian strategic partnership.

Chinese President Xi has taken to calling all this the "evergreen tree of Chinese-Russian friendship", or you could think of it as Putin's strategic "pivot" to China. In either case, Washington is not exactly thrilled to see Russia and China beginning to mesh their strengths: Russian excellence in aerospace, defence technology, and heavy equipment manufacturing matching Chinese excellence in agriculture, light industry, and information technology.

It's also been clear for years that, across Eurasia, Russian, not Western, pipelines are likely to prevail. The latest spectacular Pipelineistan opera—Gazprom's cancellation of the prospective South Stream pipeline that was to bring yet more Russian natural gas to Europe—will, in the end, only guarantee an even greater energy integration of both Turkey and Russia into the new Eurasia.

## Seventh Meeting of BRICS at Ufa, Russia

The joint BRICS and SCO summit in Ufa has been organized by Moscow as the simultaneous holder of both the rotating chairmanships of the BRICS and the SCO. It is no coincidence, however, that the Seventh BRICS and Fifteenth SCO summits have been amalgamated as one large international summit. The

Kremlin has used the opportunity to bring Russia's partners together. This is part of the integration process of the Silk World Order. There will be joint BRICS and SCO sessions and many important exchanges and discussions about a new archetype for the world.

The US is clearly worried about the Silk World Order that is emerging. It has begun to pull out all the stops, from courting Brazil on the eve of the summit in Ufa to calls for the European Union to not join China's banking project. The Pentagon's 2015 Military Strategy that addresses the possibility of confrontation with an updated (Axis of Evil) composed of China, Russia, Iran, and North Korea is catered to Washington's proclivity to confront the countries that are challenging a US-dominated international order.

The BRICS New Development Bank (NDB), the first institution of the BRICS, is being launched by Brazil, China, India, Russia, and South Africa. It is joined by the SCO Development Bank and by the recently launched Asian Infrastructure Investment Bank (AIIB) in the assault on Bretton Woods. Gone are the days of unchallenged US domination. The architecture of the post-Second World War or post-1945 global order is now in its death bed and finished. With or without Washington, a Silk World is emerging and its coming is being trumpeted from Ufa as the SCO strengthens and the BRICS institutionalizes itself as the cornerstone of a new multi-polar world order.[12]

## Conclusion

Given the contours of the Sino-Russian strategic partnership and its likely durability, what should be the US response? Perceiving this partnership as a full-fledged alliance, directed across the board against the US interests, is a mistake. The common rhetoric is easy to sustain, but what will happen if the United States negotiates with Russia in earnest on an antiballistic missile compromise? Would Chinese opposition to changes in the regime really block a bilateral deal? Are China's interests really engaged in NATO enlargement?

Sino-Russian cooperation will not markedly change questions on issues such as Taiwan or NATO enlargement. These issues remain bilateral or regional; the outside partner has little standing. Moreover, issues such as these remain subject to a dynamic outside the control of the distant partner. Russia will act in its own interests in Europe, and China in Asia. For example, China remains comfortable with a framework in Korea that excludes Russia and Japan. Russia's European interests could well lead it much closer to Europe and the European Union in the years ahead. Chinese analysts cannot confidently exclude the European turn they feared in the early 1990s. Chinese economic interests place the United States, Japan, and a wide variety of Asian countries far ahead of Russia.

Although Sino-Russian economic ties have expanded, they have not reached the levels outside the arms trade that many in Moscow expected or hoped. Sino-Russian cooperation at the UN could make future peacekeeping operations more difficult to negotiate (e.g. Macedonia) or make vetoes more likely as both countries now hold leverage over this body. Although current US–Russian differences are serious, US–Russian strategic talks on missile defence could yield a satisfactory outcome for Moscow that would complicate the situation in Beijing. Moreover, serious challenges have not yet arisen in Central Asia, though the next decade will bring changes of leadership, regional instability, and other problems there. If sustained Chinese migration pressure appears in the Russian Far East, the current strategic partnership will be difficult to maintain. Washington still controls many levers of influence, and the most ambitious bilateral expressions of solidarity and cooperation have yet to be tested.

The most important near-term consequence of Sino-Russian partnership is a negative one: the Russian contribution to Chinese military modernization. For the foreseeable future, China will have an enduring need for Russian military technology and systems, while Russia will have a variety of reasons to sell. Official statements from senior Russian defence officials indicate that they believe Russia has a long lead on China in key military capabilities and thus that current sales do not create a military threat to Russia itself. Russia's own economic problems and the ideological motivations of some in the Russian foreign policy community create incentives for sales, not restraint. These sales—and the broader defence and technology cooperation that is linked to them—could in time alter regional military balances in areas of vital US interest in East and Southeast Asia or the Taiwan Strait. China does not need to match the military of the United States and its allies to affect this alteration. It need only develop capabilities that substantially raise the cost of US intervention in the region. At the very least, the upgrading of key Chinese military capabilities places an added burden on the United States and its regional allies in future crises.

## NOTES

1. Rouben Azizian and Boris Reznik. 2006. "*Russia, America, and Security in the Asia-Pacific*", Asia-Pacific Center for Securities Studies, Honolulu, pp. 23–33.
2. Anton Barbashin, "A Pacific Vision for Russia and USA", *The Diplomat*, December 6, 2013.
3. Qimao, Chen. 1999. "Sino-Russian Relationship after the Break Up of the Soviet Union", in Chaufrin Gennady (eds.), *Russia and Asia: Emerging Security Agenda*, New York: SIPRA, OUP.
4. Gorbachev, Mikhail. 1987. "*Perestroika: New Thinking for our Country and the World*", London: Collins, pp. 123–8.
5. Chufrin, G. 1999. "*Russia and Asia: The emerging Security Agenda*", New York: Sipri Oxford University Press, pp. 292–6.

6. Jingjie, L. 2000. "Pillars of the Sino-Russian Partnership", *Orbis*, 44(4): 527–39.
7. Saiget, Robert J. 2000. "*China, Russia beef up cooperation on Ethnic Separatism, Taiwan, Terrorism*", Hong Kong: AFP, pp. 102–10.
8. Moltz, Clay. 1995. "Regional Tensions in Russo-China Rapprochement", *Asian Survey*, 35(36): 23–54.
9. Menon, Rajan and Charles E. Ziegler. 2002. "The Balance of Power and US Foreign Policy Interest in the Russian Far East", in Thorton J and Ziegler E.C. (eds.), *Russia's Far East a region at risk*, London: University of a Washington Press, pp. 17–23
10. Shaumian, T.L. 2003. "Geopolitical Changes in Central Asia and Positions of Russia, China and India", *China Report*, 38(3): 361–3.
11. Mikhail Alexseev, "The Chinese Are Coming': Public Opinion and Threat Perception in the Russian Far East", *Program on New Approaches to Russian Security: Policy Memo 184* (Washington, D.C.: Council on Foreign Relations, January 2001).
12. Aliaksandr Kudrytski, "China Builds EU Beachhead with $5 Billion City in Belarus," *Bloomberg*, May 26, 2013.

# 9

# Modi Government's Afghan Policy

*D. Gopal*

United States led NATO forces have already withdrawn in December 2014. Now the entire security of Afghanistan is in the hands of the Afghan National Army (ANA) and Afghan police. In the backdrop of this much awaited withdrawal of NATO forces, it is opined by gamut of pundits of Afghan affairs that things will be chaotic in coming month. The capture of Kunduj (2015) by the Taliban for few hours vindicates this assertion. This withdrawal has also put the ANA under acid test because after 'Operation Enduring Freedom', it's the first time that Afghan security has been managed by their own developed security forces. Of course, NATO had given them due training but now in real terms they are on practical test.

Since December 1979, when Soviet Union entered in Afghan theatre, Pakistan has been working on a unique Afghan policy and that is to maintain 'strategic depth' over India in Afghanistan. Pakistan is much concerned with the possibility of any emergence of a stable Afghanistan. Before 1979, Afghanistan was relatively stable country. During those times, Afghan government was sustainable to raise the demand of Pakhtunistan. Afghanistan never accepted 'Durand Line' demarcated by the Britishers in 1893. Afghanistan has been arguing that the demarcation of this line was accepted by them under duress and according to international law any treaty inked under duress is unlawful. Due to sustainable anarchy since 1979 till date, Pakistan has been able to prevent Afghanistan to raise 'Pakhtunistan' issue. But despite prevailing 'Hobbesian nature of State' this issue still remains relevant. Even Taliban, which is considered illegitimate child of Pakistan never accepted 'Durand Line', but on some other plea, that is a Muslim does not require visa to visit another Muslim country.

In the backdrop of NATO withdrawal, security situation is getting grim.

## Islamic State Looming Threat

From Afghanistan's perspective, failure of the Afghan government and security forces to effectively respond to the threat, or an escalation of conflict in the country, could allow the IS-inspired militants operating in Afghanistan to forge alliances and try to capture some area and announce a 'caliphate'. If Kabul achieves some sort of reconciliation with the Afghan Taliban—currently efforts are under way for this purpose—hard-line factions or commanders among the Afghan Taliban, who do not believe in political reconciliation could support the IS, strengthening the IS-inspired groups already operating in the country.[1] In the backdrop of Mullah Omar departure and rising factionalism within Taliban, it may further escalate.

At the same time, the Afghan Taliban may not be able to grab hold of the reins of power but by following the IS model; in case they do not achieve reconciliation with the government in Kabul, they could carve out a part of Afghan territory and proclaim an Islamic 'caliphate'.

In the backdrop of the announcement of the death of Taliban chief, Mullah Omar, reconciliation process launched by President Ashraf Ghani seems to be derailing its scheduled path. Internal fights are on within Taliban and despite much publicized military operation against the Tehrik-i-Taliban, Pakistan, and other terror groups in the aftermath of December 2014 terror attack on military school at Peshawar, Haqqani network is still availing privileged status within power corridor in Rawalpindi. In August 2015, the US administration has refused to confirm that Pakistan is really fighting against terror groups, resulted into the prevention of aids in this direction. In the new cabinet of Taliban, Haqqani functional chief, Sirajuddin Haqqani has been given second rank and needless to say that it was not possible without the tacit understanding of the Pakistani establishment.

After the partition of the sub-continent, Pakistan emerged as a new entity. But Pakistan and Afghanistan has had bitter relationship till December 1979 Soviet intervention. In 1989 the Soviets withdrew and vacuum was created which was filled by the growth of the Taliban, which finally captured power in 1996. Taliban was illegitimately nurtured by Pakistan to pursue its goal to maintain its strategic depth over India. Since then terror remained an instrument of Pakistan's foreign policy. Afghan Jihad was consolidated by the US-led forces during Soviet intervention but later on emerged as an independent global movement led by

Osama Bin Laden. After Operation Enduring Freedom (2001) he took shelter in Pakistan and finally was killed by US commandos in May 2011 at Abbotabad. His elimination has vindicated the nexus between the Jihad factory and Pakistan.

India has invested over $2 billion dollar in Afghanistan since last one decade and emerged as $5^{th}$ largest global contributor in the reconstruction of this war-torn country. It is an open secret that NATO withdrawal will create serious questions for India's national security.

During the period of the Taliban rule in Afghanistan (1996–2001), India's internal security was badly hit due to sustainable cross-border support.

In 1999 an Indian Airlines plane was highjacked from Kathmandu and eventually taken to Kandahar. This incident dramatically underscores why New Delhi cannot take its eyes off Afghanistan and the Taliban. JM quickly became one of the most vicious terrorist groups operating in India that has long ties with Afghanistan and the Taliban (it has also enjoyed support from the ISI), threatening vital Indian national security interests.[2]

India's engagement with Afghanistan advances its position as an important power beyond South Asia, other interests in Afghanistan specifically advance regional security concerns localized in Afghanistan and Pakistan. Many of these are tied to the proliferating Islamist militant groups which have terrorized India. Virtually every Islamist militant group operating in and against India (e.g. HUJI, Lashkar-e-Taiba (LeT), and Harkat-ul-Mujahideen/Harkat-ul-Ansar among others) trained in Afghanistan and Pakistan.

Since 2001 India has upgraded its presence in Afghanistan particularly in reconstruction efforts and built many infrastructure assets. This has enraged Pakistan because it perceives that Afghanistan is their strategic backyard and Indian presence is a hurdle to sustain it. Pakistan provided tacit support to the attacks on Indian Embassy in Kabul and other personnel working across Afghanistan.

Since last two decades, hundreds of terrorist attacks involving LeT and other terror groups based in Pakistan have occurred throughout India. Former Pakistani President, Asif Ali Zardari termed them 'Non-State Actors' but the open secret is that these elements have come into India from the Pakistani soil. LeT was implicated in plots like the terrorist attacks in New Delhi in October 2005; in Bangalore in December 2005; in Varanasi in March 2006; in Nagpur in June 2006; and in July 2007 train bombings in Mumbai, November 2008 Mumbai carnage, Pune in 2013, Jammu in 2014, 2015 and July 2015 in Punjab.

Right from the commencement of 'Operation Enduring Freedom' Pakistan has remained the recipient of largesse from the United States due to its participation in 'global war against terror'. Despite that it gave safe havens to

Osama Bin Laden and Mullah Omar. More importantly, as the senior most US military officer in 2011, Admiral Mike Mullen, told the US Congress, the Haqqani network is a "veritable arm of the Pakistan's Inter Services Intelligence Agency."[3] Pakistani military has sustained the unique Afghan policy since 1979 not to stabilize Afghanistan and use it as rear base. In December 2014, NATO forces have withdrawn from Afghanistan. New Afghan President, Ashraf Ghani, has taken some conciliatory steps to garner Pakistani support for peace but since 2009 every year more than 2500 innocent people have been killed and Pakistani invisible hands are responsible for these deadly attacks. Right from 2009 till July 2015, 16,874 people have been killed in terror related violence;[4] from January 2015 to July 2015 alone 4,921 people have been killed which is self-explanatory. President Ghani showed his will to cooperate with Pakistan but increasing number of casualties has forced him to change his mind. Afghan President Ashraf Ghani lambasted Pakistan recently over a recent wave of insurgent attacks in the capital Kabul that killed at least 56 people. "The last few days have shown that suicide bomber training camps and bomb-producing factories, which are killing our people are as active as before in Pakistan," Ghani told a news conference.

"We hoped for peace but we are receiving messages of war from Pakistan."[5] President Ghani is now aware about the core motives of Pakistan. It is candidly clear from the above indications that Pakistan is not going to permit and any real stabilization in Afghanistan and perceives it detrimental to its interests. Although it is doing lip services for peace building but has maintained tacit understanding with the terror groups accountable for acceleration of violence in Afghanistan, including Afghan Taliban and Haqqani. This situation is creating a dangerous situation for Indian security. As I have already insisted that sustainability of 'Hobbesian State of Nature' in Afghanistan had proved negative for our security in the past, it may replicate in future as well if Pakistan-nurtured terror groups will have control over power in Kabul.

In this situation billion dollar question remains that how India will cope up with the situation. It is a wider question because if Afghanistan will destabilize further it will put black clouds over the security challenges in South, South West, Central Asia in particular but in the whole globe in general as well.

## Policy Options for India

But given the prevailing situation in the power corridor in Islamabad at the outset of 2015 it is clear that Islamabad has not learnt any lessons from its past mistakes. Islamabad is still hell-bent to use terror as an instrument of its foreign policy. On 26 January 2014, an outlawed militant group, the Jaish-e-Muhammad (JeM) hold a rally of the militants at Muzaffarabad.

Maulana Masood Azhar, commander of the JeM declared, "Kashmir is part of Pakistan and unless Kashmiri Muslims get their rights, there cannot be any friendship with India."[6] On May 26, 2014, under the leadership of Narendra Modi new government called PM Nawaz Sharif but he was warned by Hafiz Saeed. Indian Consulate in Afghanistan was attacked by terrorists to prevent Nawaz to visit India with the tacit understanding of Pakistani security establishment.

In April 2014, Presidential elections held in Afghanistan. In the wake of this crucial election the Taliban had stepped up its attacks. President Karzai had pointed his accusations on Pakistan directly as the sponsor of these attacks. In a phone call with US Secretary of State John Kerry, Hamid Karzai accused Pakistan of being behind March 2014 series of attacks and of blocking his government from striking a peace deal with the Taliban.[7] Pakistan is dedicated to bleed India too at thousand places. It has been revealed by Riyaz Bhatkal that Pakistan's ISI has given Rs. 26 crore to Indian Mujahideen in last three years for anti-India operations.[8] On 23 May 2014, Indian consulate in Herat was attacked and again needle of suspicion tilted towards military–Jehadi nexus in Pakistan. It is opined that this attack was an attempt to derail the goodwill created by the invitation of Indian PM designate Narendra Modi to Pakistan PM, Nawaz Sharif.[9] PM Sharif finally attended the swearing-in ceremony and had a meeting with new Indian PM, Modi. In this prevailing situation the demand of the time is that India must prepare herself to contain propelling incidents of cross-border terror. We have to face this situation as an essential reality. At the same time we must sustain our efforts to ensure peace and development in Afghanistan. Afghanistan of 2015 is different and people of Afghanistan are hell-bent to sustain peace. Since last one decade they have experienced relative peace. Over 70 per cent voting in the Presidential election despite all-round violent threat by the Taliban is vindicating the courage and dedication of Afghan people and their urge to bring back peace and participatory democracy. India must ensure close cooperation with Iran, Russia and Central Asian Republics as they had during the Taliban rule in Afghanistan.

Eminent Indian security analyst, Raja Mohan has rightly stated in November 2013, "Any nuclear deal between Washington and Tehran will immediately bring down oil prices, relieve the current macroeconomic pressures on India, and improve Delhi's energy security calculus over the longer term. US–Iran rapprochement will help to strengthen Afghanistan against the Taliban and Pakistan and expand India's room for regional manoeuvre after 2014."[10] The interim deal between Washington and Tehran has already been concluded, and it is time when Indian diplomacy must act and bring Iran and United States on the same page to ensure peace and stability in Afghanistan. Iran is an important player and it had been part and parcel of Indian efforts along with Russia and Central Asian Republics to contain Taliban and formation of the Northern Alliance during its rule over Afghanistan. (1996-2001). In July 2015, Iran and Western world has signed nuclear deal and now gradually decade-long sanctions imposed against Iran will be lifted. In August 2015, Iranian Foreign Minister, Javad Zarif had visited New Delhi and met PM and other ministers. Again it was pledged that cooperation on all fronts will be accelerated. During one-day visit of Mr. Zarif issue related to Islamic State threat, energy investments, Afghanistan and development of Chabhahar port were discussed. He also stated that India is an important player in West Asia and can play a leading role in the region. PM Modi conveyed India's commitment to work with Iran for development of the Chabahar port that would have far reaching benefit, not only for the people of India and Iran, but also for Afghanistan and the entire Central Asian region. Mr. Zarif acknowledged India's support during turbulent times. It is expected that PM Modi may visit Tehran by early 2016.[11] China is also concerned for Afghanistan. Chinese have anticipated that worsening of Afghan situation may propel terror-related violence in its western turbulent province of Xingjiang. China has already appointed special representatives for Afghanistan. Along with China, we have to solicit the support of Russia and Central Asian Republics.

Newly elected President Ghani's visited Islamabad in September 2014 and convinced Pakistan's security 'establishment' to change its strategic approach to Afghanistan. Far from a regime entrenched in hostility and resentment towards Pakistan, Islamabad found a leader who acknowledged the vital and symbiotic nature of Pakistan-Afghan relations and understood Pakistan's concerns regarding India's role in Afghanistan. All the doors of economic and security cooperation between the two countries have been opened. Most significantly, Kabul has extended active cooperation to combat the Tehreek-i-Taliban Pakistan and Islamabad has committed to preventing cross-border attacks against Afghanistan and promoting reconciliation with the Taliban.

Kabul's posture towards the US is also visibly different. During his recent US visit, Ghani was effusive in his gratitude for America's military support and sacrifices and insistent in requesting its continued security and economic support. The US has consequently agreed to keep just under 10,000 troops and two military bases in Afghanistan in place for the present and continue its financial support to Kabul.

President Ghani has shown some flexibility towards Pakistan in comparison to his predecessor, President Karzai, and after December 2014 Peshawar school attack, both countries have pledged to work together. Speaking at the Council of Foreign Relations in New York on 26 March, he said he thought "Pakistan is integral to peace efforts with the Taliban."[12] However, in the veiled attack on Pakistan he stated that both countries were working to end 13 years of hostilities. He stated ...

> "Without sanctuary, a long-term rebellion is impossible. When sanctuaries end, peace breaks out. That is what happened in Central America and Latin America, that is what has happened in Africa."[13]

In September 2014, President Ghani made his first visit to Islamabad and pledged to work together to remove the menace of terror. Pakistan also confirmed this pledge but few weeks after this visit, Sartaz Aziz, Foreign Policy Adviser to Pakistan's PM, stated that fighting with Afghan Taliban is not the duty of Pakistan because they have done nothing wrong against Pakistan. Aziz's statement is self-explanatory which vindicates that Pakistan is part of the Afghan problem and despite all-round global efforts it cannot be part of the solution. The killing of Osama Bin Laden, despite continuous denial by Pakistan in May 2011 at Abottabad, proves that since the launch of "Operation Enduring Freedom" Pakistan has played a double game. As President Ghani has rightly stated in his March 2015 Washington visit that durability of any insurgency is not possible till sanctuary is not provided by a neighbour. Since last four decades Pakistan has perceived terrorist as an asset and has used it as an instrument of its foreign policy in all the cases. It is also an open secret that Mullah Omar, Amir of the Afghan Taliban resides at Quetta and supervises the insurgency in Afghanistan with the tacit understanding of the Pakistani security establishment. The military-mullah alliance is still hopeful that Afghanistan could be a model country where shariah could be imposed. They are equally intended to use Afghanistan as a rear base against India because of lack of hinterland in the Pakistani geo-strategic ambience.

In contrast historically, Afghanistan–India relations have been cordial. Due to its dual policy, Pakistan has become extremely unpopular and due to its huge investment of over $2 billion, India is well-respected among all sections of Afghans. According to former Pakistani NSA, Mahmud Ali Durrani, "Hamid Karzai mistrusted us, I blame Pervez Musharraf also, Once I told Musharraf, you should invite him here, but he disagreed. He said he is a third class chap. The Afghan people, by and large, have far greater respect for India than they have for us."[14]

NDA-II government has multiple challenges on this front. We have witnessed since 1999 till date that whenever we are proposing high profile peace talks with Pakistan it has been reciprocated by Kargil/Mumbai/Jammu, etc. Pakistan is still trying to create new turbulence in Kashmir particularly in the backdrop of the formation of BJP–PDP government there. India must sustain its reconstruction activities in Afghanistan and in the meanwhile must sustain its dialogue with Pakistan but at a low key level beside periodical summit level talks on international foras. This front is one of the turbulent challenges for the Modi government.

The civil-political relations in Pakistan have been always tilted towards the army. Former PM, Yousuf Raza Gillani, had stated in 2012 while he was the PM that "Pakistani military is not within the Pakistani state but Pakistani state is within the Pakistani army."[15] It is important to mention here that he was leading the Pakistan People's Party coalition, his assertion is self-contradictory and proves that military is all powerful in Pakistan. But it possesses only veto when the issues related to India, Afghanistan and nuclear aspect arise. Pakistani army has portrayed India as the permanent foe and has nursed certain terror outfits to sustain its anti-India megalomania. When Benazir Bhutto took oath as the first woman PM of Pakistan in 1988, then Chief of Army Staff, General Aslam Beg took three assurances from her that she will not intervene in India, Afghanistan and Nuclear issue, and decisions will be formulated by the army on these affairs. The evidence is that she sustained the General Zia era foreign minister, Shebzada Yakub Khan as her FM also. Here it is significant to mention that Khan fought 1988 election on IJI ticket and got elected against Benazir's PPP.[16] In recent history in February 1999, PM Vajpayee rides a bus to Lahore and inked historical 'Lahore Declaration'. It was reciprocated by the army and its terror stooge through Kargil. PM Manmohan Singh had started engaging Pakistan in his first term but that was reciprocated by Mumbai terror attack in 2008. PM Modi called all SAARC leaders including Pakistani PM to be witness his swearing in ceremony. This gesture was also reciprocated by March 2015 Jammu attack. Former Pakistani NSA stressed that "The political classes, by and large, want peace. Where the difference comes in is the religious political classes. But the biggest monster is the army. The army has always felt that India is a very serious threat to us. Every military of the world has to have an enemy, a threat to point their guns at."[17]

Pakistani army is formulating and implementing Pakistan's Afghan policy since 1979. It seems that it has not changed it even today. Pakistan despite global persuasion is not going to abandon its old Afghan policy. Civilian regime is ruling elite since 2008 till date but it has no teeth in case of foreign policy particularly on Afghan and India front and it is likely to be sustainable in foreseeable future. Needless to say that situation in Afghanistan will determine security architecture of India and will make an imprint on global peace as well. India must take all possible steps to ensure peace and stability with the tacit understanding with like-minded countries in Afghanistan.

## NOTES

1. Muhhammad Amir Rana, Accessing the IS Threat, *Dawn,* Karachi, 23 August 2015.
2. Praveen Swami, "Terrorism in Jammu and Kashmir in theory and practice," *India Review*, 2, no. 3 (July 2003): pp. 55-88.
3. C. Raja Mohan, After Mullah Omar, *The Indian Express,* New Delhi, August 4, 2015.
4. 2014 among deadliest years in AF with 10 k civilian casualties, *The Times of India,* New Delhi, August 9, 2015.
5. Ashraf Ghani slams Pakistan over recent Kabul attacks, *Dawn*, Karcahi, August 10, 2015.
6. Tariq, Banned group holds rally in Muzaffarabad, *Dawn,* 27 January 2014.
7. A.P., Karzai steps up Pakistan accusations, *Dawn,* Karachi, 30 March 2014.
8. Neeraj Chauhan, ISI gave Rs. 26 cr for anti-India ops, *The Times of India*, New Delhi, March 31, 2014.
9. *Times of India*, New Delhi, 24 May 2014.
10. C. Raja Mohan, The Great Game Folio, *The Indian Express,* New Delhi, 20 November 2013.
11. Can't forget support India gave us during difficult times; Iran, *The Times of India*, New Delhi, August 15, 2015.
12. Masood Haider, Pakistan integral to peace efforts, says Ghani, *Dawn*, Karachi, 28 March, 2015
13. Ibid.
14. Idea Exchange, Mahmud Ali Durrani, *The Indian Express,* March 22, 2015, p.12.
15. Singh, Sudhir, Limits of Electoral Mandate in Pakistan, *Politico,* Vol.1, No.1, 2013, p.37.
16. Rizvi, Hasan Aksari, *Military, State & Society in Pakistan,* St Martin Press, London, 2000, p.43.
17. Ibid, op. cit., No. 43.

# 10

# Modi's "Make in India" Policy: Revisiting the Case of South Korea

*Geetha Govindasamy*

## Modi's "Act East Policy"

India's foreign policy in the last decade has not changed much, especially the "Look East Policy" which was started by Prime Minister PV Narasimha Rao in the early 1990s. Subsequently, Indian leaders like Atal Bihari Vajpayee and Dr. Manmohan Singh expanded the same policy attempting to make Southeast Asia and, later, Northeast Asia a priority in Indian foreign policy. Like every other Indian leader, Narendra Modi saw the benefits of having closer relations with noteworthy economies of China, Japan and South Korea. Similarly, Modi's main aim is also to attract investments and investors to set up industries in India.

He is determined to form "partnerships, technology and funds" with these countries in order to accomplish the flagship *Make in India* initiative.[1] In other words, the initiative aims to draw businesses from around the world to invest and manufacture in India so that the country can develop into a manufacturing powerhouse like China.[2] Primarily, India is banking on becoming a manufacturing hub in order to create employment and for sustaining a balance in exports and imports.[3] When introducing his vision a year ago, with the slogan of "Sell Anywhere but Make in India,", Modi urged potential investors to set up their manufacturing facilities in *India in areas like electrical, electronics, chemicals, pharmaceuticals, satellite and submarine.*[4]

Since the Indian government does not have the fiscal capacity to carry out large-scale investments and public–private partnerships (PPP) are still at a nascent state, foreign money is the key in developing the Indian economy. East Asian countries like China, Japan and Korea have foreign exchange reserves that India desperately needs for its "Make in India" project. It is reasonable to argue that these countries are looking for investment destinations. They are also attracted to India due to its large market and source of raw materials. According to Samir Saran of the Observer Research Foundation,

> ...China has become the biggest provider of energy-generation equipment to India and wants to build high-speed trains here. It is why South Korea wants to build nuclear reactors and ports in India. And it is why the Japanese want to set up industrial corridors in India. Asia is also the source of most of the energy needs that are indispensable to this national project.[5]

Further, almost 55 percent of India's trade transits through the Straits of Malacca making it crucial for New Delhi to play a more strategic role in the Asia-Pacific region.[6] At the same time, countries like Japan and Vietnam are looking to India to counterbalance an increasingly assertive China. Underscoring his new regional strategy, Modi rebranded the "Look East Policy" to "Act East Policy" in November 2014 during an ASEAN meet in Myanmar's capital Naypyidaw. It can be argued that the term "Act East" reflects urgency in wanting to secure ties with Northeast Asian countries. In so doing, Modi expects to revive the Indian economy through proactive engagement with the economically vibrant Asia-Pacific region. The objective is to attract investments into India and assist Indian traders and businesses to link up with the markets of the Asia-Pacific region.

The chapter discusses Modi's "Act East Policy" and its relations to South Korea-India bilateral relations. In addition, it highlights the challenges faced by foreigners in doing business with India. While China and Japan are very significant in ensuring the "Make in India" initiative succeeds, the chapter stresses that South Korea which has been slow in entering the Indian market is equally worth exploring for one main reason. Given that Korea has made tremendous progress in infrastructure, technology and has an export driven economy, there is scope for greater cooperation between India and Delhi. Thus far, Seoul has relied heavily on the Chinese market. According to the World Trade Organization data, 26.1 percent of South Korea's exports went to China in 2014.[7] China's economy is slowing down. As a result, South Korea's trading relationship with China is experiencing an export plunge. The recent devaluation of the renminbi is expected to slash further demands for Korean products in the Chinese market.[8]

On one hand, Korean small and medium enterprises are looking to diversify investment destinations that will yield better profit margins and at the same time reduce the cost of manufacturing. On the other hand, conglomerates like Samsung and Daewoo Motors invest overseas in order to expand their export markets. As South Korea has come to realize that it does not want to depend too much on China, the "Make in India" initiative which caters for both types of investments has become an attractive policy. India is capable of fulfilling a variety of Korea's needs as it has a relatively stable economic growth, a rising middle class, abundant youth demographic, cost competitiveness of setting up businesses and huge numbers of educated as well as skilled workers. In other words, Koreans can expect greater market access and opportunities to expand their businesses within India.

For Modi, comparable to China and Japan, South Korea is a key player that can help in kick starting India's economy. From his days as the Chief Minister of Gujarat, Modi had always regarded South Korea as a role model for India.[9] Collaborating with middle powers like South Korea is vital if India aims to revive its economy and consolidate its position in a changing international scenario. South Korea as a middle power has become important to India in an environment where the United States' global influence is declining and China's influence is rising.

## Bilateral Economic Ties

The diplomatic ties between India and Republic of Korea (ROK) were formally established in 1973. Bilateral trade relations have gathered momentum in recent years. According to the Korea International Trade Association (KITA), bilateral trade between South Korea and India is as follows:

**Table 1: South Korea-India Bilateral Trade between 2007 and September 2014**

*(Amount in million US$)*

| *Year* | *Total trade* | *Growth %* | *Indian exports to ROK* | *Growth %* | *ROK Export to India* | *Growth %* |
|---|---|---|---|---|---|---|
| 2007 | 11,224 | 22.35% | 4,624 | 27.03% | 6,600 | 19.3% |
| 2008 | 15,558 | 39.00% | 6,581 | 42.32% | 8,977 | 36% |
| 2009 | 12,155 | -21.88% | 4,142 | -37.06% | 8,013 | -10.7% |
| 2010 | 17,109 | 40.76% | 5,674 | 36.98% | 11,435 | 42.7% |
| 2011 | 20,548 | 20.10% | 7,894 | 39% | 12,654 | 10.7% |
| 2012 | 18,843 | -8.30% | 6,921 | -12.3% | 11,922 | -5.8% |
| 2013 | 17,568 | -0.07% | 6,183 | -10.7 | 11,385 | -4.5% |
| 2014 (up to Oct.) | 15,290 | 2.97% | 4,626 | -12.2% | 10,664 | 11.3% |

*Source*: Korea International Trade Association (KITA)[10]

Trade imbalances have become an issue in bilateral relations. As an example, while India imported goods worth $11,385 million from South Korea in 2013, its exports to Seoul were only $6183 million. In order to boost exports and address the widening trade deficit with South Korea, the Indian government has taken a number of initiatives to identify specific products with export potential. The government seems to be seeking greater market access for products related to information technology (IT), generic medicine and textiles.[11]

South Korea was one of the earliest foreign investors after India liberalized its economy in 1991.[12] Samsung, LG and Hyundai are Korean companies operating in India, with high accomplishments. Statistics indicate that between 1990 and 2014, more than 100 Korean companies have invested 3.9 billion dollars in India.[13] Major centres of investment are Delhi, Noida, Gurgaon, Chennai, and Mumbai. Manufacturing sector dominates 80 percent of this investment. In addition, small and medium Korean enterprises feature significantly in such investments. Some of these companies are part of the supply chain for bigger conglomerates like Samsung, Lucky Goldstar and Hyundai Motors.

For bigger Korean companies, India has become a manufacturing centre for domestic as well as overseas markets. For instance, Hyundai Motors which is the second largest carmaker in India, exports its manufactured cars at the Chennai plant to 123 countries globally.[14] Despite this development, South Korea has made far less investment in India than China or Japan. At the moment Korean direct investments in India are only 1.3 percent of Korea's overseas investments of US$ 282 billion.[15]

As Asia's 3rd and 4th largest economies, India and South Korea concluded a free trade agreement in 2009—the Comprehensive Economic Partnership Agreement (CEPA). Under the CEPA, South Korean firms are allowed to own stakes of up to 65 percent in Indian firms.[16] According to the Korea Trade Investment Promotion Agency (KOTRA), Korean subsidiaries established in India are either wholly owned or have joint ventures with Indian companies. Due to difficulties in the 1990s, in trying to penetrate the market through joint ventures with Indian companies, 88 percent of Korean companies are wholly owned. Wholly owned subsidiaries are preferred as it allows Koreans to operate on economies of scale, have greater leverage in negotiating with local governments, as well as initiate brand recognition more effectively.[17]

It is clear that the Modi government is gradually trying to implement economic-friendly policies, especially in encouraging industrial parks. The goal of attracting Korean investments into India will largely be realized when the 250 acre zone industrial park developed by South Korea in Neemrana region of Alwar district in Rajasthan is completed.[18] When the industrial park is up and ready, Rajasthan will become the only Indian state to host two manufacturing zones, one Korean and the other Japanese.[19]

Though both Seoul and New Delhi see a potential of $40 billion worth of trade, currently bilateral trade is estimated to be only $17 billion.[20] Facing trade imbalances and underperforming bilateral ties, Modi's visit to Seoul in May 2015 clearly had an economic agenda attached to it. Looking to secure promises of bigger Korean investments, Modi met with business tycoons from South Korea's largest conglomerates. They include Samsung Electronics president Park Sangjin; LG Electronics president Kim Jin-hong; Hyundai Motor Company president Chung Jinhaeng and Hyundai Heavy Industries' Chief Executive Officer Choi Gil-sun.[21]

Among others, since India needs to upgrade its transport infrastructure, Modi was hoping to obtain up to $10 billion in South Korean soft loans to fund infrastructure projects. Simultaneously, Modi was also sourcing out financial assistance for projects like smart cities, Digital India and Swachh Bharat Abhiyan—initiatives to improve technology and connectivity in India. The extent to which Modi was able to obtain financial assistance for his projects is unclear. What has been reported is that US$10 billion will be sponsored by the Korean government and the Export-Import Bank of Korea for Indian infrastructure projects. This will include creating 100 smart cities and building a high-speed railway as well as improving existing railroads.[22] However, the multi-billion dollar loan can only be dispensed after detailed business plans undergo feasibility studies conducted by the Korean side. Korean companies will definitely have an advantage as they will be able to provide investment proposals for a diverse range of projects in India.

During the visit, both Park Guen Hye and Modi signed seven agreements. Bilateral relations have now been upgraded to a 'Special Strategic Partnership'.[23] Among others, the agreement encourages cooperation in maritime transport and logistics, through sharing of technologies, information and experiences; signing of avoidance of double taxation and the prevention of fiscal evasion; cooperation in areas of renewable energy, smart grids and power, information and technology; transmission and distribution of electric power, energy efficiency and storage system, intelligent transport systems and electronic toll collection systems.[24]

## Ease of Doing Business in India

To a large extent, foreign direct investment flows are determined by government actions in promoting a business-friendly environment. While Modi wants to attract investments, the reality is that there are numerous challenges in doing business in India. Because of regulatory burdens, India currently ranks 142 out of 189 countries in the World Bank's 2015 study of ease of doing business index.

Recently, Goldman Sachs published a report titled "How India Can Become the Next Korea". It concluded that the Indian economy that resembles the South

Korean economy of the 1970s should adopt the Korean model to boost its manufacturing sector.[25] The Korean model refers to export led manufacturing. In order to replicate the Korean success, the report identified several objectives for the Indian government to boost manufacturing. These include focusing on manufacturing as primary objective in order to increase productivity, promote low fiscal deficit, reducing cost of business as well as bureaucratic red tape, promotion of flexible labour laws, providing of tax benefits to encourage capital accumulation, subsidizing power for industry and developing industrial parks.[26]

Unless Modi adopts strategies similar to the Korean model and takes dramatic actions to improve the effectiveness of the country's governance mechanisms, his "Make in India" initiative is going to remain a dream. It must be said that Modi has attempted to ease the process of doing business but the question remains how much of it has been successful at the lower levels of bureaucracy. Is there bipartisanship in wanting to implement Modi's "Make in India initiative"? Further, government reforms at the central level have difficulties getting full support from state leaders. Political opposition to reform remains very strong. Recently Modi was defeated when he tried to get a land acquisition bill passed. Had the bill been successful, purchasing land for infrastructure or manufacturing projects would have created a business-friendly environment. Over the years, several projects stalled on account of difficulties in getting environmental clearances on time and braving the bureaucratic red-tapes. The Modi government needs to find its way around the opposition to get the land bill passed. Delayed projects results in cost overrun, increasing the financial burden of companies.[27] Moreover, the cost of starting a business in India is said to be very is high. According to the TMF Group,

> There are 12 procedures to complete in the initial set up of a business costing 49.8% of income per capita. It takes almost a month (27 days) to complete the tasks on average, which is well above the OECD average of 12 Construction permits are also a costly pursuit, involving 34 procedures and taking 196 days... Businesses operating in India are required to make 33 tax payments a year, taking 243 hours' worth of attention. The headline corporation tax rate stands at 30%, but companies can also incur charges in the form of a central sales tax, dividend tax, property tax, fuel tax, vehicle tax, VAT and excise duty.[28]

The government needs to offer coherent policies in infrastructure, capital markets, trade facilitation and skills to boost confidence of potential investors. Therefore, urgent reforms are needed on tax, land and labor to spearhead much-needed foreign investment into India. In order to promote competitiveness among states to attract investments, India's Department of Industrial Policy and Promotion started ranking states on 'ease of doing business. This is done to ascertain which states have a business-friendly environment and to bring India into the top 50 in terms of ease of doing business within the next three years.[29] Further, such rankings are expected to push states that are lacking in investments to initiative investor-friendly practices. Regional disparities in attracting investments are a source of concern. Between 2000 and 2014, only Maharashtra and the National Capital Region (NCR) attracted 49 percent of foreign direct investments into India.[30] Further, it cannot be denied that bi-partisan support for speeding up approval for foreign investments at the state level is hard to come by as the *Bharatiya Janata Party* (BJP) is a minority party in the Upper House in parliament. Without a majority, undertaking reforms remains challenging for the Modi government, especially in encouraging reformist and investor-friendly atmosphere at the state level.

## Are Koreans Interested in Doing Business in India?

In the case of Korean investments, clearly South Koreans are wary of doing business in India. Even though past leaderships had invited Korean companies to invest in India, to date, very few Korean firms are operating in India. Korean companies have had their share of problems in building their businesses in India. In July 2013, Posco, the world's sixth-largest steelmaker by revenue, halted plans to build a steel plant in Karnataka because of delays in obtaining land leases and mining permits.[31]

Earlier, in 2005, Posco agreed to invest $12 billion in Orissa by building a steel plant in Odisha. However, Posco has encountered a series of delays in the last ten years. Posco found it hard to procure land, mining leases and obtain environmental clearance against the backdrop of opposition from local tribal groups and environmental activists. Such protests extended to kidnapping Posco staff by activities. Thus far, Posco has been unable to secure all of the 4,000 acres needed across three panchayats of Dhinkia, Nuagaon and Gadakujang in Jagatsinghpur district. Moreover, the central government decided that it will auction all mineral resources and no entity will be given a preferential treatment. This includes iron ore, a key steelmaking raw material. As a result of the new policy, Posco has to incur higher costs due to the bidding process for securing iron ore blocks and getting a new captive mining license.[32] Initially the Odisha government had promised Posco that the license will be obtained without any extra cost.

For the moment, the project has been put on hold tentatively. According to Posco's CEO Kwon Oh Joon, "business conditions at home and abroad have changed due to a drop in global steel demand, growing deficit of subsidiaries....until Indian Prime Minister Narendra Modi offers better deals,

Posco won't resume and for now will head to the west and do more downstream work."[33] Posco's decision certainly is a major setback for Modi's manufacturing ambitions.

While there is some apprehension on the Korean side, analysts argue that Modi's ongoing economic development strategies will facilitate and strengthen Korea's investment relations with India. An editorial in the Korean newspaper, *JoongAng Daily*, urged Korean enterprises to enter the Indian market since Japan and China have already made inroads. Additionally, the editorial depicted India as being in a transitional stage whereby Korean business should not miss the opportunity to tap into a growing market with a population of 1.28 billion.[34] One of the most influential Korean-language daily newspapers and as one of the three biggest newspapers in South Korea, such views from the *JoongAng Daily* infers that Koreans are indeed interested in the Indian market.

During Modi's visit to South Korea, Park Yong-maan, chairman of the Korea Chamber of Commerce and Industry commented that the Korean and Indian economy (which brings together Indian competence in science and technology with Korea's manufacturing sector), has the potential to emerge as powerful economic entities in the age of Asia.[35] Likewise, President Park Guen-hye alluded to the fact that both countries have economic growth potential and complementary trade structures, which can create a win-win partnership. In an attempt to entice Korean investors, Modi agreed to revisit the CEPA to discuss a greater opening of the Indian market to Korean exports.[36] As a prerequisite for the success of "Make in India" initiative, Modi is certainly emphasizing on fostering a stronger manufacturing base, concentrating on building 100 ICT-enabled smart cities by 2022, universalizing the Internet, heading towards implementing an e-government system and standardizing financial services.[37] Reflecting these potential changes in India's business environment, Song Song-yi, a researcher at KITA's Institute for International Trade is confident:

> As long as the 'Modi-nomics' policies are well maintained and implemented until his term ends in 2019, the Indian market will grow into an attractive place to do business.[38]

After a closed door meeting with Modi, Hyundai chairman Chung Mong-koo acknowledged that Hyundai Motor, world's fifth largest auto maker, is considering building a third auto plant, complementing its two plants in Chennai. Moreover, Chung is also planning to invest in other key areas such as construction and producing railway vehicles.[39] Three months later, in August 2015, Shin Dong-bin, the Lotte Group Chairman who is keen on overseas expansion, is planning to build Lotte culture shopping complexes in New Delhi, Mumbai and Chennai. This is on top of Lotte's investment in a newly opened confectionery plant in

Rohtak City in northern India. The 24,793-square-meter plant is expected to produce 60 billion won ($51 million) of vegetarian Choco Pie snacks annually.[40] These potential Korean investments from bigger companies or chaebols suggest that there is great interest in tapping the Indian market. If these projects are realized, then Korean small and medium companies will be part of the supply chain for the bigger companies.

## Conclusion

The Asian Development Bank, International Monetary Fund and World Bank have already assessed that India's growth for 2015 will be around 7.5 percent which is higher than China's estimated growth of 6.8 percent.[41] The "Act East Policy" is closely tied to the "Make in India" initiative. Modi has an exceptional opportunity to transform India into a manufacturing hub and unlock its full growth potential. Clearly, many have welcomed Modi's efforts on economic reforms aimed at making India a more reliable and transparent place to invest. In June 2015, Indian Ambassador Vikram Doraiswami to South Korea rightly assessed that Korea is a perfect match for India in terms of "complementary needs and capacities."[42] It can be argued that Korean conglomerates and businesses are keen to tap new markets and India can serve as a base for exporting Korean products to Asia, Middle East, Africa and Europe. Likewise, South Korea is crucial in Modi-nomics as it is viewed as a market, source of investment and expertise for realizing the "Make in India" initiative. Indian Ambassador Vikram Doraiswami equally emphasized that the words "discipline, dedication and organization" come to mind when one describes the appeal of Koreans. As such, in order to get Korean investors deeply involved in the Indian market, the red tape, high costs and long timelines involved in acquiring permits have to be addressed. In concluding this chapter, I would like to reiterate that the Modi government needs to cultivate and enhance political consensus, expand greater contacts between individual states and foreign governments, as well as implement serious reforms to its business practices or else the "Make in India" initiative will remain a dream.

## NOTES

1. Samir Saran, "Why the 'Asian Century' Might Actually Belong to India, Not China", *The World Post*, 6 February, 2015, http://www.huffingtonpost.com/samir-saran/asian-century-india-china_b_7496170.html, Retrieved 2 August 2015.
2. Anant Vijay Kala, "5 Things that Show Modi's Make in India Campaign is Working", *The Wall Street Journal*, 12 August 2015, http://blogs.wsj.com/briefly/2015/08/12/five-things-that-show-modis-make-in-india-campaign-is-working/, Retrieved 22 August 2015.
3. "PM to investors: Sell anywhere but 'Make in India,'" Rediff. Com, 15 August 2015, http:/

/www.rediff.com/business/report/come-make-in-india-modi-tells-global-investors/20140815.htm, Retrieved 12 August 2015.

4. "PM to investors: Sell Anywhere but 'Make in India," Rediff. Com, 15 August 2015, http://www.rediff.com/business/report/come-make-in-india-modi-tells-global-investors/20140815.htm, Retrieved 12 August 2015.
5. Samir Saran, "Why the 'Asian Century' Might Actually Belong to India, Not China", *The World Post*, 6 February 2015, http://www.huffingtonpost.com/samir-saran/asian-century-india-china_b_7496170.html, Retrieved 2 August 2015.
6. Danielle Rajendram, "India's New Asia-Pacific Strategy: Modi Acts East", Lowy Institute, December 2014.
7. Steven Denney, "South Korea's Economic Dependence on China", *The Diplomat*, 4 September 2015, http://thediplomat.com/2015/09/south-koreas-economic-dependence-on-china/, Retrieved 28 August 2015.
8. Steven Denney, "South Korea's Economic Dependence on China", *The Diplomat*, 4 September 2015, http://thediplomat.com/2015/09/south-koreas-economic-dependence-on-china/, Retrieved 28 August 2015.
9. "India Celebrates National Independence on Aug. 15", Embassy of India, South Korea, August 2015, http://www.indembassy.or.kr/article_features_detail.php?nid=404, Retrieved 2 September 2015.
10. Embassy of India, Seoul, South Korea, "Brief on India-Korea Economic and Commercial Relations" http://www.indembassy.or.kr/pages.php?id=23, Retrieved 22 August 2015.
11. South Korea is looking to correct trade imbalance with India: Envoy, *Business Standard*, 31 August 2014, http://www.business-standard.com/article/news-ians/south-korea-looking-to-correct-trade-imbalance-with-india-envoy-114083100128_1.html, Retrieved 2 August 2015.
12. Soyen Park, "India-South Korea Relations Under the New Modi Government", *The Diplomat*, 13 August 2014, http://thediplomat.com/2014/08/india-south-korea-relations-under-the-new-modi-government/, Retrieved 3 August 2015.
13. Tina Edwin, "We Need Make in India, Korean Style", *DailyO*, 18 May 2015, http://www.dailyo.in/business/make-in-india-south-korea-modi-korea-eximbank-Posco-soonki-kang-dipp-amitabh-kant-sagarmala-doosan-heavy-industry-hyundai-daewoo-lg/story/1/3777.html, Retrieved 3 August 2015.
14. Tina Edwin, "We Need Make in India, Korean Style", *DailyO*, 18 May 2015, http://www.dailyo.in/business/make-in-india-south-korea-modi-korea-eximbank-Posco-soonki-kang-dipp-amitabh-kant-sagarmala-doosan-heavy-industry-hyundai-daewoo-lg/story/1/3777.html, Retrieved 3 August 2015.
15. Tina Edwin, "We Need Make in India, Korean Style", *DailyO*, 18 May 2015, http://www.dailyo.in/business/make-in-india-south-korea-modi-korea-eximbank-Posco-soonki-kang-dipp-amitabh-kant-sagarmala-doosan-heavy-industry-hyundai-daewoo-lg/story/1/3777.html, Retrieved 3 August 2015.
16. Ankit Panda, "South Korean President Park Geun-hye Visits India", *The Diplomat*, 16 January 2014, http://thediplomat.com/2014/01/south-korean-president-park-geun-hye-visits-india/ Retrieved 23 August 2015.
17. Embassy of India, Seoul, South Korea, "Brief on India-Korea Economic and Commercial Relations" http://www.indembassy.or.kr/pages.php?id=23, Retrieved 22 August 2015.
18. Tina Edwin, "We Need Make in India, Korean Style", *DailyO*, 18 May 2015, http://www.dailyo.in/business/make-in-india-south-korea-modi-korea-eximbank-Posco-soonki-kang-dipp-amitabh-kant-sagarmala-doosan-heavy-industry-hyundai-daewoo-lg/story/1/3777.html, Retrieved 3 August 2015.

19. See Invest Rajasthan, http://www.investrajasthan.com/latest_news_details.php?id=34, Retrieved 18 August 2015.
20. Tridivesh Singh Maini, "The Significance of Modi's South Korea Visit", *The Diplomat*, 16 May 2015, http://thediplomat.com/2015/05/the-significance-of-modis-south-korea-visit/, Retrieved 18 August 2015.
21. Ani, "PM Modi meets CEOs of top South Korean companies", *Asian News International*,19 May 2015, https://in.news.yahoo.com/pm-modi-meets-ceos-top-south-korean-companies-050804262.html, Retrieved 20 August 2015.
22. "Korea, India to Work Closer Together", *Chosun Ilbo*, 19 May 2015, http://english.chosun.com/site/data/html_dir/2015/05/19/2015051901182.html, Retrieved 20 August 2015.
23. Neha Attre, "PM Modi in South Korea: As it happened", *Zee News*, 18 May 2015, http://zeenews.india.com/news/india/narendra-modis-south-korea-visit-live-updates_1596972. html, Retrieved 20 August 2015.
24. "India, South Korea Ink 7 Agreements to Boost Cooperation", *India Today*, 18 May 2015, http://indiatoday.intoday.in/story/modi-in-seoul-india-south-korea-ink-7-agreement/1/438800.html, Retrieved 18 August 2015.
25. "How India Can adopt Korea Model to Boost Manufacturing", *Money Control*, 15 April 2015, http://www.moneycontrol.com/news/economy/how-india-can-adopt-korea-model-to-boost-manufacturing_1069772.html?utm_source=ref_article; http://www.moneycontrol.com/news/economy/how-india-can-adopt-korea-model-to-boost-manufacturing_1069772. html?utm_source=ref_article, Retrieved 3 August 2015.
26. "How India can adopt Korea Model to Boost Manufacturing", *Money Control*, 15 April 2015, http://www.moneycontrol.com/news/economy/how-india-can-adopt-korea-model-to-boost-manufacturing_1069772.html?utm_source=ref_article; http://www.moneycontrol.com/news/economy/how-india-can-adopt-korea-model-to-boost-manufacturing_1069772. html?utm_source=ref_article, Retrieved 3 August 2015.
27. Dinesh Unnikrishnan, "Stalled Reforms, Broken Promises: How will Modi give Wings to his $75 bn UAE dream?", *First Post*, 18 August 2015, http://www.firstpost.com/business/stalled-reforms-broken-promises-will-modi-give-wings-75-bn-uae-dream-2396798.html, Retrieved 19 August 2015.
28. See TMF Group Website, http://www.tmf-group.com/en/media-centre/resources/top-challenges/apac/india, Retrieved 29 August 2015.
29. "India Difficult Place to do Business; More Reforms Needed: WB",*Business Standard*, September 14, 2015, http://www.business-standard.com/article/pti-stories/india-difficult-place-to-do-business-more-reforms-needed-wb-115091401074_1.html, Retrieved 28 September 2015.
30. Tridivesh Maini "Modi calls for reform in India: Will state governments respond?", *Global Risk Insights*, 8 July 2015, http://globalriskinsights.com/2015/07/modi-call-to-india-will-state-governments-respond/, Retrieved 6 September 2015.
31. "Posco Said to Be Backing Away from $12 Billion India Project", *Bloomberg Business*, 27 March 2015, http://www.bloomberg.com/news/articles/2015-03-27/Posco-said-to-be-backing-away-from-12-billion-india-project, Retrieved 15 September 2015.
32. "Posco Said to Be Backing Away From $12 Billion India Project", *Bloomberg Business*, 27 March 2015, http://www.bloomberg.com/news/articles/2015-03-27/Posco-said-to-be-backing-away-from-12-billion-india-project, Retrieved 15 September 2015.
33. Bhaskar Parichha, "Posco: The Cunning Businessman," 19 July 2015, http://www.economylead.com/blog/bhaskar-parichha/Posco-the-cunning-businessman-82362, Retrieved 20 September 2015.

34. "Time is Ripe to Enter India", *JoongAng Daily*, 21 May 2015, http://koreajoongang daily.joins.com/news/article/Article.aspx?aid=3004466, Retrieved 3 August 2015.
35. "South Korea, India Launch CEO Forum for Closer Partnership", *Korea Herald*, 19 May 2015, http://www.koreaherald.com/view.php?ud=20150519000710, Retrieved 2 August 2015.
36. Korea, "India to Bolster Ties in Infrastructure, Manufacturing", *Korea Herald*, 19 May 2015, http://www.koreaherald.com/view.php?ud=20150519001046, Retrieved 29 August 2015.
37. "Please 'Make in India,' Modi urges Korean firms", *JoongAng Daily*, 19 May 2015, http://koreajoongangdaily.joins.com/news/article/Article.aspx?aid=3004351, Retrieved 20 September 2015.
38. "Please 'Make in India,' Modi urges Korean firms", *JoongAng Daily*, 19 May 2015, http://koreajoongangdaily.joins.com/news/article/Article.aspx?aid=3004351, Retrieved 20 September 2015.
39. Hyundai Motor Mulls 3rd Plant in India: Chairman, *Korea Herald*, 19 May 2015, http://www.koreaherald.com/view.php?ud=20150519000849, Retrieved 2 August 2015.
40. "Lotte Seeks Shopping Malls in India", Korea Herald, 28 August 2915, http://www.koreaherald.com/view.php?ud=20150828001007, Retrieved 29 August 2015.
41. "Please 'Make in India,' Modi urges Korean firms", *JoongAng Daily*, 19 May 2015, http://koreajoongangdaily.joins.com/news/article/Article.aspx?aid=3004351, Retrieved 20 September 2015.
42. Joel Lee, "Indian officials take 'Miracle on the Han", *Korea Herald*, 28 June 2015, http://www.koreaherald.com/view.php?ud=20150628000146, Retrieved 3 September 2015.

# 11

# India's Participation in United Nations Police (UN Police) for Post-Conflict Reconstruction: A Critical Analysis

*Jayshree Tandekar*

India is one of the founding members of the United Nations. It joined the United Nations at a time when it was still a British colony. Over the years, India has emerged as a strong supporter of the United Nations in its peacekeeping efforts. The Indian participation in UN peacekeeping began in the late 1940s when it served as a member on the United Nations Special Committee on Palestine (UNSCOP) from May to August 1947. This fact finding committee was part of the preparatory stage for organizing the United Nations Truce Supervision Organization (UNTSO) (Krishnasamy 2001: 56). Till date, India has participated in about forty-four out of the total sixty-nine UN peacekeeping operations (UN website a). According to the latest figures, India has seconded 7,690 personnel to 11 UN peacekeeping operations out of the total 106,286 personnel deployed in mission areas in July 2015. Out of the total 7,690 personnel, India has sent 6,864 contingent troops personnel, 967 members of formed police units, 66 individual police officers, and 61 experts. Based on this contribution, India ranks third after Bangladesh and Ethiopia amongst the 124 contributing countries (UN website c). India has also suffered casualties of 159 personnel in UN peacekeeping operations, which is the highest amongst all the contributing countries (UN website f). There are certain principles that have shaped the Indian contribution to UN peacekeeping operations. For example, India believes that peacekeeping efforts should be undertaken only with the consent of conflicting parties and that too with the support and guidance of the United Nations. Moreover, India emphasizes that the differences between peacekeeping and peace enforcement should not be blurred (Krishnasamy 2010: 228). These are also the principles that have influenced India's participation in UN Police for post-conflict reconstruction.

This article is an attempt to present a general understanding of the Indian participation in UN Police for post-conflict reconstruction. It starts by describing the role of the UN peacekeeping operations in post-conflict reconstruction and the functions that are assigned to the UN Police as part of post-conflict reconstruction. It then provides an overview of the Indian contribution to the UN Police. The central focus of this article is to analyze the various tasks that are mandated to the Indian police officers in post-conflict reconstruction and the challenges encountered. The article ends with the lessons that can be drawn from the Indian police experience as UN Police for the Narendra Modi led NDA-II Government.

## Post-Conflict Reconstruction and United Nations Police (UN Police)

Post-conflict reconstruction is carried out in those societies that are affected by intra-state conflicts. Intra-state conflicts result from the inabilities and weaknesses of states to meet the demands of its citizens. Sometimes, they also occur due to the atrocities inflicted by states against their own people or the lack of central authority. In such situations, the individuals are the worst sufferers as their survival and security become difficult due to the chaos and lawlessness (Doyle and Sambanis 2006: 3-4). To redress the grievances of individuals and to ensure that they do not go through the ordeal of another intra-state conflict, the international community engages in post-conflict reconstruction. In particular, the United Nations has used its peacekeeping mechanism to carry out post-conflict reconstruction as this mechanism has an accepted standing in international relations (Dziedzic 1998: 6). As part of post-conflict reconstruction, the UN peacekeeping operations are given multiple civilian tasks not only to contain violence but also to establish durable peace. These tasks entail not only assuring that warring parties in intra-state conflicts obey ceasefires but also stabilizing the law and order situation; disarmament, demobilizing and reintegrating various factions; supplying humanitarian aid to the aggrieved people; setting up of government structures; re-establishing social and economic institutions; supporting the organization of elections; clearing of mines; defending and promoting human rights; and strengthening rule of law (UNDPKO/DFS 2008: 26–28).

The military personnel are the first to be sent after the setting up of UN peacekeeping operations in conflict-ridden societies. But they cannot be expected to participate in post-conflict reconstruction as they do not have the requisite skills and training. Thus, the United Nations deploys international civilian personnel who have the skills and expertise to carry out post-conflict reconstruction. Usually, these international civilian personnel are administrators, economists, police, de-miners, electoral observers, human rights monitors, civil affairs and governance specialists, humanitarian workers, communication and public information experts, judicial and correction officers, and gender specialists (UN website a). The UN Police have become one of the most critical aspects of the UN peacekeeping operations amongst all these international civilian personnel.

The UN Police are the unarmed police personnel sent by police contributing countries (PCCs). They are mandated to assist local authorities in maintaining law and order and sometimes they are directly responsible for performing policing functions in post-conflict societies or failed states. There are three different types of UN Police that are deployed in the mission areas: individual police officers (IPOs), formed police units (FPUs) and standing police capacity (SPC) experts. Of these, the IPOs are primarily responsible for post-conflict reconstruction. The IPOs have been regularly deployed in UN peacekeeping operations for carrying out post-conflict reconstruction. Currently, they are involved in post-conflict reconstruction in eight out of the sixteen UN peacekeeping operations (UN website a). As part of post-conflict reconstruction, the IPOs are required to build the capacity of local police. This is because in conflict-ridden societies, local police personnel either lack motivation or are unable to execute policing duties effectively (Schmidl 1998: 23). The incompetence of the local police in maintaining law and order not only threatens the survival of local people but it also becomes difficult for the United Nations to carry out other reconstruction activities. Also, a stable law and order situation is essential for sustainable peace and development in a post-conflict society (Day and Freeman 2005: 141). Thus, it becomes essential to equip local police personnel with skills and resources in such a manner that they are able and willing to uphold law and order even after the withdrawal of IPOs. In order to build the capacity of the local police, the IPOs perform a number of functions such as demobilization, recruitment, vetting and certification and training (each of which have been discussed in subsequent sections).

## Indian Police and United Nations Peacekeeping Operations

India is one of the founding members of the United Nations. India has a long tradition of contributing to the UN efforts in peacekeeping. The Indian participation in UN peacekeeping operations began in the late 1940s when it served as a member on the UNSCOP from May to August 1947. This fact-finding committee was part of the preparatory stage for organizing the UNTSO (Krishnasamy 2001: 56). Till date, India has participated in about forty-four out of the total sixty-nine UN peacekeeping operations (UN website a). The Indian contribution to UN peacekeeping operations includes not only military troops but also air force, navy, police and civilian personnel. It is no hidden fact that India is one of the top troop contributors to UN peacekeeping operations. But what is not widely known is that over the years, India has emerged amongst the top police contributors as well. Graph 1 depicts the Indian contribution to UN Police over the years.

India contributed to the UN Police for the first time when it sent eight police officers for the United Nations Transitional Authority in Cambodia (UNTAC) in March 1992 and by October 1992, its contribution to UN Police in the UNTAC increased to 366 (UN website b). Since then, India has regularly seconded its police personnel to UN peacekeeping operations. Like in the case of military, India's contribution to UN Police has been largely influenced by its national interests of assuming a role in shaping the future of international system, and the desire of acquiring a permanent seat in the Security Council. In consequence of the pursuit of its national interests, India has sent its police personnel to about twenty-three UN peacekeeping operations (UN websites b and c).

**Graph 1: Indian Contribution to UN Police (1992-2015)**

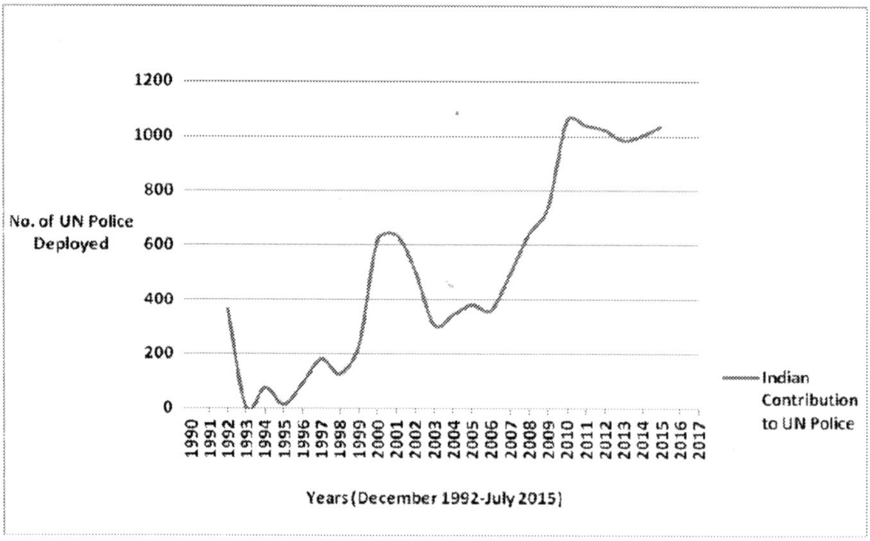


*Source:* www.un.org/en/peacekeeping/resources/statistics/contributors_archive.shtml. Accessed on 14 August 2015.

Table 1 shows the list of UN peacekeeping operations in which India has sent its police personnel. India has, on several occasions, made a much larger police contribution than the permanent members of the Security Council and the traditional peacekeepers. According to the latest figures, the Indian share in total 13,334 UN Police personnel deployed in July 2015 is 7.7 per cent which is not only higher than the share of the permanent members of the Security Council, China 1.2 per cent, United States 0.3 per cent, France 0.2 per cent, Russia 0.1 per cent and United Kingdom that contributed only four police personnel, but it is also more than the share of its neighbouring states, Nepal (7.46 per cent) and Pakistan (3.51 per cent) (UN website c). Of all the permanent members, the share of China is the highest. Even the share of the traditional peacekeeping countries such as Canada (0.63 per cent) and the Scandinavian countries such as Sweden (0.26 per cent), Norway (0.34 per cent) and Finland (contributed only one police man) is less than the Indian share (UN website c).

**Table 1: List of UN Peacekeeping Operations in which India has Sent its Police Personnel**

1. UN Peacekeeping Force in Cyprus (UNFICYP) (March 1964 – Present)
2. UN Mission for the Referendum in Western Sahara (MINURSO) (April 1991 – Present)
3. UN Angola Verification Mission II (UNAVEM II) (May 1991 – February 1995)
4. UN Transitional Authority in Cambodia (UNTAC) (March 1992 – September 1993)
5. UN Operation in Mozambique (ONUMOZ) (December 1992 – December 1994)
6. UN Observer Mission in Georgia (UNOMIG) (August 1993 – June 2009)
7. UN Angola Verification Mission III (UNAVEM III) (February 1995 – June 1997)
8. UN Mission in Bosnia-Herzegovina (UNMIBH) (December 1995 – December 2002)
9. UN Support Mission in Haiti (UNSMIH) (July 1996 – July 1997)
10. UN Observer Mission in Angola (MONUA) (June 1997 – February 1999)
11. UN Transition Mission in Haiti (UNTMIH) (August 1997 – December 1997)
12. UN Civilian Police Mission in Haiti (MIPONUH) (December 1997 – March 2000)
13. UN Observer Mission in Sierra Leone (UNOMSIL) (July 1998 – October 1999)
14. UN Interim Administration in Kosovo (UNMIK) (June 1999 – Present)
15. UN Mission in Sierra Leone (UNAMSIL) (October 1999 – December 2005)
16. UN Organization Mission in the Democratic Republic of the Congo (MONUC) (November 1999 – June 2010)
17. UN Mission in Liberia (UNMIL) (September 2003 – Present)
18. UN Operation in Cote d'Ivoire (UNOCI) (April 2004 – Present)
19. UN Mission in the Sudan (UNMIS) (March 2005 – July 2011)
20. UN Integrated Mission in Timor-Leste (UNMIT) (August 2006 – December 2012)
21. UN Stabilization Mission in Haiti (MINUSTAH) (June 2004 – Present)
22. UN Organization Stabilization Mission in the Democratic Republic of Congo (MONUSCO) (July 2010 – Present)
23. UN Mission in South Sudan (UNMISS) (July 2011 – Present)

*Source:* http://www.un.org/en/peacekeeping/resources/statistics/contributors_archive.shtml. Accessed on 14 August 2015.

Since December 2009, India has consistently emerged amongst the top five PCCs in the world. In July 2015, India ranked fourth as it contributed 1,035 police personnel to five out of the twelve UN peacekeeping operations with the UN Police (UN website c). Table 2 shows the present mission-wise contribution of India to the UN Police (in terms of IPOs as well as FPUs).

**Table 2: Mission-wise Contribution of India to UN Police (July 2015)**

| *Mission Name* | *Individual Police Officers* | | *Formed Police Unit* | |
|---|---|---|---|---|
| | *Male* | *Female* | *Male* | *Female* |
| MINUSTAH | 15 | 0 | 454 | 0 |
| MONUSCO | 0 | 0 | 265 | 4 |
| UNFICYP | 7 | 1 | 0 | 0 |
| UNMIL | 12 | 0 | 140 | 104 |
| UNMISS | 28 | 3 | 0 | 0 |

*Source:* www.un.org/en/peacekeeping/resources/statistics/contributors.shtml. Accessed on 13 August 2015.

The IPOs and FPUs sent by India have played significant part in helping the local law enforcement agencies maintain law and order, and from time to time these police personnel have been honoured for their contribution. The biggest recognition of the Indian contribution to UN Police came in October 2014 when the Indian police officer Shakti Devi working with the United Nations Assistance Mission in Afghanistan (UNAMA) was awarded the International Female Policekeeper Award (Khajuria 2014: 1). This award is given by the Police Division of the UN Headquarters in New York to a female policekeeper in recognition of her work in UN peacekeeping. Further, on some occasions, the Indian police personnel have been given the opportunity to head the UN Police components in the mission areas. For instance, Mr. Sudesh Kumar (November 2007–December 2009) and Mr Rajesh Dewan (February 2009–February 2011) were appointed as the UN Police Commissioners of the United Nations Organization Mission in the Democratic Republic of Congo (MONUC) and the United Nations Mission in Sudan (UNMIS) respectively (UN websites d and e), while Mr Gautam Sawang and Mr Sanjay Kundu were appointed as the UN Police Deputy Commissioners of the United Nations Mission in Liberia (UNMIL) and the United Nations Mission in South Sudan (UNMISS) respectively. The appointment of the Indian police personnel to lead UN Police components in mission areas is an indication of the growing reputation of India in UN peacekeeping. Similarly, the Indian FPUs have been appreciated for their contribution to maintaining stability and order in conflict-ridden societies. For instance, the 135-personnel Indian FPU-2 deployed in the Democratic Republic of Congo was awarded the UN Peacekeeping Medal in May 2013 for its 'high level commitment' in fighting criminals and maintaining peace in Goma/North

Kivu (Padovan 2013). Also, India is one of the first PCCs to send all-female FPUs to UN peacekeeping operations. India deployed two successive all-female FPUs in Liberia in 2007 and 2008 to mentor unarmed local Liberian police personnel. These all-female FPUs were even awarded the UN Peacekeeping Medal for their contribution to peace process in Liberia (UNDPI 2008).

Apart from deploying its police personnel to field missions, India has seconded its police personnel to the Police Division as well which is the nodal point of the UN Headquarters in New York responsible for the UN Police-related matters. In particular, India has the distinction of having sent two Police Advisers to the Police Division: Mr Om Prakash Rathore (1995–7) and Dr Kiran Bedi (2003–5) (Nambiar 2014). Further, there are some Indian police personnel who have served in different capacities in the Police Division. For instance, the former chief of the Mission Management and Support Section (one of the sections of the Police Division) was Mr Ajay Kashyap of Delhi Police. The appointment of the Indian police personnel to high-level posts in the Police Division not only adds to the Indian prestige but it also gives India greater opportunities to influence the UN peacekeeping decision making. However, such appointments of the Indian police personnel to the Police Division have been occasional.

## Indian Police's Participation in Post-Conflict Reconstruction and Challenges Confronted

India has deployed its police officers for post-conflict reconstruction in UN peacekeeping operations set up in Bosnia-Herzegovina, Haiti, Sierra Leone, Kosovo, Congo, Liberia, Sudan, Timor-Leste, Côté d'Ivoire and South Sudan. The objective of the Indian police in post-conflict reconstruction is to build the capacity of the local police so that the latter can carry out policing duties effectively. By doing so, the local police personnel can provide a safe and secure environment wherein people can live their lives normally and peacefully. Thus, in this way, the local police will also be able to win the trust and confidence of the local population (Groenewald and Peake 2004: 15). Currently, there are sixty-six Indian police officers (sixty-two male and four female police personnel) who have been mandated to carry out post-conflict reconstruction in four UN peacekeeping operations (UN website c). As part of the post-conflict reconstruction, the Indian police officers are assigned number of functions such as demobilization, recruitment, vetting and certification, and training. Each of these functions has been discussed in the following section.

### *Demobilization*

During intra-state conflicts, sometimes the strength of the local police exceeds the requisite numbers. This is because at times military personnel are integrated in local police so that the latter can robustly enforce law and order during civil unrest, even if it means violating the rights of people. At other times, warring factions maintain their respective police forces that are operated by separate laws, organizational structures, and command and control. Apart from the swelling numbers, occasionally the local police are characterized by the presence of such personnel who work to serve the interests of political authorities and not of local people (Celador 2005: 370).

When the Indian police officers are deployed in such situations, they are first of all required to demobilize local police. Demobilization means dismissing military personnel from local police, dismantling police forces maintained by different warring factions, and weeding out those police personnel who are politically biased. This is because these personnel have not been recruited according to merit, and also they do not have the capacity to protect public interests. The demobilization also involves stripping these personnel of their equipment, uniforms and identity cards. By demobilization, local police personnel are freed from undue pressure of serving particular interests and they are reoriented to become the true servants of public. For instance, at the time of signing of the Dayton Agreement, the Serbian, Croatian, and Muslim factions in Bosnia-Herzegovina maintained their own distinct police. As a result, there were 44,750 police personnel on duty in Bosnia-Herzegovina: 29,750 in Muslim-controlled areas, 3,000 in Croat-controlled areas, and 12,000 in the Republic of Srpska. As part of the United Nations Mission in Bosnia-Herzegovina (UNMIBH), the Indian police officers removed and reduced the size of local police from 44,000 personnel to 17,000 (Smith et al. 2007: 21).

However, the Indian police officers have faced many difficulties in demobilizing local police. The major amongst them is the reality that not all demobilized personnel find employment despite participating in the reintegration programmes. Hence with no other alternative, these demobilized personnel have often engaged in criminal activities which in turn have contributed to the destabilization of internal law and order in post-conflict societies (Neild 2001: 25). Also, sometimes these demobilized personnel are integrated in local police in an attempt to portray the success of reintegration programmes (Stodiek and Zellner 2007: 8). However, this defeats the objective of demobilization. This is because there is always a possibility that these demobilized personnel can revert to their old ways, and hence hamper the security and confidence of local people.

### *Recruitment*

Usually post-conflict societies are characterized by dwindling numbers in local police. Two reasons can be identified for this. Sometimes during conflicts, local police personnel are either killed or they leave their jobs and flee to save their own lives. Hence, there are not enough police personnel available to maintain law and order in post-conflict societies. At other times, it may so happen that after demobilization, the strength of the local police may decline. In both these situations, it becomes necessary to recruit new personnel so that the local police can be brought to the pre-conflict size. At the same time, it is necessary to ensure that the local police system represents its society. Thus, recruitment in local police is carried out on the basis of ethnicity, gender and tribe. Generally, as part of the recruitment policy, quotas are determined for minority communities. Quota-based recruitment is particularly important in those societies where ethnic or sectarian differences have driven past conflicts. Such recruitment enhances the professional conduct of local police, while maximizing their ability to develop good relations with local communities (Celador 2005: 366). For example, in the United Nations Interim Administration in Kosovo (UNMIK), the recruitment of minorities in local police was a major goal of the Indian police officers (Smith et al. 2007: 19). In recent years, the emphasis has been placed on recruiting more women in local police in order to ensure that the women and girls who have gone through the trauma are able to express themselves freely before the female police personnel. As part of recruitment, the Indian police officers have assisted local governments in advertising posts, holding exams and conducting interviews of candidates.

However, the Indian police officers have faced several hurdles in recruiting candidates in local police. For one, quota-based recruitment can undermine the establishment of efficient local police as it often prevents the recruitment of meritorious personnel. In addition, there is a possibility that the quality of personnel recruited in local police may not be up to the mark. For instance, in an effort to meet the gender targets, the Indian police officers in Liberia (UNMIL) lowered the educational standards so much for female recruits that some were incapable of performing basic police functions even after training (Durch et al. 2012: 38-39). Apart from this, sometimes inappropriate personnel are recruited in local police so as to meet the requirements of local authorities. Also, there is always a possibility that despite being recruited in local police, the personnel belonging to different communities continue to report and receive orders from their respective community leaders. Thus, their loyalty to police service becomes questionable (Stodiek and Zellner 2007: 4). Moreover, given the paucity of time, occasionally demobilized personnel are recruited in local police. Such recruitment erodes the public legitimacy and credibility of local police. Also, there are chances that this recruitment results in the continuation of old "inappropriate institutional practices and the bureaucratic culture of former security forces" (Neild 2001: 25).

## *Vetting and Certification*

Other essential functions that the Indian police officers are authorized to carry out in post-conflict reconstruction are vetting and certification. The primary objective of vetting and certification is to screen and identify all those police personnel who are fit and capable of maintaining law and order. In order to accomplish this, the Indian police officers usually set certain criteria such as educational background, training and absence of any criminal conviction. This process of screening is known as vetting. Vetting involves carrying out investigation of all the existing as well as new recruits in local police. With the help of local authorities, the names of police personnel are advertised in local newspapers so that the people can provide all the necessary information about the police personnel's past. The old police records are also checked and verified. Those found guilty are generally dismissed or suspended by local authorities (Celador 2005: 370–1). Those police personnel whose records are clean are certified and allowed to continue in the police service. Thus, vetting helps to identify and bring to account all those police personnel who have violated laws during and after intra-state conflicts. It also cements the accountability of local police as the "neutral guarantor of rights" (Neild 2001: 27). For example, in the United Nations Mission in Timor-Leste (UNMIT), the Indian police officers were involved in vetting of 900 personnel of the Polisia Nasional de Timor-Leste (PNTL) (Lemay-Hébert 2009: 400).

But the Indian police officers have confronted some challenges during the vetting and certification of local police. For instance, the Indian police officers have to deal with the indifferences of local police authorities to the investigations carried out by them. Even after vetting, local police authorities do not dismiss those police personnel who are found unfit for policing or such personnel are let off after minor punishment. This was witnessed in Timor-Leste (UNMIT) when the higher policing authorities sent back most of the files for further investigation though the files had been submitted after vetting (Lemay-Hébert 2009: 400). It means that even after found guilty, such personnel continue to serve in the police. This not only nullifies the efforts and resources invested by the Indian police officers but it also undermines the confidence of people in local police. At other times, the database (records) of local police personnel is either absent as it has been destroyed during intra-state conflicts or it is outdated. As a result, it becomes difficult for Indian police officers to conduct investigations and secure testimonies of witnesses as the former do not have suitable records to rely on.

## *Training*

Training is one of the most important functions that is assigned to the Indian police officers in post-conflict reconstruction. Training of local police is essential as it aims at transferring skills and knowledge to them, and makes sure that local police personnel acquire the necessary experience to carry out their policing duties professionally. Generally, the Indian police officers provide training to different kinds of personnel in local police such as new recruits, current serving members, middle and senior management officers, and local police trainers. As part of training, these police personnel are taught a number of topics such as crime, traffic, border, conflict resolution and mediation, forensics, crowd control, anti-terrorism, information technology, democratic policing, community policing, human rights, finance, equipment maintenance and asset management (UNDPKO 2000: 61-66).

The Indian police officers usually impart three types of training to local police: classroom training, field training, and training of the trainers. Classroom training aims at providing theoretical understanding of various policing issues and the challenges that can be confronted by local police in implementing their duties. On the other hand, in field training the local police are given practical knowledge of the topics covered in classroom training. For instance, as part of the United Nations Operation in Côté d'Ivoire (UNOCI), the Indian police officers delivered field training on fingerprinting techniques, judicial photography (descriptive images and crime scene) and criminal investigations (methodology of criminal investigation) to seventy Ivorian police officers (UNDPKO 2012: 6). The field training helps local police in developing and enhancing their basic skills such as response time, crime scene preservation, identifying and interviewing witnesses, and obtaining and safeguarding physical evidence. Sometimes, the Indian police officers impart training to the local police trainers so that the latter can train their fellow police personnel. The training of the trainers not only saves time and money but it also has a snowball effect. For example, the Indian police officers of the United Nations Stabilization Mission in Haiti (MINUSTAH) trained Haitian National Police (HNP) trainers in 'First Aid Instructor Training Programme' so that these local trainers could train other local police personnel in basic life saving techniques (UNDPKO 2012: 10). In some cases, Indian police officers have also helped local police authorities formulate training curricula on number of issues such as gender and human rights.

However, occasionally it becomes difficult for the Indian police officers to train local police. Several reasons can be identified for this. The chief amongst them is the unwillingness of local police personnel to train under the Indian police officers. This is because sometimes local police consider the UN Police as outsiders who have little or no knowledge of the former's culture and society. Thus to avoid training, local police personnel put forward such conditions that cannot be met by the UN Police. Such situations were experienced by the Indian police officers of the UNMISS. Also, given the emphasis on early exit strategy, training of local police is often limited to short periods. Consequently, it becomes difficult for the Indian police officers to cover all the topics and address individual concerns of all participants at the same time. Moreover, training can be undermined by the absence of requisite infrastructure and resources. For example, in Sierra Leone, the three regional police training centres at the provincial capitals of Bo, Kenema and Makeni were destroyed during conflict, and the police training school at Benguema could accommodate only 200 trainees per intake. The lack of adequate building infrastructure made it impossible for the Indian police officers of the United Nations Mission in Sierra Leone (UNAMSIL) to train more police personnel at one time and it also resulted in the reduction of classroom training duration from six months to twelve weeks (Meek 2003: 108).

## Conclusion

India has emerged as one of the largest contributors of police to UN peacekeeping operations. India has deployed significant number of IPOs for post-conflict reconstruction. But these police officers have faced several problems while performing the tasks of demobilization, recruitment, vetting and certification, and training. Also, as is evident from Table 3, the Indian contribution to IPOs for post-conflict reconstruction has declined since 2010.

**Table 3: Indian Contribution to Individual Police Officers (2009-2015)**

| | *Individual Police Officers* | | |
|---|---|---|---|
| | *Male* | *Female* | *Total* |
| December 2009 | 96 | 7 | 103 |
| December 2010 | 99 | 5 | 104 |
| December 2011 | 65 | 4 | 69 |
| December 2012 | 44 | 5 | 49 |
| December 2013 | 26 | 8 | 34 |
| December 2014 | 64 | 5 | 69 |
| July 2015 | 62 | 4 | 66 |

*Source:* http://www.un.org/en/peacekeeping/resources/statistics/contributors_archive.shtml. Accessed on 14 August 2015.

Based on the Indian police experience as UN Police, one of the first lessons that can be drawn for the Narendra Modi led NDA-II Government is that despite the challenges confronted by the Indian police officers in post-conflict reconstruction, India cannot afford to decrease its contribution to the UN Police. Two reasons can be identified for this. For one, India faces stiff competition from its neighbouring countries in terms of the contribution to the UN Police. As can be seen from Table 4, Bangladesh, Nepal and Pakistan have emerged amongst the largest police contributors to UN peacekeeping operations. In particular,

Bangladesh and Nepal have consistently ranked amongst the top five PCCs since December 2005. In fact, since December 2005, Bangladesh has seconded more police personnel than India. If India has to maintain its leverage in the developing world, it has to not only increase its deployment of IPOs but also contribute more than Bangladesh. At the same time, India has to understand that its contribution to UN Police in peacekeeping operations not only helps it to shape its image positively as a 'good international citizen' that is committed to global responsibilities but it also provides an opportunity for India to increase its presence within the United Nations. Given the vast reservoir of the UN Police experience, India can stake claims in the important decision-making posts in the Police Division at the UN Headquarters in New York.

As far as the challenges are concerned, India can take several steps to ensure that its police officers do not face the same problems again and again in post-conflict reconstruction. India can begin by establishing a post of the Police Adviser in its permanent mission to the United Nations. Like in the case of many other UN member states, the police related matters in the Indian permanent mission are dealt with by the Military Adviser. It is not reasonable to expect the Military Adviser to understand the difficulties that are faced by the Indian police officers. This is because military and police are two separate security institutions that have their own distinct identity, culture, doctrine, and command and control structures. Further, it would be useful if the Indian police officers are deployed

**Table 4: Ranking of India and its Neighbouring Countries amongst Police Contributing Countries (2000-2015)**

| | *India* | *Nepal* | *Bangladesh* | *Pakistan* |
|---|---|---|---|---|
| December 2000 | 2 | 17 | 10 | 6 |
| December 2001 | 3 | 19 | 14 | 6 |
| December 2002 | 2 | 18 | 13 | 5 |
| December 2003 | 4 | 10 | 13 | 9 |
| December 2004 | 5 | 3 | 17 | 2 |
| December 2005 | 6 | 3 | 2 | 5 |
| December 2006 | 7 | 4 | 2 | 3 |
| December 2007 | 8 | 5 | 1 | 3 |
| December 2008 | 6 | 5 | 1 | 4 |
| December 2009 | 5 | 4 | 1 | 3 |
| December 2010 | 3 | 5 | 2 | 4 |
| December 2011 | 3 | 6 | 1 | 4 |
| December 2012 | 3 | 5 | 1 | 6 |
| December 2013 | 4 | 5 | 1 | 6 |
| December 2014 | 4 | 5 | 2 | 7 |
| July 2015 | 4 | 5 | 3 | 7 |

*Source:* http://www.un.org/en/peacekeeping/resources/statistics/contributors_archive.shtml. Accessed on 14 August 2015.

for longer durations in the mission areas. This would enable them to build good relations with local authorities and local police personnel which in turn would help them to carry out their tasks more effectively. Also, a system of debriefing should be established wherein those Indian police officers who have already served in UN peacekeeping operations are able to record their experiences. Such a system would facilitate the identification of lessons learned and the consequent formulation of policies by the Indian government.

Moreover, India should learn something from its neighbouring countries as well. China, one of its neighbours, has established the Peacekeeping CIVPOL (Civilian Police) Training Centre in Lanfang City. This is significant because the Chinese contribution to UN Police has been minimal. According to latest figures, in July 2015, China sent only 161 police personnel, which is almost seven times less than the Indian contribution. The establishment of this training centre signifies the Chinese determination to second competent police personnel to UN peacekeeping operations (Choedon 2013: 220). Given the Indian contribution to UN Police, it would only be better if India could set up a training institute that is dedicated entirely to cater to the needs of its potential UN Police personnel. This centre would teach and train the Indian police officers in tackling some of the challenges that are confronted by them in post-conflict reconstruction.

## REFERENCES


Celador, Gemma Collantes (2005), "Police Reform: Peacebuilding Through 'Democratic Policing'?", *International Peacekeeping*, 12. 3: p. 366; 370–1.

Choedon, Yeshi (2013), "India and Chinese Engagement in UN Complex Peacekeeping Operations: A Comparative Perspective", *China Report*, 49. 2: p. 220.

Day, Graham and Christopher Freeman (2005), "Operationalising the Responsibility to Protect—The Policekeeping Approach", *Global Governance*, 11. 2: p. 141.

Doyle, Michael W. and Nicholas Sambanis (2006), "Introduction: War-Making, Peacebuilding and the United Nations", in their book *Making War and Building Peace – United Nations Peace Operations*, Princeton: Princeton University Press, p. 3-4.

Dziedzic, Michael J. (1998), "Introduction", in Oakley, Robert B., Michael J. Dziedzic and Eliot M. Goldberg (Ed.) *Policing the New World Disorder – Peace Operations and Public Security*, Washington D.C.: National Defense University Press, p. 6.

Durch, William J., Madeline L. England and Fiona B. Mangan with Michelle Ker (2012), *Understanding Impact of Police, Justice, and Corrections Components in UN Peace Operations*, Future of Peace Operations Program, Washington D.C.: The Henry L. Stimson Center, p. 38-39.

Groenewald, Hesta and Gordon Peake (2004), *Police Reform Through Community-Based Policing – Philosophy and Guidelines for Implementation*, New York: International Peace Academy, p.15.

Khajuria, Sanjay (15 October 2014), "UN Peacekeeper Award for J&K Woman Cop in Afghanistan", *The Times of India*, p. 1.

Krishnasamy, Kabilan (2001), "'Recognition' for Third World Peacekeepers: India and Pakistan", *International Peacekeeping*, 8. 4: p. 56.

Krishnasamy, Kabilan (2010), "A Case for India's Leadership in United Nations Peacekeeping", *International Studies*, 47. 2-4: p. 228.

Lemay-Hébert, Nicolas (2009), "UNPOL and Police Reform in Timor-Leste: Accomplishments and Setbacks", *International Peacekeeping*, 16. 3: p. 400.

Meek, Sarah (2003), "Policing Sierra Leone", in Malan, Mark, Sarah Meek, Thokozani Thusi, Jeremy Ginifer, and Patrick Coker (Ed.) *Sierra Leone: Building Road to Recovery*, Pretoria, South Africa: Institute for Security Studies (ISS), p. 108.

Nambiar, Satish (26 January 2014), "India and United Nations Peacekeeping Operations", mea.gov.in, 16 December 2014, http://mea.gov.in/articles-in-indian-media.htm?dtl/22776/India+and+United+Nations+Peacekeeping+Operations.

Neild, Rachel (2001), "Democratic Police Reforms in War-Torn Societies", *Conflict, Security and Development*, 1. 1: p. 25; 27.

Padovan, Clara (15 May 2013), "Indian Formed Police Unit-2 honoured with the UN Peace Medal in Goma", monusco.unmissions.org, 23 November 2014, http://monusco.unmissions.org/Default.aspx?tabid=10662&ctl=Details&mid=14594&ItemID=19806&language=en-US.

Schmidl, Erwin A. (1998), "Police Functions in Peace Operations: An Historical Overview", in Oakley, Robert B., Michael J. Dziedzic and Eliot M. Goldberg (Ed.) *Policing the New World Disorder – Peace Operations and Public Security*, Washington D.C.: National Defense University Press, p. 23.

Smith, Joshua G., Victoria K. Holt and William J. Durch (2007), *Enhancing United Nations Capacity to Support Post-Conflict Policing and Rule of Law*, Stimson Center Report No. 63, Report from the Project on Rule of Law in Post-Conflict Settings – Future of Peace Operations Program, Washington D.C.: The Henry L. Stimson Center, p. 19; 21.

Stodiek, Thorsten and Wolfgang Zellner (2007), "The Creation of Multi-Ethnic Police Services in the Western Balkans: A Record of Mixed Success", www.ssoar.info, 12 November 2014, http://nbn-resolving.de/urn:nbn:de:0168-ssoar-260323.

United Nations (website a), http://www.un.org/en/peacekeeping/operations, 10 August 2015.

United Nations (website b), http://www.un.org/en/peacekeeping/resources/statistics/contributors_archive.shtml, 14 August 2015.

United Nations (website c), http://www.un.org/en/peacekeeping/resources/statistics/contributors.shtml, 13 August 2015.

United Nations (website d), http://www.un.org/en/peacekeeping/missions/past/monuc/leadership.shtml, 14 August 2015.

United Nations (website e), http://www.un.org/en/peacekeeping/missions/past/unmis/leadership.shtml, 13 August 2015.

United Nations (website f), http://www.un.org/en/peacekeeping/fatalities/documents/stats_2.pdf, 14 August 2015.

*UN Department of Peacekeeping Operations (2000), *United Nations Civilian Police Principles and Guidelines*, New York: United Nations, p. 61-66.

UN Department of Peacekeeping Operations (2012), *UN Police Magazine*, January 2012 (8th edition), New York: United Nations, p. 6; 10.

*UN Department of Peacekeeping Operations and Department of Field Support (2008), *United Nations Peacekeeping Operations: Principles and Guidelines*, New York: United Nations, p. 26-28.

UN Department of Public Information (14 November 2008), "Indian Female Police officers inspire women to join Liberian Police to support Rule of Law", UNIC/Press Release/171-2008, www.unic.org, 23 November 2014, http://www.unic.org.in/display.php?E=1178&K=India.

# 12

# Narendra Modi: Re-Drafting the Foreign Policy Objectives

*K. Jayaprasad*

The Indian politics witnessed a fundamental change in 2014. After 30 years, a single party got absolute majority in the Parliament. Under Prime Minister Narendra Modi, the nation's domestic policies as well as foreign policy switched towards dynamic, positive and development oriented formulations. He re-drafted relations with the neighbours and major powers of the world. Within a short span of time, the nation's will asserted its dignity, self-respect, strength and gave the message of friendship and co-operation.

Prime Minister Narendra Modi opened a new and confident Foreign Policy and succeeded in participating high-powered bilateral and multilateral Summits within seven months in office. No previous Indian prime minister has such a record in office. Like Prime Minister Atal Behari Vajpayee in 1998, Narendra Modi took the mantle from a weak government at home and its feeble and confused Foreign Policy record. For example, from 1989–98 India had a succession of weak governments with poor leadership. The collapse of the USSR further confused the leadership. But in 1998 Vajpayee changed the Foreign Policy by asserting India's prestige, power and national interest. He had contributed much to raise India's national self-confidence both in internal and external affairs. He reverted the Nehruvian Foreign Policy and dogmatic orientations and placed a pragmatic Foreign Policy. He took the realistic approach and a strategy of peace through strength. As a result, India declared herself as a nuclear weapon state. Even though the USA and its allies imposed sanctions against India, within two years they were compelled to accept the nuclear policy of India. India received much recognition from Super Powers only after changing the label of a 'soft State'. The NDA Government under Vajpayee changed the traditional Foreign Policy objectives of India and asserted security, economic development and peaceful world order. Thus discarding idealism, Vajpayee government followed a foreign policy that restored India's national self-confidence and power.

Also from 2004 to 2014, India witnessed a week foreign policy under UPA government headed by Dr. Manmohan Singh. The lack of leadership, dynamism, vision and confidence were clearly evident in Manmohan Singh's Foreign Policy. The dual leadership of UPA system further confused the matter. A vibrant Foreign Policy can sustain only on the foundation of a strong domestic policy. The Prime Minister Dr. Manmohan Singh had no command in the ruling UPA but the Chairperson Mrs. Sonia Gandhi controlled the power. India lost ten years because of inaction, confusions and compromise, both internally and externally. Prime Minister Manmohan Singh's two terms can be called as the 'lost decade' for India strategically. Despite economic growth, the nations opted weakness and inability. This shows that, the GDP growth itself cannot translate into strong Foreign Policy in the absence of dynamic, forward-looking leadership and strategic goals. However, the UPA under Manmohan Singh–Sonia Gandhi rule failed to protect the national interest and national prestige.

Hence, the Prime Minister, Narendra Modi had a huge task to reassert the Indian interest. On the lines with Vajpayee he asserted national interest. But Vajpayee Government initially faced the sanctions of the super powers including USA, but Narendra Modi has been welcomed by all. The world endorsed the new leadership in India.

Every country's Foreign Policy had elements of continuity and change following a change in government. India's Foreign Policy under BJP Government led by Narendra Modi is not different. It is interesting that, immediately after the elections to the parliament in 2014, many experts were not confident on Narendra Modi's Foreign Policy initiatives. They looked through the 'prism' of political colour and predicted a dark picture of future foreign policy. Also Narendra Modi faced visa denial from USA for 10 years previously. They believed that domestic priorities would dominate the scene. But soon Narendra Modi succeeded in building the foundation of a strong domestic policy and a vibrant and progressive foreign policy with strong commitments to the protection of national interests.

It is noted that in the swearing-in ceremony, Modi as Prime Minister itself was a diplomatic success and all the Chiefs of eight neighbouring SAARC Countries along with Mauritius attended the function. The "neighbourhood first policy" of Narendra Modi changed the outlook of neighbours on India. As a gesture to Modi's invitation for the swearing-in ceremony both Pakistan and Sri

Lanka released hundreds of Indian fishermen who were imprisoned for a long period.

## Changes in Foreign Policy Objectives

Asserting the dignity of India and its national power Narendra Modi changed the idealistic conceptions and replaced by national interest and progressive ideas and policies. The Ministry of External Affairs, headed by Sushma Swaraj, the first woman to hold the office since Indira Gandhi, is free from so-called "Experts" from foreign service. Bureaucratic role has been limited to executional level. Policy making role is now entirely with the political executive. Modi Doctrine contains such dynamic policy initiatives. As a result, soon after the new government took over the office all-important nations and world leaders expressed their willingness to work with Modi government to strengthen their relations with India. All five permanent member-States of UN Security Council sent their envoys to India immediately after Prime Minister Narendra Modi assumed his office. The Prime Minister has succeeded to demonstrate his foreign relations capabilities.

i. Change in economic objectives
   Narendra Modi declared economic and technological objectives of his Government's foreign policy. His motto is "India First". "India First" means that India's basic requirements like sanitation, food security, employment generation, defence and space technology will be expressed with greater clarity and specificity to other countries.
ii. Greater link between domestic and foreign policy objectives
   The domestic policy and interest will represent the nation's foreign policy. "Make in India" is not a mere slogan, but an economic foreign policy initiative. He declared, "the entire world is looking at India. Demography, Democracy and Demand are attracting the world to India."
iii. Greater emphasis on National Power
   Due recognition of economic power and military power is the hallmark of Modi's foreign policy. Prime Minister Modi holds the National Interest but pragmatism prevailed in all dealings.
iv. Concern with Border
   Modi was against compromises on border. That message has already given to both Pakistan and China. Border firings from Pakistan will not be tolerated. Chinese incursions have been strongly opposed.
v. Rejection of Pakistan orientated Foreign Policy
   India wishes for friendship with Pakistan. But our concern is not merely Pakistan and it is not the sole enemy. India offered friendship without compromises. For the first time, India, asserted the "Lakshman Rekha". Prime Minister Modi stated that "building trust between the two nations

is pre-requisite to any further meaningful moment on the relations". Pak Officials' meeting with Separatists in India was a violation of "Lakshman Rekha", hence a trust-breaking step. Therefore India suspended all dialogue with Pakistan. Pakistan has the responsibility. Definitely, India will have a positive response.

vi. Non-alignment to realignment
Non-alignment was relevant during cold war period. India's alignment with world powers for economic development and technological advancement is for national interest. India's foreign policy is now not based on any dogmas, but on country's interest and development. Discarding the non-alignment here means projecting the national interest. Non-aligned India until the collapse of USSR played second fiddle to the ideological goal. Thus the Nehruvian policy has been totally rejected by Narendra Modi.

vii. Economic Relationship with Potential Adversaries
India's economic relationship, especially with China is independent of its security relationship. Modi has already met Chinese President Xi Jinping at three occasions both in India and abroad. But no compromise is expected on India's stand in border conflict and India's strategic partnership with Japan. At the East Asia summit Narendra Modi called for new maritime norms, aiming China's aggressive role in South China Sea. He knows that China respects only strength and not the 'Panchsheel'. Until a democratic system comes to China, there is a need for special care.

viii. Relationship with one country will not be a constrain with others
There are serious efforts for strategic partnership with Japan, USA, Australia, etc. India-Russia relations improved and the Indo-US relations entered into a new peak. India's relations with all superpowers improved within a short span of time.

ix. Participation of NRI towards the development of India
Modi addressed the India diaspora at New York and Sydney and gave greater emphasis on "Soft Power" and inspired them to contribute to the country's economic and technological development. Modi's skill development project needs the support of Indians in abroad.

x. Look East Policy to "Act East Policy"
Over the past year Indian Foreign Ministers visited East Asian countries. East Asia Summit held on November 2014 in Myanmar opened new avenues for Prime Minister Modi. He reassured the East Asian leaders about the investment friendly climate of India and offered changes in policies to do business in India.

xi. Neighbourhood concern is a priority in Modi's Foreign policy
His first foreign visit was in Bhutan. He held bilateral talks with all the

eight neighbours immediately after assuming power. He also held multilateral talks with the neighbours during the SAARC summit on November 26 and 27, 2014 at Katmandu in Nepal. Except Pakistan, relations with all the SAARC countries improved. During the UPA rule, our neighbourhood relations were very poor and China occupied its role in the region in that period. Unfortunately, due to the policy lapses of the Congress rule, China dominated the entire South Asia, not only economically and militarily but also strategically.

xii. Indo-US Relations attained a new chapter
Emergence of China and its imperialistic ambitions necessitated new strategic relation with USA. But the priorities are economic growth and meeting energy needs. But at the same time India never compromised in WTO Trade Facilitation Agreement. In WTO India asserted its right of food security. The USA also compelled to accept the Indian stand. However, the US President Obama's visit to India to participate in the Republic Day celebrations on 26 January 2015, inaugurated a new chapter in Indo–US relations.

xiii. Modi's Multilateral Engagement set a new positive record
Within six months, he participated in five major multilateral engagements, including summits like BRICS, ASEAN, East-Asian Summit, SAARC, G-20 and his engagement with UN. In all these summits, Prime Minister Modi was well received and elevated to the status of a world leader. The reception he got in USA, Australia, Germany, China, Sri Lanka, Bangladesh, Japan, Bhutan and Nepal needs special mention. Within seven months Modi held bilateral talks with all Superpowers and economic powers, including USA, Russia, UK, Japan, China, Canada, Germany, Australia, Brazil, France, Israel, etc.

xiv. Rejection of Ideology, but full of ideas
Modi's foreign policy rejected the tradition of Nehruvian ideological norms. The dream world of Nehruvian diplomacy was discarded. As a pragmatic Prime Minister, Modi highlighted the Indian values in international politics. He projected the "Vasudaiva Kudumbhakam" in the BRICS summit at Brazil. At the UN speech he stood for "G All" instead of varying Global Groupings. During his Japan visit, he projected the idea of "Vikasvad", i.e. development, and rejected "Vistarvad" (Chinese ambitions in the region). At the East Asia Summit, he demanded new Maritime norms to constrain China's claim in South China Sea. Also in G-20 Summit in Australia he sought the help of member States in getting black money and information regarding money transfer became a matter of debate in G-20 meet. At UN Modi emphasized the importance of Yoga and pursued the UN to declare June 21$^{st}$ as International Yoga Day.

xv. Israel-Palestine Conflict

India took a moderate role in the Israel-Palestine conflict. During the conflict in Gaza India asked Israel to stop "disproportionate use of force" in Gaza. It was a departure from tradition of more vocal supports for the Palestinian cause. India has already declared its willingness for friendly relations with Israel and Palestine. Also Indo-Israel relations entered into new areas.

xvi. Stand against terrorism and ISIS

India asserted its fight against terrorism and gave full support to world organizations like UNO to ban terrorist organizations like ISIS. With the concurrence of Myanmar Government Indian military crossed the border of that State to destroy the militant camps which were sponsoring terrorist killing in North-Eastern States. India's "cross-border" strike gave a message to all concerned groups especially in Pakistan which were sponsoring cross-border terrorism in India.

xvii. Indians in Conflict Zones

Narendra Modi Government played a major role in assisting the Indian nationals stranded in conflict zones like Iraq, Syria, Libya and Yemen. The External Affairs Minister personally intervened in all these issues and succeeded in the safe evacuation of all Indians. In India's Yemen operation, nationals of 43 countries benefited. Also, 46 Indian nurses abducted by the ISIS from Iraqi town of Mosul were rescued.

xviii. Para Diplomacy

One of the innovative ideas of Modi Government is the introduction of elements of para diplomacy in India's Foreign Policy. Under this policy, Indian states and cities would be encouraged to forge special relation with counties or federal states of another country. As a result agreement has been already signed between Mumbai and Shanghai, Ahmedabad and Guangzhou, Varanasi and Kyoto. Also Gujarat signed the treaty with Guangdong province of China.

## Conclusion

It is a fact that, "Narendra Modi's foreign policy appears geared to re-invent India as a more competitive, confident and secure country". (*The Hindu*, 4th December, 2014). It is a result of a strong domestic policy and concern with national interest. As a realist, the focus is on economic development but the final goal is a developed, peaceful world. India stands for peace but not rejecting the role for strength for maintaining that peace. Narendra Modi being a realist follows the legacy of Prime Minister Vajpayee with new vigour, and dynamism and definitely discards the Nehruvian foreign policy model and the world of "dreams". In short, realism is the hallmark of Narendra Modi Government's Foreign Policy.

# 13

# India's Soft Power Approaches in Southeast Asia: Challenges and Expectations

*Koushiki Dasgupta*

The question of soft power is one of the re-invented issues that is picking up in the foreign policy debates in India. Traditionally, power in global politics has always been focussed in terms of military politics or economic strategies, but the idea of soft power has evolved as one of the most visible components of foreign policy strategies of many nations including India. The concept was originally given by Joseph S Nye J and it was used to describe the potentials of American influence beyond the spell of its military and allied dominance. Nye's idea of soft power could be traced from his major works like, *Bound to Lead* (1990), *The Paradox of American Power* (2002), *Soft Power* (2004), *Power in Global Information Age* (2004) and the *Future of Power* (2011). According to him power could be executed either by coercion (sticks), inducement (carrots) or by attraction (soft power). If one is able to attract others, he can economise on the sticks and the carrots. Therefore, soft power is 'the ability to get preferred outcomes through the cooperative means of agenda setting, persuasion and attraction.[1] A variety of agents like the NGOs, cooperative institutions, transnational and individual actors could become useful in creating the atmosphere of trust and credibility. However, the agents need to show some special attributes to attract others. Benignity, competence, and beauty are the three pillars of soft power capabilities and in case of the states the choice of agents is itself very important.[2] Culture, political values and foreign policies are thee sources of soft power, however, all have their own limitations. While his initial thesis on soft power was published in 1990, later Nye brought out a series of schemes which might be worth mentioning in case of India.[3] Nature and modalities of soft power in India might be discussed under the following heads: i. Soft Power is Cultural Power; ii. Economic Strength is Soft Power; iii. 'Soft Power is more humane than Hard Power; iv. Hard Power can be measured, and Soft Power Cannot; v. Soft Power is difficult to use; vi. Soft Power is irrelevant to the current terrorist threat.[4] Whatever the modern propositions of soft power, the concept is not new in India. As far as South East Asia is concerned, since ancient times Hinduism touched all parts of the region except a few places. Interestingly the influence of Indian civilization of these parts of the region was not conditioned by dominance, coercion or violence rather the Indian priestly class, the navigators and the merchants introduced India to this region in forms of religion, culture, art, architecture script and others. It was the instance of India's natural spread of soft power over this region. It included giving attention and active support to the aspects of Indian society and culture that the world would find attractive. Definitely the advent of Islam in northern India and the subsequent era of cultural stagnation had left some depressing impact on the execution of soft power, south Indian rulers did not misuse the time and kept on exporting Indiato the region. But in the modern period, particularly the transitions of international politics changed and snapped the cultural linkages between India and Southeast Asia. In post-cold war period India took a serious note on the Look East Policy and turned towards her Southeast Asian neighbours, but her fundamental interests on economic imperatives somehow cornered India's soft power approach in this region. However, no one can ignore the fact that soft power could have been useful only when backed by hard power strategies and in post-1990s decade expectations began to rise on the ground of India's growing economy and lucrative markets. New developments were adopted in the Look East Policy, however, these were far less than the actual prerequisite for soft power strategies specially when China has already grown as a leader in soft power mechanisms in that region. China's involvement into the regional affairs of the SAARC as well its growing soft power foreign policy bought some moments of discomfort too. It is to be mentioned here that Chinese soft power had been functioning under the purview of the state and it was backed by the economic achievements of Chaina, while India's soft power was mostly steered up by its culture and cultural agencies.[5] India's soft power was looking more defensive without having any seeds of progressive transformations. It is not the case that India was not aware of China's trading and economic dominance over south and South Eeast Asian region and India also took several steps on number of matters like bilateral trade, financial assistance, abolition of terrorism between the South Asian regional states. However, in a broader South Asian context such steps were not enough to meet the needs. One question remains pertinent here: in the Indian case what should be the actual relation between hard power and soft power? Does India need both the powers simultaneously to attain the status of a big power?

Do the one partly cover the other in certain situations? How did the rise of liberal economic growth after 1990s in India complement India's budding needs of soft power mechanisms? Discussing on the relationship between soft power and hard power considerations, former Union Minister of State of External Affair Shashi Tharoor argued, 'soft power is one arrow in a nations security quiver, it is not an all-purpose panacea. And we have to accept that those who have suggested that our soft power can solve all our security challenges are wrong. When we seek of leveraging our soft power, we must ensure that we do enough to keep our people healthy, well-fed and secured not just form jihadi terrorism but the daily terror of poverty, hunger and ill health. At the same time it is not enough just to take care of basic needs. We have to preserve the precious pluralism that is such a civilizational asset. Our democracy, thriving free media, contentious NGOs, energetic human rights groups, and the repeated spectacle of our remarkable general elections—all these have made India a rare example of the successful management of diversity in the developing world.[6] According to him it has already become a belief that India had tried to concentrate more on soft power to get a majority status in her sphere of influence. In case of military strength and economic dominance India was lagging behind her nearest competitors like China in a case but India has the potential to tell the 'better story' in the language of Bollywood films, yoga, ayurveda, social diversity and a tradition of liberal thinking through the ages. "...India must remain the land of the better story.....India has an extraordinary ability to tell stories that are more persuasive and more attractive than those of its rivals Now this is not about propaganda. Indeed it will not work if it is directed from above, least of all by the government but its impact, through intangible, is enormous."[7] No doubt the task of telling the 'better story' could not be completed out of the preview of the government. The government must have a clear view on what to tell and how. The mechanisms and resources of soft power cannot be measured in a way hard powers are measured. For example, no one can compare how India and China represented their civilizational values in the world and in the South East Asian region. To what extent is it possible to measure the influence of Indian culture and values on a country and, if any, how the concerned country had executed its adherence and love for India on foreign policy mechanisms. No doubt such a measurement is tough to define but a basic outline of soft power qualities could be drawn to make India more familiar and appealing to others. In post-1990s decade the government of India took major steps in this regard, particularly in 2007 the India-ASEAN Students Exchange programmes were introduced to build mutual understanding between the two regions covering all aspects of history, culture, economy, politics and other. It became a window of the Southeast Asian students to know India better and such visits no doubt strengthened the bonds of trust and accountability. Apart from this, in the ASEAN-India Commonwealth Summit held in December 2012, two events were organized in this respect. The Shipping Expedition of INS Sudarshini to ASEAN countries and the ASEAN India Car Rally. The shipping expedition was carried through the ancient trade route along the monsoon winds and spotted India's old and new maritime linkages with South East Asia. It also acknowledged the inter-linkages between the two regions in terms of trade, culture and intellectualism. The ASEAN-India Car Rally was started from Yogyakarta, Indonesia and traversed through 8 of the 10 ASEAN nations and came to an end at New Delhi. The Car Rally was organised to show India's proximity to the ASEAN. It also wanted to promote tourism and public awareness on both o the regions. On June 21, 2013, the ASEAN-India Centre (AIC) was inaugurated. The Centre was envisaged in the ASEAN-India Vision Statement, adopted at the ASEAN-India Commemorative Summit on December 20, 2012, and the Government of India took multiple steps towards linking Indian higher education institutions with the ASEAN higher education system. Research initiatives were taken in the area of biotechnology, information technology and bio-medics, as well as exchange of scholars and students in Social Sciences and Economics. In this regard the Indian Council for Cultural Relations (ICCR) has done well too. It has marked a print on Indian soft power in nurturing mutual understanding on the ethos of culture. But in an overall analysis it has become prominent that India exhibited limited success in projecting its soft power when comparing it with China. If the economists talked about the strategic failure of India in projecting its cultural capabilities along security lines, others hold the view that India has not yet resolved its national identity questions, and hence failed to show its soft power resources on virtue of her national identity. Critics may be well acquainted to the limitations of India's hard power strategies as a cause of her lack of enthusiasm in soft power approaches. No one can ignore that India is lagging behind far from China in using her democratic strengths as the most potential soft power recourse. Even though there seems to be little room for expectations on India's success in Southeast Asia, it remains a truth that if soft power is the ability of a nation to structure a situation so that other nations develop preferences or define their interests in ways consistent with one's nation, India had been successful and could see more success in the days ahead. The tradition of India's public democracy, pluralism all had created a space for others living peacefully and in this respect India's slow but steady steps towards Southeast Asian region would not pose a cultural treat to others and it would not go or any civilizational clash with China in respect of soft power.

In recent times Prime Minister Narendra Modi put forward a comprehensive network of foreign policies and the basic mode of principles were reflected already in his party's election manifesto in 2014. One of the most striking features of his new policy was to build-up regional forums and how India could be linked up with it. The BJP adopted more or less similar agendas even in its last election manifesto, but in that case specific policies were highlighted in case of selected countries. In the new policy framework, Prime Minister Modi has elaborately stressed on a number of points like development of interlocking relationship on the basis of India's national interest; taking up uniform judgments on the internal issues lie terrorism and global warming; strengthening of regional forums like SAARC and ASEAN and to make way for interactive dialogues between the global forums like BRICS, G20, SCO or others. Infact, India's new soft power strategies took up a balanced attitude towards the states in terms of her own interest and not for any big powers' interests. Accordingly steps were taken in favour of putting together the soft power avenues into external affairs through the selective modes of spiritual, cultural and philosophical magnitudes. Soft power is inherent in the history, culture and polices of a country and regional organisation could best be evolved as a source of consolidating the soft power by providing assistance to the states, which are eager to make them attractive. India's new foreign policy evolved as a proactive foreign policy which tried to drive events as opposed to just reacting to them and started looking more active rather than being neutral only. It seems to handle multiple relations at one time and keen to leave an impact on the world. This new policy is opposed to the stand of taking a lower profile and maintaining a balanced and indirect approach. The new foreign policy under Narendra Modi picked up soft power as one of the prime components of foreign policy building as seen in case of the celebration of World Yoga Day and promotion of India's culture and heritage worldwide. Already the Indian film industry had evolved as the largest and arrest reaching medium of Indian culture, and Indian soap operas have reached a growing global audience that has become increasingly familiar with Indian society and culture. Other than the electronic medium, Indian spices, cuisine and cricket diplomacy also came out as the mediums of soft power. But it's a question that how these elements of India's soft power could best be utilised to fulfil its foreign policy objectives in the coming decades in Southeast Asian region because references to Indian culture, to its Diaspora, to its socio political values and to its economic development have been used as the rhetoric for image-polishing since a last few decades. During the Prime Ministership of Narendra Modi, expectations of change started gathering momentum over a few subjects. One such subject of soft power is eventually Buddhism. It must not be viewed as the new wine in an old bottle rather a definite shift in India's Look East policy is going on with an extra emphasis on what is called Buddha diplomacy. Commenting on PM Modi's three-day visit to China in May 2015, *South China Morning Post* expressed, ' Buddhism and Yoga will form part of Indian Prime Minister Narendra Modi's soft power diplomacy as he visits China...and tries to increase his nations influence on the world's second largest economy. With a vast population of Buddhists in east and Southeast Asia,

India is seeking help or the revival of Buddhist sites and is also helping to revive ancient temples in South and Southeast Asia including the Angkor Vat and Ta Prohm temples in Siem Reap in Cambodia, Vat Phou temple in Laos, Ananda temple in Myanmar and others. India has a plan to rope in the Mahayana Buddhists from China, South Korea, Japan, Taiwan, Singapore and Vietnam; Theravada Buddhists from Cambodia, Thailand, Laos, Myanmar and others. Buddha diplomacy thus, has emerged as a tool of soft power of India in South and Southeast Asian region.[8] Such cultural exchanges and people-to-people contact might have been proved worthy of resolving contentious political issues in the near future. However, the question is can the Modi government attract foreign direct investment for the rejuvenation of the Buddhist sites and to what extent India's Buddha diplomacy would sort out hard power issues in the region. Soft power has now become an active element of India's diplomacy in parallel to its hard power resources. India has understood that these two dimensions of power should not be placed in opposition to one another and India will need to resolve its lack of social and economic equality and she needs to improve her overall economic performances if India's wants to continue as a soft power in the near future in the Southeast Asian region.

## NOTES

1. Joseph S. Nye, Jr. The Future of Power. New York: Public Affairs 2011, p.16.
2. Ibid.
3. Joseph Nye, 'Soft Power', Foreign Policy, No. 80, Twentieth Anniversary (Autumn, 1990), pp.153–71.
4. Joseph Nye, 'Think Again: Soft Power', Yale Global Online, foreignpolicy.com/2006/02/23/think-again-soft-power. Last downloaded on 25 April, 2015.
5. Suzuki, Shogo, ed. The Myth and Reality of China's Soft Power. Edited by Inderjeet Parmar and Michael Cox, Soft Power and Us Foreign Policy: Theoretical, Historical and Contemporary Perspectives London: Routledge, 2010.pp.200-201.
6. Shashi Tharoor, 'India as a Soft Power', *India International Centre Quarterly Weekly*, Vol. 38, No. 3/4: The Golden Thread; Essays in Honour of CD Deshmukh, Winter 2011-Spring 2012, pp, 330–43.
7. Ibid.
8. www.globalresearch.ca/india-and-eas-asia by Ashok Sharma, Global Research, November 5, 2014.

## REFERENCES

Garver, John W., ed. China's Influence in Central and South Asia: Is It Increasing? Edited by David Shambaugh, Power Shift: China and Asia's New Dynamics, Berkeley: University of California Press, 2005.

Joseph S. Nye, Jr. *Bound to Lead.* New York: Basic Books, 1990.

Joseph S. Nye, Jr. *The Paradox of American Power.* New York: Oxford University Press, 2002.

Joseph S. Nye, Jr. *Power in a Global Information Age.* London: Routledge, 2004.

Joseph S. Nye, Jr. *Soft Power—the Means to Success in World Politics.* New York: Public Affairs, 2004.

Joseph S. Nye, Jr. *The Future of Power.* New York: Public Affairs 2011.

Raghavan, V.R. "Soft Power in the Asia-Pacific." In After the Unipolar Moment: Asia and Regional Global Order. Singapore: IISS London and The Stanley Foundation US, 31 May 2007.

Suzuki, Shogo, ed. The Myth and Reality of China's Soft Power. Edited by Inderjeet Parmar and Michael Cox, Soft Power and Us Foreign Policy: Theoretical, Historical and Contemporary Perspectives London: Routledge, 2010.

Wagner, Christian. "India's Soft Power: Prospects and Limitations." *India Quarterly: A Journal of International Affairs* 66, no. 4 (2010).

# 14

# Indo-Japan Conviviality under the NDA-II Administration: New Government, New Sunrise

*Mohor Chakraborty*

The Prime Minister of India, Narendra Modi's selection of Japan as the first port of call (31 August–3 September 2014) outside the immediate neighbourhood has indeed opened new vistas of cooperation and greater engagement between the two regional economic powers, which have been tethered with bonds of historical commonalities and complementarities. The pertinence of this diplomatic sojourn may be viewed in the context of the National Democratic Alliance–II (NDA-II) Government's "Neighbourhood First" policy, in the scheme of which, the South, Southeast and East Asian regions have assumed a niche.[1] With respect to the Southeast, East Asia and the wider Asia-Pacific regions, the NDA–II administration has ambitiously proclaimed its graduation from "Look East" to "Act East" policy, thereby broadening the ambit of engagement and cooperation with India's "extended neighbourhood", in the scaffold of which, Japan has emerged as a protagonist. Its policy impetus and focus on the South, Southeast, East Asian and Asia-Pacific neighbourhood was clearly enunciated in the *Election Manifesto* (2014), released in the build-up to the Sixteenth Lok Sabha Elections (May 2014). While visualising a fundamental reboot and reorientation of the content, process and goals of its foreign policy, the Manifesto harped on its execution in a manner that would locate India's global strategic engagement in a new paradigm and on a wider canvas. Besides, it would not only be limited to political diplomacy, but also include India's economic, scientific, cultural, political and security interests—both on the regional and global promenade. Such a vision emerged from a conviction that "political stability, progress and peace in the region are essential for South Asia's growth and development." Towards this developmental end, the NDA-II Government aimed at crafting a "web of allies to mutually further our interests.... There is a need to integrate our soft power avenues into our external interchange, particularly, harnessing and focusing on the spiritual, cultural and philosophical dimensions of it."[2] It is in this perspective of heralding a "proactive diplomatic" foreign policy posture that the Election Manifesto laid down the Government's *Guiding Principles of Foreign Policy*, among which, the most significant was:

> Instead of being led by big power interests, we will engage proactively on our own with countries in the neighbourhood and beyond. In our neighbourhood we will pursue friendly relations. However, where required we will not hesitate from taking strong stand and steps. We will work towards strengthening Regional forums like SAARC (South Asian Association for Regional Cooperation) and ASEAN (Association of Southeast Asian Nations).[3]

In keeping with these avowed principles, Prime Minister, Narendra Modi has broadly and vigorously adhered to his Party's Election Manifesto, with a major focus on invigorating economic, strategic, diplomatic and cultural ties in the Asian region. With respect to the Southeast and East Asian neighbourhood, Modi's address at the Ninth East Asia Summit (EAS),[4] held in Nay Pi Taw (Myanmar), on 13 November 2014, acknowledged his Government's action-oriented approach, signalling a clear shift from India's "Look East" Policy to the new "Act East" Policy, when he said: "Since entering office six months ago my government has moved with a great sense of priority and speed to turn our 'Look East Policy' into 'Act East Policy'."[5] It is in this backdrop of the NDA -II Administration's renewed momentum and enthusiasm to "act" East, that the present article attempts to trace the dynamics of political and strategic ties under the new Government between India and Japan and underscore the imperative and potential for further engagement in the near future.

## Major Trends in Indo–Japan Relations under NDA-I and UPA Governments

Before embarking on the NDA-II Government's strategic interactions with Japan, particularly in the wake of Prime Minister, Narendra Modi's official visit to Japan (31 August – 3 September 2014), a brief background study of the trajectory of mutual ties under its predecessors (NDA-I and United Progressive Alliance/UPA) may be recalled. The momentous expansion of India's "Look East" policy beyond the ASEAN countries, heralding the ushering in of the Second Phase (Phase-II) saga of this celebrated policy was emphasized when the then Indian Minister of External Affairs, Yashwant Sinha, (of the NDA-I administration) officially pronounced the Second Phase (Phase II) at the Second ASEAN-India Business Summit, held in New Delhi, on 4 September 2003. In the Plenary Session of this Summit, Yashwant Sinha announced:

> India's Look East Policy has now entered its Phase II. Phase I was focused primarily on the ASEAN countries and on trade and investment linkages. Phase II is characterized by an expanded definition of 'East' extending from Australia to China and East Asia with ASEAN as its core. Phase II marks a shift in focus from exclusively economic issues to economic and security issues including joint efforts to protect sea-lanes, coordination on counter terrorism etc. On the economic sphere, Phase II is also characterized by arrangements for FTAs (Free Trade Areas) and establishment of institutional economic linkages between the countries of the region and India.[6]

It is a fact that, the introduction of the Second Phase of the "Look East" domain brought New Delhi into the frame of greater engagement with the ASEAN Plus Three (China, Japan and South Korea) as well as into the spectrum of the extended multilateral notch – East Asia Summit/EAS – in December 2005, which was lauded as a historic meeting-place for India, ASEAN and China, Japan, South Korea, Australia and New Zealand – India's "Move East" partners. The EAS was representative of a logical step forward from the ASEAN+3 process as well as the precursor of an East Asian Community on the footsteps of the European Union (EU), and a landmark decision to create a forum for dialogue on broad strategic, political and economic issues of mutual interest, with the ultimate aim of promoting peace, stability and economic prosperity in the Asia-Pacific region. This was reinforced with India's membership of the elite ASEAN Defence Ministers+8 forum (ADMM+8) in 2010. The task began by the NDA-I administration was carried forward by its successor, the UPA, and a few significant milestones which paved the cooperative pathway under the latter's tenure are: *first*, the successful State visit of the Japanese Prime Minister, Junichiro Koizumi to India in April 2005 followed closely by the return visit by his Indian counterpart, Manmohan Singh to Japan in December 2006. In the wake of the latter, bilateral relations were upgraded to a **'Global and Strategic Partnership'**, involving closer and enhanced political and diplomatic collaboration in bilateral, regional, multilateral and global issues; comprehensive economic engagement; stronger defence ties; greater technological cooperation as well as working towards a quantum increase in cultural ties, educational diplomacy and people-to-people contacts.[7] Thus, the 'Global and Strategic Partnership' signed between Manmohan

Singh and his Japanese Counterpart, Shinzo Abe, embraced a series of measures, among which, the launch of negotiations for the bilateral Comprehensive Economic Partnership Agreement (CEPA) was remarkable.

*Secondly,* in a predominant step to heighten the pedestal of Indo-Japan relations, the Japanese Prime Minister, Yukio Hatoyama paid a State visit to India in December 2009, in course of which, he pitched for intensifying bilateral trade, by issuing a '**Joint Statement on the New Stage of India-Japan Strategic and Global Partnership**'[8] and boosting investment, particularly in ship-building; solar and renewable energy; infrastructure and technology.

*Thirdly*, amidst the optimistic trajectory in bilateral economic ties, the State visit undertaken by Manmohan Singh to Japan in October 2010 was a significant endeavour, within the framework of which, the Indian leader and his Japanese counterpart, Naoto Kan directed their authorities to work towards the early entry into force of the Indo-Japan CEPA (IJCEPA) and its smooth implementation for deepening economic engagement, in terms of trade in goods and services, investment and cooperation. Following this visit, the CEPA was signed between the Indian Commerce Minister, Anand Sharma and the Japanese Foreign Minister, Seiji Maehara in Tokyo on 16 February 2011 (operational from 1 August 2011), thereby paving the way for the most comprehensive of all such agreements concluded, insofar as embracing more than 90% of the trade, a vast gamut of services, rules of origin, investments, Intellectual Property Rights (IPR), customs and other trade-related issues were concerned. Therefore, the NDA-I and UPA governments had laid an impressive foundation for the development of bilateral conviviality between New Delhi and Tokyo and the newly-installed NDA-II administration has been adept enough to sustain the legacy of its predecessors.

## The NDA-II Saga: Enhanced Politico-Strategic Rhythm

The inauguration of the NDA-II Government in India unveiled the floodgates of bilateral cooperation with Japan and this enthusiasm was demonstrated by the Japanese Chief Cabinet Secretary, Yoshihide Suga's congratulatory message to Prime Minister of India, Narendra Modi (on behalf of the Japanese Premier, Shinzo Abe), immediately after the declaration of the results of the May 2014 Lok Sabha Elections, when he said: "We would like to extend our sincere congratulations. We expect to further deepen our political and economic relations with India."[9] On a personal note, while whole-heartedly welcoming the new Government in New Delhi, the Japanese Premier, Shinzo Abe expressed his ardent desire to continue mutual cooperation, in addition to "trilateral cooperation including our two countries", thereby paving the trajectory of a more peaceful and prosperous Asia-Pacific.[10] This gained added significance in the backdrop of Tokyo's unveiling of its maiden National Security Strategy (NSS) calling on the country to make a "proactive contribution to peace" based on international cooperation. These efforts are premised on the belief that Japan, as a "Proactive Contributor to Peace", needs to contribute more actively to the peace and stability of the region and the international community, while coordinating with other countries[11] in the scaffold of which, India assumes a responsible role as well. It is in this framework that New Delhi can express solidarity and enhanced convergence with Japan for sustaining and bolstering Asia-Pacific security, both traditional and non-traditional, in order to facilitate the realization of the latent potential of the region and its people in a concerted, peaceful and responsible manner. The most remarkable tune in the orchestration of Indo-Japan ties in the wake of Narendra Modi's assumption of power was his selection of Japan as his first port of call outside the immediate neighbourhood (South Asia). The choice of Japan as his maiden destination outside the South Asian neighbourhood indeed underscored "the high priority that Japan receives in our foreign and economic policies. It is also a reflection of Japan's paramount importance in my vision for development and prosperity in India and in peace, stability and prosperity in Asia at large."[12] Modi's Japan sojourn opened the vistas for a holistic interaction with leaders across the entire political spectrum, in addition to regional leaders, captains of business and industry and fellow citizens, thus scripting "a new chapter in the annals of the relations between Asia's two oldest democracies".[13]

A significant outcome of this visit was the elevation of Indo-Japan relations to **Special Strategic and Global Partnership**, ushering the dawn of a new era for continuing progress and prosperity for their people and advancing peace, stability and prosperity in Asia and the world. Within the broad ambit of this Special Partnership, the two leaders attached primary importance to the dialogue between their National Security Advisors, the launch of which was decided in January 2014, soon after the creation of the National Security Secretariat in Japan as a key instrument of building deeper mutual understanding and cooperation across the full range of security issues. This was in addition to underscoring the 2 plus 2 Dialogue, involving Foreign and Defence Secretaries, aimed at mutual strategic partnership and devising means to intensify the same. Among the defence-related agreements signed or negotiations undertaken by the two Prime Ministers in course of Modi's visit, the most remarkable were: *first,* the Memorandum of Cooperation and Exchanges in the Field of Defence, in the context of which, the regularization of bilateral maritime exercises, Japan's continued participation in the Malabar series of exercises, the existing dialogue mechanism and joint exercises between Indian and Japanese Coast Guards were emphasized; *secondly,* pertaining to Japan's policy on transfer of defence equipment and technology, both sides directed the Joint Working Group to accelerate the discussions and preparations for a road map for the development of the Indian aircraft industry through US-2 amphibian aircraft cooperation including the transfer of the aircraft and its technology to India; *thirdly*, defence officials were directed to launch working-level consultations with a view to promoting defence equipment and technology cooperation.[14] In other areas of strategic cooperation, particularly relating to energy resources, the signing of a Memorandum of Understanding between the Ministry of New and Renewable Energy of India and the Japan Bank for International Cooperation (JBIC) in the field of new and renewable energy on the one hand and the signing of the loan agreement between the State Bank of India and the Japan Bank for International Cooperation (JBIC) for the super-critical coal-fired power project in Meja in Uttar Pradesh, on the other, were important steps towards mutual cooperation. Furthermore, the mutual intention of collaborating and securing energy, including in the fields of energy efficiency, renewable energy and coal-fired generation technology through the India-Japan Energy Dialogue; enhanced cooperation in construction of highly efficient and environment-friendly coal-fired power plants; progress on cooperation in Clean Coal Technologies (CCT) such as renovation and modernization of the plants; progress of efforts in energy efficiency improvement, including steel, cement, and mechanical tools in India; and most importantly, substantial agreement on the commercial contract between Indian Rare Earths Limited (IREL) and Toyota Tsusho Corporation (TTC) for the production of rare earths, paved the way for bolstering the contours of the India-Japan Strategic and Global Partnership. The agreement on rare earth metals—a key input for the production of high-technology devices (ranging from smart phones, computers to aircraft)—is especially significant since the proposed cooperation could act as a spanner in Chinese monopoly in this sector.[15]

The strategic import of the defence and security-related cooperation between India and Japan within the scaffold of Prime Minister, Narendra Modi's visit to Japan deserves analysis in the context of the politico-strategic regional ambience, dominated by factors like: *first*, China's assertive ascendance in the region, which was referred to as Modi as "expansionist" approach, "encroaching on the land and in the waters of other nations."[16] This statement was directed at China's territorial assertiveness vis-à-vis India and maritime conflicts in the East China Sea pertaining to Japan. Taken from such a perspective, the Indo-Japan strategic partnership is not only important, but also "indispensable" for ensuring peace and prosperity "in particular, in the interconnected Asia, Pacific and Indian Ocean regions".[17] *Secondly*, as a natural corollary of this endorsement, an elevation in the US (United States)-India-Japan trilateral alliance gains momentum. Given this premise, the Indian Prime Minister and his Japanese counterpart discussed the potential avenues of raising Indo-Japan-US Joint Secretary-level trilateral dialogue to the level of Foreign Ministers.[18] Besides, the resolve of the trilateral alliance to further expand and regularise the scope of cooperation has been reflected through the conduct of 'Exercise Malabar'—a complex, high-end operational multilateral series of exercise among the India, Japanese and US Navies, aimed at enhancing their maritime relations, mutual security issues and interoperability in the region. Although India has been holding the 'Malabar' annually with the US (at the bilateral level) since 1992 (except for a brief interregnum after the 1998 Pokhran II nuclear tests), Japan has participated in only three editions of the same—2007, 2009 and 2014. In the 18th edition of the most recent 'Malabar', the "harbour phase" (24-26 July 2014) and the "sea phase" (27-30 July 2014) of which were held in Japan's Sasebo Port and the Western Pacific Ocean respectively, the significance of such a cooperative venture was testified to with the participation of an ambitious fleet representing the sea-muscle of the three participants. While the Indian side was represented by three Indian warships, guided-missile destroyer INS Ranvijay, stealth frigate INS Shivalik and tanker INS Shakti, along with their Kamov-28 and Chetak helicopters; Japan fielded its destroyers, JS Kurama and JS Ashigara, as well as the US-2i ShinMaywa amphibious aircraft; and the US' show was led by nuclear-powered aircraft carrier USS George Washington, Ticonderoga-class destroyer USS Shiloh, Arleigh Burke-class destroyer John S. McCain and nuclear submarine USS Columbus, apart from P-3 Orion aircraft and MH-60R helicopters, engaged in carrier strike operations, surface and anti-submarine warfare, as also VBSS (visit, board, search and seizure).[19] Indeed the MALABAR exercises have been invested with greater vigour and strategic quotient in the context of the United States' 'Pivot to Asia' policy, also famous as the Obama Doctrine. This exercise was conducted in addition to bilateral exchanges between the Indian and Japanese Navies and Coast Guards. While the two Navies have jointly participated in several multilateral exercises, the first bilateral exercise (naval) – Japan India Maritime Exercise/JIMEX – 12 – was held on 9 June 2012 in the Bay of Sagami off Tokyo. The successive edition of JIMEX was conducted from 19-22 December 2013 in the Bay of Bengal in order to bolster the bilateral content of maritime cooperation, particularly in the face of China's assertive forays in the regional waters. Furthermore, the Coast Guards have maintained the tradition of joint exercises since its launch in 1999 and in January 2014, the 13th edition of their joint war games—"Sahayog-Kaijin 2014"—was held in Kochi. It may be mentioned here that Japan has the second largest Coast Guard fleet in the world. While emphasizing the rationale of the exercise, Vice-Admiral and Director-General of the Indian Coast Guard, Anurag G. Thapliyal, not only underscored the interoperability of the two forces in order to be able to work together in a better fashion by understanding each other's operating procedures, but also outlined the "areas of benefit to both forces which include cooperation in search and rescue

(SAR), pollution response, training and capacity-building and maritime law enforcement."[20] (Besides, it was in course of Modi's Japan visit that the decision to conduct the next joint Coast Guard exercise between the Indian and Japanese sides off the coast of Haneda in October 2014 was taken. It may be added in this backdrop of the increased strategic collaboration between India and Japan that recently, on 14 January 2015, the Japanese Premier, Shinzo Abe has approved its largest-ever defence budget for the 2015-2016 fiscal year, aimed at stepping up surveillance of territorial waters in the face of a continuing spat with China. The present defence budget, hailed by the Japanese Defence Ministry as "the largest budget ever", has an allocation of 4.98 trillion yen ($41.97 billion).[21]

Interestingly enough, the heightened pitch echoed by Japan for stronger maritime security cooperation with India, urging it to "proactively" assume responsibilities to ensure "open and stable seas" in the Asia-Pacific region, in course of the Japanese Foreign Minister, Fumio Kishida's visit to India on 16-18 January 2015, to attend the Eighth Strategic Dialogue may be judged in this perspective as well. Since both India and Japan have a sea of interests in the region extending from the Indian Ocean through the South China Sea to the Pacific, it is mutually incumbent for the two countries to expand their web of strategic cooperation so as to ensure the "Open and Stable Seas". In course of his Lecture at Sapru House, while suggesting measures to further strengthen maritime interactions between the Indian and Japanese Navies, Kishida outlined efforts such as joint maritime exercises between defence authorities and the implementation of dialogue and combined exercises between coast guards. Furthermore, the emphasis on India and Japan yielding the maximum benefits of their Special Partnership was reflected when Kishida said:

> Both India and Japan are maritime countries whose interests depend on the safety of sea lanes. Japan intends to contribute to building a new era for the Indo-Pacific region, based on the special partnership with India. It is important to further strengthen our cooperation through defence equipment cooperation including the US-2 amphibian aircraft and Japan's continued participation in the India-US Malabar maritime exercises.[22]

## The Way Ahead

Therefore, taking a holistic view of the strategic content of Narendra Modi's Japan sojourn, though the success of this visit and its deep-rooted impact for the development of Indo-Japan relations cannot be overlooked, in the same vein, the failure to clinch the bilateral civil-nuclear deal has to be acknowledged as a pending issue and a metaphorical thorn in the otherwise unblemished visage of relations between New Delhi and Tokyo. This failure could be attributed to the inability of narrowing down differences over Tokyo's insistence for a tougher safeguard regime and "no nuclear test" clause in the bilateral Agreement for Cooperation in the Peaceful Uses of Nuclear Energy. Moreover, Japan wants India to guarantee that it would not undertake nuclear tests and emphasises more stringent inspections of its nuclear facilities to ensure that spent fuel is not diverted to make bombs. Although India has been insisting on self-imposed moratorium on its tests, it does not subscribe to Japan's insistence on the clause in the text of the Agreement that provides for automatic termination of nuclear ties if India conducts nuclear tests in future. However, India's efforts in the field of non-proliferation, including the affirmation that goods and technologies transferred from Japan would not be used for delivery systems for Weapon of Mass Destruction (WMD) were congratulated by Shinzo Abe, who, while addressing a Joint Press Briefing with his Indian counterpart acknowledged:

> In recent months, we have made significant progress in our negotiations on civil nuclear cooperation. Today, we have discussed this issue at length. We have reached better understanding of each other's positions through this discussion. We have agreed to instruct our negotiators to work expeditiously to conclude the negotiations at an early date so that we can further strengthen our strategic partnership.[23]

Finally, the two leaders, while affirming their commitment to work together for India to become a full member in the four international export control regimes: Nuclear Suppliers Group, Missile Technology Control Regime, Wassenaar Arrangement and Australia Group, purporting to strengthen the international non-proliferation efforts, sincerely looked forward to enhancing the momentum of cooperation in this sector and ironing out the differences.[24]

Summarily then, the forward stride taken by the NDA-II Government under the able leadership of Narendra Modi has catapulted Indo-Japan relations to an impressive height, attested to by Modi's "action-oriented" maiden official sojourn to Japan, which has gained distinction as the first port of call outside the immediate neighbourhood. This has, indeed, proved the centrality of the Indian Government's vision of "Acting East" – a marked graduation from the "Move and Engage East" doctrines. In particular, this visit has emboldened the strategic-economic content of bilateral ties, in the framework of which, greater thrust has been exerted on defence and commercial ventures. In this respect, the emphasis of the two Asian leaders—Narendra Modi and Shnizo Abe—on forging "a closer and stronger strategic partnership between India and Japan" as indispensable for securing the future of both neighbours as well as for advancing peace, stability and development of the Asia-Pacific region as a whole, has emerged as the crux of the bilateral deliberations. Towards this end, it is now contingent on the Indian and Japanese leadership, fuelled by political will to seamlessly tether their shared values, convergent interests, and complementary skills and resources to usher in shared economic development on the one hand. By the same token, the proactive engagement with other regional and extra-regional powers (particularly the United States) to address the security challenges in the region—both traditional and non-traditional in nature—would go a long way in promoting regional cooperation, integration and peaceful resolution of pending disputes with other countries—both territorial and maritime in nature. As a matter of fact, India's "Look East" Policy and its consultative fora (ASEAN Regional Forum/ARF, East Asia Summit/EAS, ASEAN Defence Ministers' Meeting+8/ADMM+8) have opened up vistas for multilateral consultations among India, Japan and important regional actors on a plethora of politico-strategic, economic and social issues of concern. Furthermore, the official-level Trilateral Security Dialogue exclusively among India, Japan and the United States is set to be elevated to the level of the Foreign Ministers—a move which signals growing convergence in strategic interests of the three nations in the Asia-Pacific. Given this backdrop, within the framework of the January 2015 visit of the US President, Barack Obama to India as the Chief Guest at the Republic Day celebrations, the Indian Prime Minister and the visiting dignitary have singled out their Navies as the primary instruments of their military ties, which could be seen as a development that looks set to overwhelm in-principle statements on technology-sharing in the region reeling under the silhouette of a "rising" China. In addition to the Joint Statement and the Delhi Declaration of Friendship, India and the US released a document specific to the Asia-Pacific and the Indian Ocean region where maritime disputes between China and other claimant nations are escalating. The Joint Statement read:

> Prime Minister Modi and President Obama express satisfaction over the efforts made by both countries to deepen co-operation in the field of maritime security, as reflected in the 2015 Framework for the US-India Defence Relationship. To this end, they agreed that the navies of both sides would continue discussions to identify specific areas for expanding maritime cooperation. They also reiterated their commitment to upgrading their naval exercise Malabar.[25]

Given this strategic anchorage, the successful visit of the Indian Prime Minister to Japan has unveiled novel avenues of bilateral cooperation, by exploiting which, the fullest potential of mutual ties could be experienced. The broad and impressive spectrum of cooperation between the two Asian neighbours, ranging from politico-defence, economic, metropolitan, infrastructure to socio-cultural sectors, as identified within the framework of this visit has established the solid foundation for further collaboration at the bilateral echelon. In addition to a plethora of defence agreements signed in course of the Prime Ministerial sojourn, the economic dimension of this visit, particularly pertaining to Abe's commitment to realize 3.5 trillion Yen of public and private investment and financing, including Overseas Development Assistance (ODA) to India in five years, financing appropriate public and private projects of mutual interest, viz. in the areas of next generation infrastructure, connectivity, transport systems, Smart Cities, rejuvenation of Ganga and other rivers, manufacturing, clean energy, skill development, water security, food processing and agro industry, agricultural cold chain, rural development, etc., have been viewed as a promised trajectory of further coordination as well. In this context of bilateral optimism, as India and Japan are poised to walk hand-in-hand to realise the vision of the 21st Century as the Asian Century, it is contingent on the political and diplomatic circuits of both the partners to sustain a development-oriented political will, so as to facilitate 'vikas vaad' (development), which has been rightly acknowledged as a driving force for regional peace, progress and humane aspirations.

## NOTES

1. Bharatiya Janata Party (BJP) Election Manifesto 2014, Bharatiya Janata Party, New Delhi, 2014, p. 39, http://www.bjp.org/images/pdf_2014/ful_manifesto_english_07.04.2014.pdf (accessed on 26 November 2014)
2. Ibid., p. 40
3. Ibid.
4. East Asia Summit (EAS), formed in 2005, is an annual conclave of the Association of Southeast Asian Nations/ASEAN – 10 members, the ASEAN Plus Three members (China, Japan and South Korea), Australia, New Zealand and India
5. Prime Minister of India's Remarks at the Ninth East Asia Summit, Nay Pi Taw, Myanmar, 13 November 2014, Website of the Prime Minister of India, New Delhi, http://pmindia.gov.in/en/news_updates/english-rendering-of-pms-remarks-at-the-east-asia-summit-nay-pyi-taw/ (accessed on 5 January 2015)
6. Statement of the Indian Minister of External Affairs, Yashwant Sinha, Plenary Session, Second ASEAN-India Business Summit, New Delhi, Ministry of External Affairs, Government of India, New Delhi, 4 September 2003, p. 1, http://meaindia.nic.in/mystart.php?id=53016849, (accessed on 5 January 2015)
7. For details see "Towards Japan-India Strategic and Global Partnership", Text of Joint Statement by Japanese Prime Minister, Junichiro Koizumi and Indian Prime Minister, Manmohan Singh,, Ministry of Foreign Affairs, Government of Japan, Tokyo, 15 December 2006, http://www.kantei.go.jp/foreign/abespeech/2006/12/15joint.pdf (accessed on 5 January 2015)
8. For details see "New Stage of Japan-India Strategic and Global Partnership", Text of Joint Statement by Japanese Prime Minister, Yukio Hatoyama and Indian Prime Minister, Manmohan Singh, Ministry of Foreign Affairs, Government of Japan, Tokyo, 29 December

2009, http://www.mofa.go.jp/region/asia-paci/india/pmv0912/joint.html, (accessed on 5 January 2015)

9. "Japan Says it Aims to Deepen Ties with India under Modi", The Statesman, 19 May 2014, p. 9
10. Keynote Address by Shinzo Abe, Prime Minister of Japan, 13[th] IISS Asian Security Summit, Shangri-La Dialogue, Singapore, International Institute of Strategic Studies, 30 May 2014, p. 2, http://www.iiss.org/en/events/shangri%20la%20dialogue/archive/2014-c20c/opening-remarks-and-keynote-address-b0b2/keynote-address-shinzo-abe-a787 (accessed on 6 January 2015)
11. For details, see Defense of Japan, Annual White Paper, Official Website of the Ministry of Defense, Government of Japan, Tokyo, 17 December 2013, http://www.mod.go.jp/e/publ/w_paper/2013.html (accessed on 6 February 2015)
12. Prime Minister of India's Departure Statement Ahead of his Visit to Japan, Press Information Bureau Prime Minister's Office, Government of India, New Delhi, 29 August 2014, p. 1, http://pib.nic.in/newsite/PrintRelease.aspx?relid=109178 (accessed on 6 January 2015)
13. Ibid., p. 2
14. Factsheet: India and Japan—Partners for Common Development, Press Information Bureau, Prime Minister's Office, Government of India, New Delhi, 1 September 2014, Clauses 37-39, http://www.mea.gov.in/outoging-visit-detail.htm?23967/Factsheet+India+and+Japan++Partners+for+Common+Development (accessed on 7 January 2015)
15. Ibid: Clauses 16-21
16. Prime Minister of India's Keynote Address at the Luncheon Hosted by Nippon Kiedanren – the Japanese Chamber of Commerce and Industry and the Japan-India Business Cooperation Committee, Tokyo, Official Website of Prime Minister of India, Government of India, New Delhi, 1 September 2014, p. 1, http://www.narendramodi.in/pms-keynote-address-at-the-luncheon-hosted-by-nippon-kiedanren-the-japanese-chamber-of-commerce-and-industry-and-the-japan-india-business-cooperation-committee (accessed on 7 January 2015)
17. Tokyo Declaration for India-Japan Special Strategic and Global Partnership, Tokyo, Ministry of External Affairs, Government of India, New Delhi, 1 September 2014, http://mea.gov.in/bilateral-documents.htm?dtl/23965/Tokyo_Declaration_for_India_ _Japan_Special_Strategic_and_Global_Partnership (accessed on 7 January 2015)
18. Ibid.
19. Rajat Pandit, "India, US and Japan to Kick off Malabar Naval Exercise Tomorrow", *Times of India*, 23 July 2014, p. 2; See also "Malabar 2014: A Multilateral Naval Exercise Starts", Press Release, Indian Navy, Government of India, New Delhi, 23 July 2014, http://indiannavy.nic.in/press-release/malabar-2014-multilateral-naval-exercise-starts (accessed on 7 January 2015)
20. "India, Japan Coast Guards to Firm Up Ties", *The Hindu*, 16 January 2014, p. 3
21. "Japan Reveals Record Defense Budget as Tensions with China Grow", *The Guardian (UK)*, 14 January 2015, http://www.theguardian.com/world/2015/jan/14/japan-reveals-record-defence-budget-as-tensions-with-china-grow (accessed on 7 February 2015)
22. "Special Partnership for the Era of the Indo-Pacific", Lecture by H.E. Fumio Kushida, Minister of Foreign Affairs of Japan, 15[th] Sapru House Lecture, Indian Council of World Affairs, New Delhi, 17 January 2015, p. 6, http://www.icwa.in/pdfs/pressreleases/2014/Pressrelease 17012015pre.pdf (accessed on 8 February 2015)
23. Joint Press Briefing by the Prime Ministers of India and Japan, Tokyo, Press Information Bureau, Prime Minister's Office, Government of India, New Delhi, 1 September 2014, http://pib.nic.in/newsite/PrintRelease.aspx?relid=109222 (accessed on 8 February 2015)
24. Tokyo Declaration for India-Japan Special Strategic and Global Partnership, Tokyo, n. 17
25. US-India Joint Strategic Vision for the Asia-Pacific and the Indian Ocean Region, Ministry

of External Affairs, Government of India, New Delhi, 25 January 2015, http://www.mea.gov.in/incoming-visit-detail.htm?24728/USIndia+Joint+Strategic+Vision+ for+the+AsiaPacific+and+Indian+Ocean+Region (accessed on 8 February 2015)

## REFERENCES

**Documents**

"Malabar 2014: A Multilateral Naval Exercise Starts", Press Release, Indian Navy, Government of India, New Delhi, 23 July 2014, http://indiannavy.nic.in/press-release/malabar-2014-multilateral-naval-exercise-starts

"Special Partnership for the Era of the Indo-Pacific", Lecture by H.E. Fumio Kushida, Minister of Foreign Affairs of Japan, 15th Sapru House Lecture, Indian Council of World Affairs, New Delhi, 17 January 2015, http://www.icwa.in/pdfs/pressreleases/2014/Pressrelease17012015 pre. pdf

"Towards Japan-India Strategic and Global Partnership", Text of Joint Statement by the Japanese Prime Minister, Junichiro Koizumi and Indian Prime Minister, Manmohan Singh, Ministry of Foreign Affairs, Government of Japan, Tokyo, 15 December 2006, http://www.kantei.go.jp/foreign/abespeech/2006/12/15joint.pdf

"New Stage of Japan-India Strategic and Global Partnership", Text of Joint Statement by Japanese Prime Minister, Yukio Hatoyama and Indian Prime Minister, Manmohan Singh,

Ministry of Foreign Affairs, Government of Japan, Tokyo, 29 December 2009, http://www.mofa.go.jp/region/asia-paci/india/pmv0912/joint.html

Bharatiya Janata Party (BJP) Election Manifesto 2014, Bharatiya Janata Party, New Delhi, 2014, Website of the Bharatiya Janata Party, http://www.bjp.org/images/pdf_2014/ful_manifesto_english_07.04.2014.pdf

Defense of Japan, Annual White Paper, Official Website of the Ministry of Defense, Government of Japan, Tokyo, 17 December 2013, http://www.mod.go.jp/e/publ/w_paper/2013.html

Factsheet: India and Japan—Partners for Common Development, Press Information Bureau, Prime Minister's Office, Government of India, New Delhi, 1 September 2014, http://www.mea.gov.in/outoging-visit-detail.htm?23967/Factsheet+India+and+Japan++Partners+for+Common+Development

Joint Press Briefing by the Prime Ministers of India and Japan, Tokyo, Press Information Bureau, Prime Minister's Office, Government of India, New Delhi, 1 September 2014, http://pib.nic.in/newsite/PrintRelease.aspx?relid=109222

Keynote Address by Shinzo Abe, Prime Minister of Japan, 13th IISS Asian Security Summit, Shangri-La Dialogue, Singapore, International Institute of Strategic Studies, 30 May 2014, http://www.iiss.org/en/events/shangri%20la%20dialogue/archive/2014-c20c/opening-remarks-and-keynote-address-b0b2/keynote-address-shinzo-abe-a787

Prime Minister of India's Keynote Address at the Luncheon Hosted by Nippon Kiedanren – the Japanese Chamber of Commerce and Industry and the Japan-India Business Cooperation Committee, Tokyo, Official Website of Prime Minister of India, Government of India, New Delhi, 1 September 2014, http://www.narendramodi.in/pms-keynote-address-at-the-luncheon-hosted-by-nippon-kiedanren-the-japanese-chamber-of-commerce-and-industry-and-the-japan-india-business-cooperation-committee

Prime Minister of India's Remarks at the Ninth East Asia Summit, Nay Pi Taw, Myanmar, 13 November 2014.

Prime Minister of India's Departure Statement Ahead of his Visit to Japan, Press Information Bureau

Prime Minister's Office, Government of India, New Delhi, 29 August 2014, http://pib.nic.in/newsite/PrintRelease.aspx?relid=109178

Statement of the Indian Minister of External Affairs, Yashwant Sinha, Plenary Session, Second

ASEAN-India Business Summit, New Delhi, Ministry of External Affairs, Government of India, New Delhi, 4 September 2003, http://meaindia.nic.in/mystart.php?id=53016849

Tokyo Declaration for India-Japan Special Strategic and Global Partnership, Tokyo, Ministry of External Affairs, Government of India, New Delhi, 1 September 2014, http://mea.gov.in/bilateral-documents.htm?dtl/23965/Tokyo_Declaration_for_India__Japan_Special_Strategic_and_Global_Partnership

US-India Joint Strategic Vision for the Asia-Pacific and the Indian Ocean Region, Ministry of External Affairs, Government of India, New Delhi, 25 January 2015, http://www.mea.gov.in/incoming-visit-detail.htm?24728/USIndia+Joint+Strategic+Vision+ for+the+ AsiaPacific+ and+Indian+Ocean+Region

Website of the Prime Minister of India, http://pmindia.gov.in/en/news_updates/english-rendering-of-pms-remarks-at-the-east-asia-summit-nay-pyi-taw/

**Articles in Newspapers**

(14 January 2015), "Japan Reveals Record Defense Budget as Tensions with China Grow", The Guardian (UK), http://www.theguardian.com/world/2015/jan/14/japan-reveals-record-defence-budget-as-tensions-with-china-grow

(16 January 2014), "India, Japan Coast Guards to Firm Up Ties", The Hindu, p. 3

(19 May 2014), "Japan Says it Aims to Deepen Ties with India under Modi", The Statesman

Pandit, Rajat, (23 July 2014), India, US and Japan to Kick off Malabar Naval Exercise Tomorrow", Times of India

**Newspapers**

The Guardian; The Hindu; The Statesman; and Times of India.

**Internet Sources**

http://indiannavy.nic.in/press-release/malabar-2014-multilateral-naval-exercise-starts

http://mea.gov.in/bilateral-documents.htm?dtl/23965/Tokyo_Declaration_for_India__Japan_Special_Strategic_and_Global_Partnership

http://meaindia.nic.in/mystart.php?id=53016849

http://pib.nic.in/newsite/PrintRelease.aspx?relid=109178

http://pib.nic.in/newsite/PrintRelease.aspx?relid=109222

http://pmindia.gov.in/en/news_updates/english-rendering-of-pms-remarks-at-the-east-asia-summit-nay-pyi-taw/

http://www.bjp.org/images/pdf_2014/ful_manifesto_english_07.04.2014.pdf

http://www.icwa.in/pdfs/pressreleases/2014/Pressrelease17012015pre.pdf

http://www.iiss.org/en/events/shangri%20la%20dialogue/archive/2014-c20c/opening-remarks-and-keynote-address-b0b2/keynote-address-shinzo-abe-a787

http://www.kantei.go.jp/foreign/abespeech/2006/12/15joint.pdf

http://www.mea.gov.in/incoming-visit-detail.htm?24728/USIndia+Joint+Strategic+Vision+for+the+AsiaPacific+and+Indian+Ocean+Region

http://www.mea.gov.in/outoging-visit-detail.htm?23967/Factsheet+India+and+Japan++ Partners+for+Common+Development

http://www.mod.go.jp/e/publ/w_paper/2013.html

http://www.mofa.go.jp/region/asia-paci/india/pmv0912/joint.html

http://www.narendramodi.in/pms-keynote-address-at-the-luncheon-hosted-by-nippon-kiedanren-the-japanese-chamber-of-commerce-and-industry-and-the-japan-india-business-cooperation-committee

http://www.theguardian.com/world/2015/jan/14/japan-reveals-record-defence-budget-as-tensions-with-china-grow

# 15

# Rise of the 'Islamic State' and Its Implications

*Nazmul Arifeen*

## Introduction

Following the decapitation of its top leaders and battered by persistent attacks in Iraq and Afghanistan-Pakistan border, Al-Qaeda's activity was largely confined to producing video messages of its leaders and intimidating with threats of further attacks. Some analysts reckoned that terrorist organisations' ability to orchestrate further major attacks and inflict considerable damage on the West would significantly wane.[1] But in recent times, the withdrawal of multinational forces from Iraq witnessed the rise of another terrorist organisation, forked out of Al-Qaeda, which is known as the Islamic State in Iraq and al-Sham (ISIS) in the political landscape of the Middle East. The emergence of ISIS and its coming to prominence recently have questioned how analysts and policy-makers previously predicted the gravity of threats emanating from international terrorism.[2]

Not only has the emergence of ISIS caused bewilderment among political regimes in its Arab and non-Arab neighbourhood, the terrorist organisation has also taken control over swathes of territories and declared a state in the domains under its control. The relative pace of its rise is, to some extent, unprecedented and unforeseen. No one could imagine that a non-state actor could quickly sweep across vast areas transcending borders and pose existential threats to nation-states by redrawing boundaries, triggering mass influx of refugees and causing internal displacement of people.

The rise of ISIS has, therefore, garnered the interests of policy-makers as well as academicians at different levels. While the adversary has caused serious concerns for the countries in the region and beyond, analysts are preoccupied with explaining its rise and governments how to confront the new threat. One particular conundrum is that, ISIS has blurred the difference drawn between what constitutes a traditional threat and what falls within the ambit of non-traditional threats. With formidable forces that continue to pose serious security challenge to neighbouring countries and other extra-territorial actors like the coalition forces, it commands and governs bands of militia and territories. Whether it is to be considered a traditional threat or a non-traditional threat also requires understanding how it capitalised on the political situation, sectarian divide and its "military" clout. Since understanding a threat is *sine qua non* for military actions or otherwise, defining ISIS and understanding its far-reaching implications have become important in order to effectively address the challenge.

Some analyses did predict a distant possibility of terrorist organisations becoming state actors *viz.* taking control of territorial states,[3] but these predictions failed in explaining the rise of ISIS in two ways. First, the terrorist organisation[4] rose to prominence sooner than anticipated. Second, the same group of analysts also believed that the centre of such events would likely to be Afghanistan-Pakistan border.[5] Therefore, there are some pertinent questions that deserve explanation. What conditions preceded such prompt ascendance of a terrorist group? What factors best explain the ascendance of ISIS that its predecessor Al-Qaeda could not materialise? What implications do these developments herald for regional politics in particular and international politics in general? These are the questions that have been analysed in this paper.

This paper seeks to answer a few questions as to what are the causes of rise of ISIS and to look at its possible implications. It might be easier to analyse the causes of an ongoing crisis, but reaching a conclusion about the far-reaching implications is difficult as new developments unfold every day. The paper addresses these issues in five sections. Following an introduction, the genesis of ISIS has been examined in Section Two. Section Three analyses the causes that gave rise to ISIS. It also puts forward some arguments as to the possible implications of its rise. Finally, concluding remarks have been drawn in Section Five based on the preceding discussions.

## A Background of ISIS

The parent organisation of ISIS was Jamaat al-Tawhidwal-Jihad, founded by a Jordanian national Abu Musab al-Zarqawi, which operated in Jordan and Iraq. After the attack of multinational forces in Iraq in March 2003, al-Zarqawi pledged allegiance to Osama bin Laden and changed the organisation's name to Tanzim Qaidat al-Jihad fi Bilad al-Rafidayn, which translates into Al-Qaeda in the Land of Two Rivers.[6] It was popularly called Al-Qaeda in Iraq (AQI) and Al-Zarqawi was its Emir. His organisation merged with six other terrorist outfits with similar agenda in 2006 for a brief period into Majlis Shura al-Mujahedin (MSM) until he was killed in June 2006. After his demise, Abu Ayyub al-Masri, taking the helm of MSM, disbanded and renamed the organisation as Islamic State in Iraq (ISI) in October 2006. After he was killed in a raid in April 2010 along with Abu Omar al-Baghdadi, Abu Bakr al-Baghdadi rose to the power of ISI in May 2010. He was not a leader of AQI to begin with, but of a smaller faction which joined Majlis Shura al-Mujahedin.[7] It is interesting to note that none of its leaders is known by their actual names, rather it has become customary among ISIS leadership to assume *nom de guerre* or "war names".

## *Nomenclatural Complexities Revolving the Notion of 'Islamic State'*

Since its birth, as discussed earlier, the entity which is popularly known as ISIS has assumed a number of names and changed when necessary and as it grew in strength. This was because the names did not adequately embody its objectives of the time being. When it flexed its muscle into neighbouring states, the name Islamic State in Iraq confined its scope to move beyond Iraqi territorial boundaries. Therefore, the name was expanded to incorporate the Levant region.[8] However, as it continues to capture new provinces and its ambitions become inflated, ISIS has dropped the Levant region from its name in June 2014 and calls itself only 'Islamic State (IS)', which is much broader in sense and not confined by geographical terrain.

**Table 1: A History of ISIS Names**

| *Group Name* | *Years in Use* |
|---|---|
| Jamaat al-Tawhidwal-Jihad (JTJ) | 1999–2004 |
| Al-Qaeda in the Land of Two Rivers(more popularly known as al-Qaeda in Iraq, or AQI) | 2004–2006 |
| Majlis Shura al-Mujahedin (MSM) | 2006 |
| Islamic State of Iraq (ISI) | 2006–2013 |
| Islamic State of Iraq and al-Sham or the Levant (ISIS/ISIL) | 2013 June 2014 |
| Islamic State (IS) | June 2014–present |

*Source:* The table is modified and updated by the author from Aaron Y. Zelin, "The War between ISIS and al-Qaeda for Supremacy of the Global Jihadist Movement", The Washington Institute for Near East Policy Research Notes, No. 20, June 2014.

There is considerable debate over the use of its newly assumed name "Islamic State" as it is subject to various political as well as religious interpretations. ISIS has also exhibited state-like characteristics and performs governance activities in the region under its control. This also causes a theoretical problem whether this "state" would require assimilation into the international system. This political question also entails the boundaries and territorial limits of the so-called "Islamic State". On the other hand, the religious conundrum of calling it the "Islamic State" or "Caliphate" as it calls itself begins with the question whether it should have the religious authority of Caliphate that Islam had during the seventh century onwards. The question on authority over all Muslims of the world had caused conflicts between ISIS and Al-Qaeda as well.

Owing to the same reason, international community never acknowledged its new name. Officially the Western countries call it ISIL or ISIS. A United Nations (UN) resolution passed condemning the brutalities of ISIS described the entity as ISIL.[9] This paper, however, uses the name ISIS which is widely used by international media.

### *Ideological Predilection of ISIS*

Any academic discussion about ISIS also requires understanding of ideologies that the organisation adheres to. More so, because despite the fact that it was previously known as Al-Qaeda in Iraq, it recently has severed ties with Al-Qaeda Central. Its ideological basis requires scrutiny and, as the following discussions will further explore, estrangement with Al-Qaeda owing to ideological disagreements also benefitted ISIS in Iraq and Syria. It should be noted here that, there is a tendency even among scholars to confuse between Wahhabism and Salafism which some scholars also called neo-Wahhabism.[10] John Esposito argues that the notions of Wahhabism and Salafism have often been inaccurately used as "a blanket term for Islamic fundamentalism, religious extremism, and radicalism".[11] However, some Salafists believe that "Wahhabism was not sufficiently rigorous in adhering to the Prophet's example".[12] ISIS adheres to Salafism ideology which is, therefore, more puritan than Wahhabism. It should be noted here that not all Salafists or Wahhabists are terrorists; rather, there are certain elements among those who believe in those ideologies resort to violent means to attain their political objectives.

## The Causes of Rapid Rise of ISIS

The sudden emergence of hitherto unknown ISIS in political scenario of the Middle East has stirred considerable interest and uneasiness in the region and beyond. Although the name ISIS was barely heard before the departure of the multinational forces in Iraq, its origin dates back to more than a decade as briefly discussed earlier. The reason it was unheard of is because it originated as an independent entity, not directly linked with Al-Qaeda. Later, after the multinational forces' attack of Afghanistan, Al-Zarqawi pledged allegiance to bin Laden and changed its name to AQI. The US has targeted AQI and regularly decapitated its leadership in the past. It gained considerable attention from the international community because of its brutal killings, beheading of foreign nationals, sudden capture of lands and finally declaring a state out of nowhere. There are various reasons behind this rather confounding triumph of ISIS.

The rise of ISIS can be attributable to two different causes. There are certain "root causes" that built on over a long period of time and finally exploded. The rest of the causes can be identified as the "triggering causes" that immediately led to its recent upheaval that include the withdrawal of coalition forces from Iraq and subsequent political vacuum. While the root cause seeks to theoretically explain its causes of ascendance, the triggering causes explain how the recent development in the Middle East politics added momentum to ISIS objectives.

## *Favoured by Changing Strategic Landscape*

The rise of ISIS is a simultaneous coincidence of two developments of international politics: namely the "Arab Spring" and the withdrawal of multinational forces from Iraq while the democratic institutions in the country were still very weak and political stability was not attained. Arab Spring gave rise to several democratic forces in the Middle East; among them was Free Syrian Army (FSA) supported by Western countries to fight against the Assad regime.[13] FSA was greatly empowered by the supply of weapons. This has made it a formidable adversary against the Assad regime. However, it did not have the capacity to retain and run functions of a state in the territories it previously captured. FSA could not continue to hold the control over the large cities it captured in Syria.

Western countries were convinced that democracy promotion was one of the most effective ways to counter radicalisation. For example, Michael Boyle explained why two successive US governments have taken the policy of democracy promotion as a remedy for terrorism.[14] As a continuation of such policies, the West has overtly or sometimes covertly supported the popular uprisings in the Middle East during the Arab Spring. However, by linking democracy promotion and fighting terrorism resulting in the policy of "regime change", the traditional autocratic governments were weakened in some countries leading to an internal political vacuum in the region.

Situation already deteriorated in Iraq because of the sectarian and ethnic divide. The coalition forces' withdrawal from Iraq created a vacuum in that country that ISIS did not waste time to take advantage of. The Iraqi provinces of Mosul and Diyala which were once the epitome of the multinational forces' presence have fallen to ISIS. The widely known Abu Gharib prison was attacked by ISIS fighters to help several hundred war prisoners escape. These incidents changed the landscape following the departure of coalition forces. Lakhdar Brahimi noted that the West's top priority in the region had been to defeat ISIS, shifting away from toppling Assad regime.[15] Nevertheless, Western countries appear to be reluctant to commit to another bout of prolonged conflict in the region.

Neighbouring countries including Turkey, Iran, Saudi Arabia and others also have contradicting objectives, priorities and diverging national interests in these areas. For example, threats emanating from ISIS are not considered "immediate" by Turkey which is claimed to have negotiated with the terrorist group to free its diplomats.[16] International state-actors were also caught in the dilemma of arming the Syrian rebels or discontinuing it, as it turned out to be benefitting ISIS. Weakening Assad regime, which can be a major force to mount considerable opposition to ISIS, will embolden the latter. In addition, in the recent months, several factions from Syrian rebels joined ISIS along with the weapons supplied to them by the West. On the flipside, Western countries cannot 'ethically' arm Assad regime. This dilemma and the lack of decisive policy to collectively face a common enemy like the ISIS have actually emboldened it further.

There have also been policy shifts of major Western countries regarding the regions where the Global War on Terror (GWoT) should be fought. Explaining US President Obama's intention to pull out force from Iraq, Trevor McCrisken noted that his administration believed the "real war on terror" should not be pursued in Iraq, rather in Afghanistan and Pakistan border.[17] Moving away from what Obama called a 'distraction' in the war on terrorism, the US decided to leave the Iraq theatre; while at the same time, sponsoring democracy promotion in the region by international community. The political vacuum that was created in the process was filled up by other non-state actors within the country.

Apart from these international political calculations, there are internal strategic considerations that greatly favoured ISIS. Many battered political forces have supported the ISIS not because of ideological predilection but tactical reasons which can be summed up in Kautilyan dictum "my enemy's enemy is my friend." It is understandable as to why top leaders of the ISIL military leadership come from the former Ba'athist army of Saddam Hussein. Saddam Hussein's daughter living-in-exile in Jordan also supported the cause of ISIS mainly because she holds personal vendetta against the current regime in Iraq. These developments, certainly along with many others, factored in the rapid rise of ISIS in the region.

### *Materialisation of 'Caliphate Dream'*

Another important factor that gave impetus to the sudden rise of ISIS is its ability to deliver on its promises. Some analysts claim that ISIS is more successful than

Al-Qaeda.[18] Indeed, favoured by the political situation and circumstances, as well as a power vacuum created by the outgoing coalition forces in the region, ISIS captured swathes of lands including important border crossings and strategic cities declaring itself the so-called 'Islamic State'. In June 2014, the ISIS leader Abu Bakr al-Baghdadi declared himself the Caliph of the 'Islamic State' assuming the title Caliph Ibrahim-II. For many global jihadists[19] who were disillusioned by the failure of their ideological cause in such areas as Chechnya and Afghanistan, the victory of ISIS is a dream coming true. For them, no other organisation has been able to deliver so much in the name of "Jihad", let alone capturing foreign lands with foreign fighters. Although the Taliban came close to that level, but at its inception, the Taliban was mainly an internal political force within Afghanistan. During the Taliban takeover of Afghanistan in the late 1990s, despite question of their political legitimacy, they were not a terrorist organisation *per se.* Later, the group's intimacy with the Al-Qaeda and harbouring Osama bin Laden led to the invasion of Afghanistan by NATO forces in 2003.

Such claim of Caliphate also increased the appeal of ISIS. Even its parent organisation Al-Qaeda feels uneasy with the notion of "Islamic State". In recent months, cleavage between Al-Qaeda and ISIS became public when ISIS claimed authority over al-Nusra Front which, according to ISIS claims, was sent by al-Baghdadi to open battle front in Syria. In an audio message, al-Baghdadi declared that al-Nusra Front would merge with ISIS which was soon opposed by both Ayman al-Zawahiri, the current leader of Al-Qaeda Central, and Abu Musab al-Zawlani, the leader of al-Nusra Front.

Apparently, 'internationalisation' of terrorist agenda also helped ISIS attract more foreign fighters. Many foreign fighters who joined the "Syrian jihad" with al-Nusra Front are foreign terrorists who travelled to the country to fight Assad regime. Laurent Vinatier argued that Al-Nusra Front's reluctance to join ISIS going beyond Syrian territories apparently disgruntled foreign fighters who were deserting the Front to join ISIS because of its global agenda.[20]

The tangible success, perceived by radical ideologues of Salafism and Wahhabism, of establishing the so-called Caliphate has, therefore, made certain appeal to terrorists from all over the world. Foreign fighters swarmed in the domain controlled by ISIS on an unprecedented scale. One estimate suggests that currently there are 12,000 foreign fighters from as many as 81 countries including the US, Britain, France and Australia in the West and Malaysia, Indonesia, Pakistan and India from the East.[21] What is more interesting is the fact that amongst the foreign fighters, there are also women who travelled mainly from Western countries to join the battle.[22] One estimate suggests that approximately sixty women joined from Britain alone.[23] While there may be various motivations, at the same time, it depicts the degree of appeal that ISIS has been able to create.

### *Political Economy of ISIS Rise*

Financing terrorist activities and control over interrupted flow of monetary supply have always been the lifeline of Al-Qaeda and the likes. Al-Qaeda was severely crippled by the stringent financial regulations put in place to deprive it of outside financial assistance. It has been argued that terrorist organisations benefitted from extortion, trade in narcotics, illicit arms deals as well as endowments received from sympathisers. But ISIS has been successful in breaking away from that tradition by diversifying its sources of finance. Not only does it sustain the economic burden of running an organisation like itself, analysts also claim that ISIS regularly pays its militia.[24]

Capturing major oil fields and selling antiques and precious metals immensely helped ISIS rise.[25] Evidence shows that ISIS income generated from oil revenue alone is approximately US$2 million a day.[26] However, there is debate over what parties this oil is being sold to. Apart from oil, there are other sources of income from extortion, robbery of banks and other financial institutions and endowments from its sympathisers. This implies that while Al-Qaeda was mainly financed by its patrons in the Gulf States, ISIS on the other hand, is largely autonomous. No terrorist organisations in the recent decades have known to have so much resource.

Despite this, the sustainability of such economic activity remains under question. The Middle Eastern countries adjacent to ISIS territories are already oil rich. This implies that there is no market for ISIS-produced oil in the vicinity. The government and the opposition in Syria blame each other for buying oil from ISIS. Despite the fierce animosity between Assad regime and ISIS, the two belligerent parties continued to benefit from each other in economic terms. As Valérie Marcel argues, ISIS sells its oil to Syrian regime "in exchange for immunity against air strikes".[27] Some claim that Turkey is one of the state buyers of ISIS oil.[28] Nevertheless, ISIS' capacity to refine oil is very limited. It mostly sells oil in the local market for electricity production and majority of its oil is sold through black market. Lack of formal trading mechanism will reduce the possibility of ISIS to continuously depend on oil revenue. This limited opportunity will not allow it to grow further economically.

### *Identity Politics in the Middle East*

Identity politics is another root cause of the emergence of ISIS which was fanned deliberately during the Iraq war by different groups. The coalition forces attempted to empower minority groups and communities that were marginalised during the previous regime. To a great extent, therefore, the emergence of ISIS is the result of identity politics in the Middle East. It was also a historical phenomenon that was engrained during the partition of these countries that cut across tribes erecting virtual state-boundaries between and among different ethnic groups and sects, while at the same time depriving large groups like the Kurds of statehood. In the recent past, its rise is also attributable to the Western policies that Sunni population, who once enjoyed political power during the regime of Saddam Hussein, feel alienated and marginalised. It is, thus, also a result of political exclusion of the Sunni population from the power of Iraq.[29] There is certainly a sectarian element in the ongoing battle between ISIS and its adversaries most of whom are Shi'ites. However, trying to view the problem through only sectarian lens would result in oversimplification of the problem.[30] In this particular case in Iraq and Syria, sectarian identities have been used for political ends.

After the defeat of Saddam Hussein, the multinational forces instated the government of Nouri al-Maliki, a Shi'ite political leader, and Jalal Talabani, an ethnic Kurd, in the political power of Iraq. Both Shi'ite and Kurds were subjected to state repression during the Saddam Hussein era. As such, the new government took policies that deprived the previous political elites from the amenities that they once enjoyed. These reversals make a large number of the Sunni population feel alienated.[31] ISIS has taken advantage of this sense of alienation among the Sunni population. At the same time, while both Al-Qaeda and ISIS are terrorist organisations, the fundamental difference between the two is that the latter has a clear identity-based agenda. Fareed Zakaria noted that Al-Qaeda had a pan-Islamic approach and its goal was "to rally the entire Muslim world to jihad against the West". On the contrary, the terrorist elements that later emerged as ISIS deliberately adopted an anti-Shi'itestance because of existing resentment between the two groups.[32] It was also conducive to attract Sunni support. Therefore, ISIS politicised sectarian identity so as to achieve its political goals.

Apart from the Shi'ite-Sunni divide, Muslims are also divided in ideological line as well, namely Salafism and Wahhabism. Although not all Wahhabists and Salafists are terrorists, at least, some of those who subscribe to these beliefs are radical extremists. The ideology of ISIS is also responsible for deliberate fanning of sectarian violence. As mentioned before, ISIS believes in Salafist ideology which is more puritan than Wahhabism. Both Salafism and Wahhabism are Sunni ideology but their beliefs are not exactly the same. Al-Qaeda is mainly a Wahhabi organisation; on the contrary, ISIS is mostly a Salafist one which is also known as neo-Wahhabism. Coupled with increasing hatred against Shi'ite population caused by change in the political landscape, ISIS has found a safe haven in Iraq.

### *Intensifying Recruitment in Cyberspace through Social Media*

One striking feature of ISIS was the relatively fast pace of its membership growth.

Experts have previously showed how terrorist organisations like Al-Qaeda made extensive use of internet and social media.[33] But as it appears, ISIS has taken that to whole new level. This can be attributable to innovative ways ISIS has taken advantage of newer media and social communications. While Al-Qaeda was dependent on clandestine website requiring passing security checks, ISIS has utilised online communication and social media to reach to its recruits. It maintains a twitter account, developed an Android application that allows users to remain constantly updated and always connected with upper chain of command. While Al-Qaeda communication medium was limited to producing audio/video messages once in a while, ISIS has frequently released videos. It regularly publishes an e-magazine called *Dabiq*[34] and relayed its messages through this. The online activity campaign also paid off as foreign terrorists are moving in the battlefield to join the ISIS.

## *Confronted by Weaker Adversaries in Iraq and Syria*

Another reason that explains the relatively unchallenged rise of ISIS is the existence of weak Iraqi national forces left alone by the multinational forces' withdrawal and battered foes like Assad regime which already lost control of many strategic areas. Iraqi cities like Mosul, Falluja, Tikrit and in Syria, Raqqa and Aleppo fell.[35] The newly formed Iraqi army severely lacks both training and capacity to wage a war against such an organised and experienced "militia" as ISIS. When Syrian rebels already took control of major cities in Syria supported by multinational forces' airstrikes, it was relatively easier on part of ISIS to drive away Syrian rebels from those territories.

The battle is being waged on several fronts in Syria as well: between Assad regime and the rest of the oppositions including Free Syrian Army, between Free Syrian Army and Al-Qaeda elements like al-Nusra Front and finally between ISIS and al-Nusra Front. Opening up a number of fronts in the battle has weakened all parties concerned and caused mutual destruction. However, ISIS remained comparatively less battered and became victories in the multifrontal battle. As previously mentioned, estrangement with al-Nusra Front, the Al-Qaeda affiliate in Syria, has also helped ISIS. The reason behind the animosity was the former's reluctance to internationalise its battle agenda beyond the Syrian theatre. But the Front was already supported by foreign fighters who migrated from faraway lands to join the battle and as such already had a global approach to jihad. When these groups left al-Nusra Front for ISIS, they brought in arms and ammunition supplied by the West and other regional actors.

The preceding analyses do not presume that the rise of ISIS can only be explained through the above-mentioned causes. Certainly, there were other factors involved. However, a deeper analysis reveals that these factors could better explain the relative rapidity of ascendance of ISIS in Iraq and Syria.

## Implications of Rise of the 'Islamic State'

The rapid rise of ISIS also heralds multifarious ramifications for global and regional politics. Needless to say, the heat of its growing influence is being felt in the neighbourhood of ISIS-controlled territories. Apart from Iraq and Syria where ISIS currently operates, Turkey, Jordan, Yemen and Saudi Arabia are likely to be among the first nations to take the blow. In the longer term, however, its impact will spread. Gradually its impact will reach faraway places from the epicentre of the crisis as the following sections argue.

### *Will there Be Domino Effect?*

One possible outcome of the rise of ISIS in the neighbouring countries can be explained through the 'domino effect'. In international relations context, domino theory[36] denotes that the success of an actor in a given region may trigger chain reaction *e.g.* encourage others in its vicinity to do the same. For example, the civil uprisings dubbed as the 'Arab Spring' itself triggered a domino effect in the region.[37] The chain reaction of what started as a street protest in Tunisia soon swept across the Arab world including Egypt, Libya, Yemen, Bahrain and Syria; either leading to change of regime or being forcefully quelled. Therefore, instability can sometimes be contagious in international politics. Likewise, originating in Iraq, the ISIS crisis already spilled over to Syria. Just the way Arab Spring spread over to neighbouring countries; inspired by the success in Iraq, ISIS leadership ordered its comrades to cross over to Syria and recruit forces which soon became a formidable threat in that country.

Nevertheless, this will be a sheer exaggeration to suggest that mass people of the Middle East are likely to follow the path of ISIS by extending their support for it. Rather, in this particular case, what is more important is the likelihood of other terrorist organisations joining ISIS. As Jack Snyder noted, intrinsically connected with the domino effect is the concept of 'bandwagon', which implies an actor's alignment with stronger forces in international politics. An actor's triumph often encourages other actors with a similar agenda to jump on the former's bandwagon.[38] By the same token, emboldened by the success of ISIS, terrorist organisations elsewhere may be encouraged to follow suit, extend support or even merge with ISIS. There are already evidences of such developments. Nigeria-based terrorist organisation Boko Haram—which previously supported the ideological cause of ISIS—recently captured a town called Gwoza in Borno State of Nigeria and declared it a new "part of the Islamic Caliphate".[39] In South Asia, two terrorist organisations including the Pakistani Taliban (also known as

Tehrik-e-Taliban or TTP) pledged allegiance to ISIS.[40] Such actions can be interpreted to be similar to getting on the bandwagon. Further bandwagoning with ISIS might be observed in the days ahead.

But given the inherent dearth of accommodative attitude in ISIS, it remains to be seen whether it will able to bring considerable number of such terrorist groups under its umbrella. Of late, ISIS had a fall out with its parent organisation Al-Qaeda and engaged in fratricidal brutalities by killing fellow comrades of other terrorist organisations including al-Nusra Front. This also casts doubt on the possibility that ISIS will be able to sustain its appeal to other terrorist organisations.

## *New Polarisation in the Region*

The emergence of the force within a relatively short period of time has brought to the forefront the question of reordering current polarisation in the region. Because, what is alarming for regional as well as global politics is that ISIS is not a conventional terrorist organisation, rather it has an expansionist agenda that seeks to carve out a "Caliphate" in the region undermining status quo and altering long-demarcated geographical boundaries. And given its recent success and resources at its disposal, it would be difficult for any country in that region to face the challenges singlehandedly. Therefore, analysts talked about changing the balance of power by creating new security architecture that accommodated regional powers to fight the common enemy.[41]

It is true that there has been no significant sign of shift in existing balance of power in the region so far, but latest developments in the regional politics of the Middle East would make new polarisation inevitable. First, Western countries appear to be hesitant over the decision to arm the Syrian rebels, as it was previously revealed that weapons—intended for Kurdish *peshmerga* fighters to fight against ISIS—had ended up in the hands of ISIS.[42] Its previous policies of weakening Assad regime had actually benefited ISIS. Scholars also argued that arming Syrian rebels would not actually prevent ISIS' rise either.[43] As a result, the West has moved away from its previous priority of toppling Assad regime in the short term.[44] Assad regime, therefore, is no longer the arch-enemy of the West in Syria, rather it can be an effective tool in neutralising the threats of ISIS. Such temporary shift in the Western countries' policies has created new polarisation in the region.

Second, another notable indicator of change in the regional political alignment is faster sign of rapprochement between Iran and the West.[45] Iran is perhaps the only country that is not likely to side with ISIS, because the country is an antithesis to what ISIS stands for. Iran is the only Shi'ite country in the region with considerable clout as well as interest in defeating the ISIS. It is true that after the departure of Mahmood Ahmadinejad, the former Iranian President, from the political scene of the country, the present regime showed interest to recommence negotiation with the West. Nevertheless, now there is another reason *viz.* the common threat of ISIS for the West and Iran to forget their differences and focus on one common enemy. Whatever the case, as long as the threat of ISIS persists, the West will avoid any direct confrontation with Iran.

Although there is no valid reason to believe that there will be any dramatic shift of power in regional politics of the Middle East, but as this paper discussed, there would be new political polarisation and realignment within the regional theatre of the Middle East. Indeed, it is difficult to predict how long this emerging status quo will last. After the Cold War, Western countries barely needed to align with a country that was previously considered the "axis of evil". The second sign in new polarisation, albeit for short-to-medium term, would be cooperating with the Assad regime in Syria. Despite Syrian support for groups like Hezbollah, it is also true that Assad's regime, albeit autocratic, is a secular force. Recent images and videos shown by ISIS indicate that weapons supplied to Free Syrian Army fell into the wrong hands of ISIS. For greater strategic interest, it has become imperative for the international community to cooperate with the current Syrian regime.

However, it can be argued that disintegration the courtiers like Iraq and Syria would serve greater purpose of securing the interest of the West's most important ally in the region—Israel. But in order to do so, no party would be willing to empower a Frankenstein like ISIS. These calculations would lead to a shift in the existing alignment and polarisation in the Middle East and move a step back from the Arab spring.

## *Terrorists' Homecoming*

One of possibly devastating impacts of the ISIS, both within the region and globally, would be managing the returnees from the battlefields. As seen in the previous case in "Afghan Jihad" against the former Soviet Union, when the "mujahideens" returned to their homeland, they played an active role in spreading extremist ideologies in their localities. The first leader of ISIS, Abu Musab al-Zarqawi himself was a returnee of Afghan war.[46] In the case of ISIS, the fallout will be much more dreadful as the foreign fighters will bring with them the battlefield experience of fighting trained armies and not to mention the connection with the global terrorist network. They would be far more seasoned and efficient in spreading the ideology, organising like-minded radicals and orchestrating attacks compared to home-grown terrorists.

Previously, it was revealed that the proliferation of terrorist organisations in South Asia, to a great extent, was caused by Afghan war veterans who fought alongside the Mujahedeen during the Soviet invasion of Afghanistan. But the problems would be more difficult to manage this time as discussed before. While the Afghan war veterans in South Asia were mostly confined within the walls of madrasahs,[47] however, the trends of the foreign fighters who have joined ISIS fight show that they belong to upper-middle class of the population and belonging to diaspora population abroad. Unlike the madrasah returnees with little knowledge and assimilation with the mainstream society in the previous cases, these new returnees would be more assimilated with the mainstream society and having the means and knowledge to spread the ideology through social and other online media. That alone may spread these ideas in South Asia. The second important threat to watch out for is the backward linkage or family ties of diaspora who keep active connections with distant family members back home. Scholars have claimed that "twenty-seven of the fifty most active contemporary terrorist organizations are either part of a diaspora or are supported by one".[48] This may also increase the chance of further indoctrination of terrorists elsewhere.

## *Influx of Refugees into Neighbouring Countries*

Following the crisis, people—especially minorities belonging to Kurd, Yazidi, Druze and other populations—left the conflict zone *en masse* and took shelter in neighbouring countries. Even Muslim Shi'ites who are not-so-minority in Iraq and Syria also fled the areas. One estimate suggests the figure of refugees fleeing into Turkey from Syria is about 130,000 in recent days.[49] However, according to the European Commission, 10.8 million people have been affected by the ISIS rise; among them 4.7 million are in areas that are difficult to reach.[50]

The influx of refugees has multiple implications. To begin with, it will put enormous pressure on the economies of the host countries. The question of who will share the burden is yet to be sorted out by the international community. Despite sympathies for fellow Arabs, no Arab country would be willing to permanently take the refugees as their citizens. Country like Turkey that is not an Arab nation has valid reason to be worried, as allowing refugees to stay for long term will adversely affect its demography because of interracial marriage. In addition, as it has been observed elsewhere in the world, refugee camps are fertile grounds for terrorist recruitment.[51]

## *Safety of Migrant Workers*

Another important consequence of the crisis could be reduced safety of migrant workers. It should be mentioned here that the Middle East, in general, is dependent on migrant workers from Asian countries and poorer Arab nations of the region.[52] In some cases, migrant workers outnumber indigenous population.[53] During battle between groups, migrant workers were caught in line of fire in Iraq and Syria. According to one report, many migrant workers are stranded in the zone unable to get out of the country.[54] Despite several South Asian nations' diplomatic manoeuvre to bring back their migrant workers from conflict-prone Iraq, many remain in that country. It is also difficult to assess the exact number of migrant population in Iraq as there are various channels of migration and it is difficult to keep tract of temporary incoming workers. Many people have crossed over to that country from other countries. While evacuating a large number of foreign migrant workers will be a challenge for sending countries, there are other aspects of the problem. Workers from poorer countries living in conflict zones are reluctant to come back because they are still able to earn and remit money to their families. Second, any international migration incurs huge economic cost. Leaving those countries would imply irrecoverable economic loss for people who migrated there for a better life.

Nevertheless, since the inception of Iraq war, the number of South Asians, for example, in that country greatly reduced as home countries took evacuation measures. If the crisis continues, economies of other gulf countries will take the blow resulting in short-to-medium term economic stagnation. This, coupled with security concerns, is likely to lead to further reduction of migrants in those countries. South Asian countries have dependence on money remitted by their diasporas all over the world. It is not that only migrant workers of Iraq and Syria will dwindle because of the crisis. It has been predicted that as the ISIS crisis turns into a protracted conflict, international business is likely to reduce investments in crisis zones in the Middle East. Thus, the economies of neighbouring states will be affected in the medium term, if not immediately. Therefore, should the crisis persist, remittance flow from the Middle Eastern countries will reduce drastically.

## *Impact on South Asia in Future*

Terrorism induced by similar religious causes has been a common menace in several countries in South Asia. The relative proximity of this region to the epicentre of ISIS controlled territories has made it more prone to the fallout of the crisis. While the state of complete lawlessness which has facilitated the rise of ISIS cannot compared with India and Bangladesh with their democratic tradition and history of religious tolerance, nevertheless, the rise of ISIS can pose serious threats to these countries in the future.

The most likely impact of burgeoning influence of ISIS in South Asia will be intensified radicalisation among the youth. The state-of-the-art means of the group to reach out to young people will likely to impact India and Bangladesh at an alarming rate in the days ahead. It was reported that there were more than a dozen 'missing' individuals in India who were presumed to have joined ISIS.[55] These numbers cannot be said with accuracy in case of any country of the region and the actual figure may, in fact, be a cause of concern for all. Praveen Swami notes, "Perhaps most important, support for the Islamic State is blossoming in underground blogs and chat-rooms. Islamic State propagandists have, in particular, been calling for educated volunteers, especially engineers and doctors, to help build an Islamic utopia."[56]

It has been claimed, as discussed before, migrating to ISIS-territories is actually a well-paid job, compared to the idea of voluntarism prevailing in case of many other terrorist organisations.[57] Given that fact that people of South Asian countries are poor, it makes them more susceptible to brainwashing and radicalisation. The proximity of the region with Iraq and Syria may increase such migration and recruitment in the future.

In fact, such phenomenon has already been observed. Several individuals in Bangladesh[58] and India[59] were arrested in the past over suspected connection with ISIS. It was also reported that ISIS has intensified recruitments of Indians in the recent times.[60] British nationals of South Asian origins such have found to have migrated to ISIS territories with their families. These developments bear ominous signals of further radicalisation among South Asians.

However, the greater challenge will come when these individuals choose to return to their ancestral homes. Along with the likelihood of indoctrinating more people with radical ideas, perhaps even bigger threat they pose is orchestrating attacks inside these countries. Situation will be more complicated to manage if radicalised citizens of democratic nations such as India and Bangladesh mount terrorist attacks in their own soil.

It may never be possible for ISIS to bring its battles to the frontiers of India and Bangladesh due to various reasons like lack of popular support in these countries, democratic traditions and presence of strong security forces. Nevertheless, its ability to disturb peace and stability, mount attacks in various places within these counties is very much feasible. Returnees with real battlefield experience of fighting trained armies will pose unforeseen security challenges.

## Conclusion

As the paper shows, certain political developments in the region created conducive space for the rise of ISIS. Owing to multinational forces' departure from Iraq, there was no strong opponent in Iraq to counter its burgeoning influence. This has emboldened ISIS to continue its spread across the country. Weakened political regimes in Syria and elsewhere were by-products of Arab Spring and, in the process, caused a political vacuum. This also catalysed its rise. The imminent crisis may threaten countries in the neighbourhood, nevertheless, there is a lack of urgency among abutting states to confront an enemy that would require attacks in other sovereign states. Therefore, ISIS faced little resistance from international community barring a few airstrikes. Its apparent success in materialising what it calls the "Caliphate" by capturing lands bred further success as terrorists from other countries keep joining its bandwagon. Its state-of-the-art tactics on cyberspace also allowed it to reach more audience and recruit globally. Finally, diversification of financial resources by capturing oil fields gave it the required capital to run an organisation like itself.

This paper also argues that the rise of ISIS would encourage other like-minded terrorist organisations to join hands with ISIS and is likely to further revitalise international terrorism. If it continues to increase in power, this may lead to a "domino effect" in the region as other terrorist organisations would rally behind it. In case of its demise caused either by leadership decapitation or collective military action by other state actors in the region, those who joined ISIS and became a part of a larger terrorist network would return to their home countries and may spread terrorist ideology or even orchestrate further attacks elsewhere. That could be one of the devastating consequences of this crisis. However, as refugee situation deteriorates with more people crossing over international borders or also becoming internally displaced, there is a possibility that neighbouring countries would put aside their differences in the short-term as long as the crisis persists. This may also lead to new polarisation in the region by bringing former enemies like Iran, the Western countries and Saudi Arabia in the same platform to fight a common adversary.

## NOTES

1. Fawaz A. Gerges, *The Rise and Fall of Al-Qaeda*, New York: Oxford University Press, 2011.
2. International terrorism or transnational terrorism is acts of terrorist violence that has implications for more than one countries and, therefore, requires international cooperation to be addressed. See, B. Peter Rosendorff and Todd Sandler, "The Political Economy of Transnational Terrorism", *Journal of Conflict Resolution*, Vol. 49, No. 2, 2005, pp. 171–82.
3. Rick Nelson *et. al.*, "Confronting an Uncertain Threat: The Future of Al-Qaeda and Associated Movements", Center for Strategic and International Studies (CSIS), September 2011.
4. There are considerable debates among scholars as to what constitutes a terrorist organisation. This paper uses the definition provided by Colin Wight which stipulates that terrorism is "form of violent political" expression and that violence "illegitimate"; it involves "deliberate targeting of non-state actors and institutions" despite the fact that the "victims are not the intended recipients of the political message". See Colin Wight, "Theorising Terrorism: The State, Structure and History", *International Relations*, Vol. 23, March 2009, pp. 99–106.
5. Rick Nelson, *op. cit.*
6. Gordon Corera, "Unraveling Zarqawi's al-Qaeda Connection", *Terrorism Monitor*, Vol. 2, No. 24, 2005.
7. Peter Beaumont, "Abu Bakr al-Baghdadi: The ISIS chief with the Ambition to Overtake al-Qaida", *The Guardian*, 12 June 2014.
8. The Levant (or al-Sham in Arabic and widely used in Islamic texts) is a biblical name of a

region that once was comprised of present day Syria, Lebanon, Jordan, Palestine, Israel and Southern Turkey.

9. United Nations Security Council Resolution No. S/RES/2170 (2014), adopted by the Security Council at its 7242nd meeting, 15 August 2014.
10. Colin Wight, *op. cit.*
11. John L. Esposito, *Unholy War: Terror in the Name of Islam*, New York: Oxford University Press, 2002, pp. 105-106.
12. David Commins, *The Wahhabi Mission and Saudi Arabia*, New York: I. B. Tauris, 2006, p. 173.
13. Zeke J Miller, "Congress Votes to Arm Syrian Rebels", *Time*, 18 September 2014.
14. Michael J. Boyle, "Between Freedom and Fear: Explaining the Consensus on Terrorism and Democracy in US Foreign Policy", *International Politics*, Vol. 48, No. 2/3, 2011, pp. 412–33.
15. Paper presented by Lakhdar Brahimi, Former UN and Arab League Special Envoy to Syria, on "Syria's Conflict and the Impact on its Neighbours: The Long View" in The Royal Institute of International Affairs, 14 October 2014.
16. Alessandria Masi, "Turkey Freed 46 Turkish Hostages From ISIS Using 'Diplomatic And Political Negotiations'", *International Business Times*, 22 September 2014.
17. Trevor McCrisken, "Ten Years On: Obama's War on Terrorism in Rhetoric and Practice", *International Affairs*, Vol. 87 No. 4, 2011, pp. 782–3.
18. See, Jay Sekulow, *Rise of ISIS: A Threat We Can't Ignore*, New York: Howard Books, 2014.
19. The Arabic word *jihad* can have several meanings with religious connotations as described in Islamic scriptures or without. Transnational terrorist groups have often used the word to justify their violent political means. For a detailed discussion on *jihad* and its various connotations, see, Richard Bonney, *Jihad: From Qur'an to bin Laden*, New York: Palgrave Macmillan, 2004.
20. Laurent Vinatier, "Foreign Jihadism in Syria: The Islamic State of Iraq and al-Sham", Security Assessment in North Africa, *SANA Dispatch*, No.4, April 2014.
21. Abdul Basit, "Foreign Fighters in Iraq and Syria–Why So Many?" *Counter Terrorism Trends and Analysis*, Vol. 6, No. 9, 2014, pp. 4-8.
22. Richard Barrett, "Foreign Fighters in Syria", The Soufan Group, June 2014, available at http://soufangroup.com/wp-content/uploads/2014/06/TSG-Foreign-Fighters-in-Syria.pdf, accessed on 07 September 2014.
23. Abdul Basit, *op. cit.*
24. Michael Jonsson, "Following the Money: Financing the Territorial Expansion of Islamist Insurgents in Syria", Swedish Defence Research Agency, *FOI Memo*, No. 4947, 23 May 2014, available at http://foi.se/Global/V%C3%A5r%20kunskap/S%C3%A4kerhetspolitiska%20studier/Asien/Rapporter_och_memon/FOI%20Memo%204947.pdf, accessed on 15 August 2014.
25. Jay Sekulow, *op. cit.*
26. David Sanger and Julie Davis, "Struggling to Starve ISIS of Oil Revenue, U.S. Seeks Assistance from Turkey", *The New York Times*, 13 September 2014.
27. Valérie Marcel, "ISIS and the Dangers of Black Market Oil", Royal Institute of International Affairs, 21 July 2014, available at http://www.chathamhouse.org/expert/comment/15203, accessed on 02 September 2014.
28. *Ibid.*
29. Andrew Phillips, "The Islamic State's Challenge to International Order", *Australian Journal of International Affairs*, Vol. 68, No. 5, 2014, pp. 495–8.

30. F. Gregory Gause, "Beyond Sectarianism: The New Middle East Cold War", Brookings Doha Center Analysis Paper, No. 11, July 2014.
31. Michael Lipka, "The Sunni-Shia Divide: Where They Live, What They Believe and How They View Each Other", Pew Research Center, 18 June 2014, available at http://www.pewresearch.org/fact-tank/2014/06/18/the-sunni-shia-divide-where-they-live-what-they-believe-and-how-they-view-each-other/,accessed on 27 September 2014.
32. Fareed Zakaria, *The Post-American World*, New York: W. W. Norton & Company Ltd, 2008, pp. 11-12.
33. Brian Michael Jenkins, "Is Al Qaeda's Internet Strategy Working?", RAND Corporation, 06 December 2011, available at http://homeland.house.gov/sites/homeland.house.gov/files/Testimony%20Jenkins%20.pdf, accessed on 15 August 2014.
34. "The Islamic State's (ISIS, ISIL) Magazine", The Clarion Project, 10 September 2014, available at http://www.clarionproject.org/news/islamic-state-isis-isil-propaganda-magazine-dabiq, accessed on 17 September 2014.
35. "Areas Under ISIS Control", *The New York Times*, 12 June 2014.
36. Domino theory also guided many US policies during the Cold War era. In simplest terms, the theory suggested that if one country fell to communism, adjacent nations would follow suit. For further discussion on 'domino effect' in international relations, see, Jerome Slater, "The Domino Theory and International Politics: The Case of Vietnam", *Security Studies*, Vol. 3, No. 2, 1993-94, pp. 186–224.
37. Parag Khanna, "The Domino Effect of Arab Unrest" *CNN*, 02 February 2011, available at http://edition.cnn.com/2011/OPINION/02/01/roundup.jordan.egypt/, accessed on 01 September 2014.
38. Jack Snyder, "Introduction", in Robert Jervis and Jack Snyder (eds.), *Dominoes and Bandwagons: Strategic Beliefs and Great Power Competition in the Eurasian Rimland*, New York: Oxford University Press, 1991.
39. Cahal Milmo and Tom Witherow, "Boko Haram Closes in on its Dream of an African Caliphate – and ISIS Gives its Blessing, and Advice on Strategy", *The Independent*, 08 September 2014.
40. Najib Sharifi, "ISIS Makes Inroads in Afghanistan, Pakistan", *Foreign Policy*,30 September 2014.
41. Marco Vicenzino, "Confronting ISIS through a New Balance of Power in Middle East", *The Huffington Post*, 11 September 2014, available at http://www.huffingtonpost.com/marco-vicenzino/confronting-isis-through-_b_5804618.html, accessed on 22 September 2014.
42. Ted Thornhill, "ISIS Arming Themselves with US-Made Military Hardware to Wage Jihad across the Middle East after Seizing Weapons from Syrian Rebels and Iraqi Soldiers", *The Daily Mail*, 09 September 2014.
43. Marc Lynch, "Would Arming Syria's Rebels Have Stopped the Islamic State?", *The Washington Post*, 11 August 2014.
44. David Ignatius, "Obama Wants Assad to Go, But Not too Soon", *The Washington Post*, 19 June 2013.
45. David Usborne and Nigel Morris, "Iraq Crisis Prompts Reconciliation between Iran and the West: From Great Satan to the Great Rapprochement", *The Independent*, 16 June 2014.
46. Gordon Corera, *op. cit.*
47. Taj Hashmi, "Islamic Resurgence in Bangladesh: Genesis, Dynamics and Implications", in Satu Limaye, Robert Wirsing, and Mohan Malik (eds.), *Religious Radicalism and Security in South Asia*, Hawaii: Asia-Pacific Center for Security Studies (APCSS), 2004, pp. 40–1.
48. Louise Richardson, "The Roots of Terrorism: An Overview", in Louise Richardson (ed.), *The Roots of Terrorism*, London: Routledge, 2006, p. 6.

49. Ben Hubbard, "Raids by ISIS Push Flood of Refugees Into Turkey", *The New York Times*, 22 September 2014.
50. European Commission, *ECHO Fact Sheet*, October 2014, available at http://ec.europa.eu/echo/files/aid/countries/factsheets/thematic/civil_protection_en.pdf, accessed on 23 October 2014.
51. Gabriel Sheffer, "Diasporas and Terrorism", in Louise Richardson, *op. cit.*, pp. 120–1.
52. Toby Shelley, *Exploited: Migrant Labour in the New Global Economy*, London: ZED Books, 2007, pp. 1–10.
53. *Ibid.*
54. Syed Zain Al-Mahmood, "South Asian Migrant Workers Stuck in Wartorn Iraq", *The Wall Street Journal*, 02 July 2014.
55. Praveen Swami, "ISIS Group Draws More Indians, Alarm Bells in Delhi", *The Indian Express*, 26 August 2015, available at http://indianexpress.com/article/india/india-others/islamic-state-draws-more-indians-alarm-bells-in-delhi/, accessed on 27 August 2015.
56. *Ibid.*
57. Keiligh Baker, "ISIS Offers Fighters up to £1,000 Starter Home Bonus and Honeymoon in Their Stronghold Syrian City of Raqqa" *The Daily Mail*, 26 May 2015, available at http://www.dailymail.co.uk/news/article-3098235/ISIS-offers-fighters-1-500-starter-home-bonus-free-honeymoon.html, accessed on 24 August 2015.
58. "4 Suspected ISIS Men Arrested" *The Daily Star*, 20 January 2015.
59. Harmeet Shah Singh and Laura Smith-Spark, "Indian Police Arrest Man Suspected of Running Pro-ISIS Twitter Account", *CNN*, 13 December 2014, available athttp://edition.cnn.com/2014/12/13/world/asia/india-isis-twitter-arrest/, accessed on 27 August 2015.
60. Abhishek Bhalla, "ISIS Goes on Recruitment Spree in India: IM Members Turn Headhunters with Focus on Grooming Youngsters Online", *The Daily Mail*, 31 July 2015, available at http://www.dailymail.co.uk/indiahome/indianews/article-3181759/ISIS-goes-recruitment-spree-India-IM-members-turn-headhunters-focus-grooming-youngsters-online.html, accessed on 25 August 2015.

# 16

# Sino-India Bustle for Securing Hydrocarbons in Africa: Zero-Sum or Win-Win?

*Pranav Kumar*

Energy Security of a nation can best be described as long-term measures to adequately maintain the required supply of energy at all times and at a reasonable price to support its sustained economic, commercial and developmental activities (Kumar 2007: 1). Man's survival has always dependent upon his ability to derive sufficient energy as it is the supply of energy that increases supply of food, improves physical comfort, decides the level of development and expands the quality of his life (Loftness 1998: 3). Unlike traditional security, to have sustainable and sustained energy security many dimensions—economic, political, military, social, cultural, environmental—have to be taken into account and various 'levels', like human, state and systemic have to be factored in (Buzan 1991: 146). Energy security ranges from exploration, production, and transportation, to physical security, strategic reserves and even foreign policy (Malakar 2006: 132). Structural change in the economy, transformation in demographic composition, shift in the government policy for the power generation, increasing defence and space related fuel requirements and growing environmental concerns all these call for strenuous demands on the hydrocarbon sector for the supply of India's and China's energy needs. But faced with inadequate energy production the Asian giants' energy security needs are directly linked with the external supply of the hydrocarbons. India and China increasingly see energy security as a national priority and central aspect of their foreign policy. This is mainly driven by the recognition of the countries' increasing oil and gas import dependence and the need to employ a multi-pronged strategy to address its energy security concerns

(IEA 2005: 244). Energy security is improved by managing energy demand, increasing domestic energy supply, or increasing the reliability of imported or domestic supplies.

## The Asian Giants' Energy Security and Expanding Geopolitical Space

There has not been a single period in modern and industrial history when either European and/or North America have/has not been a major force propelling global economic growth and, in turn, determining the pattern of global energy demands. However, one of the most important visible global trends of twenty-first century is the rise of emerging economies from the South or the East. The BRICS countries—Brazil, Russia, India, China, South Africa—have been a major source of economic growth in the recent past (Kelly 2015). These countries, unlike the West, have been defying stagnant economic growth post the financial crisis and have been growing way faster than the developed world (Kelly 2015). Rise of their share in global economy has been exponentially transforming global energy consumption trajectory wherein their relative share has been zooming with each passing year. The pattern seems to continue in the foreseeable future. The uneven spatial distribution and its persistence centrality in propelling development of major economies of hydrocarbons, it remains to be one of the most significant strategic commodities shaping the geopolitics of the world since early 1970s. Since then the only visible change is that on the place of the West, China and India are leading the demand for hydrocarbons abroad.

China has proved to be the engine pushing global energy demand vigorously. During the two decades following China's opening of its economy in early 1980s, China's economy grew with an averaged 9 per cent (Naidu and Martin 2006: 69). Until early 1990s, China was one of the major oil exporters in the East Asia. Since 1993, however, China has been importing oil. Securing energy sources abroad has become one of the major imperatives of China's 'peaceful rise'. During 1993–9 Chinese policy makers realized that production of oil can no longer meet domestic demand. The Government started to conduct reform to increase competitiveness of the State Owned Enterprises (SOEs) so that they can start to seek oil in foreign markets. Subsequently, under the slogans of "Go global" during 2000–8, and "Go abroad and buy" (Jian 2011: 6), China has been aggressively pursuing its hydrocarbon diplomacy, mainly with the help of SOEs and track-one channels. China has become the second largest importer of energy (Zweig and Jianhai 2005: 25). The US Department of energy expects that China's imported oil will climb to 9.4 million per day by 2025 (Zahirinejad and Vrushal 2010: 63). IEA's projection predicts that around 2030 China is going to overtake the European Union in gas consumption (IEA 2014a).

Similarly, for India, a country that has been defying trends of global economic meltdown at the large extant and has been growing at a brisk pace; no other factor would be more pertinent than to support its economic growth with sustained supply of resources—natural and human—at affordable price. Needless to mention that securing constant flow of energy ranks the highest amongst all. Despite the fact that the energy source diversification has been high on India's agenda and her domestic hydrocarbon production bases are expanding, more than 80 per cent of its hydrocarbon energy demand is being fulfilled by the external sources. Thirty per cent of India's energy needs are fulfilled by oil and around 70 per cent of oil is imported. The IEA predicts that in order to nourish present growth, India will have to increase its energy consumption by 3.6 per cent annually. India's energy demand is to double by 2015, compelling it to import 90 per cent of its hydrocarbon supply (Hate 2015).

The dependence on imported oil is not going to end in foreseeable future; it may well increase, judging by the Integrated Energy Policy, which projects import dependence in excess of 90 per cent for crude oil, up to 50 per cent for natural gas, and up to 45 per cent for coal (Desai 2013). During the four decades since 1970s, i.e. from 1970–71 to 2010–11, the Compound Annual Growth Rate (CAGR) of production of coal, lignite, crude petroleum, natural gas, and electricity (hydro and nuclear) generation was 5.0 per cent, 6.1 per cent, 4.3 per cent, 9.1 per cent, and 4.0 per cent respectively. In terms of energy equivalent of all the primary energy sources in 2010-11, the shares of coal and lignite, electricity (hydro and nuclear), and natural gas were 52 per cent, 28 per cent and 11 per cent respectively (GOI 2013: 233).

Domestic annual production of crude oil has been stagnant at around 38 million tonnes in the last four years (GOI 2015: 98). Faced with inadequate energy production India's energy security needs are directly linked with the external supply in the vital energy sectors with special emphasis will remain on hydrocarbons. The vagaries of petroleum supply from the Persian Gulf and over dependence on the region create an atmosphere of insecurity for India and hamper its economic and developmental prospects. Even though the global price of oil has been dwindling of late, the unreliability in the supply pattern of the Persian Gulf emanates from the dynamics of regional geopolitics, internal political instability, use of production as a strategic commodity and the proactive role played by oil cartel OPEC in the region.

In the last few years Indian policy-makers have recognized the fact that increased dependence on the Persian Gulf for oil supply can impede India's vital security interests. India has been keen to diversify her petroleum supply options. The diverse supply patterns would reduce her sense of vulnerability against any supply disruption. In view of an unfavourable demand-supply ratio of hydrocarbons in the country, acquiring equity oil and gas assets overseas has been an important strategy for enhancing energy security for last ten years or so. The government is encouraging state-owned companies to purchase oil from foreign sources (Roy-Choudhary 1998: 1671) and to aggressively pursue equity oil and gas opportunities overseas. ONGC Videsh Limited (OVL) has produced about 8.753 MMT of oil and equivalent gas during the year 2011–2 from its assets abroad in Sudan, Vietnam, Venezuela, Russia, Syria, Brazil, South Sudan, and Colombia (GOI 2013: 239).

## Rise of Africa on Global Hydrocarbon Map

Africa's rise on global hydrocarbons map is parallel and complementary to the skyrocketing external energy demand of India and China. Africa is rich in energy resources. Even the most conservative estimates are to be believed; Africa accounts for 10 per cent of the world's oil reserves; 8 per cent of the natural gas reserves; 5 per cent of the coal reserves; 38 per cent of uranium reserves; and 12 per cent of global technical hydropower potential (Sikhwati 2009). Almost 30 per cent of global oil and gas discoveries made over the last five years (2009–14) were in the continent. Rising output from Nigeria, Angola and a host of smaller producers, means that sub-Saharan Africa remains an important source of global oil supply. The region emerges also as an important player in gas, as development of the major east coast discoveries off Mozambique and Tanzania accompanies increased production in Nigeria and elsewhere (IEA 2014b). According to International Energy Agency (IEA), Oil production in Africa will exceed 6 million barrels per day (mb/d) in 2020 before slightly falling back to 5.3 mb/d in 2040. The countries that will lead the African production would be Nigeria and Angola. Demand for oil products is supposed to double to 4 mb/d in 2040, and Gas output reaches 230 billion cubic metres (bcm), led by Nigeria, and increasing output from Mozambique, Tanzania and Angola. LNG exports will triple to around 95 billion cubic meter (bcm) (IEA 2014a).

The Gulf of Guinea, an arm of Atlantic Ocean, has a large amount of hydrocarbon energy resources. Eleven African Countries—Ivory Coast, Ghana, Benin, Togo, Nigeria, Cameroon, Gabon, Equatorial Guinea, Democratic Republic of Congo, Republic of Congo and Sao Tome and Principe share its continental shelf. Among these, Nigeria, Gabon and Cameroon are major petroleum producers. Furthermore, Angola which can also be considered to be an extension of the Gulf is the second most important oil producer in Africa. Until very recently the oil discoveries, exploration and production in sub-Saharan Africa (with the exception of Chad and Sudan) has been found in countries located along the Atlantic coast. While prospects for oil in Namibia and South Africa look promising, and while oil has been found in the waters off Mauritania, most of the major known reserves of any magnitude are concentrated in an area that spans the Atlantic littoral from Nigeria to Angola. Moreover, the crude oil from the region is of very high quality, i.e. light and with low sulphur content. Furthermore most of oil in the region is found and extracted from open sea platforms that are offshore, far away from the dire and often troubled mainland of the respective states (Kumar 2007: 83).

Nigeria is Africa's largest oil producer. The proven oil reserves of the country are approximately 30 billion barrels and it produces approximately 2 million barrel per day of crude oil (Beri 2005: 374). Approximately 65 per cent of Nigerian crude oil production is light and sweet, making it particularly suited in the context of growing environmental concerns (Valle 2004: 53). Nigeria has the potential to increase its crude oil production significantly in the next few years as recent deep-water discoveries come on stream. Existing and new producers, such as Angola, Gabon, Equatorial Guinea and São Tomé and Príncipe, are going to continue to develop new oil and gas reserves in the coming years. The Petroleum industry is the principal economic mainstay of Angola (Hughes 2006: 81). Angola has estimated reserves of 1.6 trillion cubic feet of natural gas (IEA 2006: 133).

The North African country Algeria holds the third-largest amount of proven crude oil reserves in Africa, all of which are located onshore because there has been limited offshore exploration. According to Sonatrach, about two-thirds of Algerian territory remains largely underexplored or unexplored. According to the *Oil & Gas Journal* (OGJ) estimates, released in January 2014, Algeria held an estimated 12.2 billion barrels of proved crude oil reserves (EIA 2014: 5). EIA Study also estimates that Algeria contains 707 trillion cubic feet (Tcf) and 5.7 billion barrels of technically recoverable shale gas and oil resources (EIA 2014; 2). The country's all of proved and unexplored oil reserves are held onshore because there has been limited offshore exploration.

West and North Africa has long held the spotlight as a major oil province, but recent discoveries in other areas of the continent have catapulted Africa on the global energy map. Barely appearing on the energy radar until very recently, eastern Africa has become one of the world's hottest spots for oil and natural gas reserves. Beyond Tullow's success in Uganda, the offshore East Africa is attracting attention from various international players. With successes in Mozambique and potential growing in Tanzania, Kenya and Madagascar, East Africa is emerging as a new hydrocarbon province. During past 10 years, East Africa, on account of its offshore and onshore discoveries, has emerged as the world's most promising hydrocarbon frontier. 2.3 billion barrels of recoverable oil have been discovered in Uganda and Kenya; and more than 50 tcf natural gas in Tanzania (Manson 2015).

## Under Shadow of the Red Star

China has a much larger presence in Africa than India, in terms of both acquiring energy deals and government engagement. Chinese oil companies have been investing heavily in the continent. For instance, in Nigeria the Chinese oil giant China's National Offshore Oil Corporation (CNOOC) has owned a 45 per cent stake in deepwater block Offshore Mining License (OML) 130 since 2009 (Europetrole 2009). Furthermore, as a part of purchase of Nexen— a Canadian country—by CNOOC clinched significant offshore oil reserves in Nigeria. Yet another Chinese company CNPC has purchased shares in Nigeria, buying rights to blocks OPL 298, 471, 721, and 732 from the Nigerian government in 2006. This purchase was followed by a purchase of the rights to blocks OML 64 and OML 66 in 2012. The Chinese oil giant Sinopec also has made inroads in Nigeria, including a deal with Total to pay $2.5 billion for a 20 per cent share in block OML 138 in 2012 (Patel 2012). Almost all of these investments by Chinese companies are in buying shares in blocks, not sole control, so the Chinese often rely on their partners to do most of the actual production work for them, releasing them from the technological demands that come with offshore drilling. While there are a number of onshore fields that Chinese companies have stakes in, most of the oil-rich fields are offshore, so they are not quite as vulnerable to the population of the areas hurting their production (Quigle 2014).

Angola has emerged as one of the major African partners accounting for lion's share. China has made a large amount of diversified oil investments in Angola, spending over $92 billion between 2009 and 2012 in joint ventures and energy acquisition (Quigle 2014). Overall, the Chinese oil companies are operating in nearly 20 African countries in both the upstream and downstream activities (IDE-JETRO 2015). However, the state-owned companies are the major actors that China is using for venturing in the continent.

## India's Engagements

As part of its international strategy to diversify suppliers, the government's oil exploration and production enterprise, the Oil and National Gas Corporation (ONGC), has ventured into Africa. Nigeria is already India's second largest supplier, with 15 per cent of the share. ONGC Videsh, the international arm of the agency, has acquired shares in oil exploration ventures in Libya and Nigeria. It has also made substantial investments in Sudan's hydrocarbon sector and plans to invest in offshore drilling in the Ivory Coast. Reliance Industries, one of India's largest privately held energy companies, is also negotiating energy collaborations for refining with several African countries including Angola and Nigeria. In 2010–11, India imported 20,726 million USD worth of crude oil from Africa, accounting for 21.6 per cent of India's total crude oil imports (Department of

Commerce 2013). Nigeria, followed by Angola, commanded a major share of this, accounting for 50.85 and 24.5 per cent respectively. These nations are followed by Algeria, Egypt and Libya together contributing around 17.5 per cent of India's oil import.

**Table 1.1: India's Crude Oil Imports from Africa (2010–1)**

| *S.No.* | *Country* | *Values in US$ million* | *% Share of Africa* | *% Share of total import* |
|---|---|---|---|---|
| 1. | Nigeria | 10,536.92 | 50.85 | 11.37 |
| 2. | Angola | 5,089.12 | 24.5 | 5.49 |
| 3. | Algeria | 1,704.30 | 8.2 | 1.84 |
| 4. | Egypt | 983.82 | 4.75 | 1.10 |
| 5. | Libya | 961 | 4.6 | 1.04 |
| 6. | Sudan | 565.77 | 3 | 0.61 |
| 7. | Congo P Rep | 478.65 | 2.3 | 0.52 |
| 8. | Gabon | 211.85 | 1 | 0.23 |
| 9. | Cameroon | 117.98 | 0.5 | 0.13 |
| 10. | Guinea | 76.83 | 0.3 | 0.08 |
| | **Total: Africa** | 20,726.62 | 100 | 22.4 |
| | **Total: Import** | 92,651.77 | | |

*Source:* Compiled from export import data bank, http://commerce.nic.in/eidb/ecntq.asp

Apart from the import, ONGC Videsh (OVL) has been one of the most active public sector companies in Africa. The company has its exploration projects in Africa, one in Libya, two in Nigeria, one in Egypt and one in JDZ: Nigeria-STP. There are also two production projects which are in Sudan (one of them is the Greater Nile project). The main countries of interest with confirmed reserves of oil are Angola, Nigeria, Equatorial Guinea, Ghana, Cote d'Ivoire, and Sierra Leone. The projects in Sudan are currently the only examples of state-owned companies extracting hydrocarbons. The other public sector companies in Africa are Oil India Limited (OIL), Bharat Petroleum (BP) and Hindustan Petroleum (HP). Oil India Ltd has interests in three blocks in Libya, two in Egypt and one in Nigeria, Bharat Petro Resources has interests in a block in Mozambique and Hindustan Petroleum has interests in two Egyptian blocks (Deccan Herald 2011). Bharat Petro Resources also announced a major natural gas discovery offshore Mozambique in 2010 (Kulkarni 2010).

Unlike the Chinese case, the Indian private sector has also been making inroad into the oil and gas sector in Africa. Reliance Industries, India's largest private sector player in the energy sector made its first major overseas acquisition through buying a majority stake and management control of Gulf Africa Petroleum Corporation (GAPCO) in 2007 (ENS Economic Bureau 2007). Another private sector company, Essar Energy Overseas Limited has a 50 per cent stake in the

Kenya Petroleum Refineries Limited since 2009. Both RIL and Essar have been bidding to acquire assets of British Petroleum in Zambia, Malawi, Botswana, Namibia and Tanzania (Barman 2010).

## Zero-Sum Game

The main driver for both Asian giants in Africa is energy. Interestingly, it is against the backdrop of Africa's energy landscape that India and China have started seriously engaging Africa. They have been competing against each other for the African Oil. Nonetheless, India has lost several lucrative oil deals to China and so far India seemingly lacks the obstinate strategic drive that Beijing has skilfully displayed in the African continent (Hate 2015). For instance, Sinopec prevailed over India's state-owned ONGC-Videsh Limited (OVL) to acquire Shell Oil's 50 per cent stake in Block 18 in Angola, operated by BP-Amoco. To ease out Indian bid China used 'carrot policy', by extending US$2 billion loan to Angolan government and by partnering in reviving Lobito refinery (IDE-JETRO 2015).

## Win–Win Scenario

**Partnership**: India and China have also cooperated in hydrocarbon sector. One of the earliest ventures in Africa by India and China was joint venture. In 1997, China National Petroleum Corporation (CNPC) and Oil and Natural Gas Corporation, the state owned companies of India and China respectively, jointly ventured in the Greater Nile Oil Project (GNOPC) alongside Sudan's Supdapet and Malaysia's Petronas (IDE-JETRO 2015). Even though today the venture may not be considered as a great success story as the region has been marred by civil discontent in which Chinese role has also been sensed, it proves that political will and complimentary interest can pave the way for cooperation between perceived competitors (Tiezzi 2015).

**Balancing the Energy Order in Africa:** Energy sector of Africa has been considered as theatre of the East-West rivalry and indicator of shifting geopolitical and geo-economic focus from the West to the East. Analogous to the 'New Great Game' being played in the other oil rich regions, Africa has also been kept on witnessing a scramble for hydrocarbon resources that includes a number of stakeholders. Earlier it was the colonial powers which were active there. Later, during the cold war, America and other western players started to make inroads there in a big way. During last two decades China's and India's entry to the region has compounded the scenario. Like the Gulf of Guinea and other onshore oil rich regions, Asian state-owned oil companies are making forays in the contest for East Africa's energy reserves and are gaining power in export projects that Western explorers used to dominate earlier (Mining Review 2013). China and

India have been entering to the region via joint ventures (equity shares). China has forged joint ventures with a number of local state-owned companies so that it can remain to be close to policymakers of the country. This has been evident in joint ventures with Nigerian National Petroleum Corporation (Nigeria), Sonangol (Angola), Sonatrach (Algeria), Sudapet (Sudan). Moreover, China and India have been involved in upstream and downstream activities of hydrocarbon rich countries. For instance, China has been involved in hydrocarbon related upstream activities in at least 20 countries and in downstream activities in at least half a dozen countries (Mining Review 2013). Hence, unlike the western model, they have redefined the nature of engagement with the oil producing countries by linking hydrocarbon sector with overall development of the region.

**South-South Cooperation:** Oil Geopolitics in the region, like other oil rich regions, is closely associated with intervention and interference of external forces, countries, multinational companies, and multilateral international bodies in the domestic spheres. In this context oil companies have played a pivotal role and the French company Elf's intervention in the region is a striking example of this fact.[1] The costs of oil imports include political ties to unstable countries. Prospects of those countries achieving greater political stability simply by acquiring oil wealth are slim, as historical experience amply demonstrates (La Vine 2004: 18). More often, oil wealth has triggered power struggles among governmental, socio-political and industrial fractions. Such rivalries, social divisions and developmental distortions can threaten price and supply stability and incur escalating protection cost. As fights over oil revenues become the reason for ratcheting up the level of pre-existing conflict in a society, oil may even become the very rationale for starting wars. This is especially true of economies that are not stable, as is the case of the continent. Petroleum revenues are also a central mechanism for prolonging violent conflict, and only rarely a catalyst for resolution.[2]

The West's involvement in Africa has provoked much debate and discussion. The involvement of the western energy hunters has been scrutinized on the ground that whether their energy relationship in the Gulf is based on 'Core-Periphery' model or they are also interested in overall development of the region? Although, China has been proclaiming that her engagement with Africa is based on principles of 'south-south cooperation' and 'all weathered friendship' (Kumar 2015: 189), China's footprints in Africa have also been perceived as asymmetrically skewed in favour of China. China's dubious role has been discerned and deliberated upon in Sudan. India, however, riding on its public sector enterprises, has been more carefully crafting its energy engagement with Africa. Indian and Chinese policy makers have been conscious of the fact that this sort of image may hurt their Energy security and overall prospects in Africa very badly in long term and can loom large on their relations with the continent and elsewhere. India's Energy

Security is cardinal to its relation with the region. At any cost it cannot be groomed on the shaky normative grounds of 'Dependency' and 'Neocolonialism'. They must adhere to the framework of "South-South Cooperation". Initiatives taken under the aegis of BRICS may be instrumental in this context in near future.

**Securing Energy Sea Lane of Communications (SLOCs):** So far as assuring uninterrupted supply of African hydrocarbon to their home is concerned, for both the countries energy security and maritime strategy are irrevocably intertwined (Jacob 137). One facet of energy security though well-known but the implications of which are usually not fully appreciated, is the fact that almost all the hydrocarbon acquired in Africa is transported by sea lanes (Desai 2013). The Sea Lanes of Communication (SLOCs) are channels through which goods, energy and to some extent people are transported from one state to another. The sea-bound transportation of goods and commodities is an essential component of the contemporary world's transnational and international interactions.

The protection of sea lanes has been one of the essential components of energy security of both the countries. As Mahan narrates, 'the necessity of a navy, in the restricted sense, springs from the existence of peaceful shipping' (Mahan 2004: 29). Sea power protected vital commercial flows when other, more peaceful, methods had failed (Blunden 2012: 117). Today, more than 90 per cent of intercontinental trade and two thirds of the all hydrocarbon supplies transverse through sea (Kaplan 2010: 7).

Uninterrupted supply of hydrocarbons from Africa to both the countries has been closely linked with the protection of its SLOCs and the effectiveness of navy in the Indian Ocean. China's has been expanding its influence in Indian Ocean and protection of its SLOCs has been main imperative of its 'vertical ambitions' (Raja Mohan 2013: 110–1). The future projections of emerging patterns of the Sea Lanes of Communications (SLOCs) augur that the region is going to be more significant during the foreseeable future, wherein the Indian Ocean will remain to be important trade route. India, being a major geostrategic player in the region and owing to its geographical location, is bound to face plethora of challenges and is supposed to get scores of opportunities under the backdrop of the undergoing situation and future scenario.

## Conclusion

From the perspective of energy security, Africa has emerged as a happy but strenuous hunting ground for both India and China. The two Asian countries have been successful in loosening the western Multinational Companies' noose on Africa's hydrocarbons. So far as their energy diplomacy in Africa is concerned, they have been anticipated as rivals in the second largest continent. This assumption, nonetheless, is not misplaced as there have been numerous instances in which they found themselves in a zero-sum pay-off matrix. On the contrary, however, there have been occasions, although handful in number, wherein both the countries forged effective cooperative ventures to extract hydrocarbons. Although miles to go, they are learning to calibrate their diplomatic tools in order to balance their acts in Africa in energy sector by co-operating when it is possible and by competing when necessary. Geopolitics of African hydrocarbons pits the Asian giants in the game of 'prisoners dilemma' wherein strangeness can be detrimental to meaningful cooperation but repeated interaction and an apt assessment of ground realities may induce congruous synergy. The trans-regional international institutional frameworks like BRICS and philosophy of 'South-South Cooperation' can be a guiding force in transcending 'zero-sum' situation into a 'win-win' scenario. There has been no big difference when it comes to the normative framework that guides their engagement in Africa. However, when it comes to execution there has always been a big mismatch between the strategies adopted by India, a doer, and China, a preacher, in Africa.

## NOTES

1. Because of the presence of oil, among other reasons, France covertly supported the secession of Biafra where the petroleum was located. Elf was asked to pay the royalties to Biafra instead of Nigeria. The money was used to buy weapons and fuel the war on account of humanitarianism. The Gabon became, for a long period, heart of the oil empire of Elf. This explains the leading position of the country and of its president within Francophone Africa. Equatorial Guinea is an emerging producer; while the productions of Gabon and of Cameroon are stagnating, the productions of Congo are on the rise, and this increases the strategic importance of Angola from a geopolitical point of view. Elf has been directly involved in the civil war in Congo-Brazzaville and more indirectly in Angola financing or helping simultaneously and successively both camps. The civil war in Congo, between the former Marxist President, Sassou Nguesso and Pascal Lissouba, the newly elected one, was related to the process of democratic transition. Elf has been massively helping financially and militarily to regain the power by its friendly forces in these countries. For detail see http://www.icai-online.org/xp_resources/icai//oil_companies//elf_oilandwar.pdf accessed on 13 May 2005.
2. See Fearon, James D, "Why Do Some Civil Wars Last So Much Longer than Others?" paper presented to 'Civil Wars and Post Conflict Transition,' University of California, Irvine, May 18-20, 2001. This study includes data from 122 civil wars between 1945-1999.

## REFERENCES


Barman, Arjit (4 August 2010), "RIL, Essar to bid for BP's African Petrol Pumps," *Business Standard*, 22 August 2015, http://www.business-standard.com/article/companies/ril-essar-to-bid-for-bp-s-african-petrol-pumps-110080400092_1.html.

Beri, Ruchita (2005), "Africa's Energy Potential: Prospects for India" *Strategic Analysis* ( New Delhi), vol. 29 no. 3 July – September 2005.

Blunden, Margaret (2012), "Geopolitics and the Northern Sea Route," *International Affairs*, vol. 88 (1), p. 117.

Buzan, Barry (1991), *People, States and Fear: An Agenda For International Security Studies in the Post-Cold War Era*, 2e, Hertfordshire, Harvester Wheatsheaf.

Deccan Herald (4 September 2011), "India's Interest Growing in African Oil, Gas Assets," *Deccanherald.com,* 22 August 2015, http://www.deccanherald.com/content/188348/indias-interests-growing-african-oil.html

Department of Commerce (Government of India) (2012), *Export Import Data Bank*, 3 April 2013, http://commerce.nic.in/eidb/ecntq.asp

Desai, Nitin (17 April 2013), "How to Secure India's Energy," *The Times of India*, 20 April 2013, http://www.business-standard.com/article/opinion/how-to-secure-india-s-energy-113041700600_1.html

Europetrole (12 March 2009), "CNOOC Limited Announces Start-up of OML130 in Nigeria," *Europetrole*, 22 August 2015, http://www.euro-petrole.com/cnooc-ltd-announces-start-up-of-oml130-in-nigeria-n-i-2078

ENS Economic Bureau (4 September 2007), "In First Major Foreign Foray Reliance Buys Gulf Africa Petroleum," *Indianexpress.com*, 22 August 2015, http://archive.indianexpress.com/news/in-first-major-foreign-foray-reliance-buys-gulf-africa-petroleum-/214536/

Government of India (GOI) (2013), *Economic Survey 2012-13*, New Delhi, Ministry of Finance.

Government of India (GOI) (2015), *Economic Survey 2014-15,* Vol. II, New Delhi, Ministry of Finance.

Hate, Vibhuti (22 August 2015), "India in Africa: Beyond Oil," Centre for Strategic and International Studies, 22 August 2015, http://csis.org/story/india-africa-moving-beyond-oil

Hughes, John (2006), "Economy," *Africa South of Sahara 2007*, London, Routledge.

Institute of Developing Economies-Japan External Trade Organization (IDE-JETRO) (2015), *China in Africa*, 22 August 2015, IDE-JETRO, http://www.ide.go.jp/English/Data/Africa_file/Manualreport/cia.html

International Energy Agency (IEA) (2005), *Energy Policies of IEA countries: 2005 review,* Paris, Organisation for Economic Co-operation and Development (OECD) Publication.

IEA (2006), *World Energy Outlook 2006*, Paris, OECD Publication.

IEA (2014a), "Africa Energy Outlook," *World Energy Outlook 2014*, Paris, OECD Publication.

IEA (2014b), "Executive Summery," *World Energy Outlook* 2014, Paris, OECD Publication.

Jacob, P.J. (2006), "Maritime aspects of Energy Security and the Gulf", in Malakar, S.N., ed., *India's Energy Security and the Gulf*, Delhi, Academic Excellence, pp. 137–8.

Kaplan, Robert D. (2010), *Monsoon: The Indian Ocean and the Future of American Power*, New York, Random House Trade Paperbacks.

Kelly, Evan (21 August 2015), "This Week in Energy: A Dangerous Trend is Emerging," *oilprice.Com*, 22 August 2015, http://oilprice.com/Energy/Energy-General/This-Week-In-Energy-A-Dangerous-Global-Trend-Emerging.html

Kumar Pranav (2015), "Dragon's Footprints in Africa: Diplomacy and Dilemmas," China Yearbook 2014, New Delhi, Magnum Book Pvt Ltd, pp. 189–98.

Kumar, Pranav (2007), *India's Energy Security: Potential of the Gulf of Guinea*, Unpublished Ph.D. Thesis submitted to Centre for West Asian and African Studies, School of International Studies, Jawaharlal Nehru University, New Delhi.

Kulkarni, S.V. (25 November 2010), "BPCL Announces Major Natural Gas Discoveries in Offshore Mozambique," A Communication to Secretary, Bombay Stock Exchange Ltd from S.V. Kulkarni, Company Secretary, BPCL, Bharat Petroleum Corporation Ltd., 22 August 2015, http://www.petrowatch.com/BPCL291110.pdf

La Vine, Victor T.(2004), *Politics in Francophone Africa*, Boulder, Lynne Rienner Publication.

Loftness, Robert L. (1998), *Energy Handbook*, New York, Van Nostrand Reinhold.

Mahan, A.T. (2004 ), *The Influence of Sea Power upon History, 1660–1783*, Project Gutenberg eBook, release date 26 Nov. 2004 (first pub. 1890).

Malakar, S. N. (2006), *India's Energy Security and the Gulf*, Delhi, Academic Excellence.

Manson, Katrina (12 February 2015), "Falling Crude Price Hits Prospects for East Africa," 22 August 2015, ft.com, http://www.ft.com/cms/s/0/0961f6a2-b13c-11e4-831b-00144feab7de.html#axzz3jbXUAiOV

Mining Review (18 April 2013), "Asia Makes Inroads in Contest for East African Energy Reserves," 18 April 2013, http://www.miningreview.com/node/22092

Naidu, Sanusha and Martyn Davies (2006), "China Fuels its Future with Africa's Riches", *South African Journal of International Affairs*, Vol.13, Issue 2,winter/spring, 2006

Patel, Tara (19 November 2012), "Total Sell Nigeria Oil Field to Sinopec for $2.5 Billion," *Bloomberg.com*, 23 August 2015, http://www.bloomberg.com/news/articles/2012-11-19/total-sells-nigeria-oil-field-to-sinopec-for-2-5-billion

Quigley, Sam (01 June 2014), "Chinese Oil Acquisition in Nigeria and Angola," The American University in Cairo, 22 August 2015, http://www.aucegypt.edu/huss/pols/khamasin/Pages/article.aspx?eid=14

Raja Mohan, C. (2013), "China Eyes the Indian Ocean," *Samudra Mandhan: Sino-Indian Rivalry in the Indo-Pacific*, New Delhi, OUP.

Roy-Choudhary, Rahul (1998), "An Energy Security Policy for India: The Case of Oil and Natural Gas," *Strategic Analysis*, Feb 1998.

Shikwati, James (2009),"Africa as a new frontier", in R. Beri & U.K. Sinha,eds., *Africa and Energy Security: Global Issues, Local Responses*, New Delhi: Academic Foundation, pp. 41–2.

Tiezzi, Shannon (13 January 2015), China in South Sudan: Practical Responsibility, *The Diplomat*, 23 August 2015, http://thediplomat.com/2015/01/china-in-south-sudan-practical-responsibility/

# 17

# Great Game in Central Asia: Where Does India Stands?

*Pramod Kumar Sharma*

In July 2015, Prime Minister Narendra Modi became the first Indian Prime Minister to visit all the five countries of Central Asia since 1990, giving a clear indication that India under the new Government is determined to develop a new bound of ties with the countries of Central Asia. Needless to add, these countries have assumed huge significance for India for various reasons, one being the fact that they can prove to be instrument in meeting India's growing energy requirement in the coming years. The CAR region has also risen to prominence in the backdrop of "Operation Enduring Freedom" launched in 2001 as far as the global efforts against counter-terrorism is concerned. It is in this context that this chapter attempts to understand the significance of Central Asia for India and to examine as to what extent India and the Countries of Central Asia have been able to deepen and expand their relations.

## II

India is the 5$^{th}$ largest global energy consumer and will become the 3$^{rd}$ largest country by 2020. The prevailing anarchy in the Middle East, which has remained an important source of natural oil and gas for us, has caused concerns for India. At the same time, containing terror and drug trafficking have emerged another areas of common interests between CAS and India. Nursing the ambitions of emerging global power it is our moral duty to ensure peace and stability in this extended neighborhood. The Central Asian republics of Kazakhstan, Kyrgyzstan,

Tajikistan, Turkmenistan and Uzbekistan became independent in the 1990s. Since then, these countries have remained diplomatically engaged with India. In fact, New Delhi has developed strategic partnership with three of the five republics. In 2012, India announced the 'Connect Central Asia' policy and also announced to hold an India-Central Asia Dialogue at Track II annually in one of the republics. These measures have indeed contributed significantly in strengthening India's bilateral relations with the countries of Central Asia. For Instance, the recent inauguration of Kazakhstan-Turkmenistan-Iran railway line has given the region a short access to the Indian Ocean. India, on the other hand, has been making investment in Iran's Chabahar port. This alternative route has eased the business connectivity between the outside world with this region. This route has provided an alternative route to Afghanistan and reduced its dependence over Pakistan (Karachi port). Central Asia has already been connected by Zarnej–Delaram road constructed by India in Afghanistan and linked to Chabahar port. The BJP-led Government under the Prime Minstership of Narendra Modi in 2014 has already outlined its foreign policy priorities, in which Central Asia acquires a special place. This became very apparent in July 2015 when Prime Minister Modi visited all five nation states of CAR.

## III

From the onset of the Cold War till the disintegration of the USSR, the Countries of Central Asia remained under the control of the Soviet bloc. However, the collapse of the Soviet Union freed these countries to choose a new path for their future. In addition, Central Asia's stature further got scaled up in the international era, given the fact that other countries view this part of the world very crucial in securing access oil and gas. In fact, since the late 1990s, the International Energy Agency has viewed Central Asia as one of the largest undeveloped energy reserves in the world, especially for the production of oil and natural gas.[1] Given increasingly pressing problems with energy supply and its sequential impact on the global economy as we enter the 21st century, Central Asia has become a more significant region for energy studies. The five Central Asian nations of Kazakhstan, Kyrgyzstan, Tajikistan, Uzbekistan and Turkmenistan have emerged firmly onto the global energy stage.[2] Since the end of the last century, Barry Buzan, who co-worked with Wæver and de Wilde, has suggested five distinct sectors of security concern in the contemporary era: military, political, economic, environment and societal. "Economic" security naturally includes the securing of natural resources.[3]

To facilitate energy competition in the region, the major powers have found it increasingly necessary to rationalize their ambitions ideologically. The United States works from a platform of liberal democracy and "human rights above sovereignty", Russia proffers its own idea of "sovereign democracy" to the Central Asians, and China portrays itself as a non-interventionist "responsible state" in the region. As one of the powers in the region, India lacks a unique ideology to increase its influence in Central Asia. However, India may play the cocktail of soft and hard power and under the dynamic leadership of Prime Minister Modi India can effectively exercise the amalgam of soft and hard power in Central Asia in order to serve its national interests.

From the perspective of nation-states, interests always trump ideologies because blindly following ideologies could result in deviation from national interests. If the two are in conflict, excessively fanatical ideological pursuit would be discouraged; and reporting of the regime's sacrificing the mere pursuit of ideologies would be toned down. Ideologies energy diplomacy has to retain flexibility for the regimes: that is the general acceptance in the home countries housing the energy resources. Without showing concern for the actual situation, fanatically following ideologies can go against the national interest, just as an authentic follower of Marxism can go against the perceived national interests of a Marxist government.[4] In statist regimes, excessively fanatical ideological pursuit would be discouraged; in less state-centric regimes, reports of the regimes' sacrificing the ideological pursuit would also be toned down. In other words, without the energy concerns, it is difficult to preach these ideologies with any sincerity on their own and once their dogmatic interpretations no longer serve state interests, they are effectively redundant.

## IV

Scholarly interest in Central Asia, which is commonly perceived as "landlocked, poor, peripheral, fearful, defenseless, Muslim, and undemocratic", has become widespread since the five republics gained independence.[5] There are many aspects to the importance of the region. Some scholars stress the significance of its Islamic religion while discussing security issues in Central Asia.[6] for some, geopolitics plays a greater role in the region, which has been described as the "second Persian Gulf", the new "grand chessboard", the "heartland of the heartland" or the "Great Game II".[7] The Cold War complex also haunts the republics. Despite this unease, energy politics seem to be of the greatest concern on this grand chessboard. Of the global powers that have prime energy interests in the region, the US, Russia and China are the leading competing forces, although nations such as Japan and India also have their sights on the region.[8]

Various studies on energy encroachment in Central Asia share two common assumptions: the stakeholders are rationalist-based, and realist- or neo-realist-orientated.[9] Although early scholars and realist practitioners may not have obviously included economic concerns in their works, latecomers have started featuring energy resources in the political realist analysis of international relations.

Gilpin regards Thucydides' work on the History of the Peloponnesian War to be partially driven by energy competition; at that time it was wheat to fuel human bodies.[10] In the contemporary world, natural oil and gas has become the lifeline of energy and India is growing rapidly. Thus, how India will cop up with these challenges, it is an important challenge before Modi government is to ensure uninterrupted energy supply to accelerate India's economic growth in coming decades.

Given the policies used by the US, Russia and China, one may well question whether another great power candidate adjacent to Central Asia, i.e. India, could apply the same strategy. Undoubtedly, India also has strong interests in Central Asia. As the second largest growing economy in the world, India relies heavily on energy imports to sustain its domestic economic expansion. According to the International Energy Outlook, India was the fifth largest oil consumer in 2007 and its demand grew to almost 3 million barrels per day (bbl/d) in 2008.[11] In 2009, 68 percent of its oil was imported, and its dependency on oil imports is expected to increase to 92 percent by 2020.[12] In this context, considerable progress by India to obtaining Central Asian resources has been made. For instance, since 2004, India has invested US$3 billion in the Sakhalin-3 oil field and the joint Russian-Kazakh Kurmangazy oil field in Central Asia. India also signed an agreement with Uzbekistan to launch a US$60 million joint venture for India's state-owned gas utility.[13]

The countries of Central Asia are endowed with significant hydrocarbon and mineral resources and are close to India geographically. Kazakhstan is the largest producer of uranium and has huge gas and oil reserves as well. Similarly, Uzbekistan is also rich in gas, and is an important regional producer of gold along with Kyrgyzstan. Tajikistan has vast hydropower potential besides oil deposits, and Turkmenistan has the fourth largest gas reserves of the world. Geographically, the strategic location of these countries makes them a bridge between different regions of Asia and between Europe and Asia. Although the significance of the region in India's economic and energy security is clear, lack of direct surface connectivity has been affecting the economic engagement. However, the recent inauguration of Kazakhstan-Turkmenistan-Iran railway line has given the region a short access to the Indian Ocean. India, on the other hand, has been making investment in Iran's Chabahar port. This alternative route has eased the business connectivity of the outside world with the region.[14]

India and Iran have already got connected in Central Asia through this port while construction of the Delaram-Jarnej road in western Afghanistan will further improve connective between India and Central Asia. In fact, in April 2015, India's Surface Transport Minister Nitin Gadkari during his visit to Iran stressed on the point that the newly developed Chahbhar port jointly built by India & Iran can prove to be instrumental in cementing relations between India and Central Asian countries. Prime Minister Modi's visit to this part of the world further witnessed many bilateral agreements ranging from energy supply to defense cooperation. Iranian President Rouhani and Indian Prime Minister Modi met in Ufa (Russia) in July 2015 and had a 90 minutes bilateral talk. During this meeting it was pledged that India and Iran will accelerate their bilateral relations. In July 2015, Iran and the western world have I inked a nuclear deal and now the whole gamut of the decade long sanctions imposed against Iran will gradually be lifted. In August 2015, Iranian Foreign Minister Javad Zarif visited New Delhi and met Prime Minister Modi and other ministers. Again it was reiterated that cooperation on all fronts will be accelerated. During one day visit of Mr. Zarif issues related to Islamic State threat, energy investments, Afghanistan and development of the Chabhahar port were discussed. He also stated that India is an important player in West Asia. Prime Minister Modi 'conveyed India's commitment to work with Iran for development of the Chabhahar port that would have far reaching benefit, not only for the people of India and Iran, but also for Afghanistan and the entire the Central Asian region. Mr. Zarif acknowledged India's support during turbulent times. It is expected that Prime Minister Modi may visit Tehran in early months of 2016.[15] Iran has enormous energy reserves therefore relationship between the two countries took a natural way of deepening. India is currently 5$^{th}$ largest global energy consumer and by 2022 will be 3$^{rd}$ largest energy consumer leaving Japan and Russia behind. It is also opined by sections of global economic pundits that by 2042 India will be representing 23% of the global GDP. For the sustainability of India's growth saga, sustainable and diverse supply of energy is a must.

Iran is not only important for fulfilling India's energy needs but due to its geographical proximity it is emerging India's gateway to Central Asia. In addition, due to the connections between regional terrorist groups in Central Asia and the insurgents in Kashmir and the Punjab, the region's cooperation is seen as instrumental to India's anti-terrorist security. India is also seen by the Central Asian countries as an important gatekeeper of regional terrorism: once the Kazakh President Nazarbayez publicly invited India to join the Shanghai Cooperative Organization (SCO) for the sake of facilitating anti-terrorism.[16] Consequently, in July 2015, India formally joined it. Hence, Central Asia is also involved in the Indian-Pakistani rivalry. In 2004, Uzbekistan was commissioned by the Indian Air Force Mid-Air-Refueling Squadron (MARS) to build three giant IL-78 MKI refuellers. Kazakhstan also signed a military cooperation agreement with India in 2002 for joint production of military hardware such as torpedoes and heavy machine gun barrels.[17] All these gestures have irritated Pakistan. Indeed, India has shown its intention to respond to great power diplomacy in Central Asia by challenging the Big Three as well. For instance, Phunchok Stobdan, former Director of the Indian Cultural Center, once suggested that the US's growing presence in the region "forms a compelling reason for India's reclaiming its geopolitical rights and responsibilities in Central Asia".[18]

## V

As far as India's inter-state diplomacy, the Mandala concept in Kautilya's *Arthashastra* precisely portrays a quasi-balance of power tactic in interactions among states. The Vijigishu, who intends to establish its hegemony over others, should be aware of the motives of the other eleven kings of the Mandala in order to secure peace.[19] The circumstance of friends and foes changes with the existing political and economic situation. When the nation is situated on the circumference, the Vijigishu is the enemy (ari). Next to the ari is the ally (mitra), then the enemy ally (arimitra), one's ally's ally (mitra mitra) then the enemy's ally's ally (arimitra mitra).[20] A smart and inscrutable leader should be required to play the political field with wit and strategy. As can be seen, protection rather than expansion is more important in state governance and the complex mandala concept is easy to ensure in case of Central Asia but successive Government has failed to do that. India till recently was pursuing its Central Asia policy in a low profile manner but since the arrival of the Modi Government in 2014, it has scaled up its central Asia policy and hell bent to ensure its national interests.

Prime Minister Modi's visit to five countries of Central Asia in July 2015 has indeed been viewed as a major initiative towards bridging the gap between India and Central Asia. Central Asia is extremely important for the promotion of our national interests. Energy security is of utmost importance. Kazakhstan, Turkmenistan and Uzbekistan are endowed with enormous hydrocarbon reserves. Two of these countries Kazakhstan and Turkmenistan are in the Caspian littorals, thereby promising to open the door to other energy rich Caspian states. Connectivity through the North-South Transport Corridor featured in Modi's speeches in both countries as much as the impending implementation of the two gas pipelines. These are implementable but hinges on the political situation in Pakistan and Afghanistan.[21] After the nuclear deal Iran could be important facilitator of our interests in Central Asia. Prime Minister Modi has visited entire Central Asia and pledged a lot, now it is the time to implement possible assurances to promote our national interests. It is the demand of the hour. India has enormous soft power in the region and unlike Russia and China, India is always welcome by CAR. Accelerating our bilateral relationship with CAR will be one of the challenging foreign policy tasks for the Modi Government.

## NOTES

1. International Energy Agency, Caspian Oil and Gas: The Supply Potential of Central and Transcaucasia (Paris: OECD Publications, 1998).
2. Shai Feldman (ed.), *After the War in Iraq: Defining the New Strategic Balance* (Brighton; Portland, Oregon: Sussex Academic Press/Jaffee Center for Strategic Studies); Richard Heinberg, *The party's over: oil, war and the fate of industrial societies* (Gabriola Island, B.C.: New Society Publishers, 2003).
3. Barry Buzan, Ole Wæver, Jaap de Wilde, *Security: A New Framework for Analysis* (London: Lynne Rienner Publisher, 1998).
4. Van Ness, *Revolution and Chinese Foreign policy; Peking's support for wars of national liberation* (Berkeley: University of California Press, 1971).
5. Charles William Maynes, "America Discovers Central Asia," *Foreign Affairs,* 82, 2 (March/ April 2003): 120-33.
6. David Hoffman, "Iran's Drive to Rebuild Seen Posing New Challenges to West," *The Washington Post,* February 2, 1992; Jim Nichol, "Central Asia: Regional Developments and Implications for U.S. Interests," CRS Report for Congress, November 13, 2008.
7. Zbigniew Brzezinski, *The Grand Chessboard: American Primacy and Its Geostrategic Imperatives* (New York: Basic Books, 1997); Mehdi Amineh, *Globalization, Geopolitics and Energy Security in Central Eurasia and the Caspian Region* (The Hague: Clingendael International Energy Program, 2003). Sally Cummings (ed.), *Oil, Transition and Security in Central Asia* (New York: Routledge Curzon, 2003); Robert Legvold, "Greater Power Stakes in Central Asia," in Robert Legvold (ed.), *Thinking Strategically: The Major Powers, Kazakhstan, and the Central Asian Nexus* (Cambridge, MA: MIT Press, 2003).
8. Annete Bohr, "Regionalism in Central Asia: New Geopolitics, Old Regional Order," *International Affairs,* 80, 3 (2004): 485-502; Neil MacFarlane, "The United States and Regionalism in Central Asia," *International Affairs,* 80, 3 (2004): 447-6; Dianne Smith, "Central Asia: A New Great Game?" Research Monograph from Strategic Studies Institute, 1996, p. 20, http://www.strategicstudiesinstitute.army.mil/pdffiles/PUB117.pdf, (December 18, 2009).
9. Xu Xiaojie, "The Oil and Gas Links between Central Asia and China: A Geopolitical Perspective," OPEC Review: Energy Economics & Related Issues 23, 1 (1999): 33-54; Ariel Cohen, "U.S. Interests and Central Asia Energy Security," November 15, 2006 <http://www.heritage.org/Research/Reports/2006/11/US-Interests-and-Central-Asia-Energy-Security> (April 6, 2010); Andrew Monaghan, "Russia's Energy Diplomacy: A Political Idea Lacking a Strategy?" Southeast European and Black Sea Studies 17, 2 (2007): 275-88.
10. Thucydides, *History of the Peloponnesian War* (Chicago: University of Chicago Press, 1989), p. 293.
11. International Energy Outlook 2009 <http://www.eia.doe.gov/oiaf/ieo/>
12. Shiv Kumar Verma, "Energy Geopolitics and Iran-Pakistan-India Gas Pipeline" *Energy Policy,* 35, 6 (2007): 3280-3301.
13. Scott Moore, "Peril and Promise: A Survey of India's Strategic Relationship with Central Asia," *Central Asian Survey,* 26, 2 (2007): 279-291.
14. Athar Zafar, India-Central Asia: Finding New Synergies for Greater Engagement, Indian Council of World Affairs Policy Brief, New Delhi, 9 July 2015.
15. Can't forget support India gave us during difficult times; Iran, *The Times of India,* New Delhi, August 15, 2015.
16. Rahul Bedi, "India and Central Asia," *Frontline* 19, 19 (2002).
17. Amit Mukherjee, "IAF to get 5th IL-78 refuellers soon," India times, September 29, 2004.

18. Ibragim Alibekov, "India set to expand presence in Central Asia," Eurasianet, March 12,2003
19. Roger Boesche, *The first great political realist: Kautilya and his Arthashastra* (Lanham: Lexington Books, 2002), pp. 77-78.
20. Donald Mackenzie Brown, *The White Umbrella: Indian Political Thought from Manu to Gandhi* (Berkeley: University of California Press, 1953), pp. 59-60.
21. P.L. Dash, When Central Asia Calls, *The Indian Express*, New Delhi, July 27, 2015.

# 18

# India and the Tibetan struggle for Right to Self-determination: A National Security Perspective

*Rakhee Viswambharan*

India inherited the British policy of keeping Tibet as a buffer zone. In the post-communist revolution India urged China to maintain Tibet's autonomous status, as it suits India's security interest to minimise China's military presence in the region. However, the invasion of Tibet by People Liberation Army of China in 1951 put an end to Tibet's status as a buffer zone. It exposed the India-China border as undefined and invalidated the agreement between Tibet and British India on border delineation. In 1951 Tibet was forced to sign a 17 point agreement with China and Tibet become part of People's Republic of China. Though, China termed its invasion of Tibet as 'peaceful liberation' gross human rights violations had taken place in Tibet. By the end of 1950s, Tibetans rose in an attempt to independence known as 'National Uprising'. The Tibetan system of government was replaced and Dalai Lama and his followers were forced to seek asylum in India. The Tibetans in India formed a government in exile at Dharamsala. India's decision to provide asylum to Dalai Lama and his followers was one of the irritant in Indo–China relations. Ultimately it resulted in the Indo–China war of 1962 and China had annexed a large part of strategically important territory of India. Tibetans are distinct people with their own language and culture. They also form a large majority of the population of Tibet. The UN General Assembly passed a resolution in 1959 in support of the right to self determination of the people of Tibet. The disintegration of Soviet Union and the formation of a large number of new nation states in Eastern Europe on the basis of right to self-determination of the people once again brought the Tibetan issue before the international and regional organization. As a major stake holder in the Tibetan issue India's stand assumes great significance. Further if the Tibetan struggle for self-determination eventually results in Tibet's autonomous status, it very well serves India's security interest to minimize China's military presence in the region.

## The Tibetan Struggle for Right to Self-determination

The Tibetan issue is embedded in the history of Tibetan nationalism and Tibet-China relations. The history of Tibetan nationalism and the Tibet-China relations may be divided into four main periods (Smith 1996; Goldstein 1989; Grunfeld 1987). The first phase (630-842) is that of the consolidation of the Tibetan state from the beginning of Tibetan history up to the fall of the Tibetan empire in 842.

Tibet was not again politically unified until the mid-thirteenth century when Tibetan Lamas established a political—spiritual relationship known as 'cho-yon' or 'priest-patron' relationship with the Mongol empire. Tibet was a dependent state under the Mongol Yuan (1260–1368) and Manchu Ching (1644–1911) dynasties. Tibet was independent of Chinese influence during the native Chinese Ming dynasty (1368–1644). During the second phase, Tibet was under the direct rule of China for a short span of three years from 1911–4.

In the third phase (1914–50), Tibet experienced modern imperialist pressures and Tibetan nationalism was aroused. Tibetan nationalism was stimulated in the early 20th century by the British imperialist interest in Tibet and Chinese attempt to impose more direct control over Tibet. With the British patronage Tibet managed to achieve de facto independence, however, it failed to gain international recognition to its independence.

In the fourth period (1950 to the present) Tibetan independence was forcibly eliminated. The People's Liberation Army (PLA) marched into Tibet in the 1950 and annexed Tibet through a 'peaceful liberation'. Under the pretext of peaceful liberation China had generally imposed its will on the Tibetan people. Tibet was forced to sign an agreement with China in 1951 known as the '17-Point Agreement on Measures for the Peaceful Liberation of Tibet'. The Chinese consider this agreement as a measure to liberate Tibetan territory from imperialist forces. However, it is well known that when the PLA marched into Tibet there were no imperialist forces present in Tibet. Therefore from the Tibetan perspective such 'peaceful liberation' was imposed and promises of autonomy stated in the agreement were not being followed by the Chinese. And the Tibetan national identity comes under intense pressure from China for the 'socialist transformation' of Tibetan society. The Tibetan culture was subjected to assimilationist pressure during the Cultural Revolution (1966–76). However, the Tibetan nationalism survived and grew under the Chinese rule. After 1980, in the period of liberalized Chinese policies in Tibet, Tibetan culture and nationalism revived. During this phase Tibetans gained international support to their plea for right to self-determination (Smith 1996).

The great power game was well visible in Tibet from the beginning of 20th century. In 1904 the British troops entered Tibet and forced it to sign an agreement. This move on the part of Britain was mainly based on then Viceroy Lord Curzon's perception regarding the Russian moves in Central Asia and in particular the Russian interaction with Tibet. However, the British government in London did not approve the invasion of Tibet and the Chinese suzerainty was once again brought into force. The 1907 convention by Russia, China and British India approved the Chinese suzerainty over Tibet. However, the fall of Manchu dynasty in 1913 once again had given Tibet the de jure independent status. In the 1914 Shimla convention, Tibet attended along with British India and China (Tibetan Centre for Human Rights & Democracy, Human Rights Situation in Tibet, Annual Report 2009). The final outcome of the convention was the McMohan line which demarcates the border between British India and Tibet. There is difference of opinion regarding the Chinese approval to the final outcome. However, given the weak power position of China at that time it had only limited option but to accept the Shimla convention of 1914. Thus, in the Shimla convention of 1914 the Tibetan plenipotentiary attended it along with China and British India and this clearly shows that Tibet enjoyed independent status to negotiate with others. This status of Tibet continued till the entry of People's Liberation Army (PLA) in 1950-51 and annexed Tibet.

It is important to note that though Tibet was never formally recognized by the League of Nations or the United Nations, Tibet in the period 1913–51 had an independent government, currency, army, judicial and postal systems, and administration. Furthermore, the Tibetan government enjoyed formal bilateral relations with the neighbouring countries of Mongolia, Nepal, India, and Bhutan, and concluded treaties with China and Britain. The Tibetan claim that they have every right to self-determination as China had illegally occupied their territory in the name of 'peaceful liberation of Tibet' in 1951. The China's annexation of Tibet in fact once again altered the geostrategic position in the Himalayan region and also nullified the outcome of Shimla convention of 1914. It is interesting to examine how Tibetan issue forms a significant factor in India–China relations.

## Tibet as a Factor in India–China Relations

It appears that there are four major issues which form Tibet as a factor in India–China relations. They are:

i. The status of Tibet
ii. Tibetan refugees in India
iii. The India–China border dispute
iv. Common security concerns

## *The status of Tibet*

India's position on the status of Tibet has changed from the British policy of recognising the de facto independence of Tibet—'completely Autonomous State'—under ambiguous form of Chinese suzerainty to Tibet as 'autonomous region of China'.

Independent India was not very sympathetic to the Tibetan demand for independence. However, when the PLA entered into Tibet, India did not hesitate to deplore China's invasion of Tibet. (Mehrotra 2000: 14). In a note dated October 26, 1950, the Ministry of External Affairs, Government of India, told the Chinese foreign office how it looked at the event:

> In the context of world events, invasion by Chinese troops of Tibet cannot but be regarded as deplorable and in the considered judgment of the Government of India, not in the interest of China or peace. This statement clearly shows India's stand on the Tibetan issue in the initial period.[1]

Again, when the PLA entered into Tibet, the Indian Prime Minister, Jawaharlal Nehru stated in the Indian Parliament on 7th December 1950:

> It is not right for any country to talk about its sovereignty or suzerainty over an area outside its own immediate range. That is to say, since Tibet is not the same as China, it should ultimately be the wishes of the people of Tibet that should prevail and not any legal or constitutional arguments—the last voice in regard to Tibet should be the voice of the people of Tibet and of nobody else.[2]

Jawaharlal Nehru's statement at the Indian Parliament was significant in many respects. It reflected India's stand on right of the people. It also manifests a clear understanding of the Tibetan question.

In the beginning India had supported the Tibet's claim for self-determination. However, a marked change in India's stand on self-determination was visible after the Indo–China bilateral agreement of 1954, known as Panchasheel.[3] As per the agreement India had accepted China's claim on Tibet. Thus on 29 April 1954, India relented to the Chinese insistence on referring to Tibet as 'Tibet Region of China'. Though India failed to provide any support to the Tibetans right to self-determination when it was taken up at the UN General Assembly in 1958, India had provided political asylum to Dalai Lama and his followers in 1959.

After the 1962 border war, India often merely used 'Tibet' until the 1988 visit of the then Indian Prime Minister, Rajiv Gandhi when the 'Sino–Indian Joint Press Communiqué' referred to Tibet as 'an autonomous region of China'. Again in 2003, Prime Minister Atal Bihari Vajpayee signed a declaration which recognised 'that the Tibet Autonomous Region is part of the territory of the People's Republic of China' (Declaration on Principles for Relations and Comprehensive Cooperation between the People's Republic of China and the Republic of India, 25 June 2003). However, India's acceptance of Tibet as a part of China is conditional upon Tibet's enjoyment of autonomy. China, therefore, demands stronger and more unambiguous statements from New Delhi on China's sovereignty over Tibet, which India has resisted so far.

## *Tibetan refugees in India*

India's consistent official Tibetan policy has been to disallow anti-Chinese activities by Tibetan refugees on Indian soil. However, India has allowed the Tibetans to run a government-in-exile, the Central Tibetan Administration. India refuses to bend to Chinese pressure by reducing or suspending its support to Tibetan exiles in India. India will and should continue to support Tibetan refugees because it is in India's national interest. For the foreseeable future, India's material assistance and facilitating role for the Tibetan struggle will continue. This is one of the major irritants in India–China relations. The Chinese complain that such open encouragement and support given by the government of India to the Tibetan in their 'anti-China activities' constitute interference in China's internal affairs and obstruct the progress of India-China relations. It appears that India's gravest threat to China lies in Tibet because of the political asylum that India had provided to over 80,000 Tibetans in India. So long as the exiled community exists, Tibetan nationalism and the demand for self-determination will remain a major apprehension for the communist China. (Suresh R. 2011: 246)

## *India–China Border Dispute*

The border dispute continues to avoid a resolution ever since India and China have acquired a common border when the PRC occupied the Tibet in1951. The historical roots of the Sino–Indian border dispute can be traced to the imperial period when the great game between British India, Czarist Russia and Qing China over Tibet and Central Asia. Empires thrived on uncertain borders—frontiers were more preferable to imperial powers—as clearly demarcated borders constrained their own ambitions and strategic ûexibility. In addition, the inhospitable terrain of the high Himalayas, the absence of sophisticated surveying technologies and existence of a functioning Tibetan state made the delimitation of India's northern border either unnecessary or difficult.

Nevertheless, ultimately in the Shimla convention of 1914, in fact, made the border line between British India and Tibet. However, in the mid-20th century, when two equally nationalistic and territorial states gained control over the Indian and Chinese empires, China was not ready to accept the British proposed McMohan line. This stand of China was well reflected especially after the signing of the 'India–China Agreement on Trade and Intercourse between Tibet Region of China and India' (April 29, 1954) in which India for the ûrst time accepted Tibet as a part of China. On the Indian side Prime Minister, Jawaharlal Nehru at the time of signing of Panchsheel agreement thought that the boundary was no longer an issue, and that the China had accepted the historical status quo.

Jawaharlal Nehru wrote about this to the Chinese Premier, Zhou Enlai in 1958 as the border issue heated up:

> When the Sino–Indian Agreement in regard to the Tibet region of China was concluded, various outstanding problems, including some relating to our border trade, were considered.... No border questions were raised at that time and we were under the impression that there were no border disputes between our respective countries. In fact we thought that the Sino–Indian Agreement, which was happily concluded in 1954, had settled all outstanding problems between our countries.[4]

He had also expressed shock at seeing maps printed in China showing certain 'Indian' areas to be parts of China.

The India–China border problem is embedded in Tibet as China had no border with India except through Tibet and India's border with Tibet was a well-settled border negotiated at the Shimla conference of 1914. [5] Thus it appears that a solution to the Indo–China border problem lies in the implementation of the Tibetan claim for the right to self-determination and the restoration of Tibet's historical status as a buffer zone between India and China.

Further it appears the communist regime in China is also not very serious about finding an amicable settlement of the border problem due to two important reasons. First, the prevalence of successful democratic system in India poses a challenge to the communist system in China. Any close cooperation and interaction with democratic India would be detrimental to the continuance of the totalitarian system in China. Secondly, the present communist regime in China wanted to keep the border problem unresolved so that they can divert the attention of its own population from the serious domestic issues and also a rationale for its huge defence spending and heavy force deployment along Tibet.

### *Common Security Concerns*

It appears that Tibet is an important factor in security paradigm of both India and China. Since its geopolitical position has wedged it between two great powers, it has to be dependent on either China or India, having no other choice. Tibet has always had a high degree of spiritual identiûcation with India. The Republican Chinese officials way back in1910 expressed similar assessments when they stated: 'Tibet is a buttress on our national frontiers—the hand, as it were, which protects the face—and its prosperity or otherwise is of the most vital importance to China'.

India has its reciprocal fears arising from Chinese military presence in the Tibetan plateau. The true extent of China's military presence in Tibet cannot be gauged, given the extreme secrecy surrounding information about the Peoples Liberation Army. The presence of Chinese strategic forces on the Tibetan plateau adds another dimension to India's China threat perception. Again India's security perceptions also centred on the China's management of water resources originating from Tibet, which in fact feed the Indian subcontinent. The historical memory about betrayal and humiliation on account of the 1962 war that continues to casts a shadow over India's perceptions of China.

In essence, the complex of security concerns connected to Tibet underpins the strategic rivalry between the two major Asian players, India and China. Consequently, China and India have common security concerns that are connected to Tibet. These issues can be well addressed only through mutual trust and confidence building measures. Though there are mechanisms to resolve the border dispute amicably since 1988 through the joint working group (JWG), little progress was reported so far. Meanwhile the external powers exploit the conflicting situation to their advantage through various overt and covert moves.

## Conclusion

Tibetans are distinct people with their own language and culture. They also form a large majority of the population of Tibet. The UN General Assembly passed a resolution in 1959 in support of the right to self determination of the people of Tibet. The disintegration of Soviet Union and the formation of a large number of new nation states in Eastern Europe on the basis of right to self determination of the people once again brought the Tibetan issue before the international and regional organization. As a major stake holder in the Tibetan issue India's stand assumes great significance. Further if the Tibetan struggle for self-determination eventually result in Tibet's autonomous status, it very well serves India's security interest to minimize China's military presence in the region.

## NOTES

1. Quoted in L.L. Mehrotra, India's Tibet Policy: An Appraisal and Options, Tibetan Parliamentary and Policy Research Centre, New Delhi, 2000.
2. Ibid., p. 14.
3. (i) Mutual respect for each other's territorial integrity and sovereignty; (ii) mutual non-aggression (iii) mutual non-interference in each other's internal affairs; (iv) equality and mutual benefit; and (v) peaceful co-existence.
4. Notes, Memoranda and letters Exchanged and Agreements signed between The Governments of India and China White Paper III, MEA, Government of India, New Delhi.
5. Indian Parliament on Issue of Tibet, Lok Sabha Debates 1952–2005, Tibetan Parliamentary and Policy Research Centre, New Delhi, 2006.

## REFERENCES

Goldstein, Melwyn C (1989): *A History of Modern Tibet, 1913-1951*, Munishiram Manoharlal Publishers Pvt Ltd.

Grunfeld, A. Tom (1987): *The Making of Modern Tibet*, Oxford University Press, Delhi.

Lama, Dalai (1988): *Five Point Peace Plan for Tibet*, Information Office, Central Tibetan Secretariat, Dharamsala (H.P.), India.

Mehrotra, L.L (2000): *India's Tibet Policy: An Appraisal and Options*, Tibetan Parliamentary and Policy Research Centre, New Delhi.

Smith. Jr, Warren W. (1996): *Tibetan Nation: A History of Tibetan Nationalism and Sino-Tibetan Relation*, Westview Press, Oxford.

Suresh R (2011): "Tibetan Right to Self Determination and Sino Indian Relations", *International Journal of South Asian Studies*, Vol. 4, No. 2.

Tibetan Centre for Human Rights & Democracy (2009): "Human Rights, Situation in Tibet", Annual Report 2009, Dharamsala, Himachal Pradesh.

UN Doc. A/CONF.157/23.

Zhao, Suisheng (1996): "The Implication of Demilitarization of Tibet for Sino-Indian Relations and Asian Security", *Asian Affairs*, Vol. 22, No. 4, Winter.

# 19

# India and Australia: Closer and Closer?

*R.F.I. Smith*

## Introduction

In the big shift of economic and political power back to Asia the prospect of closer relations between India and Australia are tantalizing for Australia. That Prime Minister Modi included Australia in his spectacular round of outreach visits in his first year in office has raised high expectations on both sides. But there is a long way to go. Turning a multiplicity of hitherto weak ties into robust, mutually rewarding relationships will take persistence, skill and time. At this stage firming up potential agreements, especially on international security and trade and investment, may depend as much on firming up mutual understanding of how to talk to each other as on expecting immediately fruitful negotiations on perceived interests in common. Following expressions of goodwill by both national leaders, four threshold challenges stand out: identification of a robust range of mutually interesting opportunities; negotiations on an initial set of issues that lead to substantive results; building up capabilities for more wide ranging collaboration; and accommodating divergent interests. A positive sign is that interest in the task is high.

This paper begins with a summary of the differences in background that hinder closer relationships. It then examines, first, relationships between India and Australia in the Indo-Pacific region and opportunities for strategic convergence, and second, trade cultural and other initiatives which may help build stronger relationships. It concludes that India and Australia have much to benefit by getting closer to each other. But hopes for big initiatives are likely to place large demands on two scarce resources: continuing political commitment at the highest level; and the ability of participants on both sides to work across differences of interests, scale and culture.

## Differences

The search for productive relationships begins from very different standpoints. Both countries recognize the significance of the rising economic and political power of Asian states. But asymmetries of history, location, perception and aspiration get in the way. India's experience of colonization was of foreign institutions and practices superimposed on local ones; contemporary Australia began as a set of British settler colonies in which indigenous peoples were dispossessed, recognition of their prior occupancy remains politically contested, and national identity is enmeshed with the European origins of much of its population. India occupies a subcontinent with far reaching geographical and historical links to West, Central, East and South East Asia; Australia occupies a large island continent at the far eastern tip of South East Asia to which it is not only adjacent but also distant (Darwin is closer to Bali than to Melbourne, but New Delhi is further from Melbourne than from London).

With its size, ancient and sophisticated civilization, pre-colonial significance as an economic and trading power astride the Silk Road and the Indian Ocean, young population and current economic potential, India aspires to great power status. But in the meantime it needs to handle the immediate problems of soft borders in a troubled South Asian neighbourhood. Its internal affairs are complex, demanding and resistant to change. Internationally it wishes to maintain an independent stance and links with other states in the non-aligned movement in which it played a leading role. It has found it hard to change old positions or commit to new ones. Discussions about foreign policy are subject to competing views. Continued reliance on incremental adjustments to positions adopted first under Prime Minister Nehru has cogent and influential advocates. But so does determination to wring more benefit out of established positions (Hall), advocacy of much bigger changes, and recognition of its ability over the long term to respond to new challenges (Varghese: 13).

In comparison, Australia is a small, natural resource endowed country with a developed economy and a population enriched since 1945 not only by European but also more recently by Asian migration (100,000 Australians speak Hindi at home; approximately 450,000 residents of Australians are of Indian origin). It seeks to build up its profile as a middle power (Evans 2012, Andrew Carr) and to be influential in international forums dominated by the great powers. Since the 1950s its trade links have shifted decisively towards Asia (Harcourt). Indeed, for a quarter of a century its major trade partners have been in East Asia—China, Japan and Korea. Significantly, trade with India, while growing is nowhere near as substantial. Despite bruising and inward looking partisan conflict, it enjoys broad continuity in foreign policy. But the mismatch between its traditional links and the trade patterns that drive its recent economic success is stark. Closer economic integration with Asia, continuing close cultural and security links with the United States and Europe, and adjusting to its developing multicultural and multiracial identity, coexist in uneasy accommodation (for a particularly insightful book length discussion see Wesley 2011).

Even characteristics shared by both India and Australia lead to parallel rather than converging perspectives (Grare). For both, China is the major trading partner (although unlike India Australia has a favourable trade balance). Both also have significant relationships with the US. But while the prospect of increasingly competitive relationships between China and the US is a source of shared fascination and not a little apprehension, progress towards closer engagement has been slow. Following the collapse of the Soviet Union, India has tended to follow a pragmatic course of interest based multilateral arrangements. It seeks to maintain strategic autonomy and to resist the emergence in Asia of any one dominant power. A generally closer relationship with the US has nevertheless been characterised by ebbs and flows. Relations with China are pragmatic on trade but testy on borders.

In contrast Australia continues to rely very substantially for security in Asia on alliance with the US. As the US turns more closely towards Asia it looks to Australia for support and facilities. Australia also actively pursues multilateral as well as bilateral strategies of engagement with Asian states, but not at the expense of the US alliance. Despite its fundamental importance to the economy, trade with China is partitioned off. The significance of power shifts within Asia is acknowledged (Grare), but both sides of politics affirm that no choice between the US and China is necessary (see for example, Bob Carr). While dissenting voices exist—a former conservative prime minister has advocated increased independence from the US (Fraser a.), Australia's first ambassador to China has suggested a focus on 'security in rather than from Asia' (Fitzgerald), a leading strategic analyst advocates that the US make space for a rising China (White) and a former foreign minister, Gareth Evans, has said that Mr Fraser's recent book (Fraser b.) is a major contribution "to the debate Australia has to have" (Tingle)—official and effective public engagement with the issues they raise has yet to emerge. Indeed Fitzgerald (2015) bluntly cautions against expecting big shifts from current political leaders: 'they have no foreign policy framework and seem frightened of big ideas'.

Finally, a recent diplomatic history of relationships between India and Australia (Gurry) offers a cautionary tale in which consistent efforts since before independence by committed Australian diplomats were frustrated by diffuse and diverging interests, lack of empathy with Asia by some Australian prime ministers, fluctuating interest in India by others, unwillingness to commit resources to relationship building, adverse impacts of the White Australia Policy and perceptions of continuing racism. While current prospects are much more promising, the differences in culture through which interests are identified remain daunting (consider the implications, for example, of the contrast between the conjunction of motor cycles, mobile phones and Mahabharata in the lives of newly arrived entrants to the middle class in India and the privileged, secular, hard-working but pleasure loving lives of upwardly mobile workers in Australia's service industries). Closer relationships between India and Australia may still rely on both countries playing a long game.

## Indo-Pacific

India and Australia's strategic interests meet most directly in the Indian Ocean. In a sense they are neighbours (Singh), with India to the north and Australia to the south of an ocean the significance of which has dramatically re-emerged.[1] The contemporary rise of the ocean as the world's 'busiest and most strategically significant trade corridor' is a potential turning point for both countries (Medcalf: 3). The 'crossroads of the Indian Ocean and the Western Pacific' (Medcalf: 3) connects both countries to wider relationships, in 'a very new and yet very old framework' (Kaplan: xii). Significantly, in doing so it focuses attention on the relationships of both countries with China and the US.

Medcalf (2014) and Rumley (2013) outline the rationale for an Indo-Pacific region. It draws its strength less from geography (because of the multiplicity of very different littoral states) than from activities and relationships. In its current incarnation, for which Kaplan provides indispensable background, it has been incorporated in the thinking by defence strategists in Australia, has received bipartisan acceptance by Australian governments and has the potential to support pragmatic policy initiatives by India (Varghese: 9). The basis for the region is that (Medcalf: 2):

> The accelerating economic and security connections between the Western Pacific and the Indian ocean region are creating a single strategic system.

This system is about (Medcalf: 2-3):

> ...the arc of trade routes, energy flows, diplomatic bonds and strategic connections between the two oceans. These links in turn emerge especially from the rise of China and India as outward-looking economic and military powers, the expansion of their economic interests, and

> their strategic and diplomatic imperatives in what each might once have considered its primary maritime zone of interest.

For India, the Indo-Pacific encompasses existing interests in the Indian Ocean, puts it in the company of China and the US and extends its perspectives beyond South Asia (Chacko). For Australia, the Indo-Pacific gives it standing in Asia as a member state (Medcalf) and unlike Gareth Evans's concept of an 'East Asian Hemisphere' (Evans 1995) gives it reasons to look more closely towards South Asia.

However, the idea of the Indo-Pacific is controversial. By its potential to connect India to tensions between China and the United States it extends the arena in which contested adjustments to a changing world order are taking place. It lays bare a number of strategic and conceptual sensitivities. For example, it can be seen as a 'manufactured super region' (Pan: 453), a device for building coalitions against China, a token by which Australia can attract attention in India, a means to bind Australia even more tightly to the US, and to put the sea lanes between the Pacific and Indian Oceans at risk of militarisation (Pan, Wilson, Bisley and Phillips, Gordon). It is thus an idea to be used with care; using it as a frame of reference directs attention to India and Australia's overlapping security interests in the Indian Ocean, their complementary relationships with countries in South East Asia, and their potentially shared approaches to wider issues in international affairs. Its greatest value may be to stimulate exploration of otherwise overlooked possibilities.

## India's Interests

India's interests of particular relevance to Australia begin in the North East Indian Ocean and extend from there into South East Asia. These are a subset of India's interests in the Indian Ocean littoral which extend from the Gulf Region in the west, along the east coast of Africa, and across to South East Asia and Australia. In the North East Ocean India, despite past apprehensions about Myanmar as a possible host to a naval presence by China, has a dominant role. It has also fostered cooperative security arrangements with ASEAN states bordering the Bay of Bengal/Andaman Sea (Brewster: 128) From there, as Brewster explains, India's defence facilities in the Andaman and Nicobar Islands potentially project its influence into the South East Asian trade routes and from there into the South China Sea (Brewster: 127). The key is the ability to control access to the western end of the Malacca Strait. Echoing an old proverb that 'Whoever is lord of Malacca has his hands on the throat of Venice' (Kaplan: 7) Brewster has argued:

> The Indian Ocean is the one area in which India holds a clear military advantage over China and the potential to control the Malacca Strait reinforces that advantage. (Brewster: 131)

As traffic through the strait on which China depends continues to increase (one estimate suggests that by 2030 up to 80 per cent of China's oil and 50 per cent of its gas will be imported through the strait) (Dupont) the sensitivity of India's role will continue to grow.

However while India is well-positioned to 'look outward', and has an increasing need to do so, it has hitherto been hesitant about entering into arrangements to formalise such a role. It has tried to position itself in South East Asia as a 'benign security provider to the region as a whole' (Brewster: 133) but this aspiration remains unconsolidated; although Mr Modi's recent visits may help. Further, proposals from the US and Japan for multilateral security arrangements involving India for many years did not draw support. While Singapore became India's 'advocate' in South East Asia strategic relationships did not develop as Singapore would have liked. Similarly, India's relations with Vietnam, which date from the Cold War, did not develop as Vietnam sought. Proposals for closer ties with other South East Asian states, especially Indonesia, and with South Korea for long remained proposals. Moreover, India's potential for leadership too was not accepted by all South East Asian states. India thus found itself building up military relationships bilaterally or with groups of states (including the US, Japan, Singapore and Australia) while also continuing to place a high value on autonomy and restraint.

India's strategic interests in South East Asia are complemented by its 'Look East' economic policies, emphatically restated by Prime Minister Modi. The thinking behind the liberalisation initiatives in the Indian economy in 1991 followed close interest by Indian ministers and advisers in the sources of economic growth in Malaysia and other South East Asian countries (Mukherji). The economic crisis that crystallised policies of liberalisation prompted a drive to expand trade and investment links. India became a 'dialogue partner' of ASEAN in 1995 and it is the institutional vehicle for pursuing economic links in South East Asia. Since 2002 an India-ASEAN summit has taken place each year and India has promoted other sub-regional forums for economic cooperation in the Bay of Bengal and with Indochina (Brewster: 134). India also promotes ASEAN as a forum for discussions on security and participates in meetings of Ministers of Defence from ASEAN plus Australia, China, Japan, New Zealand, Russia, South Korea and the US. However, ASEAN provides only a limited forum for deliberations on security. Whether an alternative vehicle for such discussions will emerge and what part, if any, India might play in it remains to be seen. In the meantime India has developed webs of interactions with South East Asian states and the many other states with interests in this region and the wider Indo-Pacific. Also, through active participation in BRICS Summits India not only extends links beyond the Asia-Pacific but facilitates relationships with Russia and China.

The experience gained from these interactions provides a foundation on which to craft more ambitious relationships in the Indo-Pacific Region. The renewed impetus to 'Look East' by the Modi government suggests that in both trade and security India will seek to do so.

## Australia's Interests[2]

Australia's interests of most relevance to India begin also in South East Asia. But from there it also looks up towards its trading partners in East Asia and across the Pacific to North America. Despite a long exposure to the Indian Ocean on its western coast Australia had found the diversity of interests represented by littoral states hard to grapple with (Bisley and Phillips). Until rising trade flows solidified the definition of the Indo-Pacific, relationships with South Asia in general and India in particular remained fuzzy and easily dissolved (Gurry and Weigold). However, the heightened salience of Indo-Pacific trade routes and maritime security provides a persuasive reason for exploration of potential interests in common. For Australia, as for India, ASEAN and its related forums has provided a vehicle for engagement. However, Australia has been much keener than India to go beyond 'soft security and dialogues' (Grare: 7). In a variety of statements and forums involving a range of stakeholders, including state governments and business groups, Australia has outlined opportunities for closer bilateral cooperation (Cerule Consulting, Grare: 5). In 2008 India and Australia signed a joint security declaration which 'established a framework for the further development of the security relationship' (Grare: 6). Australia also removed the irritant of a ban on uranium sales to India, which recalled the even greater irritant of Australia's reaction to India's nuclear tests. However a 'quadrilateral security dialogue' initiated earlier by then Secretary of State Colin Powell and involving the US, Japan, India and Australia dissolved (Garnaut). In 2013 Australia's Defence White Paper (Grare: 7) reiterated the importance of relationships with India and the then Defence Minister for India made the first visit of such a minister to Australia. In 2014 the election of the Modi government dramatically revived possibilities for stronger security arrangements.

In July 2014, in a move that linked security in the Indo-Pacific with wider security issues in the Pacific associated with the rise of China, India and Australia agreed to strengthen military ties. The agreement with India took place as Australia was drawing closer to both the US and Japan. These steps sparked renewed interest in a four-way relationship between the US, Japan, India and Australia, with a possible extension to include Indonesia. Following renewed US interest in Asia, governments of both persuasions in Australia have agreed to provide improved facilities for the US, for example facilities for US Marines in northern Australia (Gillard Labor government) and improved military communications (Abbott

Liberal National government). The US officials and former officials have also been urging Australia to increase expenditure on defence. However in other areas of the Asia-Pacific, uncertainty about US preparedness to come to their assistance in the face of rising Chinese assertiveness influenced countries to form their own coalitions. In this context Japan sought to increase its defence partnerships. It looked to the Philippines, Vietnam, India and Australia. It also moved away from post 1945 pacifism to a policy of 'collective self defence' in which Japanese forces can be deployed alongside those of allies.

## Sensitivities

The moves to closer ties between India and Australia have thus taken place in sensitive circumstances in which the management of relations with China is a major driver. China is concerned about being surrounded by unfriendly neighbours. It has many land borders and maritime neighbours extending from East to South East Asia. However, other powers are concerned about growing Chinese naval strength, territorial claims, an expanded air defence zone, land reclamation, military facilities on existing and newly created islands and other initiatives to project Chinese influence in the South China Sea. They are also trying to extend relationships with China without inhibiting closer ties with current or potential allies. Experiments with overlapping relationships in which consultation and collaboration, including the US, China or neither, take precedence over formal and confrontational alliance building are taking place. However, Chinese comments indicate that the difference between say, a 'consultative security forum' or a 'countervailing coalition' and a 'military alliance' is a matter of interpretation (Garnaut, J 2014; Kerin a.). While multi-track strategies or strategies of multi-polarity and multi-alignment continue to be explored (for example Australia's joint exercises with the US and China [Kerin b.] and India's joint exercises with the US and Japan [Aneja]), the extent to which they are sustainable has yet to be determined. In this context the appreciations that India and Australia make about China and the kinds of responses they make to Chinese assertiveness may be critical to the further development of relations with each other.

What is also important is how adeptly they manage relationships with each other and with other participants with interests in the Indo-Pacific. In addition to ASEAN and related forums, India and Australia participate in other forums where shared interests can be explored. The East Asia Summit is one. Others include the Indian Ocean Rim Association and the Indian Ocean Naval Symposium. While the absence of a single regional institution which spans the whole of Asia is often noted, the more important question may be how to make the best use of those that exist. When former Australian Prime Minister Rudd proposed the creation of a new Asia-Pacific Community the importance of relationship management was reinforced (Ayson and Taylor). There was little enthusiasm for a new structure but a 'high degree of interest in discussing further how cooperation processes may be enhanced' (Frost). As Ayson and Taylor have proposed (Ayson and Taylor: 193):

> The most important *institutions* of regional politics are not the formal organisations that hold regular summits, but the rules and patterns of behavior that operate between the major actors on a daily basis. Such an informal approach would suggest that the basis of Asia's strategic future, including China's role, is not a regional architecture—which seeks to organise and perhaps even to control the actors—but a set of regional bargains that nourish and support their most important strategic relationships. One of these bargains is an effective but informal compact between the United States and China that they will recognise each other's leading role in regional affairs.

From this perspective there are already enough forums. However, using them creatively to manage competition, promote cooperation and avoid zero sum games will be a major challenge.

How effectively India and Australia approach this challenge will be influenced by how they balance internal policy drivers with existing and emerging interests. In different ways both countries face internal challenges that spill over into how they present themselves to the world. In India the most prominent challenges are about how to create sustainable economic opportunities that meet the expectations of a restless electorate and enhance its standing in international forums (for a review of India's challenges through the prism of its relations with the European Union see Winand *et al*, especially pp. 338–58). In Australia the most prominent challenges are about how to manage a developed economy subject to painful structural change while growing beyond the electoral temptations of fear of 'the other' and to operate more confidently beyond the Anglosphere.

## Closer and Closer?

With closer military ties in prospect questions arise about how far they will extend, whether they will be accompanied by thickening economic and social ties, and whether indeed effective cooperation on security will depend on thicker ties in general (Varghese). The extended gestation period between the identification by security analysts of opportunities for cooperation and recent official announcements is a reminder that analysis alone does not drive policy change. Similarly, the webs of business, institutional and personal contacts between India and Australia that now exist (for example, two way foreign direct investment, state government business development strategies and offices in India, cultural programs in both countries, Bollywood enthusiasts, enrolments from India in a recent MOOC on India presented by the Australian National University and another presented in 2015 by the University of Melbourne, engineering consulting services, participation by Indian civil servants in programs of the Australia and New Zealand School of Government, extensive programs of the Australia India Institute, high level round table discussions, agreements on vocational education and training, and links between universities and individual scholars) do not guarantee thicker ties. Earlier economic, scholarly and social contacts (for example, Australian economic planners in India in the 1950s, Hindustan Machine Tools investments in Australia in the 1970s, Victorian agricultural scientists in India in the 1970s and the continuing work of Queensland semi-arid tropics scientists with ICRISAT in Hyderabad) were often discontinuous or remained specialised. More recent connections such as Indian student enrolments in universities and other institutions of further education have been troubled. However, overall the variety of current links, including those provided by a continuing flow of immigrants from India to Australia and a return of student enrolments, provides a stronger basis than before on which to build connections that link military, economic and soft power.

Realising this potential will demand conscious efforts by both countries. Indian interest in doing so is underpinned by Prime Minister Modi's emphasis on the soft power of 5Ts: trade, tourism, talent, technology and tradition (Mattoo). In Mr Modi's nearly twenty international visits he has not only been enthusiastic about improving bilateral ties with countries in South Asia, participation in forums such as the BRICS Summit in Brazil (Ministry of External Affairs) in 2014, and complementing strategic tensions with China with economic common ground (for example, allying with China to urge reform of the international financial order and inviting Chinese investment in India) but has also demonstrated a consistent determination to look outwards.

Modi's visit to Australia marked an 'unprecedented level of engagement' (Rajendram). His rapport with Prime Minister Abbott, following an earlier visit to India by Mr Abbott, was strong; his address to a joint sitting of the Australian parliament (delivered in English) was eloquent, witty and warm. In Sydney Indian community groups greeted him with extraordinary enthusiasm. Business leaders, including the most influential, queued up for introductions. Following the visit interchanges between the two countries proceeded with enhanced energy and enthusiasm.

Two agreements stood out: a Framework for Security Cooperation; and, following free trade agreements with Japan, China and South Korea, the beginning of negotiations for an agreement between India and Australia. However, getting the most out of these initiatives will focus attention on the extent to which the expectations of the two countries are aligned and their capabilities to work together commensurate with likely difficulties. Pursuit of both security and trade agreements will generate internal debate. In India the news about the Framework for Security Cooperation drew not only favourable comment but also an astringent critique under the title 'In the Making—An Asian NATO?' (*Economic and Political Weekly:* 8) In Australia satisfaction that Australia is no longer at the periphery of India's vision (Rajendram) was accompanied also by criticism that enthusiasm for security arrangements directly aimed at China was too hawkish. Neither country wants polarisation in Asia. However, from Australia's perspective Michael Wesley (2014) has observed that avoiding it will require three things: to maintain regional institutions that include all of the rival great powers and smaller states; to disentangle key bilateral relations with Japan, China, the US and India from each other while making each relationship as strong as possible; and to strive to ensure that rival institutions promoted by the big powers do not encourage regional polarisation (Wesley).

Building trade and investment links will encounter challenges. In India the liberalisation initiatives of 1991 are still widely criticised, opening up domestic markets is resisted, and the Modi government has moved with caution on further steps towards market based reform. Market access for foreign firms is especially sensitive. By contrast, despite the reservations about the value of free trade agreements by the Productivity Commission (2015: 62), the Australian government's own in house source of policy advice, the prospect of such an agreement with India has been promoted by the government as a way into a huge and growing market. Two comments by Australian leaders suggest that expectations may be overheated: the Minister for Trade, Andrew Robb (2015) has said that India could be 'China all over again' while the Prime Minister, when asked what drove his China policies, replied 'Fear and greed' (Garnaut, J 2015). A focus on prospects for coal and other energy exports and fostering of business contacts mainly through very large companies has generated sceptical comment (Sainsbury). Caution has been expressed also about the extent to which the two countries' service industries may align. As an experienced Australian manager of engineering services in India observed, his firm was more able to sell India based services to Australia than to sell Australia based services to India (Walters: 45). Moreover, the range of educational, cultural and other contacts suggests that whatever the fate of particular trade and investment prospects, organisational links are expanding.

To underpin the task of turning opportunities into tangible results, keeping up momentum and fostering a widening range of links, unofficial as well as official, deserves high priority. The high level discussions of the 2014 Australia–

India Roundtable produced a number of practical suggestions (Lowy Institute). Three of the suggestions that stand out are:

- Federalise the bilateral relationship, encouraging dynamic states and cities in both countries to connect more with each other.
- Improve business and regulatory environments to enable cross-investments by the private sectors in the two countries, including in the entire energy chain.
- Foster champions for the bilateral relationship among leaders and opinion-makers in both countries, as well as encouraging the further growth of people-people relations (Lowy Institute).

The first recognises the trend for sub-national authorities in each country to look outwards and their potential to strengthen a wide range of practical links. It is especially important following the Modi government's federalising initiatives in national policy making and funding for the states. The second directs attention to the difficulties businesses in both countries have experienced, sometimes substantially, with barriers to foreign investment. The vicissitudes of the Adani Group's proposal for a major new coal mine in Queensland, even without taking into account the merits or otherwise of the business case and funding basis for the proposal, illustrate the range of issues involved. The second priority is also relevant to the argument that greater economic complementarity will help drive improved ties on security (Grare, Earl, Varghese). The third recognises that ultimately the deployment of power, whether hard or soft, depends on strategic relationships between people. Seeding opportunities for specialist dialogues on topics of mutual interest, for example, to national, state, city, business, cultural and educational participants could be a mutually rewarding investment. A program to send Australian students to study in Asia is already taking shape. For both countries the size and influence of the Indian diaspora in Australia is a strategic resource. Initiatives by Indian immigrants in Australia and Australian residents and visitors in India are also helpful. A burgeoning of such people to people contacts will be a good sign that momentum is being maintained.

But further systematic efforts are essential. Reminders of the risks of discontinuity are plentiful. On election the Abbott government summarily archived the Gillard government's Asian Century White Paper and its implementation plans designed to refocus private and public sector attention on change in Asia (DPMC). In turn the Asian Century White Paper traversed ground covered by an overlooked report commissioned by the Hawke government in the 1980s (Garnaut R). Further, high quality diplomatic representation remains essential. Australian representatives in India have been of exceptionally high quality. Indian representatives in Australia have also been well regarded. However, the diplomatic services of both countries are spread thinly and timely recommendations from posts have often fallen on stony ground at home (Gurry).

## Conclusion

There is now no doubt that India and Australia have a wide range of mutually interesting questions to explore. The good relations between the Modi and Abbott governments provide the high level official support lacking earlier. However, the task of deepening relationships, especially on security and trade, has yet to mature into strings of significant results. Meaningful convergence on specific issues is likely to depend on much more exploration of questions of mutual interest and potential complementarities. In turn this will turn attention to capabilities and persistence. A positive sign is that interest in the task is high. But each country will need to become far more aware of what the other can offer and work systematically to turn opportunities into achievements. How tricky this may be is illustrated by recalling that while Mr Modi addressed the Australian parliament in English and a recent Australian prime minister addressed Chinese audiences in Mandarin, the prospect that an Australian leader might be able to address the Indian parliament in Hindi seems remote. Two final questions arise: does this matter? And if so, how might it be remedied? How such questions are answered will tell us something about the depth of the progress being made.

## REFERENCES

Aneja, Atul (2014), "India, U.S., Japan joint naval exercise in Pacific today", *The Hindu*, 24 July

Ayson, R & Taylor, B (2009), "Architectural alternatives or alternatives to architecture?", in Ron Huisken (ed), *Rising China: Power and Reassurance*, ANU ePress, Canberra Australia, pp. 185–99.

Bisley, N and A Phillips (2012), The Indo-Pacific: what does it actually mean? *East Asia Forum,* 6 October, http://www.eastasiaforum.org/ (access 28 May 2015)

Brewster D. (2013), "India's Defence Strategy and the India-ASEAN Relationship", in Ajaya Kumar Das (ed.), India-ASEAN Defence Relations, RSIS Monograph No.28, Singapore: S. Rajaratnam School of International Studies.

Carr, Andrew (2015), *Winning the Peace: Australia's Campaign to Change the Asia-Pacific*, Melbourne, Melbourne University Press.

Carr, B (2014) *Diary of a Foreign Minister,* Sydney, NewSouth

Cerule Consulting, India Country Strategy-Australia http://www.slideshare.net/CeruleConsulting/india-country-strategy-australia (access 14 July 2014)

Chacko, Priya (2014), "The rise of the Indo-Pacific: Understanding ideational change and continuity in India's foreign policy", *Australian Journal of International Affairs,* 68:4, DOI: 10.1080/10357718.2014.891565

DPMC (Department of Prime Minister and Cabinet) (2014) https://asiancentury.dpmc.gov.au/ (access 14 July 2014)

Dupont, A (2014), "China's Maritime Power Trip", *The Australian*, 24 May.

Earl, G (2014), "Weight of global expectations rests on Modi's shoulders", *Australian Financial Review*, 1 July.

Evans, G (1995) Australia, ASEAN and the East Asian Hemisphere, 2 August, http://www.gevans.org/speeches/old/1995/020895_australia_asean_eahemisphere.pdf (access 19 June 2015)

Evans, G (2012) Idealism and Realism in Australian Foreign Policy, Hedley Bull Lecture University of Sydney, 14 August 2012 http://www.gevans.org/speeches/speech482.html (Access 14 July 2014)

Fitz Gerald, Stephen (2015), "An independent foreign policy requires our leaders to take on fear of the US and China", *The Age*, 11 May

Fraser, M (2014a) Foreign Policy in the Asian Century, Fabian Essay, July 2014, http://www.fabian.org.au/files/FabianEssay-MalcolmFraser-July2014.pdf (access 14 July 2014)

Fraser, M (2014b), *Dangerous Allies,* Carlton, Melbourne University Press.

Frost, F (2009), Australia's proposal for an 'Asia-Pacific Community': issues and prospects, Parliament of Australia, Parliamentary Library, 1 December

Gordon, S (2012), Indian Ocean: don't militarise the 'great connector', East Asia Forum, 10 April, http://www.eastasiaforum.org/ (access 28 May 2015)

Garnaut, J (2014), "Australia and India to strengthen military ties", *The Age*, 2 July

Garnaut, J (2015), "A bet each way: our China policy is rational", *The Age*, 22 May

Garnaut, R (1989), *Australia and the Northeast Asian ascendancy: report to the Prime Minister and the Minister for Foreign Affairs and Trade*, Canberra, Australian Government Publishing Service.

Grare, F (2014), The India-Australia strategic relationship: Defining realistic expectations, Carnegie Endowment for International Peace, March 2014, http://carnegieendowment.org/files/india_australia_strat_rel.pdf (access 14 July 2014)

Gurry, M (2015), *Australia and India: Mapping the Journey 1944-2014,* Carlton, Melbourne University Press

Kaplan, Robert D (2010), *Monsoon: the Indian Ocean & the Battle for Supremacy in the 21st Century*, Collingwood (Vic), Black Inc.

Harcourt, T (2014), Unfinished business: Labor, free trade and structural reform in the Asian century, Fabian Essay, March 2014 http://www.fabian.org.au/files/FabianEssay-TimHarcourt-March2014(web).pdf (access 14 July 2014)

Hall, I (2015), "Is a 'Modi doctrine' emerging in Indian foreign policy?" *Australian Journal of International Affairs,* 69:3, DOI: 10.1080/10357718.2014.1000263

Kerin, J (2014a), "Dangerous liaisons: Australia's alliances leave China cold", *Australian Financial Review,* 7 July

Kerin, J (2014b), Australia to host US-China war games, *Australian Financial Review*, 24 July

Lowy Institute (2014), 2014 Australia-India Roundtable—Outcomes Statement http://www.lowyinstitute.org/publications/2014-australia-india-roundtable-outcomes-statement (access 14 July 2014)

Medcalf, R (2014), "In Defence of the Indo-Pacific: Australia's new strategic map", *Australian Journal of International Affairs,* DOI: 10.1080/10357718.2014.911814

Mattoo, A (2014), A doctrine of economic levers, soft power, *The Hindu*, 12 June http://www.thehindu.com/todays-paper/tp-opinion/a-doctrine-of-economic-levers-soft-power/article6106020.ece (access 14 July 2014)

Ministry of External Affairs (2014), Sixth BRICS Summit—Fortaleza Declaration http://www.mea.gov.in/bilateral-documents.htm?dtl/23635/Sixth+BRICS+Summit++ Fortaleza+Declaration (access 24 July 2014)

Mukherji, R (2009), "The State, Economic Growth, and Development in India", *India Review,* 8: 1, 81-106

Pan, Chengxin (2014), "The 'Indo-Pacific' and geopolitical anxieties about China's rise in the Asian regional order", *Australian Journal of International Affairs, 68:4,* DOI: 10.1080/10357718.2014.884054

Productivity Commission (2015), *Trade & Assistance Review 2013-14*, Annual Report Series, Canberra, Productivity Commission, June, http://www.pc.gov.au/research/recurring/trade-assistance/2013-14/trade-assistance-review-2013-14.pdf (access 25 June 2015)

Rajendram, D (2014), Modi in Australia: An unprecedented level of engagement, *Lowy Interpreter,* 19 November, http://www.lowyinterpreter.org/post/2014/11/19/Modi-in-Australia-An-unprecedented-level-of-engagement.aspx?COLLCC=2685195111& (access 19 November 2014)

Robb, A (2015), quoted in *The Sydney Morning Herald,* 10 January.

Rumley, D (ed) (2013) *The Indian Ocean Region: Security, Stability and Sustainability in the 21st Century,* Australia India Institute http://www.aii.unimelb.edu.au/sites/default/files/IOTF_0.pdf (access 14 July 2014).

Sainsbury, M (2015), Australia bets it all on India's coal market, *Crikey,* 19 January.

Singh, Sudhir (ed) (2015), *India in Emerging Asia*, New Delhi, Pentagon Press, p. 18.

Tingle, L (2014), "We need to talk about our relationship with the US", *Australian Financial Review*, 30 May

Varghese, P (2013), Our Journey with India, Australia-India Institute Oration, 16 May, http://www.aii.unimelb.edu.au/events/our-journey-india-australia-india-institute-annual-oration (access 19 June 2015)

Walters, G (2014) Engineering a future in India, in Kanga M and A Mattoo (ed) Hullabaloo The Fuss About The India-Australia Relationship, Carlton, Australia India Institute, http://aii.unimelb.edu.au/events/buy-now-hullabaloo (access 5 January 2015)

Weigold, A (2013) in Brennan L and A Weigold (ed) *Re-thinking India: Perceptions from Australia,* New Delhi, Readworthy

Wesley, M (2011), *There Goes the Neighbourhood,* Sydney, NewSouth

Wesley, M (2014), "Face of the Future: Australia has hard strategic choices to make amidst a complex rivalry over leadership and order in the Asia-Pacific", *Australian Financial Review,* 20 November

White, H (2010), *Power Shift: Australia's Future between Washington and Beijing,* Quarterly Essay, September, Collingwood, Black Inc

Wilson, T (2014), The 'Indo-Pacific': absent policy behind meaningless words, *East Asia Forum,* 19 September, http://www.eastasiaforum.org/ (access 28 May 2015)

Winand, P and M Vicziany and P Datar (2015), *The European Union and India: Rhetoric or Meaningful Relationship,* Cheltenham, Edward Elgar

# 20

# "Redesigning Priorities and Affirming Presence": A Pessimistic Perspective on Indo-Latin America Relations

*Sabu Thomas*

## Introduction

Designing a foreign policy is a complex game. It has many contexts and conditions, each suitable for a particular time frame. After the end of a cold war this task become more intricate since a number of new players entered into the arena of international politics. The most difficult assignment was selection of new friends without damaging existing relations. This also coincided with the ever-growing importance of economic dimension of foreign policy. Trade and economic relations became a crucial factor in the designing of foreign policies. The result was the emergence of new alliances and relations.

The foreign policy of India is shaped by several factors including its history, culture geography and economy. Preservation of national interest, achievement of world peace and disarmament have been important objectives of India's foreign policy. These objectives are sought to be achieved through some principles viz. Panchsheel, non-alignment, anti-colonialism, anti-imperialism, anti-racism and strengthening the UN system. Since the end of the cold war India emerged as a vibrant actor in the international scenario. In regional politics, India became an unquestioned actor by virtue of its economy and politics. The country is actively involved in strengthening the regional ties through many regional forums and alliances.

In the international scenario, the Indian position is well established by the Indian presence in economic forums and global groupings. The Indian links with Latin America are also a part of its global strategy to promote international peace and secure national interests. With respect to the Latin American region, its foreign policy was much isolated due to the geographical disadvantages and traditional dependence on United States. By and large Latin American countries were absent from mainstream international politics for a long time in history. However, the Indian association with Latin America can be traced back to the early period of Indian independence. In order to ensure a share in the new global politics collective voices became a necessity. This culminated in the birth of Non-Alignment Movement. India and Colombia are members of that movement. However, the Indo-Latin America relations are still at its infancy and there are many steps to initiate and complete. The region requires special attention from the policy quarters as there are large potentials and profits both for India and Latin America.

## Shared Culture and Shared Concerns

Foreign policy becomes sustainable only in the background of commonalities. If the policy participants are having common concerns and bonds the relations will become more stable and friendly. In this respect India and Latin America have many common issues and concerns. Latin America suffered four hundred years of colonial domination till the beginning of the twentieth century when the continent was finally free. This story of colonial domination is a common thread between both. India was under colonial domination for a considerable part of her history. The colonial exploitation and consequent damages to national morality, economy and politics is at the same pitch in both areas. India is not a 'distant', 'strange' land for the Latin Americans in a cultural sense. Indian Yoga and meditation has won many followers in the region. In many ways India and Latin American countries are natural partners because of their shared understanding of the values of democracy, rules of law, justice and equality.

The politics of Latin America is more in favour of leftist ideology. It is observed that the majority of the countries in Latin America have leftist governments. However, the regional politics is more pragmatic and admits private sector in the economy to create more wealth. Today, Latin America can be considered as a land of flourishing democracy. There are regular elections and active political parties and military coupes are history. The liberalization wave has already reached the area and India can find many understanding partners here.

Trade and commerce makes foreign policies more spicy and vibrant. With regard to trade relations, India-Latin America trade relationship can be considered at an infant stage. Potentials are many, but there is a long way to go. As of 2010 estimates India and Latin American region traded just $23 billion in goods. It comes to barely one-sixth of the region's trade with China. However, the scenario is very bright since Latin America's trade with India is growing fast. Latin America provides a large market of 600 million populations with a combined GDP of US$ 6.9 trillion and a trade turnover of US$ 2.1 trillion. Foreign Direct Investment (FDI) flows into Latin America touched a record high of US$ 166 billion in 2012. In the late 1980s Latin American countries had a trade-to-GDP ratio roughly equal to the trade-to-GDP ratio of China and two times larger than the trade-to-GDP ratio of India (Lederman, Olarreaga, & Perry, 2009).

A few years back the economic scenario in the Latin American region was dismal with high inflation, heavy external debt and stagnant economy. But the liberalization process has changed the equations. In the case of external debt, the figure is around 21% of GDP. The high growth rate of the region and the enormous size of the market is a big attraction to Indian investors. Combined with calm politics, the Latin America offers a big business venue. This potential was well realized by China much earlier and they established high volume trade relations. They have a heavy volume of trade with the area that comes around ten times of Indian trade.

Indian business has a strong presence in the Latin America. In the Information Technology sector Indian companies have set up software development centres, business process outsourcing, knowledge process outsourcing and call centres. Indian companies are also active in the agrochemical sector as well as in hydrocarbons and minerals. In the automobile sector Indian companies have set up assembly plants for automobiles. Latin American region offers a significant and growing market for India's pharmaceutical engineering, textile, handicraft and other exports. It is hoped that the immense endowments of natural resources including hydrocarbons agricultural land fresh water minerals and bio-diversity in the area have been increasingly recognized for their potential contribution to India's energy and food security. Understanding the potential of the area, the Commerce Ministry, Government of India started an integrated programme titled "Focus: LAC" in November 1997.

## The BRICS Factor

The term BRICS stands for Brazil, Russia, India, China and South Africa. This term was coined by the Chief Economist of Goldman Sachs in 2001 in a paper titled 'Building Better Global Economic BRICs' which looked at the growth prospects of the four largest emerging economies that are culturally and geographically disparate. The major finding of the paper was that BRICs has a potential role in changing the global economy. It is visualized as a new economic bloc catering for the emerging markets. South Africa was later introduced into the group, making the term BRICS. The organization emerged in a period when global financial structure was in great trouble due to the financial crisis. The BRICS countries managed to stay stable in the storm of economic crisis. This was a clear signal to the advanced economies. They alone cannot operate the economic structure. Global economy needs an integrated approach to include the lesser powerful actors. Economic blocs like BRICS gained more relevance in this context. BRICS is also a forum for promoting multipolarism in the post-cold war world.

BRICS countries together account for more than 40 per cent of the global population It also has nearly 30 per cent of the land mass and a share in world GDP (in PPP terms) that amounts to nearly 25 per cent as of 2010 figures (Finance Ministry, 2012:IX). In the BRICS organization Brazil plays an important role. Brazil is major exporter of agricultural products. In the social sphere the Brazil model of conditional cash transfers proved to be an effective check to poverty in the country. This model was later taken by India to address its poverty issues. Amidst the turbulent waters of global financial crisis Brazil stood as an unchallenged economy due to its strict regulatory framework and monetary policies. Brazil and India are two giants of their respective regions and they have a unique and important relationship. Brazil and India rank among the largest democracies and economies in the world and share similar development goals.

**Table 1: India-Brazil Bilateral Trade (2008-2014) (in US Dollar millions)**

| *Sl No* | *Year* | *India's Exports* | *India's Imports* | *Balance of trade for India* | *Total trade* | *Growth %* |
|---|---|---|---|---|---|---|
| 1 | 2008 | 3564 | 1102 | 2461 | 4666 | 49.23 |
| 2 | 2009 | 2,191 | 3,415 | -1224 | 45605 | 20.12 |
| 3 | 2010 | 4242 | 3492 | 750 | 7734 | 37.97 |
| 4 | 2011 | 6081 | 3201 | 2880 | 9282 | 20 |
| 5 | 2012 | 5043 | 5577 | -544 | 10620 | 14.41 |
| 6 | 2013 | 6357 | 3130 | 3227 | 9487 | -10.67 |
| 7 | 2014 | 6635 | 4789 | 1846 | 11424 | 20.40 |

In the BRICS Indian trade with Brazil gives a positive growth in the period 2013-14 with a 20.4% growth. However, the graph is not steady and shows negative trends in certain periods. The conclusion is that the prospects of bilateral trade remaining highly positive, the benefits are yet to be reflected in economic sphere. This demands larger attention for bilateral trade.

## Prospects of Partnership

The liberalization of economy is a major propellant in foreign relations. This liberalization process started in India and countries in Latin America at the same time. One result of that policy shift was more international investment opportunities and deeper global economic ties. India and Latin America share a growing young population and price-sensitive consumers. India lacks natural resources whereas Latin America exports them. This relationship has the potential to generate mutual benefits for both the Indian and Latin American economies.

The government of India has expressed growing interest in fostering Latin American connections. There are frequent high level visits between the two countries in recent times. In September 2014, Indian Prime Minister Narendra Modi paid a visit to Brazil for the BRICS Summit. During the visit he met the leaders of twelve South American countries. These meetings opened a new door to the deliberations between India and the region.

## Conclusion

The historical disinterest between India and the Latin American Countries is almost over. There is greater understanding between the two, particularly in the era of globalization. The enormous distance between the two areas is not a disadvantage in the new foreign policy paradigm. The economic concerns and trade relations are rewarding both for India and Latin America. Jorge Heine who was Ambassador of Chile to India opines:

> "At the beginning of the second decade of this new century the appeal that India is starting to exercise in Latin America is considerable. Its vigorous parliamentary democracy its growing economy its high-tech achievements in combination with its millenarian spiritual traditions make for a heady mix. To make the most of this appeal however requires a much more proactive policy towards the region one that realizes that in this new international order that is emerging by working together India and Latin America have much to gain" (Heine, 2011:27).

The end of the cold war and the new international politics demands closer association with like-minded powers. Here are serious issues like climate change, terrorism, natural calamities, human rights etc. These issues can be addressed by global efforts effectively and Indo-Latin America collective can contribute to this issues. The problem of combating narcotic trafficking is another problem area in the relations. The grave issue of narcotics can be handled only by the interaction of the actors. The emergence of a turbulent international politics and new global problems demands more and more close collective forums. India and Latin

America can be such a potential forum for bringing global order and peaceful human life.

## NOTES

1. It is argued that there was an evident reluctance from the part of some Latin American countries to take part in the global politics. This situation is well evidenced by Heine (2011). He says, "The reluctance of some Latin American countries in the not-too-distant past to stand for election as non-permanent members to the UN Security Council (even when according to the rotation principle it was their turn) is a good example of this international shyness. This derives from a feeling that there is little to be gained and much to be lost by engaging global issues on a platform like the Security Council. See Heine (2011: 22).
2. See External Affairs Minister's Speech on "India-Latin America & Caribbean: The Way Forward" at the CII India-LAC Conclave Valedictory Session, December 10 2013, http://www.mea.gov.in/SpeechesStatements.htm?dtl/22605/External+Affairs+ Ministers+ Speech+ on+ IndiaLatin+America+amp+Caribbean+The+Way+Forward+at+the+CII+IndiaLAC+ Conclave+ Valedictory+Session, Accessed on 16-06-2015
3. The non-dogmatic leftism of Latin America is well explained by Ambassador (Retd) R. Viswanathan at his extempore talk at Jadavpur University, Kolkatta on 18 April 2015. He observes "MN Roy was a founder of the Communist Party of Mexico before he came back to found the Communist party of India. He spent over two years in Mexico from 1917 to 1919. He became a communist during his stay in Mexico. .... Roy called Mexico as 'the land of his rebirth'. Today the house where he stayed in Mexico City has been converted into a vibrant bar/night club with the name MN Roy". Source,http://www.mea.gov.in/distinguished-lectures-detail.htm?279, accessed on 22-06-2015.
4. However presently China's and India's combined share of world exports is 50 percent larger than LAC's share.
5. Venezuela and Argentina are the exceptions to this statement. However, they also possess many potentials and they can easily emerge from the problems, many of which are self-created.
6. The stability of the economies of individual countries in the region has been reinforced by the regional integration through Mercosur Andean Community UNASUR and SICA. Mexico is part of NAFTA. In April 2011 another economic grouping, the Pacific (Ocean) Group was formed by Mexico Peru Colombia and Chile with the objective of economic integration. Through these groups the barriers are being removed for free movement of goods services capital and people and there is growing intraregional trade and investment. Mercosur has emerged as a formidable trading bloc of the region. The other groups are in various stages of integration. The pace of integration might be slow but regional integration is the clear destination in the long term. See Viswanathan (2011: 9).
7. Source, http://www.mea.gov.in/articles-in-indian media.htm?dtl/22142/Fusing+ adventure+ with+ diplomacy+Indias+Latin+America+odyssey, accessed on 18-06-2015.
8. Focus LAC programme aims at: 1. Sensitizing the organizations viz. Export Promotion Councils Chambers of Commerce & Industry EXIM Bank ECGC etc. involved in trade promotion efforts; 2. Granting various incentives to Indian exporters and launching of export promotion measures; 3. Focussing on the Latin American region with added emphasis on major trading partners of the region; 4. Focussing on the following major product groups for enhancing India's exports to the Latin American region: (a) Textiles including ready-made garments carpets and handicrafts; (b) Engineering products and computer software; (c)

Chemical products including drugs/pharmaceuticals. *Source*: Ministry of Commerce, Government of India.

9. "BRICS is strengthening global multipolarity in the world. This is how it should be. It is important that it does not take us back to the bi-polar world of the Cold War. Fortunately there is no reason for such apprehension. Each of the BRICS members has close economic ties with the West and wishes to promote cooperation with it. BRICS must repose trust in a cooperative approach both with the West and with the rest. BRICS should also endeavour to gain the trust of other developing countries through its developmental activities". See Amb (Retd) Dilip Sinha, Role of India in BRICS, Distinguished Lecture, Visva Bharati West Bengal, April 18 2015, *Source*: http://www.mea.gov.in/distinguished-lectures-detail.htm?285, accessed on 23-06-2015.
10. Ambassador R. Viswanathan observes: "Latin America has undergone a paradigm shift in the last two decades. The region has come out of the past curses of political and economic instability and cycles of booms and busts. A stable and prosperous New Latin America is emerging. The New Latin Americans are looking forward to the future with confidence and optimism. India needs to recognize this new scenario and take strategic steps to engage this region enhance cooperation and promote trade and investment". See Viswanathan (2011: 7)
11. "India and Colombia are victims of terrorism. India's neighbourhood has emerged as the epicenter of world terrorism. Cross-border terrorism continues to impinge on our security. The fight against international terrorism needs a strong commitment from the world community both in the form of actions and multilateral frameworks. India's proposal for a Comprehensive Convention on International Terrorism (CCIT) assumes importance in this regard. We are confident that with the support of countries like Colombia we will be able to ensure its early adoption", See Katju (2011: 6).

## REFERENCES

Finance, M. O. (2012). *The Brics Report.* New Delhi: Oxford University Press.

Heine, J. (2011). "Much to Gain by Working Together in the Emerging International Order", *Indian Foreign Affairs Journal,* 6 (1), 19–27.

Katju, V. (2011). "Growing Awareness between India and Latin America", *Indian Foreign Affairs Journal,* 6 (1), 3-6.

Lederman, D., Olarreaga, M., & Perry, G.E. (2009). "Latin America's Response to China and India: Overview of Research Findings and Policy Implications", in D. Lederman, M. Olarreaga, & G.E. Perry, *China's and India's Challenge to Latin America Opportunity or Threat?* (pp. 3-39). Washington DC: The World Bang.

Mathur, S., Dasgupta, M., & Sirohi, P. (2013). "Trade Policies and Institutions of BRICS", in S. Mathur, & M. Dasgupta, *BRICS: Trade Policies, Institutions and areas of Deepening Cooperation* (pp. 1-158). New Delhi: Centre for WTO Studies, Indian Institute of Foreign Trade.

Schmid, A. P. (2004). "Frameworks for conceptualing terrorism", *Terrorism and Political Violence,* 16 (2), 197–221.

Viswanathan, R. (2011). "The New Latin America and the Next Steps for India", *Indian Foreign Policy Affairs,* 6 (1), 7-17.

# 21

# India-China-US Relations: Prospects for a Strategic Triangle

*Shyna V.V.*

## Introduction

The 21st century is witnessing the rise of two home-grown maritime powers against the backdrop of US dominion over the global commons. Their aspirations for power status and, above all, their quests for energy security has compelled both Beijing and New Delhi to redirect their gazes from land to the seas. There are mutual convergences and divergences of interests and objectives among the three nations. But the bilateral relationship between all the three countries has grown significantly in the recent years. Among these, the US, the only superpower today, and its strategic interests in Asia must account for the concerns of its two rising powers, China and India. Each has almost 37-38% of the world's population and a great domestic economic transformation of these two countries, thus, has major international implications. But, China's political future remain a big question mark, as China may have undergone increasing economic liberalization, but its polity continues to be marked by a Communist monopoly over political power. Being a democracy, India has an institutionalized political system, and transfer of power between different political parties or alliances is a regular political occurrence.[1]

The last two decades have witnessed dramatic improvements in Indo-US ties, a reduction of tension in bilateral Indo-China relations and the progression of Sino-US relationship from a strategic partner under the Clinton administration to a strategic competitor under the Bush Government and ambivalence under

President Barack Obama.[2] However, the nature of interaction among the Indo-China, Sino-US and Indo-US couplets is currently far from hostile and full of uncertainties at the dawn of the new millennium. The trio is showing a remarkably consistent and restrained reciprocity towards one another. It is unclear what pattern the triangle will evolve into; some speculate about a Indo-US alignment on issues where they share common interests, vis-à-vis China. Others emphasise on India and China, who might join hands to build a multi-polar world. And some viewed a conflict between India and Pakistan might witness the US and China joining hands against India.[3] Hence, the strategic triangle is an inherently restricted triangle, with the degree of its restriction varying in different situations.

With the economic and military rise of China and India, both countries have become considerably strong regional powers that shift the unipolar position of the US. Considering the fact that the US aims to pursue its balance of power strategy in Asia, it increasingly ties up with India in order to counterbalance China's powerful rise.[4] However, the question is how India will play the game in the changing international power structure: should it go along with the US and contain China? Or, should it play an equiproximity game, maintaining closeness both with the US and China? Thus, the challenge for India is how to boost its relationship with the US that can provide an impetus to its economy and defence capability building without antagonising China. Therefore, the present Government led by Narendra Modi is expected to pursue a more robust and assertive approach and enhance India's influence and prestige on the global stage. Accordingly, the current paper highlights the existing competitive interests between the three countries and tries to find out the ways and means which will strengthen the co-operation. The paper analyses the triangular relationship in reference to three themes: firstly nuclear proliferation, secondly militarization, and thirdly the international political and financial economy. But it is necessary to have a look at the bilateral relations between all the three countries.

## India-China: Competition or Cooperation?

China and India were the ancient civilizations that together comprise nearly two-fifths of humanity. Their entire 4,057-kilometre long border, one of the longest in the world—remains in dispute without a clearly defined line of control in the Himalayas separating the rival armies. The disputes and tensions between the two countries hold significant implications for international security and Asian power dynamics. China is a big power in East Asia while India is a big power in South Asia and each enjoys advantages and influence in their respective regions. However, the cooperation in the areas include a burgeoning economic relationship, greater dialogue on issues like Afghanistan and counter terrorism, as well as cooperation in multilateral forums, including BRICS and on multilateral issues such as climate change.[5]

China's concerns about the presence of the Dalai Lama and other Tibetan leaders in India, as well as India's concerns about Chinese dam construction on its side of the Brahmaputra river and cyber espionage and cyber security threats led to a conflicting interest between the two countries. As Ashley Tellis rigtly pointed out that Beijing's and New Delhi's divergent behaviours are shaped by the unique histories governing their formation as modern states, the stark contrasts in their respective political regimes, and their ongoing territorial disputes and geopolitical rivalries.[6] In fact, India fears an encircling by China in South Asia while China fears an encircling in South East Asia and East Asia, by US and its allies, including India. This mistrust led to a geopolitical competition, has been sharpened by China's strategic projects around India including new ports in Sri Lanka and Pakistan and transportation links with Myanmar, Nepal, and Pakistan, as well as China's own major upgrades to military infrastructure in Tibet.[7] These factors make the three countries important strategic partners for China, while India's relations with these countries will remain an issue for China unless there is an understanding on mutual interests.

As far as the security is concerned, Sino-Pakistan bilateral relationship has been a source of concern, especially its military, missile and nuclear aspects. Delhi viewed China's issuance of stapled visas to Indian citizens from the state of Jammu and Kashmir as a deviation from China's neutrality in the dispute between India and Pakistan and a questioning of Indian sovereignty.[8] The interesting thing is that India wants China to show that India-China relation is a central priority. As long as China allies itself with Pakistan, there will be little hope for improved Sino-Indian relations.

The simmering Sino-Indian tensions threatened to become an open conflict in 2013 when Chinese troops stealthily crossed the disputed Himalayan border at night in the Ladakh region. China then embarked on coercive diplomacy and withdrew its troops three weeks later only after India destroyed a defensive line of local fortifications. This episode showed that stoking tensions with Japan, Vietnam, and the Philippines over islands in the South and East China Seas did not prevent an increasingly assertive China from opening yet another front. The fact is that, with its 'peaceful rise' giving way to an increasingly sharp-el bowed approach to its neighbours, China has broadened its 'core interests' and territorial claims while showing a growing readiness to take risks to achieve its goals.[9] But the recent visit of the Xi Jinping to India on September 18, 2014, symbolizes the beginning of a new stage in the development and formulated several agreement between the two countries. It cover a variety of areas including investments into the road and port infrastructure of India, cooperation in space and in nuclear energy, construction of industrial parks in India, joint efforts in combating terrorism, cultural cooperation and a twin cities agreement between Mumbai and Shanghai.[10]

At the economic level, China is one of the most crucial trade partners of India. But the bilateral trade has actually fallen over the last few years from $74 billion in 2011 to about $65 billion in 2013.[11] China's new premier Li Keqiang said, "We are not a threat to each other, nor do we seek to contain each other," and pledged to open China's markets to Indian products to address the trade imbalance and boost commerce to $100 billion a year. While the trade has increased between the two countries becoming a binding factor in improving relations, the ever-widening deficit has become a major stumbling block, especially for India, whose exports were hit by depreciating rupee and also by declining exports of iron ore which previously was the main stay of Indian exports.[12] Anyhow, their bilateral relationship will be characterized more by competition than cooperation because the issues that bind them are also the issues that divide them. Neither power is comfortable with the rise of the other.

## India and US: Friendship on Fast Track

In the past decades the Indo-US relationship was like a Stock Exchange, which had its ups and down. The relationship between the two countries was wounded of mismatched obsessions of India with Pakistan and America with the erstwhile USSR. The Pokhran II tests in May 1998, resulted in a review of the relationship and the Clinton visit to Delhi of March 2000 marked the beginning of the thaw. However, the more radical decision to admit India into the global nuclear framework was enabled by then US president George Bush in mid-2005 and reached fruition in late 2008.[13] Hence, the US has comprehended India as major partner and both countries agreed to work cooperatively to promote stability, democracy, prosperity and peace throughout the world. It was, however, the offer of the US to "work to achieve full civil nuclear energy cooperation with India, seek agreement from Congress to adjust US laws and policies and work with friends and allies to adjust international regimes to enable full civil nuclear energy cooperation and trade with India." That was symbolic of the new phase of ties between the two countries.[14] Therefore, the synergy in energy contributed a turning point in the evolution of India's relations with the US. It saw a drastic change in the international community's stance towards India on the nuclear issue.

At the security level, both countries are:

- trying to help Bangladesh to cope with it aggressive, radical Islamic movement and to stop Bangladeshi support to IIGs;
- advising Nepal on how to bring back democracy and to resolve the Maoist movement;

- trying and convince the parties in Sri Lanka to agree to a cease-fire;
- supporting the initiative of Kofi Annan's new initiative on democracy promotion worldwide;
- planning on undertaking practical exercises in anti-narcotic operations and in countering piracy; and
- working jointly to fight global HIV/AIDS in worldwide.

But there are some serious differences of opinion about Iran, Burma, and Pakistan. Even today, the United States is actively trying (for now, unsuccessfully) to force India to support an American initiative to reform the WTO, which, if it should be implemented, would lead to the ruin of hundreds of millions of Indian farmers. Additionally, both countries have divergence over the 'Af-Pak' region and the Middle East, the evolving situation in Asia could well provide the basis for a new bonding. The breakthrough also signalled a significant diplomatic victory for India's stand that it would not dilute its liability law.[15] The nuclear liability issue has remained a stumbling block in Indo-US relations over the past four years. While in opposition, the BJP opposed the nuclear deal and pushed for liability legislation that complicated US companies' ability to invest in civil nuclear projects in India.[16] But President Obama has made a historic visit to India, the first US head of state to attend India's Republic Day and the only sitting US President to visit India twice, has given an opportunity to discuss misgivings over the liability law and also meet foreign governments and the supplier community halfway on the issue.

Inspite of these issues, both share core values and strategic interests, including mutual concern about militancy in Pakistan and the rise of China. Therefore, the relationship has success stories. These include robust economic relations, maritime cooperation and a 3-million-strong Indian American diaspora.[17] Besides, the American and Indian militaries have participated in a number of bilateral exercise including Yudh Abhyas, Cope India, Malabar and Vajra Prahar. India conducts more military exercise with the US than with any other country.[18] Thus, PM Modi has referred to the two nations as natural allies. As he noted, "the true power and potential in this relationship is that when the oldest and largest democracies come together, the world will benefit."[19]

As far as the economy is concerned, the bilateral trade between the two countries has increased 60 per cent in the past couple of years to a record $100 billion, but India's exports to the US were still less than 2 per cent of all American imports.[20] The US is India's largest trading partner, but there is immense room for growth. Because China-US trade, for example, is over five times more than Indo-US trade. However, the new Government has promised to open the economy to more private investment, improve the GDP growth rate, create jobs for the rapidly growing youth population, and quicken the pace of India's defence modernization. It will open numerous opportunities for expanded Indo-US cooperation on a range of issues.[21] If India needs US investments and strategic support in Asia where China's futuristic moves are narrowing India's space, the US equally needs the world's largest democracy for its market and for maintaining a fair balance of power in the region.[22]

## China-US: Ambivalence Powers

The Sino-US relation has graduated from an environment of hostility to engagement. The two sides welcomed all efforts conducive to peace, stability and development in South Asia. They support the efforts of Afghanistan and Pakistan to fight terrorism, maintain domestic stability and achieve sustainable economic and social development, and support the improvement and growth of relations between India and Pakistan.[23] But there are some differences on issues regarding Taiwan, trade imbalances, China's growing military power, China's global and regional activities, human rights, and domestic and political matters. The state of human rights in China, the situation in Tibet, and the treatment of other minority communities such as Uighur Muslims in Xinjiang remains an important human rights and religious freedom concern for the US.[24] Needless to say, as the relation between the US, the world's great power, and China, the world's rising power is one of the most important yet complicated bilateral relationships in the world today.

China's greatest strategic fear is that an outside power or powers will establish military deployments around China's periphery capable of encroaching on China's territory or meddling in its domestic institutions. At the same time, the US fear, sometimes only indirectly expressed, is of being pushed out of Asia by an exclusionary bloc. If China and the US come to regard each other's trade-pact efforts as elements in a strategy of isolation, the Asia-Pacific region could devolve into competing adversarial power blocs. The key decision facing both Beijing and Washington is whether to move toward a genuine effort at cooperation or fall into a new version of historic patterns of international rivalry.[25]

At the economic level, both countries have expanded substantially over the past three decades. The total Sino-US trade rose from $2 billion in 1979 to $562 billion in 2013. China is currently the US second-largest trading partner, its third-largest export market, and its biggest source of imports. Besides, China is estimated to be a $350 billion market for US firms (based on US direct and indirect exports to China and sales by US-invested firms in China).[26] Although China's comprehensive capabilities have been growing rapidly for the past three decades, almost all analysts inside and outside of China agree that there is still a huge gap between China and the US in terms of comprehensive capabilities, particularly when the US is far ahead of China in military and technological realms. China's economy has passed the US economy as the largest one in 2014, but the quality of China's economy still remains a major weakness for Beijing. Thus, it would be a serious mistake for China to challenge the US directly given the wide gap of capabilities between the two.[27]

On 12 November 2014, President Barack Obama sat down with Chinese President Xi Jinping at the Asian Pacific Economic Cooperation (APEC) summit to discuss joint co-operation on a range of international issues. Obama managed to leave Beijing with a guarantee that China would cut greenhouse gas emissions and increase the share of non-fossil fuels in primary energy consumption—a development that was heralded as a diplomatic coup for the US. However, the issue of climate change was not a sensitive issue in the same way that cybersecurity and South China Sea issues are today. In a best case scenario, we could see both sides acknowledging a divergence of opinion on these matters in a joint statement.[28] Moreover, President Xi Jinping's state visit to the US is expected in the month of September 2015. The important topics might be on the agenda, including progress on a bilateral investment treaty (BIT), military confidence building measures and agreement on what approach to take at December's climate change conference to be held in Paris.[29] However, the 2015 is an important year in Sino-US relations, and making headway both on areas of cooperation and making headway on areas of concern.

## Challenges for the Triangle

On the one side US is promoting mutual cooperation, where the mighty and average would work together to reap the benefits of inter-dependence to maintain a peaceful world order. But on the other side, US does not want Asia to be dominated by any single power and, much more, its own exclusion or marginalisation in the Asian geo-strategic architecture.[30] Because there are a number of strategic directions China could take depending on which domestic and external factors emerge as key determinants of Chinese national security policy. And which path China will follow remains unknown, however, and this uncertainty complicates the formulation of an effective policy for managing China's rising power throughout the Asia-Pacific region.

As Asia and its maritime spaces emerge as a major arena of contest between Washington and Beijing, the US and India are drawing closer in their respective policies to the region. It is in this context, India's new triangular dynamic with the US and China added significance and plays out most clearly in the Asia-Pacific.[31] However, a beneficial triangular relationship presupposes, as a minimum, a long-term common goal. India, China, and the US that share a similar long-term vision of prosperity and stability in the Indo-Pacific. Even the Pentagon agrees, viewing India not only as a "regional economic anchor", but also as a "provider of security in the broader Indian Ocean region."[32] But the query is how to cooperate effectively with both US and China without seeming to favour the relationship with one at the cost of the relationship with the other? It will be one of the main concerns in the coming decades. Therefore, we can identify the challenges through three important angle-military, nuclear and economy.

## Military Confrontation

In regard to militarization, both China and India are increasing their military expenditures in relation to the US. With the Taiwan straits, the Sino -Indian border disputes and recent escalations with the Philippines over the nine--dashed line in the South China Sea amongst others, there is potential for military confrontation in Asia.[33] Besides, China's claims over the entire South China Sea as well as the Spratly and Paracel islands, which sit astride vital sea-lanes through which 25 percent of the world's shipping passes. It is one of the biggest potential flashpoints in the Asia-Pacific region, as it affects virtually all countries in the South China Sea including Vietnam, Malaysia, Taiwan, the Philippines, and Brunei.[34] However, its increasing military re-assertion, many Asian countries seem to seek an alliance with the US to counterbalance China's rise. At the same time, US naval forces are trying to play a major role in a South China Sea contingency, access to the region for US land-based fighter aircraft would complicate Chinese calculations, because of the serious difficulties China would face in establishing air superiority for its naval forces operating in the South China Sea.[35]

Simultaneously, China is closely watching the prospering Indo-US relations with suspicion because it perceives that the expanding multifaceted relationship between India and the US is finally aimed at the containment of China. China doesn't want to see India become a major power in the world and the relationship with the US is the key to India achieving this objective.[36] One of the eminent strategic analysts S.D. Muni examined that strategically the Asian countries are seeking assurance in the heightened US presence in the region and a new strategic balance to be created with greater involvement of Asian powers like India, Australia and Japan. All these countries want to prevent China's domination in the region. But the exceptions, such as Iran and Pakistan have no problem with a rising and assertive China.[37] Therefore, the question is will India play a balancing game for US. The Indian Government has always upheld that it does not propose to follow an aggressive policy towards China and has declined to be an American proxy or bulwark under any circumstances. But from a geopolitical point of view, if a US policy strategically confines or weakens China in the region, it is unlikely that India would mind, even though it does not want to be directly involved in any anti-China strategy.[38]

Another issue that ties in with this argument is the continuingly unresolved Taiwan question. Taiwan has been an important geostrategic partner for the US throughout the era of the Cold War and the containment of contender states. According to Bruce Cumings, the US geopolitical interests determined the successful development of Taiwan to a considerable extent. Whereas China still claims the 'One-China' solution, Taiwan is very likely to tie in with other Asian countries to form a closer alliance with the US.[39] In the future it will be interesting to see if China has the ability to balance out military power and a careful rise without making its neighbours too nervous.

## Issue of Nuclear Proliferation

On the one hand, India has upheld that its weapons are deterrent against China but on the other hand Pakistan also maintained that its weapons are a deterrent against India. At the centre of this nuclear climax, if India decides to speed up its nuclear programme whether it is civilian or military, there will be a ripple effect through the region. Consequently, the basic point worth stressing here is that the Indo-US nuclear agreement could prompt Pakistan to go for similar deal with China on the principle that an enemy's enemy is a friend.

The interesting thing is that the US wants India's assistance in dealing with a range of dangerous contingencies involving Pakistan. As we know that, Pakistan is already a proliferation risk: Pakistani nuclear scientist A.Q. Khan's unlawful nuclear network, revealed in 2004, shocked the world with its brazen trade of nuclear technology. In fact, many of the nuclear proliferation problems of today are directly linked to the A. Q. Khan network. Parallel with Khan's efforts, China has provided loans and technical assistance to Pakistan for building two atomic power reactors. It has now been revealed that China has signed a US $2.375 billion agreement for supplying two 340 MW power reactors (Chasma-3 and Chasma-4) to Pakistan. Beijing would also loan some 80 percent of the project cost. It is a matter of concern for the US. But the Chinese official is arguing that the supply of Chasma-3 and Chasma-4 was included in the earlier agreement of 1985 pertaining to the supply of Chasma-1 and Chasma-2.[40] It will indeed be an uphill task for the new Indian Government to get China to discuss nuclear security matters with India. However, nuclear confrontation is a great concern in the coming decades.

## International Economic Competition

The growing economic interests of the three countries is another concern. Indian interests now extend from Aden to Singapore, from the Straits of Hormuz to Malacca and New Delhi will economically integrate with Asia, and work closely with Hanoi and Tokyo. Consequently, the US wants to assign important strategic role to India from Strait of Hormuz to Strait of Malacca. Because the US is the most powerful military power in this region for its Central Command and Asia-Pacific Command. India is strategically located between these two naval task force. Thus, its location can be beneficial for both the US commands.[41] Moreover, the US has vital strategic interests in the world's largest reserves of energy lying in the Middle East, Gulf region and South Asia and India occupies the strategic location linking the Indian and Pacific Oceans.[42] As Harsh V Pant rightly noted that US would like a strong US-India alliance to act as a 'bulwark against the arc of Islamic instability running form the Middle East to Asia and to create much greater balance in Asia.'[43] At the same time, China, in turn, is exploiting the chaos in Afghanistan and Pakistan to extend its influence in the region and into Central Asia.[44] The interesting thing is that China has not categorised India as a threat or challenge even though it considers India as a 'future strategic competitor'. Therefore, managing these interests is significant in the 21$^{st}$ century.

Another aspect is the billions of dollars US corporations are pouring into China. Much of what the largest American supermarket chain, Wal-Mart, sells today—from small appliances to refrigerators is made in China. Dell, among the largest producers of personal computers, assembles its laptops and desktops in China. The toys for American children are manufactured in China. The more Chinese economy grows and expands, the more resources China will have for military modernization and for 'broadcasting' its power in the world.[45]

Additionally, nearly 70 percent of China's trade is through the Strait of Malacca, the Indian Ocean, and the Suez Canal. The predominance of the US and Indian navies along these sea-lanes of communication (SLOCs) is viewed as a major threat to Chinese security. To protect its long-term economic security interests, China is now laying the groundwork for a naval presence along maritime chokepoints in the South China Sea, the Malacca Straits, the Indian Ocean, and the Strait of Hormuz in the Persian Gulf through acquisition of naval bases in Cambodia, Burma, Bangladesh, and Pakistan. India has countered by promoting defence cooperation with Iran, Oman, and Israel in the west while upgrading military ties with Burma, Singapore, Maldives, Thailand, Vietnam, Taiwan, the Philippines, Australia, Japan, and the United States in the east. India's new naval doctrine is to influence events around the Indian Ocean and beyond. However, the maritime competition is likely to intensify as Indian and Chinese navies show off their flag in the South China Sea and the Indian Ocean with greater frequency.[46]

## Prospects for Strategic Cooperation

The emerging strategic triangle has all three states having their mutual convergences and divergences and also having ongoing strategic partnerships or dialogues amongst them. Each state has partnerships with the other working together on some issues, but finding themselves in disagreement on others without forming any firm or enduring alignment. Hence currently, the strategic triangle is a complex and shifting one, which is highly fluid, as proposed by Harry Harding, the Director, Research and Analysis, Eurasia Group, USA. It means each pair of countries working together on some issues, but finding themselves in disagreements on others, without forming any firm or enduring alignment.[47]

The fluid nature of the India-China-US triangle generates uncertainty, since there are elements of cooperation as well as conflict involving all the three bilateral relationships. The hope for stability lies in mutual accommodation.[48] The three countries share common concerns—including those related to Afghanistan (and even Pakistan), the Middle East and climate change—and this offers the prospect of cooperation, or at least, consultation in the future.[49] In the case of Afghanistan, India worries about stability in its front yard, China is concerned about its economic investments and American fears terrorism. Each has a considerable stake in keeping Afghanistan from becoming a failed state. The three powers have much more in common than not when it comes to stabilizing Afghanistan.[50]

Moreover, the US role in the ongoing global war on terrorism, the Uighur problem in China, and India's counter-terrorism initiatives in Kashmir find commonality of purpose. Hence, it is very likely that all three states may work in concert to pursue convergences such as the rising threat of terrorism in near future, other transnational problems, economic inter-dependence and trade benefits, and to curb global developments inimical to their national interests and in furtherance of global peace and prosperity. Similarly, with recent increases in violence in Xinjiang, Beijing is concerned about the flow of militants across national boundaries. On October 31, 2014, Chinese Foreign Ministry Spokesperson Hong Lei told reporters at a press conference that, "China is willing to start cooperating with the international community in striking out against terrorism." Driving this newfound willingness to engage with the US on counterterrorism is a recent event in China's far western province Xinjiang.[51]

Further cooperation can be enhanced through trade. Successful initiatives such as the Joint Commission on Commerce and Trade (JCCT) and the Strategic Economic Dialogue (SED) between the US and China will have to be further strengthened to boost economic cooperation. Correspondingly, there is a need for India to increase its trade with both China and the US. The existing forums developed as part of the US-India Economic Dialogue must seek ways to resolve outstanding economic and trade issues and boost trade.[52] Another important area of convergences on the energy and environmental issues as well. Initiatives such as the APEC Energy Security Initiative and Asia-Pacific Partnership on Clean Development and Climate are aimed at collaborative efforts to implement projects that will improve energy security, air pollution, climate change, and efficiency in a variety of energy-intensive sectors.[53]

There is a need for confidence building measures such as a trilateral military and security dialogue and transparency in military matters among all three states. India must maintain transparency and reiterate its adherence to the global non-proliferation norms to dispel Chinese fears about the Indo-US nuclear cooperation. India must also examine the Chinese offer for nuclear cooperation based on its merits. Efforts must be made to promote joint military exercises and exchanges among all three states. Equally, China must maintain transparency about its military modernization and trade issues such as the WTO.[54] The US must also initiate a military and nuclear dialogue besides the ongoing strategic dialogue in the case of US-China. This will in turn lead to stabilizing patterns and preventing a nuclear arms race by China.

In addition to this, the strategic triangle will turn more cooperative if all three states must have equitable representation and play an active role in global and regional forums such as the United Nations Security Council (UNSC), G8 summit, Shanghai Cooperation Organization (SCO), Association of Southeast Asian Nations (ASEAN), ASEAN Regional Forum (ARF), East Asia Summit (EAS) and South Asian Association for Regional Cooperation (SAARC). This will act as a confidence building measure and allay current fears which have manifested due to either restrained participation or exclusion of one of the three states from some of these institutions.[55]

In the case of strategic issues, it is time to include the navies in the on-going Indo-China bilateral military exercises and dialogue, as a confidence-building measure. This is especially important given the trend of Chinese submarines conducting long-range patrols into the Indian Ocean and seeking to defend trade routes, even as our own ships venture into the South China Sea. The Indian Ocean has four of the six major maritime chokepoints and serves as a maritime super highway for in-demand energy resources that drives the world's largest economies. Accordingly, the three sides should immediately compare notes on their own Indian Ocean strategies because the secure maritime navigation from Africa and the Middle East to East Asia is vital to energy and resource access. Forty percent of the world's oil and commerce is commuting through the Indian Ocean. Almost 68 percent of India's, 80 percent of China's and 25 percent of the US' oil is shipped from the Indian Ocean Region.[56] Recognising mutual interests in the Indian Ocean and in the South China Sea should also be explored, rather than the chess game that is now going on, which adds to the tensions, and where the real beneficiaries are the countries of the region playing -off India and China against each other.[57]

In the aspect of traditional security cooperation, China maintains stable military relationship with the US and India. For instance, China and India joined the RIMPAC naval exercise with the US in 2014 for the first time and held the joint military exercise, 'Hand-in-Hand' in Chengdu in November 2014. And India has also participated in RED FLAG with the US.[58] It's a positive move for trilateral cooperation. However, as the world's three largest economies and major players that shape Asia's political and security context, proper management of the trilateral India-China-US relationship has become more important than ever.

## Conclusion

Though, the prospects for strategic triangular relationships are looked with some degree of scepticism, the potential benefits of participating in tri-lateral ties are significant for all the three countries in the 21st century. But managing these expanding relations will increasingly be a key challenge for Washington, Beijing and New Delhi. Also the major characteristic of this emerging strategic triangle lies in that it is still in an evolutionary phase and has not assumed a strong and mature form similar to the Sino-Soviet-US strategic triangle during the Cold War. It's a complex and dynamic triangle that stands for the linkage of cooperation and conflict and all of them are involved in a hedging strategy. Among the three side of a triangle Sino-Indian dyad is sensitive to triangular impacts. The India-US relation has been the facilitator in this triangular regime, and the China-US relation has served as the driving force. As of mutual strategic distrust, China and India could not overcome the conflicts in various spheres and this has created a 'drag' in terms of the development of the triangular cooperation regime. If India, China, and the US can develop strong and amicable economic ties with one another, it will therefore ensure the prosperity of the world as a whole. But because of the geopolitical competition and territorial disputes, we cannot expect the advent of strategic cooperation in the near future. The most likely possibility is a combination of competition and cooperation.

## NOTES

1. Ashutosh Varshney, *A New Triangle: India, China and the US*, available at http://www.india-seminar.com/2006/557/557%20ashutosh%20varshney.htm, accessed on December 11, 2014.
2. Ananya Chatterjee, "India-China-United States: The Post-Cold War Evolution of a Strategic Triangle," *Political Perspective*, vol. 5, no.3, 2011, pp. 74-95, p. 75.
3. Sun Xun, "New Nuclear Triangle and China's Role in South Asia," *Regional Centre for Strategic Studies*, Sri Lanka, 2005, p. 7.
4. Annemarie Detlef, "An Analysis of Contemporary US-China-India Relations," July 7 2012, available at http://www.e-ir.info/2012/07/07/an-analysis-of-contemporary-us-china- india-relations/, accessed on December 12, 2014.
5. Tanvi Madan, "The Modi-Xi Summit and China-India Relations," September 16, 2014,

available at http://www.brookings.edu/research/opinions/2014/09/16-modi-xi-summit-and-china-india-relations.html, accessed on December 11, 2014.

6. Ashley J. Tellis and Sean Mirski, *Crux of Asia: China, India, and the Emerging Global Order*, Carnegie Endowment for International Peace, 2013, p. 4.
7. Brahma Chellaney, "An Uneasy Strategic Triangle: the Troubled China India Relationship and US Asia Policy," *JPRI Occasional Paper*, no.48, January 2014, available at http://www.jpri.org/publications/occasionalpapers/op48.html, accessed on 11 December, 2014.
8. C. Raja Mohan, "India, China and the United States: Asia's Emerging Strategic Triangle," *Strategic Snapshots,* MacArthur Foundation, Loy Institute for International Policy, February 2011,
9. Brahma Chellaney, op.cit.
10. Boris Volkhonsky, "India- China relations: A factor of stability or tension in Asia?" September 24, 2014, available at http://in.rbth.com/blogs/2014/09/24/india-china_relations_a_factor_of_ stability_or_tension_in_asia_38523.html, accessed on December 11, 2014.
11. Tanvi Madan, "India- U.S. Relations in 14 Charts and Graphics," Brookings Institution, September 26, 2014, available at http://www.brookings.edu/blogs/up-front/posts/2014/09/26, accessed on January 13, 2015.
12. "India's trade deficit with China rose to $37.8 billion in 2014," *The Economic Times*, 13 January 2015.
13. India, China, US will be in uneasy strategic triangle, *Business Standard News,* September 2, 2013, available at http://www.business-standard.com/article/news-ians/india-china-us-will-be- in-uneasy-strategic-triangle-113090200647_1.html, accessed on 11 December 2014.
14. Gopalan Balachandran, "Nuclear Real Politik: The prospects for Indo-US Relations", *Australian Journal of International Affairs*, Vol.61, No.4, 2007, p. 546.
15. Suhasini Haidar, "N-deal Logjam Cleared: Modi, Obama Agree not to Dilute Liability Law," *The Hindu,* January 27, 2015.
16. Lisa Curtis, "The Quality of the Indo-U.S. Relationship Matters more than the Quantity of Dialogues," August 18, 2014, available at http://www.americanbazaaronline.com/2014/08/18/quality-indo-u-s-relationship-matters-quantity-dialogues/, accessed on January 13, 2015.
17. Michael Kugelman, "It's time for the US to Reset Relations with India," May 18, 2014, available at http://www.latimes.com/opinion/op-ed/la-oe-kugelman-india-election-20140519-story.html, accessed on December 11, 2014.
18. Tanvi Madan, op.cit
19. "Obama's trip a defining and exciting time in Indo- US Relations: Nominee for US ambassador to India," *The Times of India,* December 3, 2014.
20. Puja Mehra, "Modi's reforms enthuse Obama," *The Hindu,* January 27, 2015.
21. Lisa Curtis, op.cit.
22. Seema Sirohi, "Can Modi Revive thc India - US Relationship?" September 29, 2014, available at http://www.aljazeera.com/indepth/opinion/2014/09/can-modi-revive-india-us-relati-201492872246706449.html, accessed on January 13, 2015.
23. B. Raman, "A Balancing Act," *Outlook Magazine*, November 11, 2010, available at http://www.outlookindia.com/article/A-Balancing-Act/267917, accessed on December 12, 2014.
24. Major Banit Singh Negi, op.cit, p. 70.
25. Henry A. Kissinger, "The Future of US--Chinese Relations," *Foreign Affairs,* March/April 2012,
26. Wayne M. Morrison, "China-U.S. Trade Issues," *Congressional Research Service*, December 5, 2014, available at http://www.fas.org/sgp/crs/row/RL33536.pdf, accessed on December 15, 2014.
27. Dingding Chen, Relax, "China Won't Challenge US Hegemony," *The Diplomat,* January

14, 2015, available at http://thediplomat.com/2015/01/relax-china-wont-challenge-us-hegemony/, accessed on 20 February 2015.

28. Ankit Panda, "5 Predictions for Xi Jinping's US State Visit," *The Diplomat,* February 10, 2015, available at http://thediplomat.com/2015/02/5-predictions-for-xi-jinpings-us-state-visit/ accessed on February 20, 2015.
29. Shannon Tiezzi, "Why 2015 Will Be a Great Year for US-China Relations," *The Diplomat,* February 12, 2015, available at http://thediplomat.com/2015/02/why-2015-will- be- a-great-year-for-us-china-relations/, accessed on February 20, 2015.
30. Snehalata Panda, "Global Energy and Alliances: Challenges for India," *India Quarterly: A Journal of International Affair,* Sage Publication: New Delhi, vol.62, no.92, 2006, pp.92-123, p.109.
31. C. Raja Mohan, "India, China and the United States: Asia's Emerging Strategic Triangle," available at http://www.lowyinstitute.org/publications/india-china-and-united-states-asias-emerging-strategic-triangle, accessed on December 12, 2014.
32. Karl D, "US-India Relations: Pivot Problems," Centre for Strategic and International Studies, 2011
33. Annemarie Detlef, "An Analysis of Contemporary US- China -India Relations," July 7 2012, available at http://www.e-ir.info/2012/07/07/an-analysis-of-contemporary-us- china-india-relations/, accessed on December 11, 2014.
34. Richard Sokolsky, Angel Rabasa and C. Richard Neu, "The Role of Southeast Asia in U.S. Strategy Toward China," RAND Corporation, 2001, pp. 1-2
35. Ibid, p. 72
36. China's Growing Apprehensions over India- US Strategic Relations, December 1, 2011, available at http://www.turkishweekly.net/op-ed/2915/china-39-s-growing-apprehensions-over-india-us-strategic-relations.html, accessed on 11 December 2014.
37. S D Muni, "Introduction", ed by S.D. Muni and Vivek Chanda, *Asian Strategic Review,* Pentagon Press: New Delhi, 2013, p. 5.
38. Prashant Hosur, "The Indo-US Civilian Nuclear Agreement: What's the big deal?" *International Journal,* Spring, 2010, p. 440, pp. 435–6.
39. Annemarie Detlef, "An Analysis of Contemporary US-China-India Relations," July 7, 2012, available at http://www.e-ir.info/2012/07/07/an-analysis-of-contemporary-us-china-india-relations/, accessed on 10 December 2014.
40. P.R. Chari, "Nuclear Dealing Wheeling," *Institute of Peace and Conflict Studies,* 10 May 2010, available at http://www.ipcs.org/article/pakistan/nuclear-dealin g-wheeling-3123.html, accessed on 28 October 2014.
41. Tej Pratap Singh, "Indo-US Civil Nuclear Cooperation Agreement: Implications for Asian Security," N.K. Jha, in his ed. *Nuclear Synergy Indo-US Strategic Co-operation and Beyond* (New Delhi: Pentagon Press, 2009), p. 99.
42. Mussarat Jabeen and Ishtiaq Ahmed, "Indo-US Nuclear Cooperation," *South Asian Studies,* vol. 26, no. 2, July-December 2011, p. 418, pp. 411–29
43. Harsh V Pant, *Contemporary Debates in Indian Foreign and Security Policy,* Palgrave Macmillan, 2008, p. 22.
44. Adam Segal, "India- US- China Strategic Triangle," October 25, 2010, http://blogs.cfr.org/asia/2010/10/25/india-u-s-china-strategic-triangle/
45. Ashutosh, op.cit.
46. Mohan Malik, "India-China Relations: Giants Stir, Cooperate and Compete," *Asia-Pacific Centre for Security Studies,* October 2004.
47. Major, op.cit, p. 102

48. Mohan Malik, *China and India: Great Power Rivals*, Boulder & London: First Forum Press, 2011, p. 396.
49. Tanvi Madan, op.cit.
50. "The Emerging Strategic Triangle in Indo-Pacific Asia," *The Diplomat,*
51. Kevin Peters, Can China and the US Work Together on Counterterrorism?, *The Diplomat,* December 02, 2014, available at http://thediplomat.com/2014/12/can-china-and-the-us-work- together-on-counterterrorism/, accessed on February 20, 2015.
52. Ibid., p.116
53. Major Banit Singh Negi, The United States-China-India Relationship: An Analysis of the Emergence of a Strategic Triangle, 2007, p.69.
54. Major, op.cit, p. 113.
55. Ibid., p. 114.
56. Colonel Dan McDaniel, India, "China and the United States in the Indo-Pacific region: coalition, co-existence or clash?" October 2012.
57. Mukul Sanwal, "Reappraising Relations with China: From Strategic Ambiguity to Recognising Mutual Interests," *IDSA Issue Brief*, January 22, 2015.
58. Joint Military Exercise Hand-in-Hand 2014 Begins, Press Information Bureau Government of India, Ministry of Defence, 17 November, 2014, available at http://pib.nic.in/newsite/PrintRelease.aspx?relid=111495, accessed on 10 December 2014.

# 22

# India-Taiwan Relations: Looking towards the Future

*Sumit Kumar*

While the genesis of India-Taiwan relations can be traced in the period of pre-independent India, the relationship between the two came to an end in 1950 when India not only accorded diplomatic recognition to the People's Republic of China, but also diplomatic relations with Taiwan, considering the latter as a part of the Chinese territory. However, the last decade of the 20$^{th}$ century witnessed encouraging developments in the relationship. For instance, both the countries established unofficial relations in 1995. As a part of its Look East Policy India started deepening the bilateral ties with Taiwan in several areas of common interests including economic, trade and commerce and others. Taiwan also opened the Taipei Economic and Cultural Centre (TECC) in New Delhi. At the same time, China's assertive foreign policy in recent years towards Asian countries in general and India in particular has led New Delhi to rethink its policy towards Taiwan. These and other factors have indeed played a crucial role in transforming India-Taiwan relations. This can be gauged from the fact that the total trade volume between the two countries rose to $6.1 billion in 2013.[1]

However, these positive developments notwithstanding, the relationship continues to face some inherent problems. Of course, managing China is a major problem. Though both the countries consider China as a common security threat, they do not want to jeopardy their bilateral ties with China. It is in this context that this paper tries to examine India's interests in Taiwan. It also intends to analyse areas of cooperation between the two countries. The paper also deals with the challenges both the countries are facing in deepening their bilateral ties and finally recommends some policy prescriptions for enhancing cooperation between India and Taiwan. However, proceeding further, it would be appropriate to examine the question of Taiwan's identity as an independent country in international relations.

## II

Taiwan, officially the Republic of China (ROC), claims as a sovereign state in East Asia.[2] The Republic of China, originally based in mainland China, now governs the island of Taiwan, which makes up over 99% of its territory as well as Penghu, Kinmen, Matsu and other minor islands. Neighbouring states include the People's Republic of China to the west, Japan to the east and northeast, and the Philippines to the south. Taipei is the seat of the central government. New Taipei, encompassing the metropolitan area surrounding Taipei proper, is the most populous city.

Historically, Taiwan, formerly known as "Formosa", was mainly inhabited by Taiwanese aborigines until the Dutch and Spanish settlement during the Age of Discovery in the 17th century, when Han Chinese began immigrating to the island.[3] In 1662, the pro-Mingloyalist Koxinga expelled the Dutch and established the first Han Chinese polity on the island, the Kingdom of Tungning. The Qing Dynasty of China later defeated the kingdom of Tungning and annexed Taiwan.[4] When Taiwan was ceded to Japan in 1895, the majority of Taiwan's inhabitants were Han Chinese either by ancestry or by assimilation. The Republic (ROC) was established in China in 1912 and after Japan's surrender in 1945, the ROC assumed the control of Taiwan.[5]

The Chinese-Taiwanese Conflict began in 1949, after the Chinese Communist Party, led by Mao Tse-tung, overthrew the nationalist government of the Republic of China (ROC). It was during this time that President Chiang Kai-sheck of the ROC and his political party, the Kuomintang (KMT), was forced to flee with soldiers and civilians loyal to them to the Chinese island of Taiwan and re-establish the Chinese nationalist government. In 1950, the Chinese Communist Party established the People's Republic of China (PRC) and invaded Taiwan with the aim of unifying all of China under its rule. However, the Chinese Communist Party failed completely in achieving its goal, as the US came to the rescue of the ROC by sending its naval forces and. Since then, both countries have existed in a state of neither complete independence nor integration, of neither war nor peace. The PRC claims that the ROC ceased to exist in 1949 and that Taiwan is a province of "one China." In fact, the PRC also asserts itself to be the sole legal representation of China and claims as its 23rd providence to under its sovereignty, denying the status and existence of ROC as a sovereign state. The PRC has threatened the use of military force as a response to any formal declaration of Taiwanese independence, or if it deems peaceful reunification no longer possible. The ROC also does not recognise the PRC. In fact, the ROC continues to treat itself as a lawful Government of entire China. For it, Taiwan, a Chinese territory under the two declarations, legitimately belonged to the ROC. The Taiwan crisis took an ugly turn in August 1958 when the People's Liberation Army (PLA) bombed the Taiwanese islands of Kinmen and Matsu.

Not surprisingly, the immediate reaction of the world community to the crisis was divided. As the Cold War was in full swing and the world was virtually divided between two power blocks—the US and the Soviet Union, countries took their stands on the issue in the light of the fact that which block they belonged to. This became more glaring when the Korean War and other Cold War compulsions led the US to refuse to recognised the PRC as an independent country, continuing to recognise ROC in order to prevent ROC from becoming a communist follower. The US and its allied countries also helped ROC in retaining its seat in the United Nations Security Council (UNSC). On the other hand, the Soviet Union took no time in switching over its recognition from the ROC to PRC.

However, in 1971, the ROC received a big blow when the UN General Assembly passed Resolution 2758 restoring all its rights to the People's Republic of China. The resolution also recognises the representatives of its Government as the only legitimate representatives of China to the United Nations. Consequently, ROC lost its seat to the PRC in the Security Council. This in turn made it clear that the United Nation. In 1979, the US also recognised the People' Republic of China as an independent country. And, most countries also switched recognition to the PRC. These developments indeed went against the ROC to maintain its position as an independent state and get international recognition as the representative of mainland China. Not only this, the KMT Government came under scathing criticism of western countries that there was no democracy in Taiwan. This was evident from the fact that the KMP Government had put in place martial law. There was controlled media and there was no opposition. At the same time, some dissenting voices against the Government also started being raised. Thus, the KMT Government realised that fact that if it continued to ignore the ground reality, public resentment would further increase against it, and China could use the internal crisis of Taiwan as a pretext to remove the KMP Government, annexing ROC with PRC. It was against this background that Taiwan began to witness a democratisation process in late 1980s and 1990s. The beginning of the democratisation process was indeed an important development in the sense that people genuinely got an opportunity to participate freely in the political process in the country, realising their natural right to freedom and equality. This, in turn, soon led to the formational of other parties. For instance, 1986, the Democratic Progressive Party was established as the first opposition party to the KMT. The DPP fundamentally was formed by those Taiwanese people who seek for complete independence from mainland China. In turn, the legitimacy of Taiwan's bid for international recognition as a sovereign entity was considerably boosted in the eyes of Western popular opinion by its rapid democratization under the presidency of Lee Tenghui.[6]

In the meantime, Taiwan also began to register high growth rates, becoming one of the Asian Tigers in Asia. Today, Taiwan is ranked as the 19th largest economy in the world in terms of purchasing (PPP), and as 18$^{th}$ in terms of gross domestic product (GDP). The economy of Taiwan has also been ranked the highest in Asia for 2015 Global Entrepreneurship Index (GEI) for specific strengths.[7] Certainly, Taiwan's robust and growing economy started receiving the attention of the rest of the world, with countries expressing their desire to establish economic ties with Taiwan. This is evident from the fact that Taiwan enjoys a special status in the International economic order by getting the membership of most of the International economic organisations including the World Trade Organisation (WTO), Asia-Pacific Economic Cooperation (APEC), Asian Development Bank (ADB) and others. At the same time, Taiwan has close economic ties with the United States, Japan, European and Asian Countries. By the end of July, 2015, Taiwan's foreign exchange reserves have increased to US$ 421.96 billion.[8]

Taiwan has also assumed added significance in international politics in view of its strategic significance. As most of other countries fell that a rising China would attempt to change the balance of power in its favour at least first in East Asia, these counties are of the opinion that as long as Taiwan remains independent of Beijing, much of China's increased capability and resources will be absorbed and digested by the Taiwan issue, which will effectively prevent Beijing from inflicting security threat to other neighbouring countries.[9] At the same time, a war over Taiwan would affect all states in the region and many beyond. Even in the absence of conflict, Taiwan has an important role to play in ensuring sea-lanes in its backyard.

These economic, strategic and other factors have, therefore, scaled up Taiwan's stature in international politics. Thus, despite the fact that only 21 UN member states and the Holy See currently maintain official diplomatic with the ROC, one may estimate the increasing importance of Taiwan in the world from the fact that it has unofficial ties with most other states via its representative.[10]

## III

Historically, India has close ties with Republic of China. However, following the establishment of People's Republic of China in the Mainland, India under the leadership of Prime Minister Jawaharlal Nehru decided to establish diplomatic relations with the PRC, parting with the ROC. Nehru informed Indian Parliament in March 1950 that the PRC had been recognised because "it is a question of recognising a major event in history," and because it controlled 'practically the entire mainland of China." Moreover, its Government was stable and unlikely "to be supplanted or pushed away by any force." He informed the Parliament that the recognition of the PRC and the exchange of diplomatic missions had only happened after all the facts had been carefully ascertained.[11] The successive Indian Governments also maintained the consistency in India's stand on the issue of China-Taiwan relations.

But, in the 1990s the Narsimha Rao Government reoriented India's policy towards Taiwan. More to the point, In the 1990s India faced some serious domestic and foreign policy challenges. For instance, domestically, India had to deal with one of the worst economic cissies in the post-independent era. In fact, it did not have sufficient foreign reservoirs to buy oil even for a month. Externally, India needed to adapt to a new international order which emerged following the end of the Cold War. In turn, India lost its time-tested friend—the Soviet Union, which had not only provided security cover to India, but also financial and defence assistance during Cold War time. China started flexing its political military power against India by developing close ties with India's neighbours. On the other hand, its lack of interest or oversight had resulted in complete cut off between India and China's neighbours in East Asia, despite the fact that India has historically close cultural and economic ties with these countries of East Asia. Thus, these and other factors forced India to make fundamental changes in its foreign policy orientation towards East Asia. It was in this context that the P.V. Narsimha Rao Government focused on reviving India's historical ties with East Asia Countries by initiating the Look East policy.

Of course, Taiwan figured pre-eminently in India's look east policy for various reasons. First, Taiwan's economic muscle, particularly its huge foreign exchange reserves was the main attraction for India. Second, having emerged as a major economic giant in the world, China stared modernising its military and asserting its position in the Indian Ocean. At the same time, Beijing initiated the policy of string of Pearls aimed at encircling India by winning over the South Asian neighbours. China's move forced the Indian strategists to search for options helping India in pushing back China from this region. Given its strategic location and acrimonious relations with China, Taiwan was viewed a much valued country by India to forge close ties with in order to contain Beijing.

Consequently, a delegation led by Inder Kumar Gujral visited Taiwan in 1992 with the purpose of inviting the business community of Taiwan to invest in India. The delegation met the President, Prime Minister, legislators and top-ranking officials.[12] Subsequently, India and Taiwan established 'unofficial' relations in 1995 with the establishment of the India-Taipei Association (ITA) in Taipei to promote interactions between India and Taiwan, including business, tourism and cultural and people-to-people exchanges. The ITA also serves as a de facto Indian embassy, authorised to issue visas and provide other consular services.[13] In the same year, Taiwan opened the Taipei Economic and Cultural Centre (TECC) in New Delhi.[14]

When the Democratic Progressive Party under the leadership of Chen Shi-bian was voted into power, the prospects of improving ties between India and Taiwan increased in view of the fact that the DPP had fought the election on the slogan of anti-China and pro-independence. True to the expectations, the new regime of Chen Shi-bian appeared interested in cementing the ties between the two countries. This facilitated interactions between people to people. Following the 2001 earthquake in Gujarat, the Taiwanese Government had offered a million dollar relief package and Taiwanese Vice-President Annette Lu expressed her desire to visit India. However, the Indian Government refused to give her a visa and instead, Parris H. Chang, Deputy Secretary General of Taiwan's National Security Council (NSC) came to India, bringing the relief material.[15]

On October 17, 2002, the directors of the ITA and the TECC signed the Agreement on Promotion and Protection of Investment. In 2002, Vincent Chen spent three months at the Institute for Defence Studies and Analyses (IDSA) in New Delhi as a Visiting Fellow. He was probably the first Taiwanese scholar to spend that much time in India. K. Santhanam, the then Director General of the IDSA, visited Taiwan. In 2004, Taiwan began offering the Taiwan Scholarship and Mandarin Scholarship (National Huayu Enrichment Scholarship) to Indian students and The Faculty of Social Science at the University of Delhi and Taiwan's National Chengchi University (NCCU) also signed an MOU in 2007.[16] Furthermore, China Airlines started a direct flight between New Delhi and Taipei in 2003, establishing direct air contact between Taiwan and India. The Desire for Strategic Cooperation Although the DPP government started with low-key contacts, Taiwan soon began making further efforts in the direction of strategic cooperation with India.[17] In an unexpected move, George Fernandes, former Defence Minister of India, visited Taiwan twice in his personal capacity—first in 2004 and again in 2006—at the invitation of the Taiwan Think Tank.[18] His visit was first such visit by any senior most Indian politician since India's independence. His focus on "China is India's No. 1 enemy" was seen very encouraging by the DPP Government.[19]

The DPP Government moved to explore the possibility of security cooperation with India. With this hope, the DPP Government sent several mid-level military officers to India during 2000-08 as a part of its delegations. In fact, United Daily News (UDN) quoted an unnamed military official as saying "The military cooperation is limited to exchange of military intelligence." UDN military reporter Lu Teh-yun wrote that "Taiwan has sent a military attache to its trade office in New Delhi and an Indian Air Force officer ... visited Taiwan at the invitation of Taiwan Air Force Commander-in-Chief Chen Chao-min."[20]

In 2006, the Taiwan-India Cooperation Council (TICC), a private organisation was established in Taipei, with Democratic Progressive Party (DPP) Chair-man Yu Shyi-kun elected as its first chairman. The Council aims to act as a bridge to promote economic exchanges and broader cooperation on bilateral interests between Taiwan and India. At the occasion, Yu further said:

> "India is seen as having the best potential among the four golden BRIC[21]- Brazil, Russia, India and China countries. Besides, Taiwan and India's collaboration in software and hardware and India's overall economic takeoff will provide even more opportunities for Taiwan-India economic and trade cooperation."[22]

Yu emphasised the fact that the idea to promote closer Taiwan-India exchanges is in line with the Indian government's "Look East policy," which overlaps with Taiwan's "Go South Policy." on the other hand, Brigadier Arun Sahgal, the deputy director of India's United Service Institution, attended the council's founding ceremony. He said the council provides a channel for India to reach out to East Asia, a policy the Indian government has been working toward in recent years. Arun Sahgal categorically stated:

> "India's 'Look East Policy' engages mostly with Southeast Asia, but India is looking for much greater engagement with East Asia. It is in this context that our relationship with Taiwan is extremely important. We would like to use our new-found confidence and new-found economic development model to engage to a much greater degree with Taiwan."[23]

In 2007, the ITA and the TECC signed an MOU on behalf of India's Department of Science and Technology (DST) under the Ministry of Science and Technology and Taiwan's NSC. As per the MOU, the DST and the NSC hold annual meetings alternately in New Delhi and Taipei, which are attended by four to five representatives from each side. The main purpose of the annual meeting is to invite research proposals into begin with, Taiwan Scholarship was provided by Ministry of Education (MOE), Ministry of Economy Affairs (MOEA), and the National Science Council (NSC).[24]

## IV

When The KMT Government came to power in 2008, there was a growing concern in sections of Taiwanese experts that India-Taiwan ties would not receive the same priority in the foreign policy of the President Ma Ying-jeou Government, given the fact that the KMP party carries strong inclination towards mainland China. However, the act of President Ma Ying-jeou Government did not collaborate this apprehension. For instance, Ma Ying-jeou, then as the Presidential candidate of the KMP party, had already visited New Delhi to diversify Taiwanese cooperation with Indian businesses. Apart from the reported meetings with certain mainstream political and business leaders, Ma Ying-jeou addressed a gathering at Indian Council for World Affairs at New Delhi on June 12, making it a KMT event after six decades at the same venue. While emphasising expanding relations with India, which he said are "old friends, exploring new opportunities," a major portion of his speech consisted, surprisingly, of tensions in Taiwan Straits—displaying internal political differences on a range of issues between the KMT and DPP.[25]

India and Taiwan signed the Double Taxation Avoidance Agreement in 2011 and the Customs Cooperation Agreement. This agreement clearly reflected the growing synergy between India and Taiwan, especially in the economic area. In particular, the DTA aims at establishing the taxing rights over permanent establishments in each country, while reduced withholding taxes on dividends and interest should promote a rise in the flow of capital investment. At the same time, a Customs Cooperation Agreement between the two sides was also signed on the same occasion which came into effect on August 1, 2011.[26] The Ministry of Economic Affairs of Taiwan Government established the India Task Force in 2010.[27] There are five sub-groups of this Task Force: Economic Cooperation, Industrial Cooperation, Trade Cooperation, Education Cooperation and Economic Cooperation Agreement (ECA). These sub-groups hold separate meetings with Government agencies. The Task Force has made two recommendations: the Government of Taiwan should encourage private sector companies to invest in India and the Government should send more delegations to India. Indian Federation of Indian Chambers of Commerce and Industry (FICCI) and the Taiwan External Trade Development Council (TAITRA) signed the Carnet Protocol in 2013.[28] The Chung-hua Institution of Economic Research (CIER) and the Indian Council of Research on International Economic Relations (ICRIER) conducted a joint feasibility study on a FTA/ECA. The Bureau of Foreign Trade and the office of Trade Negotiation in Taiwan supervised this study.[29]

The most significant evidence of Taiwan-India relations warming up was provided when ROC President Ma Ying-jeou made a stopover in Mumbai en route to Africa in early April, an event that went almost unnoticed by India's media. The visit, part of a phenomenon called "refueling diplomacy", is historic because India had never allowed a serving ROC president to land on Indian soil. The ROC Ministry of Foreign Affairs described Ma's stopover as a "sign of improving ties" with India, even though New Delhi itself barely remarked on the event.[30]

India's decision to green light Ma's stopover indicates that the country is slowly but surely asserting an independent position in foreign affairs, demonstrating an unprecedented nonchalance towards mainland China, which generally reacts by kicking up a stink whenever it finds Taiwan getting too close to any nation. Of course, the present state of tranquillity in the Taiwan Strait, characterised by growing trade and direct air links between the two sides, contributed to India's decision to allow Ma to land in Mumbai. India, of course, does not need mainland China's prior approval to permit visits by foreign heads of state on its soil. In addition to allowing Ma's stopover, New Delhi has been taking some "bold initiatives," to quote Indian experts, by encouraging its companies to explore for oil and gas in the disputed South China Sea with Vietnam. This is a sign of India's growing assertiveness in foreign affairs where it has, in the past, played a low-key role. At the same time, another sign of this can be seen in the island's move to open a representative office in Chennai, bringing the total on the subcontinent to two. There is no question that strengthening bilateral ties have necessitated this development.[31]

India-Taiwan bilateral trade has also grown from the 1995 levels when the bilateral trade was reportedly around $700 million. The trade volume between India-Taiwan has risen from $700 million in 1995 to $6 billion in 2013. More than 70 Taiwanese firms had invested in India by the end of 2013.[32] Bilateral business and other forms of cooperation are more evident in the IT sector. Companies such as Acer, Asus, D-link and HTC are major Taiwanese brands recognized in India. Taiwanese companies such as Hon Hai, Compal and Wintek are suppliers to multinationals such as Nokia and Motorola in India.[33] Taiwan also has an enclave on a 500 acre area in Sri City, Andhra Pradesh (property development underway for "Taiwan Formosa Industrial Park"; an exclusive zone for Taiwanese manufacturing companies in India. The park entails a total investment of around 50 million USD and over 70 companies are expected to set shop in the SEZ. In terms of institutional arrangements, one of the main agencies for promoting the India–Taiwan economic partnership is the Taiwan External Trade Development Council (TAITRA), which is a non-profit trade promotion organization under Taiwan's Ministry of Economic Affairs (MOEA). The Taiwanese construction giant, Continental Engineering Corporation (CEC) and steel giant China Steel Corporation (CSC) have business operations in India. Taiwan keeps track of India's naval build-up, and China's naval activities in the Indian Ocean.[34]

The TECC set up a new office in Chennai in 2012. The China Trust Bank opened its second branch in Sriperumbudur, Tamil Nadu. The TECC assisted and facilitated the entry of Taiwan's steel giant China Steel Corporation (CSC) into India. Initially, China Steel invested $178 million in Gujarat where it has since begun operations. The Vice-Minister of MOEA visited India in September 2013 to attend the seventh EMMA Expo held in Chennai, from 5-7 September 2013. The delegation was supposed to have economic dialogue with India's commerce ministry.[35]

The educational and academic communications between Taiwan and India have been developed smoothly in the last several years. MoU on acknowledgement of each other's university degrees was signed between Foundation for International Cooperation in Higher Education of Taiwan (FICHET) and Association of Indian Universities (AIU) in 2010, which has resulted in close and frequent academic exchange and cooperation between the two sides.[36] Now Indian students have opportunities to study in Taiwan through Taiwan Scholarships and Huayu Enrichment Scholarships provided by the Government of Taiwan. To encourage enrolment of Indian students, Taiwanese universities and colleges also provide scholarships to attract outstanding Indian students. On an average there are around 600 Indian students studying in Taiwan every year. Taiwan and India's academic cooperation is developing in fast paces. The Ministry of Education, the Government of Taiwan, established the first Taiwan Education Program (TEP) in the OP Jindal Global University in the Indian state of Haryana in 2011. Later the TEP was established in Amity University in Uttar Pradesh in 2011 in Jamia Millia Islamia in Delhi in 2013 and in the China Studies Centre, IIT, Madras in 2013. The Taiwan Education Programme, funded by The Ministry of Education, the Government of Taiwan, works under the supervision of the National Tsing Hua University (NTHU). The aim of this joint Programme of India and Taiwan is to promote learning of Mandarin Chinese language and culture among Indian students in higher education and to facilitate greater understanding and cooperation. In so doing, while Taiwan provides teachers and teaching material, the Indian universities provide them with free accommodation and some other facilities. At the same time, in 2009, The National Tsing Hua University signed MOUs with the University of Delhi, IIT Delhi, IIT Madras, the IISC Bangalore, and. Jawaharlal Nehru University, New Delhi and the IIT Kharagpur signed and National Chiao Tung University of Taiwan signed an MOU for student exchange in 2012. These MOUs have increased mobility and interactions between Indian and Taiwanese student and teachers.[37]

## V

With a new Union Government in New Delhi under the Prime Minstership of Narendra Modi, it is hoped that India would pursue a proactive foreign policy towards Taiwan. In fact, Taiwan extended its congratulations on the BJP's poll victory and on Narendra Modi to take over as prime minister and said bilateral ties are expected to be strengthened to create a win-win situation. In a letter of congratulations, the Taipei Economic and Cultural Centre in India said the Indian Lok Sabha election "went smoothly and peacefully, bearing testimony to the democratic quality and vitality of the people of India."[38] True to the expectation, Taiwan has indeed assumed an important place in Prime Minister Narendra Modi's vision of "Act-East Policy."

When Bennet Chen, deputy director general in Taiwan's economic affairs ministry's Department of Investment Services visited India in September 2014 with a 21-member delegation of automobile parts manufacturers and traders. He said:

> "In response to Prime Minister Narendra Modi's vision of 'Come and Make in India' inviting manufacturers from across the world to invest in India and help boost India's industrial growth, Taiwanese automobile manufacturers are looking forward to exploring the possibilities of business cooperation for the Taiwanese auto parts and automobile electronics makers in India."[39]

He also asserted that expanding cooperation in trade and investments highlighted the potential for further cooperation between the two countries in the manufacturing sector. Chen added that apart from the automobile sector, Taiwan looked towards India for cooperation in information technology enabled services (ITES), textiles, infrastructure development, construction and engineering.[40] Furthering Prime Minister Narendra Modi's call to foreign companies to "make in India," the India Electronics and Semiconductor Association (IESA) and Taipei Computer Association (TCA) on Thursday signed a memorandum of understanding to promote local manufacturing in the field of semiconductors and electronics.[41]

However, it is also true that unless both the sides seriously address the structural constraints hampering improvement the bilateral ties, India and Taiwan may not be able to garner the economic and other benefits they hope for. For instance, while it is true that people-to-people interaction between India and Taiwan has considerably increased over the period, yet systematic efforts have hardly be taken to increase the understanding of India among Taiwanese people. This evident from the fact that the general perceptions of Taiwanese about India is this that India is not conducive economic destiny believing India does not have good infrastructure facilities like road, electricity, proper law and order which are essential for doing smooth business. The Taiwanese business community also has the strong feeling that the Indian bureaucracy is an instrument supportive for doing business in India. They believe that unless the Indian Government takes initiatives to ease the bureaucratic hurdles in order to attract foreign investment, it would not be very difficult for them to invest in India.

China is another factor that has overshadowed Taiwan's economic relations with other countries. It has emerged as Taiwan's number one trading partner and investment destination. The total bilateral trade was worth US $ 113.2 billion in 2013 that comprised 21.57 per cent of the total trade. China is the biggest and the closest market available to the Taiwanese entrepreneurs, and is capable of satiating their appetite. At the same time, it has the advantage of nearness, shared language, culture, customs and traditions where personal connections are easy to build. In comparison, India is a distant country, with an unfamiliar civilisation and language, and where personal connections and bonds are difficult to cultivate. Besides, Taiwanese entrepreneurs are more inclined to trade with the developed world rather than with the developing economies. China's export-friendly policies have been a major attraction for them. Taiwanese companies doing business in China is, in general, export-oriented; they use China to gain access to the markets of the developed world. In the case of India, they are convinced that India does not provide better, or equal, options for export.

Taiwanese companies also face stiff competition from Japan and South Korea because of India's CEPA with Japan and South Korea, and it's FTA with ASEAN. India's CEPA with South Korea and Japan, and its FTA with SEAN are major causes of worry for such Taiwanese companies as petrochemical and steel industries. With lower import tariffs on relevant products from Japan, South Korea and some ASEAN countries, which will eventually come down to zero over a period of time, some Taiwanese products have lost their competitiveness in the Indian market. This phenomenon has not only hurt the competitiveness of Taiwanese products in the Indian market, but may also discourage Taiwanese investment in India. For instance, China Steel Corporation (CSC) indicated that the plan for the first phase of production and sales of electrical steel coils by its branch 'China Steel Corporation India Private Limited' in the state of Gujarat calls for its raw material 'cold rolled steel coils' to be supplied CSC. However, India's import tariff of 7.5 percent on cold rolled steel coils from Taiwan is excessive, and higher than the 2.5 per cent on imports from Japan and South Korea. This will significantly increase procurement costs for CSC's branch in Gujarat, seriously impacting its competitiveness and ultimately affecting the feasibility of subsequent expansion of investment in India.[42]

Another problem that India-Taiwan relations are facing is the displeasure of Taiwanese over the fact that India does not recognise Taiwan as independent of mainland China. Thus, India's policy to deny visa to Taiwanese people to the places where Chinese people are not allowed is not seen by Taiwanese in good light. The Taiwanese business community has also expressed its reservation over the fact that Taiwanese companies like the Chinese companies, have to undergo a longer review process in India, and are not given a one-time banking clearance to bring in capital.[43] KMT Government's inclination towards PRC is also viewed as a factor which hampers the consolidation of the relationship between India and Taiwan. Consequently, India does not receive the same priority from the KMT Government as it had during the DPP Government.

The China First Policy also works as a barrier in India-Taiwan ties. For instance, this policy allows Taiwan to join any those international organisations in which statehood is not a criterion, and only if China is already a member of the organisation in question. For example, China allowed Taiwan to join the WTO only after it had joined it first. This policy is not limited to international organisations. When Taiwan succeeded in having a direct flight between New Delhi and Taipei in 2002, China asserted its China First Policy by starting direct flights between New Delhi and Beijing on April 1, 2002, four days before the flight between New Delhi and Taipei was scheduled to be inaugurated.[44]

## VI

These impediments notwithstanding, the prospect of India-Taiwan relations will be determined by the extent the two sides show their commitment towards cementing their improving bilateral ties. Undoubtedly, New Delhi and Taipei have their own reasons for forging close ties with each other. First, China's assertive behaviour certainly concerns India and Taiwan. As China has emerged as an economic and military power can be felt in Southeast Asia, it would be surprising if it further uses military might to annex Taiwan and bullies all other powers like the US, Japan and India to stand off this part of the region. This fact, China has already reflected its ambition of doing so by asserting that the South China belongs to China. Therefore, both the countries need to work together to push China to regulate itself. In so doing, India and Taiwan should closely work with Japan and the US—the two countries which also have similar threat perceptions from the rising China. Second, close bilateral ties would help both the sides in accelerating its economic growing. As India has an expertise in software, and our companies are looking for markets abroad, if we can marry this with Taiwanese expertise in hardware this venture would be beneficial to both sides. Third, India can have a better understanding of China's strategic behaviour by developing security ties with Taiwan. At the same time, Taiwan has sees India as an emerging region power which can work as counter-balancer to the rising China. Fourth, India and Taiwan can also engage in information sharing and cooperation to resist China's cyber attacks. India should also understand that stability of the Taiwan Strait and South China Sea is very important for its trade interests, and it should promote a peaceful solution to regional disputes and safeguard freedom of navigation.

In the light of these common objectives, India and Taiwan need to take some concrete initiates to deepen their ties. For instance, as Taiwan has better understanding of People's Republic of China and it is also ready to host Indian military students at its National Defence University (NDU), India should utilise this opportunity to study the functioning of the Chinese military establishment. India should also promote joint bilateral military exercises, seminars and other important military engagements with Taiwan. As Taiwan expects India to allow its ships to make port visits for freshwater and fuel replenishment, India should develop naval cooperation with Taiwan at the highest level. As there is a demand of Taiwanese business community for a free trade agreement, India should address this issue in order to further facilitate trade and commerce.

At the same time, further efforts should be taken by both the sides to institutionalise their ties. This in turn would help the two sides in expanding cooperation in different areas. In so doing, a Task-Force could be constituted, either jointly or separately, by the two countries to identify possible institutional linkages and potential areas of functional cooperation between the ministries and departments on both sides. The expertise of the private sector could also be utilised to carry out more specialised sector-based studies to identify competition and complementarities within the economies.

While it is true that dialogues are held at different levels between the two sides, yet there is need for acceleration in this process. For instance, while there are interactions between think-tanks of India and Taiwan, there is need to encourage MoUs between key research institutes in India and Taiwan that have an active component of scheduled annual exchanges. It is imperative that India and Taiwan should focus on multi-level academic exchange programs (faculty exchanges, semester abroad programs with Universities, reciprocal research faculty visits, etc.) with a host of institutions across India (beyond a Delhi-centric or Taipei-centric focus) to attract domain experts (those specifically dealing with the subject matter) and allow more eclectic policy inputs to emerge.

As there is no much interaction between the people-to-people level between the two sides, there is huge lack of misgivings and misunderstandings about each other, damaging the bilateral ties. India and Taiwan should take steps to address this issue. As Buddhism is the religion of the majority of Taiwanese people and

India is the home land of this religion, India should promote religion tourism to improve contacts between the people of the two sides. This step would also add to the India's economic prosperity. High-ranking officials of the two sides should visit each other and hold meetings. These visits would play a pivotal role in cementing the ties between India and Taiwan in the sense that the two sides have ironed out their misperceptions about each other.

To conclude, while it is true that India-Taiwan relations are determined and constrained by India's acceptance of "one China policy," this does not deter New Delhi to seek close security and economic ties with Taiwan. Thus, India should take bold initiatives to reach out to Taiwan, without wittingly angering China. At the same time, India should also assert its right to decide what type of relations it wish to have with Taiwan, if China dictates India not to directly deal with Taiwan.

## NOTES

1. "ROC Says Taiwan, India to Strengthen Bilateral Economic Relations; Congratulates Modi," http://zeenews.india.com/business/news/economy/roc-says-taiwan-india-to-strengthen-bilateral-economic-relations-congratulates-modi_100024.html.
2. Christopher J. Carolan, "The Republic Of Taiwan: A Legal-Historical Justification for a Taiwanese Declaration of Independence," http://www.nyulawreview.org/sites/default/files/pdf/NYULawReview-75-2-Carolan.pdf
3. "Ministry of Taiwan," http://taiwanvisanoc.com/
4. "Taiwan," http://heyevent.com/venue/cebbl6tg2agika
5. "Taiwan," International Chamber For Service Industry (ICSI), http://www.icsiindia.in
6. Chris Rahman, Defending Taiwan, And Why It Matters, Naval War College Review, Autumn 2001, vol. 54, no. 4, pp. 70–97.
7. Economy of Taiwan, https://en.wikipedia.org/wiki/Economy_of_Taiwan
8. Pan Chi-i and Lauren Hung, "Taiwan's Foreign Exchange Reserves Increase," August, 6, 2015, Focus Taiwan New Channel, http://focustaiwan.tw/news/aeco/201508060049.aspx
9. Wu Xinbo, The Taiwan Issue and U.S.–Asia/Pacific Security Strategy, *American Foreign Policy Interests*, 24, 2002, p. 2311.
10. Foreign relations of Taiwan, https://en.wikipedia.org/wiki/Foreign_relations_of_Taiwan
11. K.P. Mishra, 'India's Policy of Recognition of States and Governments', The American Journal of International Law, Vol. 55, No. 2, April 1961, p. 401, cited in Prashant Prashant Kumar Singh, Transforming *India-Taiwan Relations New Perspectives* (New Delhi: Institute for Defence and Security Analysis, Series no. 35 April 2014), p. 47.
12. 'The India-Taipei Association: A Mission Extraordinaire', Interview with Ambassador Vinod C. Khanna, Indian Foreign Affairs Journal, 5 (2), April 2010, pp. 240–51.
13. Manesh SV, "Good Vistas for Taiwan-India Ties," Taiwan Info, June 06, 2006, http://taiwaninfo.nat.gov.tw/ct.asp?xItem=21893&CtNode=103&htx_TRCategory=&mp=4
14. The Taipei Economic and Cultural Centre (TECC) in New Delhi, http://www.roc-taiwan.org/IN/ct.asp?xItem=481336&CtNode=5053&mp=277&xp1=
15. Prashant Kumar Singh, Transforming *India-Taiwan Relations New Perspectives* (New Delhi: Institute for Defence and Security Analysis, Series no. 35 April 2014), p. 92.
16. Ibid, p. 91.

17. Ibid, p. 92.
18. Walter C. Ladwig, III "Looking East 2: East Asia and Australasia/ Oceania," in David Scott, ed., *Handbook of India's International Relations* (New Delhi: Routledge, 2011), p. 145.
19. Singh, n. 16, p. 95.
20. "Taiwan, India Develop Military Ties," *Inside China Today*, January 2, 2002, http://www.freerepublic.com.
21. BRICS became BRICS when South Africa jointed this grouping in 2010. There are five counties in BRICS—Brazil, Russia, India, China and South Africa.
22. Chang Yun-ping, "Council Established to Boost Taiwan-India Exchanges," Taipei Times, February, 12, 2006, http://www.taipeitimes.com/News/taiwan/archives/2006/02/12/2003292656
23. Ibid.
24. Annual Report 2006-2007: International Science & Technology Cooperation, Ministry of Science and Technology, Government of India.
25. "What do Growing India-Taiwan Ties Mean," Rediff. Com, June 14, 2007.
26. Mary Swire "Taiwan-India DTA Comes Into Effect" August 23, 2011, http://www.tax-news.com
27. MOEA Calls for Closer Taiwan-India Trade Ties, Taiwan Today, July 8, 2012, http://taiwantoday.tw/ct.asp?xItem=194466&ctNode=421
28. "India-Taiwan Protocol," the Federation of Indian Chambers of Commerce and Industry (FICCI), March 13, 2013, http://www.ficci.com/ficci-in-news-page.asp?nid=6989
29. Namrata Hasija, "Time India Stopped Looking at Taiwan through Chinese Prism Spotlight,) July 11, 2014 http://southasiamonitor.org/detail.php?type=sl&nid=8534
30. Manik Mehta, India's Changing Attitude toward Taiwan, 06/17/2012, Taiwan Today, http://taiwantoday.tw/ct.asp?xitem=192274&CtNode=423
31. Ibid.
32. Rupakjyoti Borah, 'Taiwan-India Relations Need an Extra Push," June 10, 2015 http://www.geopoliticalmonitor.com/taiwan-india-relations-need-an-extra-push/
33. Joe Thomas Karackattu, *The Economic Partnership Between India and Taiwan in a Post-ECFA Ecosystem* (New Delhi: Springer, 2013).
34. Ibid.
35. "150-Strong Taiwan Trade Team to Visit India," *The Business Standard* (New Delhi), 3 September 2013
36. Taiwan, India Sign Education Agreement, Taipei Economic and Cultural Central in India, http://www.roc-taiwan.org/IN/ct.asp?xItem=481336&CtNode=5053&mp=277&xp1=
37. Ibid.
38. Taiwan Congratulates BJP and Modi, *Indian Express* (New Delhi), May 21, 2014.
39. "Taiwan-based Auto Parts Traders to Visit Delhi," *Business Standards*, September 4, 2014.
40. Ibid.
41. IESA, TCA sign MoU for make-in-India push, *The Economic Times* (New Delhi), September 12, 2014.
42. Ibid., p. 106
43. Singh, n. 16, p. 107.
44. Prakash Nanda, Rediscovering Asia: Evolution of India's Look-east Policy (New Delhi: Lancer Publishers, 2003), p. 570.

# 23

# Indian Diaspora: A reckoning force, a lobby group and a friend of NDA-II government in stabilizing relations between Indian and other nations

*Salu D' Souza*

## Introduction

Often some of us leave our homeland for one or the other reason and go to a host country. We long to go back to our motherland one day; the desire to go back to homeland, the feeling of belongingness towards our motherland is the notion of diaspora. N. Jayaram who has done research on Indian Diaspora while trying to analyse the behaviour of emigration pattern opines:

> "The emigration of Indians that began in the second quarter of the 19th century continued into the early decades of the 20th century. The trickle of emigration of Indians to the industrially developed countries, which assumed phenomenal proportions in the post-colonial phase, could be noticed in the 19th century itself." (Jayaram 2004: 19)

The above observation shows that Indians have always been enthusiastic about leaving their home country and go in search of greener pastures that they find in various Western countries. Many Indians who went to foreign countries were born after Independence; hence they are aware of the various democratic principles that govern liberal democratic countries like Canada, USA and UK and conservative democratic countries like China, Cuba, Gulf countries and few

African nations. Though China is a communist country, it says it practices true communism and democracy inside the communist regime. When these Indians come to India for holidays, they are not much perplexed about the Indian system of democratic governance. Indian diaspora owes a lot to the globalization and liberalization policies that the Indian democratic administration set in motion in the 1990s where liberal policies towards NRIs and PIOs privileged them as chosen citizens of India that entitled them many concessions.

Indian diaspora, irrespective of its religion, region and language that it belongs in India, has accepted the Christian Liberal Democratic views of western social set up where multicultural atmosphere is increasingly seen in the daily lives of people. The immigrants in general in various countries and Indian diaspora in particular want to have a good life. Bikhu Parekh, who has seen a Multicultural lifestyle in Britain says:

> "A multicultural society is characterized by a plurality of cultures. Its members subscribe to different systems of meaning and significance and structure their lives differently. Although some of their values invariable overlap, others do not. And even so far as the former are concerned, they sometimes define and prioritize them differently. Unlike a culturally homogeneous society, members of a multicultural society do not share a common substantive vision of the good life, and disagree about the value to be assigned to different human activities and relationships." (Parekh 2004)

This reiterates the multicultural environment that the western countries provide to their genuine immigrants to prosper and the members of Indian diaspora reaping the benefits according to their multi-tasked role in the western society.

## Role of Indian–Americans in Influencing the Policies

The Indian—American population is growing in various cities in the USA. The diaspora communities are very active in social media. There are governors and attorneys of Indian origin in the USA. The corporate houses also controlled by Indian origin people in the USA. The prominent members of Indian diaspora constantly lobby for policies towards India. The pressure groups and the other diaspora communities have become feeding grounds for the foreign policy analysts in the USA. In a study published in Foreign Policy Analysis, Jason Kirk (2008:277) claims:

> "In 2006, two historical stories converged: one involving the ongoing deepening of the U.S.-India relationship since 1998, the other a general consolidation of organizational capacity within the burgeoning Indian community in the United States. Without the latter, it is unlikely that

> the bold U.S.-India nuclear agreement would have made it over the requisite congressional hurdles in 2006."

Kirk's case study, while being highly interesting, has two major weaknesses that this thesis seeks to address. First, the study included only one personal interview with the Chairman of the U.S.–India Political Action Committee (USINPAC), one of the two leading lobby organizations for the community, and none with other relevant actors. Second and related to this, Kirk's study paid only limited attention to other possible explanations for Congress's strong vote in favour of the controversial agreement.

In 1998 the NDA formed the government with BJP as the ruling party. Within weeks of forming the government, to be precise on May 11, 1998, India announced to a stunned world that it had conducted simultaneous tests of three devices. American reaction was angry and swift. It kicked out overnight all the Indian scientists who were working in various US-based laboratories and companies (see below), and imposed a wide range of sanctions on India. Indian diaspora consistently lobbied to lift the sanctions imposed on Indian space technology transfer. Indian–Americans have succeeded and India has benefitted.

Clinton's visit to India, the first visit of a U.S. President since Jimmy Carter, was widely characterized as a success. Interestingly, for the first time, no less than 150 Indian-–Americans accompanied the U.S. delegation and Clinton's itinerary showcased a "new India"—visiting places such as Hyderabad, "the high-tech city" (Iype 2000).27 In his address to the Indian Parliament, Clinton:

> "[...] went into an extended critique of India's decision to go nuclear. But the tone was respectful and gave the sense of debate among equals" (Mohan 2006: 20).

It was interesting to note that, Clinton had stayed five days in India; he stopped only five hours in Pakistan on his way back home. Shri Atal Bihari Vajpayee of the BJP was the Prime Minister of India in that year.

Those Indians in the Diaspora who went to USA, Canada, UK, Australia and New Zealand were surprised to see the function of liberal democracy which had many rights to their citizens. Certain Indian communities did face occasional racial abuses and discrimination. Tinker Hugh in his book *Overseas Emigrants from India, Pakistan and Bangladesh* rightly identified the ethnic complexities that govern people from South Asia in western countries,

> "With reference to countries where the ethnic relations involving Indians have become complicated, Tinker (1977: 138-9) raises the following questions, 'do the Asian Indians create their own difficulties by their own way of life, and by remaining separate from the host society; or do

> their troubles arise mainly from excess of chauvinism or racism in the country of their adoption?' Racial discrimination is a rare occurrence in the present scenario. Few in Indian Diaspora were attacked in South Africa and Australia. Sikhs are targeted by Native Americans due to mistaken identities.

Ahead of a key Senate vote which could make Vivek Murthy the youngest ever Surgeon General of the US, Indian-Americans have launched a nationwide campaign calling their Senators to support him. The United States Senate is scheduled to vote on Tuesday to confirm Murthy, 37 as Surgeon General who was nominated for the position by US President Barack Obama in November last year. (*Times of India*)

## India and its Neighbourhood: How does Indian Diaspora view its neighbouring countries?

Indian diaspora is equally concerned about the various democratic institutions that exist in its neighbouring countries which play a crucial role in sustaining the democratic system of government. A stable democratic government of Pakistan can work towards the fulfilment of people's aspirations of Pakistan and have good relations with India, Afghanistan and China. India's concern is the concern of Indian diaspora. Nepal has found it difficult to sustain itself in a democratic institution without any external influence. India is worried about the developments that are taking place in Nepal. Nevertheless, India does not lose its hold on influencing Nepal's political system and tries to wean away from any communist influence that comes from China.

Bhutan is a strong supporter of Indian democracy. However, in the last general elections in Bhutan, India found itself losing hold over Bhutanese political class but eventually the regime had the wisdom to listen to India. Bangladesh is another India's neighbour, needs India's help in many areas. The refugees from Bangladesh who are in India reckoned and non-reckoned, sometime indulged in anti-national activities that has become a headache to Indian law enforcing agencies. The development in Bangladesh is carefully watched by India. Sri Lankan affair is important to India. Tamil Nadu government and the DMK leaders keep Indian political leaders at Delhi always "informed" about the India-Sri Lanka relations. The recent election in the Maldives is a setback to Indian interests. India wants to keep Maldives and Sri Lanka in good humour to contain Chinese influence in the Indian Ocean. The developments in Afghanistan and Myanmar are keenly observed by Indian diplomats and policy makers. Indian diaspora is always worried about neighbouring countries of India.

## A Critical Appraisal

The visit of previous Australian Prime Minister to India, Ms. Julia Gillard, who emphasized on Arts and culture that could be powerful forces for bringing people together and the two countries have pledged to strengthen the bilateral cultural relationship. The recent visit of the present Prime Minister of Australia, Tony Abbot, underlined the importance of greater connectivity to support growing commercial and cultural ties, including in the education and tourism sectors.

Migrants who enter into various parts of Australia need to 'modernise' and assimilate into local culture at the same time preserve the culture of their homeland. Last month the Prime Minister of India visited Australia that was termed as a success by both Australian and Indian media. Mr. Narendra Modi who visited Australia while addressing the Australian Parliament spoke on people-to-people links that are transforming the relationship. Prime Minister Modi and Prime Minster Abbott welcomed the signing of a Social Security Agreement, which will enhance two-way mobility and lower business costs. Further, they agreed to hold a Festival of India in Australia in 2015 to display the dynamism and diversity of contemporary Indian culture. This will see increasing participation of various Indian diaspora associations and communities in enhancing the bilateral relationship between Australia and India. This relation will definitely help NDA-II led by Modi to have favourable foreign policies towards the west.

It is true that political parties in India keep on changing but the basic structure of the Constitution of India has so far not changed. Indian diaspora loves its motherland and the institution of democracy that India practices. The agenda for development in the era of globalization and liberalization should take everyone into confidence and everyone should have the right to claim the benefits irrespective of their political affiliation. Inclusive growth leads to further sustenance of our democratic institutions. Indian diaspora has strong faith in Indian democracy. They are ever ready in helping less fortunate Indians through various charitable institutions and NGOs. Indian Diaspora is always reliable during the economic crisis that the Indian economy faces time to time. In this juncture, Indian democratic institutions need to be more liberalized with delineation of certain democratic rights to Indian people in general and Indian diaspora in particular. The foreign policy and the relation that the Modi led government is been establishing with neighbouring countries and reset of the world is unprecedented. India's image has not only made Indians inside India proud and optimistic but it has also seen that members of Indian diaspora can walk keeping their head straight in the host land where Indians are migrants. The host countries have increasingly acknowledged the contribution of Indian diaspora to the growth of their economy. Thanks to the Shri Narendra Modi led NDA government's robust foreign policy that has won appreciation from the

Indian diaspora associations across the world. Indian diaspora would like to see more positive dialogues with the neighbouring countries to make India as a truly regional superpower. The coming days will herald the prosperity not only for India but also for the neighbouring countries who have supported India in all International forums.

## REFERENCES

Bhikhu, Parekh. (2004). *Limits of the Indian Political Imagination*. London: Sage Publications.

Jayaram N. (2004). *The Indian Diaspora: Dynamics of Migration*. New Delhi: Sage Publications.

Kirk, Jason (2008). *"Indian Americans and the U.S.-India Nuclear Agreement: Consolidation of an Ethnic Lobby?"*, Foreign Policy Analysis 4, (3): pp. 275–300.

Iype, George (2000). *"PM's cold shoulder upsets NRIs"*, India Abroad, March 21.

Mohan, C. Raja (2006). *Impossible Allies: Nuclear India, United States and the Global Order*. New Delhi: India Research Press.

Neerja Arun & Rakesh Saraswat (2011),. *Summarizing the History and perspectives of Global Indian Diaspora*, Ashok Prakashan Mandir: Ahmedabad

Tinker, Hugh. (1977). *The Banyan Tree: Overseas Emigrants from India, Pakistan and Bangladesh*. Oxford: Oxford University Press.

http://timesofindia.indiatimes.com/nri/us-canada-news/Indian-Americans-campaign-ahead-of-Senate-vote-on-Vivek-Murthy/articleshow/45519869.cms

# 24

# Rebalancing Policy of the US in the Asia-Pacific and India's Maritime Security Policy

*Suresh R.*

## The post-Cold War International Scenario

A quick glance into the history of international politics shows that there were various methods adopted by nation states to protect and promote their national interests. During the 19th century and early 20th century it was the policy of imperialism and colonialism. However, the end of the Second World War and the establishment of the United Nations Organization marked an end to the policy of colonialism as a means to promote national interests. The cold war period witnessed the dominance of power politics in international politics. In fact international politics had become synonymous with military power and its predominance. It was known as the period of political realism and the consequent role of military power. The realists focus was on the role of states in international politics, and how the behaviour of states is motivated by power considerations. However, without the use of military power, either conventional or nuclear weapons, the cold war has ended. This development poses a major question regarding the dependence of military power as the sole means to protection and promotion the national interests.

The unexpected disappearance of discipline enforced by the super power rivalry and competitions on nation sates prompted at least one incident of violation of sovereignty and territorial integrity of a nation in the international system. The enthusiasm shown by the international community of nations under the collective security principle to nip in the very bud the revival of use of force to endanger the sovereignty and territorial integrity of nation was also a warning to all decision makers of nation states, especially the dictators who adopt war as an instrument of foreign policy. Again the challenge posed to national security by the non-state actors such as terrorist groups was also effectively addressed with the multilateral efforts. These new challenges to national security once again demonstrate the imperatives of multilateral efforts to wipe out threats to national security.

Further the end of cold war marked the beginning of accelerated pace of globalization. The post-cold war period also witnessed some major alterations in the national security threat perception of nation states. The non-traditional threat to the security of nation states have become more grave, numerous and imminent than the traditional threat that emanates solely from other nation states. Among these threats international terrorism is the serious and looming. A viable solution to this tribulation can be found only through collective efforts of all, developed and developing, militarily strong and weak nations.

It is the responsibility of the government to frame policies to ensure security. While framing the policies both domestic and external, the security of the people should be the sole criterion. It appears that in the post-cold war period the threat to security of the people emanates mostly from non-state actors. This new situation demands a multilateral effort with the cooperation of all nations both developed and developing, militarily powerful and weak nations. It is very difficult for the decision makers to take up this new course of action based on drastic amendments in the existing security policies.

India has to revisit its external policy under the changed international situation. Commensurate with changes in the international situation the defence policy also needs reorientation. The futility of arms race and competitions are well reflected towards the end of cold war. Moreover, the vertical and horizontal nuclear weapon proliferation makes the conventional arms built up as a means for the survival of international arms business establishments. In the post-cold war deeply interdependent world, war as an instrument of foreign policy has lost its relevance. However, a minimal force is required to wage limited war and to deter any military adventure from state or non-state actors across the land or maritime borders.

## The Rebalancing Policy of the US in the Asia-Pacific

The Asia-Pacific region is important because two-third of the world's population lives in the region. The maximum number of conflicts since the 1990s has been witnessed in this region though some of them are very old. The Asia-Pacific region also accounts for more than 20 percent of the land on the globe. It is in this changed context of security threat that the rebalancing policy of the US towards the Asia-Pacific region needs to be analysed.

The rebalancing in the Asia-Pacific region by the US is not disengagement and then re-engagement in Asia. Instead, it is a matter of emphasis and priority, building on an elaborate foundation of US-Asia relations that was already in place. The United States has had powerful national interests in the Asia-Pacific region since World War II and was deeply engaged in the region—militarily, economically, and diplomatically—throughout the Cold War. The post-cold war administrations of Presidents Bill Clinton and George W. Bush were actively engaged in Asia. The defence report of Feb 2006 clearly stated the US intention in the Asia-Pacific region. The US aims with the active support of major players in the region including Russia, China and India the defeat of terrorist networks and to prevent the proliferation of weapons of mass destruction by state as well as non-state actors. The report specifically stated that it was the US's aim to encourage China to play a constructive peaceful role in Asia-Pacific region to serve as a partner in addressing common security challenges including terrorism, proliferation, narcotics and piracy.

The Obama administration's policy towards the Asia-Pacific region has evolved over time and has gone through two distinct phases. When the policy was first rolled out in 2011–2, much of the emphasis was placed on military initiatives in the region. However, due to opposition from dominant players in the region the Obama administration adjusted its approach in late 2012, playing down the significance of military initiatives, emphasizing economic and diplomatic elements, and calling for closer US engagement with China.

The policy of rebalancing in Asia-Pacific has been driven by a much broader set of strategic, economic, and political considerations. The rebalance is a region-wide, multidimensional policy initiative. In regional terms, the shift includes a stronger emphasis on Southeast Asia and South Asia to complement traditionally strong American attention to Northeast Asia. In policy terms, the rebalance entails three sets of initiatives—security, economic, and diplomatic elements.

The fundamental goals of the new US policy are to broaden areas of cooperation beneficial to the United States with regional states and institutions; strengthen relations with American allies and partners, including great powers such as China and India as well as important regional powers such as Indonesia; and develop regional norms and rules compatible with the international security, economic, and political order supported by the United States. Thus rebalancing matters not only with regards to military presence, but also as "an effort that harnesses all elements of US power—military, political, trade and investment, development and our values." The Secretary of State Kerry put forth President

Obama's four principles of growth—"strong growth, fair growth, smart growth, and just growth"—at his visit in Asia, highlighting the aim for development in the rebalancing strategy.

## Perceptions on the US rebalancing policy in Asia-Pacific

There are divergent perceptions regarding the US initiative towards rebalancing the Asia-Pacific region. With regard to the rationale of the policy it is viewed that this policy aimed at containment of China, the growing great power in the global scenario. Another perspective is that such an initiative aims at harnessing maximum benefits from growing strategic, economic and military importance of the Asia-Pacific region. This region possesses abundant human and other resources. It is also the most significant sea-borne international trade route. All these factors appear to have influenced the rebalancing policy. However, the containment of communism in China seems to be of lesser role in this policy initiative. Though the US–China relation is conditioned by lack of mutual trust, the ongoing globalisation process has tied them together in balancing the economic interests. The volume of trade interaction between these two global economic powers is the testimony to this perspective.

The US policy of protecting the interest of its strong supporters in the Asia-Pacific region also appears to have prompted for such an initiative. Thus the rebalancing policy also appears to have aims at the protection of various interests including the security interests of Japan, South Korea, Vietnam, and Philippians against any China supported offensive measures. The maintenance of power equilibrium in the region is the sine qua non, especially in the context of an unresolved South China Sea dispute existing in the region. None of the Asian countries could singlehandedly meet the military power of China. Therefore the US presence in the region not only helps to maintain power balance in Asia but also pre-empt any aggressive move on the part of non-democratic countries in the region.

The US presence in the region is also advantageous to India as long as it helps to ensure the protection and promotion of democratic regimes in the region, especially in the context of democratic transitions that takes place in the neighbouring countries. India cannot and should not afford to spend more on arms race and militarisation of the region mainly on two counts. Firstly, the human security issues confronted by India are multifarious and any further delay in addressing these problems like poverty and infrastructure development in the so far neglected area would jeopardise the internal security situation. Secondly, the possession of nuclear weapon by its immediate neighbour having an unstable regime, not only pose a direct threat to its national security but also necessitate the external power presence inevitable to maintain some kind of discipline among the players in the region.

Another major threat that India has confronted in the post-cold war period is cross-border terrorism. A solution to this problem is possible only with the involvement of external powers, especially the US. Similarly, it is the anti-terrorism moves in the immediate aftermath of the 9/11 in 2001 that brought together the world's largest democracy and powerful democracy to a common platform. Since one of the major components of the rebalancing policy of the US is anti-terrorism measures there is ample scope for collaboration and joint action between India and the US against the menace of international terrorism.

However, one of the major security predicaments in the region is that any closer interaction between India and the US will be viewed by China as part of a move towards containment of China. And any close China and the US interaction would be viewed by India as move against its national interest. Though there is balance of interests of these three major players of the Asia-Pacific region, India, China and the US, at the bilateral level they lack mutual trust. In the absence of mutual trust any minor issue may aggravate to a major national security issue. In such a scenario it would be interesting to look into India's maritime security concerns.

## India's Maritime Security Concerns in the Post-Cold War Period

The maritime security is very important to India's military, economic, energy, environment, and human security. India has a coastline of 7516 kms and an exclusive economic zone (EEZ) of 2 million sq kms. The significance of the maritime domain has long been recognized. The famous words of Alfred Tyler Mahan testify this: "whosoever control Indian Ocean dominates Asia. This Ocean is important in the seven seas, in the twenty first century the destiny of the world will be determined in its waters."

India occupies a central position in the Indian Ocean region, a fact that exercises an increasingly profound influence on India's security environment. Writing in the 1940s, K.M. Pannikar, noted the importance of the Ocean to India that "while to other countries the Indian Ocean is only one of the important oceanic areas, to India it is a vital sea. Her lifelines are concentrated in that area, her freedom is dependent on the freedom of that water surface. No industrial development, no commercial growth, no stable political structure is possible for her unless her shores are protected." In tune with the above observations the first Prime Minister of India, Jawaharlal Nehru observed, "History has shown that whatever power controls the Indian Ocean has, in the first instance, India's sea borne trade at her mercy and, in the second, India's very independence itself..."[1]

The significance of the Indian Ocean to India has also been emphasized in the Annual Report (2004-2005) of India's Defense Ministry, which noted that "India is strategically located vis-à-vis both continental Asia as well as the Indian Ocean Region."

Again the Indian Maritime Doctrine asserts: "All major powers of this century will seek a toehold in the Indian Ocean Region. Thus, Japan, the EU, and China, and a reinvigorated Russia can be expected to show presence in these waters either independently or through politico-security arrangements. There is, moreover, "an increasing tendency of extra regional powers of military intervention in [IO] littoral countries to contain what they see as a conflict situation." Thus the Indian Ocean and its littoral and hinterland area have a direct bearing in safeguarding India's maritime security interests which is closely connected to national security.

## India's Maritime Security Policy in the Post-Cold War Period

India's maritime security policy also underwent a sea change in the post-cold war period. The policy of exclusive engagement and elimination of outside powers has given place to overt engagement with extra regional powers. This has been well reflected in India's joint military exercises along with the US, Japan, France, and Australia. India no longer considers the external power presence as a threat to its security. Rather it considers a joint effort to wipe out the major threat to India and the international community posed by terrorism. It is not possible for any single nation whatsoever powerful to address the menace of international terrorism singlehandedly. India began to realize the importance of major amendments in framing its security policy objectives and pursuing it through increased naval power and active collaboration with extra regional as well as intra-regional powers. This policy shift in India's stand is visible in the maritime doctrine as well as in the Navy's vision document published by the Indian Navy.

It essentially encompasses:

(i) Shaping a favorable maritime environment in the IOR for operations in peace as well as during conflict.

(ii) Preventing incursions by powers inimical to India's national interests by actively engaging countries in the IOR littoral, and rendering speedy and quality assistance in fields of interest to them.

(iii) Engaging extra-regional powers and regional navies in mutually beneficial activities to ensure the security of India's maritime interests.

(iv) Projecting the Indian Navy as a professional, credible force and the primary tool for maritime cooperation.

India has also earmarked the area which falls within its immediate concern. "India's growing international stature gives it strategic relevance in the area ranging from the Persian Gulf to the Strait of Malacca...." India's post-cold war maritime policy had stated: "India has exploited the fluidities of the emerging world order to forge new links through a combination of diplomatic repositioning, economic resurgence and military firmness."

It appears that India has adopted a three-pronged strategy to protect and promote its national interests. Firstly through diplomatic means, India has pursued a policy of cooperation with all major players in the Indian Ocean, including extra regional powers. This policy would help India to increase further its international stature. The Indo-US civilian nuclear agreement can also be viewed as an attempt to do away with nuclear isolation. The process of globalization has also accelerated better and cordial interaction with outside powers as the movement of people as well as commodities would further cement relation between nations.

India has developed a friendly and cordial relation not only by bilateral exchange with nations but also strengthened the bilateral cooperation through interactions in regional organizations, such as ASEAN, EAS, SCO, BRICS, ASEM, IBSA, APTA, and IOR ARC. India is vigorously pursuing the objective to become a developed nation by 2020. This requires the Indian economy to maintain an annual average growth rate of 8 per cent per annum.

India has adopted "Look East" followed by "Act East Policy" in pursuance of this objective. Now the Look East policy and Act East policy are a vital part of India's foreign policy. More than an external economic policy or a political slogan, the look east policy and act east policy show a strategic shift in India's vision of the world and its place in the evolving global economy. It was also a manifestation of India's belief that developments in East Asia are of direct consequence to its security and development. Therefore India actively engaged in creating a bond of friendship and cooperation with East Asia that has a strong economic foundation and a cooperative paradigm of positive inter-connectedness of security interests. India became a member of the ARF in 1996 and considers it as an experiment in fashioning a pluralistic, cooperative security order reflective of the diversity of the Asia-Pacific region. India has also successfully clinched a free trade agreement with the ASEAN, which had come into force on 1 January 2010. India is also a member of the East Asia Summit (EAS) which includes the ASEAN members and India, China, Japan, Republic of Korea, Australia, and New Zealand. It focuses on energy, environment, climate change, and sustainable development. The look east policy of India has included not only vigorous interaction with ASEAN but also improved relation with China.

The ultimate objective, it appears, is to evolve an Asian Economic Community on the lines of EU. India has also pursued a policy of strengthening its economic and military power. It appears that in order to increase the national power India had not only declared itself as a nuclear weapon power but also augmented its non-nuclear defence capabilities manifold. India is the largest importer of weapons as per the SIPRI reports. Again the maritime doctrine of India focuses mainly on building blue water navy. India's role in ensuring the security of Indian Ocean region has been recognized by major players in the region mainly because of the major shift in its external policy through a pragmatic approach. As a result India was not hesitant to cooperate with any regional and extra regional powers. India has undertaken several innovative steps towards economic resurgence of the country. India's initiative to interact with nations at the bilateral and multilateral levels through various regional groupings appears to be based on this policy initiative. The existence of non-traditional threat to India's security also demands multilateral approach towards security with the involvement of regional and extra-regional countries. The NDA-II government, led by Prime Minister Narendra Modi, had taken several initiatives to improve India's relation with neighbouring countries and also with major powers through bilateral and multilateral engagements. The initiative to strengthen the economic and military power and also special focus on the maritime security of India are policies in the right direction.

## Conclusion

Thus a closer look into the Asia-Pacific rebalancing policy initiative of the US and India's post-cold war maritime security policy shows convergence of interests. However, with regard to the means to be applied for the achievement of these objectives there is divergence. The US as a global power has all means to achieve its stated objectives, including use of coercive power. However, India as a functional democratic developing country having a hostile border with non-democratic nuclear weapon neighbours has only limited options to achieve its objectives. In such a situation it appears that the external power presence, especially the US presence in the region is advantageous to India.

# 25

# Maritime Dimensions of China's Maritime Silk Route and India's Foreign Policy Responses

*R.S. Vasan*

## The Maritime Environment in the Background

The pre-colonial era witnessed some remarkable engagement amongst nations despite limited connectivity and communication challenges. The silk and spice routes allowed the countries in different oceans to establish contacts. The initial such exchanges between nations were predominantly over treacherous land as new frontiers over sea routes were being explored. New trade routes were being discovered through the perilous oceans simultaneously by using wind power till the discovery of steam engines. The trade winds or monsoons paved the way for sail ships and dhows to connect continents for promoting trade interests while simultaneously enhancing the people to people contact. The commodities included spices, silk, pottery, horses, precious stones etc., This in turn enabled cultural assimilation from amongst diverse cultures and religions. The dimensions of trade slowly made way to expansion of imperialist nations and led to establishment of colonies of the West notably in Asia.

The example of the setting up of the Sri Vijaya empire and the spread of Hindu influence in Indo China through both sea and land routes is an example of the influence of the silk and spice routes . Likewise, the adventurous sea journey by the Chinese Admiral Zheng he in the sixth century which took the Chinese fleet and merchandise to many ports in Asia and Africa is again an absorbing tale of the importance of the oceans for trade and commerce. The Chinese are revisting their history and are trying to learn the importance of maritime silk routes to peace and prosperity. The spinoff of such expeditions always was in the cultural, political and religious domains which led to spread of religion, culture and social practices around the world.

The end of the World War II ushered in a new era of competitive dynamics of international relations with the sea forces playing a crucial role in providing sea based deterrence and projection of power in far corners of the world. The oceans around the world witnessed the power play by the NATO and the Soviet blocks with seemingly innocuous intention of preventing the third world war. It is ironic that such a measure only led to addition of nuclear arsenal and many near misses that brought the world to the brink of war. With the breakup of the Soviet Union which was least expected, the world order changed to a uni- polar one with the US becoming the global super cop with interests around the world. Being the number one economic power with well-oiled military machinery the US was able to project power and intervenes in far off corners of the world to restore order or change the status quo according to the whims and fancies of the only super power of the world. The recent failed examples in Iraq and Afghanistan even after lengthy stays of the occupational forces and spending of trillions of dollars has not brought peace and stability. On the contrary, the region has been devastated with no sign of lasting peace. Even the enormous loss of tens of thousands of innocent victims of the so called collateral damage has not helped in achieving the desired objectives.

The 21st century, designated as the century of the sea, has indeed been extremely challenging thus far in terms of the happenings at sea. There has been string of questions raised about security and stability due to many incidents of significance to a seafarer irrespective of whether he is on a warship or on a merchant ship or a fishing vessel. The maritime environment in the Asia-Pacific region which is increasingly being referred to as Indo-Pacific region is undergoing a major transformation. There are great changes in the maritime security land scape of immense importance to the global community. Both China and India are developing maritime power potential which comes with economic prosperity.[1] Before examining the Sino-Indian maritime equations and its impact in the current century, there is a need to examine some of the important issues that would influence the bilateral, regional and international relations.

One has to examine the indisputable factors that have governed the global maritime domain and the way nations have played out their role based on national interests. These factors have remained constant through the ages. The discussions below while not being exhaustive clearly illustrate that these constants continue to hold sway in the context of politico, military, social and cultural relations between nations irrespective of their geographic location.

## Maritime Silk Route

This is a notable Chinese initiative on the lines of ancient Silk Route to revisit the past and regain the glory of the yester centuries. It was first proposed by Xi Jinping when he visited Southeast Asia in October 2013. Premier Li Keqiang, who also carried out a high-profile visit to the region, announced the setting up of a 3 billion yuan ($495 million) maritime cooperation fund, part of which would support the plan. This on the face of it appears to be an initiative to promote trade, connectivity and also provide leverages for future contingencies in the Indian Ocean.

China has decided to approach the UN this year to bid for World Heritage Status for Maritime Silk Route. It may be noted that this is the seventh in the prominent list chosen for recognisition as world heritage site. Others in the list include ruins of the Nanyue King Palace, the Nanyue King Mausoleum, Guangxiao Monastery, the Light Tower of Huaisheng Mosque, the Ancient Tombs of Muslim Sages and the South Sea God Temple.It may be noted that a Sailor's trading map shown below shows India as the fulcrum for trade routes. Both India and China's combined economy was of the order of more than 55 percent of global GDP in the 14th century and it is only a matter of time before similar position is achieved by these two Asian powers.

India's maritime neighbours have responded enthusiastically to the proposal.

Maldives Government stated that "The Maldives welcomes and supports the proposal put forward by China to build the 21st Century Maritime Silk Road, and is prepared to actively participate in relevant cooperation,"... "The two sides agreed to enhance cooperation in other areas, such as marine, economy, and security."

Sri Lanka likewise indicated its willing ness and it was indicated that the two sides agreed to strengthen defence cooperation and to cooperate in the areas of defence-related science and technology, exchange of military academics, and provide logistic support," It is important to note that Sri Lanka has an investment of over 50 billion USD with a population of just about 21 million USD. Also in the case of Maldives, with a population of just 3,30,000 people, it attracts more than 3,50,000 Chinese tourists outnumbering the local population annually. China has also investments in Maldives that is a quarter of the Maldives economy.

From the Indian point of view, The invitation for India, was extended just a week after China's naval exercises out of the Sunda Strait in the waters of the eastern Indian Ocean in February 2014 as illulstrated in the diagram below:

> This was also two weeks after the People's Liberation Army Navy (PLAN) tried to overcome the Malacca Dilemma by carrying out its first-ever drills in the Lombok Straits of the Indian Ocean near Indonesia.

MSR can be assessed to be a bid to reframe China's rise in a non-threatening manner through maritime trade with adequate provisions for Confidence Building Measures (CBMs) entirely by investments close to the ports and harbours, soft loans for improvement of maritime infrastructure and mutual visits. The possibility of expanding naval capabilities through trade, connectivity to strategic out posts in IOR cannot be ruled out with the kind of interest in the protection of energy routes and trade.

## Genesis of the MSR

Maritime trade and connectivity through the ages has always been at the centre of international relations. Trade never stopped though the centuries though it may have slowed down during periodic periods of recession. It has only registered constant upward growth except for brief periods in human history. Commercial interests provide leverages by enhanced interaction and interdependence. Such exchanges expand in to the politico strategic dimensions that change the balance at times with not too pleasant consequences.

The slant of US Policy to Asia Pacific indeed is influenced by the growing Asian power equations in that area and the diminishing importance of western economies. Asian powers China and India are expected to overtake US and Japan progressively[2]. This is also due to the fears of a rising China that compels US to try and achieve balance in the region[3]. With the withdrawal from Afghanistan US is expected to lose strategic interest in Middle East also due to its own predicted energy independence due to discovery of Shale oil and gas.

An examination of the conduct of nations in the past centuries clearly illustrate that Commercial interests (and energy interests now) spur nations to different parts of the world to conduct business while shaping their national strategies for engagement in the region. As witnessed by history, the commercial interests do have the potential of transforming the strategy of the host country depending on local conditions and opportunity. The initial commercial interests at times give raise to grand strategies to acquire political, economic and strategic clout through trade and commerce. The classic example of how the British colonized India through the East Indian Company bears testimony to this modus operandi that is available for adoption by others. The setting up of the East India Company in India a predominantly trading company illustrated how trade led to expansionism and setting of the British rule in India that lasted for over 250 years till India got its freedom in August 1947. The story is not very different in other Asian countries where colonial rule was established by the Dutch, Portuguese, British, French and other western colonial powers. The fact that most of such colonies were established through the sea and known trade routes is a telling story of the importance of the oceans which promoted and nurtured ambitions of both great and small powers. The historically recorded Sea voyages/ adventures of both China and India as seafaring nations are noteworthy as both nations did not colonise other countries. On the contrary, the connectivity through the oceans was used to promote trade, cultural and religious exchanges that enhanced the peaceful engagements without any major skirmishes at sea.

**Sea Lines of Communication** are the life lines of the world. As a form of clean and cost effective transportation there is no substitute to movement by sea for transporting large volumes of human needs. Without such movement, it has been suggested that "**Half the world will starve, the other half will freeze**"[4] and many economies will collapse with the onset of Chaos and conflict. The choke points continue to provide pivotal role in both facilitating and regulating the flow of critical goods through them. In the context of the present century, the increased importance of transporting energy goods through the critical straits and choke points cannot be underestimated. Vulnerable as they are, due to the vagaries of regional imbalances/political instability in an area it compels coordinated action to create suitable security architectures both under UN Statutes and also the United Nations Conventions on the Law of the Seas. The safety of the SLOCs and the security of shipping in the choke points is of great importance to nations who are dependent on the sea routes for economy and prosperity. The new MSR has overlapping contours with the SLOCs. Irrespective of how it is nomenclatured, these are routes for providing connectivity between nations from Asia to Africa and in the process, also throw up opportunities for promoting political strategic and economic engagements.

In the context of the South China Sea, the fact that more than 80 percent of the[5] energy goods are imported through the sea routes through the Indian Ocean and also pass through the South/East China Sea before reaching the eastern destinations brings in acute concerns on the safety of the Sea Lines of Communication (SLOCs) Nations therefore have to initiate measures to safeguard these interests. This explains why China and other navies are sending out their war ships to the troubled waters of Somalia where pirates are having a field day in taking over ships and craft to disrupt maritime trade and traffic while instilling fear in the minds of ship owners and the crew. While the disputes in East China Sea (ECS) and South China Sea (SCS) are not new, they seem to be acquiring the potential to destabilize the status quo maintained for decades. The new assertive leadership of Abe in Japan and the increased emphasis on safeguarding national/historical interests is at the core of the problem in the region. The leadership of Xi Jinping a popular leader who is on a mission to set his house in order has certain implications in the region. China will not alter its stance on going to any extent to protect the declared core interests that include sea territories around disputed Islands which are expected to yield high volumes of gas and oil.

While all the involved in the regional dispute are engaged in show of power to assert their sovereignty and ownership claims, two incidents stand out to demonstrate the resolve of those in power in the area. First, China established a province in Sansha (which is also known as Woody Island) under the Hainan province. Second the Government of Japan bought the Islands in Senkaku which were privately owned by Japanese national. This led to increased protest on both sides and jingoism that has not helped to cool down fraying tempers. The world is watching with baited breath to see if the situation would go out of control due to some mis-calculations on any side. The disputes in the region are not entirely due to either historical or sovereignty issues. The assessment is that the disputes have a lot do with the energy security aspirations of the involved nations. China and Japan, just as some of the other East Asian countries are heavily dependent on energy imports and thus vulnerable to possible intervention and manipulation of the oil prices and interruption of energy products. Any discovery of hydrocarbons/gas in the immediate neighbourhood would help to minimize the energy dependence on imports. The ownership of the disputed Islands or any other territory therefore assumes great significance for the energy thirsty nations in the region. So in the back drop of discussions above, how does this impact the MSR initiative or how it is relevant at all is a question that needs to be answered?. The sea borne interests of China traverse long distances in the Indian Ocean from the energy producing nations and then reach the energy hungry nations after passing through the Malacca Straits. The outposts in countries that have joined the MSR would provide some options for China to use the ports in these countries to provide logistic facilities for out of area operations in IOR.

The very notion of freedom of navigation has been questioned by the aggressive stance of China which has tried to bull doze its maritime neighbours both in the South China Sea and also the East China Sea. The collision of Vietnamese vessels with Chinese vessels on 05 May 2014 aggravated the situation in the SCS. The claims and counter claims in these areas are not new but with the non-resolution of such disputes, the tension is building up in these areas.

The declaration of ADIZ has complicated the matter even more as now the sea areas and the air envelope in disputed areas is sought to be controlled with the ultimate aim of cementing the ownership claims by physical presence and by such extra ordinary proclamation of ADIZ. The declaration of the ADIZ in the East China Sea on Nov. 23, 2013 has escalated the tension in another dimension. In the process of activating the ADIZ, the interception of the Japanese surveillance aircraft by the Chinese Sukhois in last week of May 2014 can be classified as a near miss as the aircraft closed to less than fifty meters from the Japanese aircraft. Any miscalculation or an unintended manoeuvre would have resulted in an avoidable accident that could propel both the sides to next level of undesired engagement. It was expected that China would also declare an ADIZ in South China Sea by end of last year. However, this has not yet happened.

The developments in the Persian Gulf also are not comforting as Iran threatened to block the Straits of Hormuz[6] if the US and the west cross a pre-determined nuclear threshold. While Iran continues to nurture its aspirations to be a nuclear weapon power, the possibility of the situation in the Arabian Peninsula going out of hand with possible impact on the movement of traffic through the world's critical maritime choke points are issues of great concern. However, the recent agreement in April 2015 to allow Iran to use nuclear energy for peaceful purposes under appropriate monitoring by the IAEA has allowed some breathing time though there are other questions of existence being raised by Israel.

**Sea based deterrence** (SBD) did not halt with the breakup of the Soviet Union. Resurgence of cold war at regional levels appears inevitable with emphasis on SBD. Mis-match between haves and have-nots of nuclear weapons will see attempts to bridge this gap by weapon programmes, delivery, command and control systems—Iran, North Korea, Pakistan and other aspirants make the list of those who would like to possess nuclear weaponry by hook or crook. The famous quote of ZA Bhutto, "We will eat grass[7] but will make a nuclear bomb"—illustrates the point about how the world will have to continue with both the existing and future challenges of nuclearisation. Would the establishiment of the MSR help in the Indian Ocean aspirations of China by locating its SBD units (SSBNs) for targeting locations in the West including USA.

While presently, China has a lead in the number of nuclear capable submarines in its inventory, India is joining the club with INS Arihant ,a nuclear submarine[8] and follow on submarines that would provide it with the SBD capability. The challenges of maintaining an SSBN[9] notwithstanding, the emphasis on Sea Based deterrence will not vanish in the coming decades. With specific reference to the MSR, it is evident that some of the recipient countries in the IOR may be in the cross hair of China for ensuring that there is turn round facility provided in times of need to the units of PLA Navy.

There are some dynamic developments which have the potential to impact in the maritime domain in the present century in the Indian Ocean in particular. The collective and individual responses to these developing situations would determine the shape of maritime safety and security architectures. Some of the important developments with potential for impacting the maritime security dimensions are discussed below in the succeeding paragraphs.

## Pivot to Asia

A lot has been said about the possible impact of what the US pivot to Asia would mean to the region and the rest of the world. The analysis for this pivot has been explained as more to do with the raise of China. USA by redeploying its maritime forces in the new areas of interest wants to remain relevant where action is. The turmoil in the South China Sea and the East China Sea has engaged the attention of the countries in this region where almost everyone seems to have a dispute with China.

The recent conflagration in the region with aggressive posturing by North Korea and the joint exercises of South Korea and the USA in the surrounding areas has added to a greater sense of instability and there are fears about the conduct of intransigent North Korea which seems to press on regardless without heeding even to the counsel of its mentor China.

With the impending withdrawal from Afghanistan, USA can exercise some flexibility in troop redeployment in other areas of interest it is the assessment of the policy makers in USA that their presence is vital and necessary to ensure that regional stability. The revised Maritime Strategy released on 13th March 2015 makes it clear that USA will not with draw from the Gulf area. On the contrary, there would be a proportionate increase of maritime forces in the region by increasing the numbers to 40 vessels by 2020.[10]

## Additional Factors in the MSR

In addition to the factors above, the challenges of 21st century include Proliferation Security Concerns, Environmental concerns, and Traffic density with more vessels which could lead to greater risk of grounding, collision and spillage which exist to a large extent along the MSR . Such accidents unfortunately come with long term impact on the fragile environment. Piracy seems to be on the rise in different parts as the navies of the world try to contain it in one part or another. Opening up of the Antarctic routes for navigation has its ascendant challenges.

Specific technologies in the recent times include AIS, LRIT, SSAS, VTMS, GPS, and ECDIS etc.,[11] have enhanced the safety of ships and also provides options for contingency planning based on data fusion. Doubtlessly, cutting edge technological advances enables safe, expeditious and efficient transportation—Advances in propulsion, marine technology, under water and over water surveillance, space based surveillance, deep sea mining, Tsunami warning systems have transformed the Safety and Security Architecture. Such technological improvements are all pervading and impact the way maritime stake holders conduct their business. The flip side is that what is available to you is also available to the tech savvy Non State Actors (Pirates, Terrorists, online fraudsters ) a fact that needs to be constantly borne in mind while drawing up security architectures and responses. These factors would need to be taken in to account by China when it plans to use the MSR for furthering not just its economic interests but also its strategic posturing.

It is in the context of the facts brought out above, that there is a need to examine the impact of the MSR in shaping the maritime contours in the Indian Ocean. This is particularly so since China is not an Indian Ocean power just as India is not a Pacific power. Yet, both the countries do have enormous interest in the respective regions for economic reasons, global prosperity and stability. The interests stem from the need to access global commons and to use the seas for the common good of the people of the two nations.

There is definitely a sense of competition due to the growing economies of Asia which would like to take center stage. India is not in a position to challenge China whose growth has been spectacular and has alarmed its neighbours with the military developmental plans. Despite the assurances by China that it is not for any offensive action, the pattern of spending on defence[12] does not bring about a sense of confidence amongst the observers. India and China have no contests in the maritime domain and the only issue apparently is related to resolving the vexed issue of land borders. The perception in India is that China has been overly aggressive with all its neighbours including India when it comes to sorting out the border and sovereignty issues. The concern has shifted to the East China and South China Sea[13] where the occurrences at sea have not reinforced any confidence that the situation would not go out of control due to over indulgence in nationalistic fervor. The diagram below illustrates the number of disputes in which China is involved. The reported disputes numbering 61 in the case of PRC is indicative of the state of flux in the region. The increased military expenditure and the investment in newer technology and weapons systems is adding to the concerns of stability in the region.

China has by and large invested heavily in breaching certain technologies to ensure that its maritime anti access capabilities[14] are fine tuned. The investment in Anti Satellite technology, Stealth aircraft, Anti-Ship Ballistic Missile (ASBM) and the Cyber war capability has provided considerable teeth to the PLA. As illustrated in the diagram below, it is clear that there is a layered kind of overlapping technologies that would provide China with the capability to take on its adversaries before they even reach the areas of conflict in its back yard. The cyber capability of which a lot is being discussed today seems to suggest that they do have an edge and are experimenting with various cyber war options that could tilt the favour one way or the other with the potential adversary including USA. For China USA and its actions of recalibration or pivot to Asia poses a serious challenge. While it faces these challenges in a hostile maritime neighbourhood both in ECS and SCS, through the MSR, it would like to have certain options in the Indian Ocean where again the USA has a dominant maritime presence. The presence of the fifth fleet since the 80s has ensured to a large extent free flow of energy goods from the Straits of Hormuz to the needy markets of the East.

Should India or China challenge the sea borne trade due to a spillover of the land dispute, and then China would like to be prepared for such a contingency by having some leverage in the Indian Oceean Littorals.

Both China and India are emerging Blue Water Navies if they are already not there. While there is a lot of debate on what constitutes a Blue Water Navy (BWN), the present day definition is as follows: "...A maritime force capable of sustained operation across the deep waters of open oceans. A blue-water navy allows a country to project power far from the home country and usually includes one or more aircraft carriers. Smaller blue-water navies are able to dispatch fewer vessels abroad for shorter periods of time." [15]

By present day classification, the classic Blue water Navies include US, UK and France, where as the one's in the making are China, India and South Korea? When one examines the operations undertaken by India, it is clear that since 1971 which is considered the turning point for the navy in India, Indian Navy has demonstrated its potential as a BWN. The details of the operations at Serials a, b and c below have been well covered in the books titled Transition to Triumph (1999), Transition to Eminence (2004) and Transition to Guardianship (2009) by the official historian of Indian Navy, Vice Admiral Hiranandani Without getting in to the details of the operations, the same are listed to highlight the range of operations which included both the peace time and the activities during hostile environment:

a) Liberation of Bangladesh in 1971[16]
b) Prevention of Coup in Maldives in 1988[17]
c) Deployment of Indian Peace Keeping Force in Sri Lanka[18]
d) Anti Piracy Patrols off Somalia (Both India and China have been engaged in anti-piracy patrols since 2008 and have been even cooperating to protect shipping passing through the high risk area)
e) Evacuation of Indian and Foreign Nationals from Lebanon, Libya and now from Yemen in April 2015.

Historically, both China and India could come under the definition of blue water navies as both ventured out to far corners of the world. So if it was Zheng he[19] who undertook the voyages in the 14$^{th}$ century and visited many ports in the Indian Ocean, it was the Chola's[20] and Pallavas of the southern Indian dynasties who extended their reach up to South East Asia and beyond. Today, China has commercial and strategic interests in the Indian Ocean just as India has renewed its interests in East Asia by its Look East Policy. India is increasing its engagement with the East Asian nations including China.

The main maritime interest is to protect the ships carrying its energy products and goods. India also possesses the capability to protect its commercial interests in different parts of the world where both China and India are engaged in the hunt for energy resources. The Chinese navy for the first time entered Indian Ocean to protect its interests off the Somali Coast where the scourge of piracy had started affecting all merchant men. The PLA-N has maintained an effective patrol in the areas of interest and it is not usual for either the Chinese or the Indian navy vessels to escort any foreign vessel and to ensure that the SLOCs remain open and secure. This reinforces the belief that the two Asian countries can come together to ward off common threats in the global commons.

While it appears that the concept of "string of pearls" a phrase coined to indicate the extent of strategic inroads in Indian Ocean by PRC[21] has been debated endlessly the perception is that China is slowly establishing its sphere of influence in the immediate neighbourhood of India that is detrimental to the national/ maritime interests of India. With the economic clout enjoyed by China coupled with the decision making and political processes that give China an edge over India, PRC has found it easy to make inroads in Sri Lanka, Myanmar, Mauritius, Bangladesh, Seychelles, Pakistan and Maldives. The huge economic investments with soft loans serve as a great incentive for the developing countries in the region. The economic investments in India's immediate maritime neighbourhood have alarmed the Indian establishment even though they concede that China has a major role to play in the economic development of the region.

The assessment is that despite the geo strategic advantage enjoyed by India, India is slowly conceding its time tested advantage in the region to the aggressive economic policies of China with long term strategic dividends in the Indian Ocean Region. While investments in port developments in Pakistan, Sri Lanka, Bangladesh, Myanmar and other investments in Maldives are not designed to create basing facilities for the PLA-Navy, the economic leverages provide a great opportunity for China to use these facilities at a future date for augmenting any naval initiatives depending on the strategic development.

The visit of the Chinese submarines to Colombo on the eve of the visit of Chinese Premier Xi Jinping in September raised the heckles in the Indian establishment. The Mahinda Rajapaksa's Government was seen as pro-China and granting numerous concessions to help China realize its ambitions in the Indian Ocean. However the change of Government in Sri Lanka consequent to the Presidential election which has brought a India friendly government changes some equations in the Indian neighbourhood. It is from this point of view that the visit of PM Narendra Modi to countries in our maritime neighbourhood takes center stage. The visit of Modi to Sri Lanka came after twenty eight years and showed the past policy makers of India and leadership in poor light as they continued to ignore the most important maritime southern neighbour post the visit of Rajiv Gandhi.

It is easy to visualise two lines of seaward defence peripheries with respect to India. The inner periphery passes through Sri Lanka, Maldivers and the A&N Islands which houses the Tri Services command. The outer line of maritime defence includes the countries such as Mauritius Seychelles and other Indian Ocean countries. The visit of the Prime Minister to Mauritius and Seychelles is an attempt to ensure that the outer periphery of our seaward defence is not breached by Chinese MSR which could lead to other initiatives using this handle.

The Foreign Policy prescriptions are very clear and lucid as for as the Indian Government is concerned. The message is that if you ignore those who are on the two lines you lose out any advantage that was conferred historically by geography and also by the percentage of Indians who have settled down in these countries of great importance to our maritime security and stability. However it is to be noted that there are other stake holders in the Pacific and the relations with Vietnam, Japan, South Korea and other South East Asian countries also need to have a high priority to ensure that there are leverages available in the Pacific to meet the futuristic strategic developments.

Whether on the MSR or in other areas of interest, the challenges for both the Indian Navy and the PLA-N are similar due to the nature and scale of maritime developments in the new world. The new era though has a very clear focus on trade and commerce also has brought us back to revisit concerns on safety and security at sea, illegal immigration, environmental degradation, piracy, asymmetric threats, Proliferation and WMD which requires the application of sea-power. The need for greater safe-guards, intelligent use of technology, Rules of Engagement (RoE) and best practices essential to prevent recurrences can hardly be overemphasized. The joining of hands of the major world powers to promote safety, stability, law and order at sea is the need of the hour. The MSR initiative which has trade and connectivity as the central theme cannot be a standalone initiative. It is a package that needs to be handled with care by all the stake holders.

The areas of engagement along the SLOCs of great importance to all the countries who use the seas obviously allude to anti-piracy, HADR, energy security, coordinated investments for resources, joint exploration and such like. Unlike India, China carries a lot more products using its own shipping fleet. China indeed is very concerned about the piracy attacks and also the vulnerability of its shipping fleet when engaged in trade and commerce in far corners of the world. China is well aware that it would serve its interests if it is part of the global initiatives such as the one witnessed in the Gulf of Aden. The cooperative initiatives of the two big giants of Asia will go a long way in augmenting the regional and global maritime security architecture. However, India somehow does not want to join the MSR initiative as it feels that it would yield strategic space through the trade and connectivity format adopted by China to engage the countries both in Asia and Africa.

There are no doubts any more about the assertion that the 21st century belongs to Asia in general, China and India in particular. This geographic entity is shaping the international landscape as never before. The interplay of major western and eastern powers in economic, strategic, political, military and cultural arenas has witnessed manifold increase due to the changing dynamics of global power play. The revolution in information technology has on one hand shrunk the globe even more and has brought about a paradigm shift in the manner in which nations interact to protect their interests and rights.

The raise of China and India both Asian powers is set to change the existing equations and would bring in new changes to the global order. The recent economic report brought out that India has pipped Japan to the number three position after US and China. These changes have far reaching impact on the military, economic and political developments in the region. US which continues to take it up on itself to be the guarantor of global security and order is recalibrating to the Indo Pacific in order to be able to intervene militarily should it be necessary to protect the interests of its allies in the Pacific and its own interests. An increasingly assertive China which has economic power and a growing modern military challenges the notion of the only super power.The fear that any vacuum created by US would be occupied by China is also a factor that has weighed heavily in the minds of the US policy makers who do not want to surrender the geo strategic advantage.

The withdrawal from Afghanistan at least theoretically allows for redeployment of certain forces in the areas of interest in the Indo Pacific. China has been aggressively pursuing its claims for territory in the East China Sea and the South China Sea by quoting historical claims.It has also displayed a tendency to resort to use of force to settle such disputes. This has not gone well with the maritime neighbours in the region who would like to use the presence and friendship of USA to counter the military might of China. The smaller neighbours such as Philliphines have even approached the International Court of Justice (ICJ) challenging the Chinese claims. USA has assured its traditional allies that it would uphold the friendship treaties with these countries should there be a need.

The impact of the pivot to Asia can be viewed in two ways. From the American point of view, it would facilitate greater security and stability in a volatile area where claims and counter claims over territory could go out of hands and lead to either localized conflict or escalate to something more bringing in extra regional players such as the US itself. Some of the recent clashes at sea and certain responses from those involved does not augur well for maritime stability and security in the region under question. From the point of China, the presence of US is an impediment and China is uncomfortable with the unwanted presence of the only super power. The recalibration and presence of US is seen as the inability of the super power to reconcile to the changed geostrategic land scape and the growth of China in the Indo Pacific region. The actions and statements of leaders from USA including from Obama are perceived as posing hurdles for the maritime military ambitions of China under the guise of peaceful raise. There are legitimate major concerns are about the freedom of navigation and the right to safe passage through various SLOCs.

## Conclusion

A quick look at the MSR strategy of China and the study of the maritime dimensions in India's neighbourhood brings out that essentially the old silk routes have become the Sea Lines of Communication (SLOCs) connecting oceans and continents sustaining the global economic interests by trade and commerce. The haves and the have nots have used the oceans to bridge the gap by engaging in sea borne trade. The energy dependent countries in Asia such as China, India and Japan have no choice but to use the sea routes to import their energy sources from far corners of the world to sustain the economic growth. China has become the manufacturing hub of the world and again has to use the seas for exporting large quantities of its industrial products for feeding the markets in the west while simultaneously importing oil, gas and other energy resources. The new silk routes therefore have become the indispensable arteries or life lines of the world which need to be protected. The challenge to these sea routes have come from Pirates and VNSAs who interfere in the safe passage of vessels of all sizes and shapes which are engaged in legitimate trade activity. It is evident that there are areas for cooperation in ensuring the free use of the global commons. It is also a foregone conclusion that the MSR would provide those desired advantages to China when more countries decide to join the initiative. India unfortunately, did lose out in the neighbourhood due to lack of good leadership and strategy to engage the neighbours in its traditional areas of influence in the IOR.

## Recommendations for recalibrating the Foreign Policy in the Maritime Domain

China and India will have to initiate measures to face the challenges. This can only be accomplished by coordinated, collaborative efforts to ensure maritime equilibrium. There are areas in which both the counties can easily join hands particularly in the maritime domain without any fear of treading on each other's toes even along the Maritime Silk Routes. Both the countries have a lot to gain by engaging each other in the maritime arena. India will continue to be weary of the Chinese overtures in the Indian Ocean Region though, for the present, it is to do more with the ability of China to invest heavily due to its own growing economy and its intention to develop a powerful maritime power potential.

There is a need to address vulnerability of SLOC and Huge volumes of Mercantile Trade that passes under the watchful eyes of the Indian establishment. Energy Security being of paramount importance to India, there is a need to ensure that it engages with all stake holder nations in the region to safeguards its interests.

India while not being in the same league as China when it comes to investments, India has no choice but to engage its maritime neighbours actively with investments and soft loans. There should be no hesitation to use its soft power in the maritime neighbourhood to obtain long term benefits.

Indian Ocean is the only ocean named after India and it is important that this definition and the import is not lost on policy planners and the leadership.

## NOTES

1. Geoffrey *Till, Sea power: A Guide for the Twenty-First Century* (Oxon, Routledge) 2013, 20, 203
2. Anil K. Gupta, Haiyan Wang *Getting China and India Right,* (San Francisco, Jossey Bass) 2009, 6, 8, 61
3. Shelly Rigger, *Tangled Titans* ed, David L Shambaugh (Maryland: Rowman and Littlefield Publishers Inc 2013 ),309
4. Tay Lim Hing ,*Maritime Security in Southeast Asia,* ed Kwa Chong Guan, John Kristen Skogan(New york: Routledge 2007), 201
5. Garver. John W, *China and Iran: Ancient Partners in a Post-Imperial World (*Washington University of Washington Press 2006),246
6. Gibson Bryan R. *Covert Relationship* (California PSI reports 2010*), 126*
7. Khab Feroze Hassan, *Eating Grass: The Making of the Pakistani Bomb* (Stanford, California 2012),87
8. Verghese Koithara *Managing India's Nuclear Forces (*Washington, Brookings Institute 2012),136
9. ibid
10. Full document rleased on 13th March 2015 and accessed by visiting http://www.navy.mil/maritime.
11. As illustrated in Integrated Maritime Policy for the EU, Working Document III on Maritime Surveillance Systems (Joint Research Centre, Ispra) ,2
12. Ed SIPRI, Sipri Year Book *Armaments, Disarmament and International Security 2011* (Oxford University Press 2011) 184.185,
13. Ibid, 110
14. Ronald O'Rourk ,*China Naval Modernization: Implications for U.S. Navy Capabilities* (Washington,CRS Report 2009), 23

15. According to the definition of Defence Security Service of USA
16. Hiranandani GM, *Transition to Triumph* (New Delhi, Lancer 2000), 181, 227, 228
17. Hiranandani G.M., *Transition to Eminence* (New Delhi, Lancer 2004), 14, 199, 242
18. Hiranandani GM, *Transition to Guardianship* (New Delhi Lancer 2009), xxvi, 52, 107
19. Michael M Yamashita, *Zheng He: tracing the epic voyages of China's greatest explorer,(White Star Publishers 2006) 14,17*
20. Krishna Reddy *Indian History (*New Delhi, Tata McGraw Hill), 2001, 64, 65
21. Ashley J. Tellis, Travis Tanner, Jessica Keough, *Asia Responds To Its Rising Powers: China and India (Seattle, NBAS 2011), 110, 111*

# 26

# Indo-Pak Relations: In the Context of Changing Security Architecture in Afghanistan

*Sudhir Singh*

India and Pakistan were one country before partition in 1947. They are biggest countries of South Asia as well. Like India, Pakistan inherited a secular state ruled through a bureaucracy led by a civil service elite recruited and organized on merit. There is little evidence that Jinnah wanted to effect major changes on many of these fronts.[1] Indian leadership established military, bureaucracy and political elite balance just after independence. But Muslim League, unlike the Congress in India, failed to make the transition from a national movement to a ruling party and soon fragmented as it failed to move quickly towards drafting a new constitution and lost both of its founding leaders, Jinnah and Liaquat Ali Khan. Muslim League used religion to garner political support and thus created third stake holders popularly known as Mullah. The troika of military, bureaucracy and the Mullah captured the canvass of national building process and instead of egalitarian state they formed a theocratic state which was detrimental for the minorities in particular and development in general. General Zia-ul-Haq (1977-1988) military regime further consolidated the power of this troika over the destiny of the country. This troika has become so much powerful that even an elected government is unable to change the direction which leads the country on the path of destruction.

This makes the domestic political environment detrimental for good relations with India. Either military or civilian every ruler is known to use an Indian card whenever they are in crisis.

In this backdrop, since their inception both countries' relations have been turbulent. Both fought limited war over Kashmir just few months after the independence. Till date both have fought three full and one half wars and three among them were fought for Kashmir. We are aware about the fact that India has grown phenomenally since the end of the cold war at the international level. Three US Presidents visited India from independence to 2000, but since 2000 three US Presidents have already visited India. Between January and June 2010 all five permanent United Nations Security Council member countries' Prime Minister/Presidents have already visited India. India is gaining respectable space at the global table of governance also. India has been maintaining the growth rate of 7% since last two decades and projections are of 8% in coming years. In contrast, 55,000 people have been killed in Pakistan between 2007 and 2014, i.e. after the assassination of former Prime Minister Benazir Bhutto in December 2007. Its economy has remained stagnant. One thing is extremely important that since 2000 the United States has started to maintain cordial relations simultaneously with India and Pakistan while maintaining neutrality on Kashmir. It is in contrast with the cold war era when the United States was inclined towards Pakistan and even after the end of the cold war, but before 2000, Rabin Raphel, US Deputy Secretary of State (first President Clinton regime, 1992-96) gave a controversial statement about Kashmir which dented Indo-US relations.

The post-Pokhran (1998) situation has enhanced Indian status at the global level. Boosted with sustainable economic development, India has achieved good progress at the strategic level as well. The end of the cold war and post-9/11 situation has further brought Asia as a dominating continent at the global table of governance. Asia is biggest in terms of geography and continent at the global level. India has emerged as an important Asian power and without India Asian balance of power is not stable. These developments have, however, put India under stress. In the given prevailing circumstances India could not be obsessed with Pakistan. The forefathers of Indian national movement had given adequate mandate to Indian foreign policy formulators to promote the tenets of justice based international order. But as Kautilya has stated that without power, a country is not an important player in the shaping of the global order. Today in contemporary global system India has the capability as well as will power to implement the mandate of its founding forefathers.

In this prevailing situation how India could reformulate its Pakistan policy? There are many divergences and fewer convergences between both traditional rivals of South Asia. How diplomacy could be used to reduce divergences and increase convergences? This focal point will be widely debated within the ambit of this paper. It has been also discussed that how far Afghan tango will make imprint on this thorny bilateral relations in the backdrop of NATO withdrawal by the end of 2014. In the wake of official death of Mullah Omar, Afghan theatre has become violent and within January–July 2015 around 5,000 people have already lost their lives due to terror resurgence. Combined right from 2009 till July 2015, 16,874 people have been killed in terror related violence.[2] Right from January 2015 to July 2015 alone 4,921 people have been killed, which is self-explanatory.

In April 2012, Pakistan's President, Asif Ali Zardari visited New Delhi although for pilgrimage of famous Sufi Dargah of Ajmer, Rajasthan but he had a lunch session with Indian Prime Minister, Dr. Manmohan Singh. All outstanding issues had been discussed and it was decided that irritants will not be preventing the normalization process. It was a maiden visit of any Pakistani President after a long time. It is an open secret that President Zardari was representing Pakistan People's Party (PPP), which was ruling the country since March 2008 till March 2013 and despite many odds completed its tenure of five years. It is the first democratic government of Pakistan to do so. It should also be noted that military still holds the key as far as Pakistan foreign policy is concerned but after the deadly avalanche in Siachen in April 2012 in which more than 130 Pakistan's military personnel had been killed, the Chief of Army Staff (Pakistan) General Pervez Asfaq Kayani had suggested that India and Pakistan must inked an agreement on Siachen because this terrain is inhospitable for human beings and weather has killed more soldiers than the actual fighting. He also expressed his concern that more military activities in Siachen will erode environmental security and water flow in Pakistan could hurt the most.[3]

In May 2014 after the general election, BJP in the leadership of Narendra Modi has taken over. The BJP and PM Modi are known for their nationalist temper. Modi invited all SAARC heads of the states to participate in his swearing in ceremony on May 26, 2014. Pakistani PM, Nawaz Sharif had also attended along other SAARC leaders. Modi and Sharif had a 50-minutes conversation and expressed their desire to resolve all outstanding issues. In last over one year both PM met many times and expressed their desire to sustain dialogue but non-state actors' interventions prevented the pace of the dialogue. Both PM met at Ufa (Russia) in July 2015 but due to sustainable terror attacks after this meeting, the enthusiasm has reduced.

After the May 2013 general election the government has changed in Pakistan. Nawaz Sharif led PML-N has taken over and Sharif has become Prime Minister third time. During election process, ruling PML-N and other parties have refrained from their pet rhetoric of anti-India megalomania. Sharif had promised during election campaign that if elected he will promote cordial relationships with India. His government has released over 350 fishermen in August 2013 as a goodwill gesture. In an interview given to *Telegraph* (London), Prime Minister

Nawaz Sharif asserted that his victory in May 2013 elections is a mandate for peace with India. He further added, "We have been in a very unfortunate arm race with India ever since partition and I think we are a very unfortunate country from that point of view." He stressed that trust deficit should end and both countries must settle all outstanding issues through dialogue and remain with peace and development.[4]

I must return on the focal issue now. What are the basic irritants between both traditional rivals of South Asia. It keeps on changing but more or less it has been sustainable. When Benazir Bhutto's PPP took over in 1988 and became first women Prime Minister of Pakistan, the Pakistani army took three assurances from her, where she agreed not to intervene. Kashmir, Afghanistan and Nuclear issue were the three arenas, which were agreed upon between Prime Minister, Benazir Bhutto and Chief of Army Staff, General Aslam Beig. More or less these three issues are still preventing cordiality between nuclear armed two biggest nations of South Asia. Terror has remained as an instrument of Pakistan's foreign policy and since early 1980s Pakistan has extended support to cross border terror activities in India. First it was done in the case of Punjab and later on in Kashmir. However, later Pakistan has revised its policy and now extended support to terror activities in entire India. Strengthening of participatory democracy could be pivotal for cordial relations between both hostile neighbours. When Nawaz Sharif was trying to accelerate the peace process, five Indian soldiers were ambushed and killed at the LOC in August 2013. Who was accountable for both provocative incidents? It is the Pakistani army. Army and the terror network have been pursuing one thing as common agenda and that is anti-India megalomania. According to Stephen P. Cohen a leading American expert on Pakistan, "A full blown democracy, in which the armed forces come under firm civilian control, will be impossible until Pakistan's strategic environment alters in such a way that the army retreats from its role as guardian of the state."[5] Army will not allow any government either democratic or military to do so, because Pakistani army has only one agenda and that is sustaining its monopoly over the system.

It has proved the argument that if violence will occur in Afghanistan it will spill over to Pakistan. Due to porous border and ethnic and religious commonality, both countries are prone to the violence of another country. Survival of Afghanistan's own democratically elected government led by Hamid Karzai has created the question of survival for Pakistan. Since 1979 Afghan war, when entire capitalist world came into Afghanistan to contain expansion of communism, Pakistan had been nodal platform of this Afghan Jihad. Militants right from Morocco to Mindanao (the Philippines) have been recruited to establish the supremacy of the Ummah. In this process, terror factory originates and after elimination of the Taliban and Al-Qaeda from Afghanistan, it has shifted its bases into Pakistan.

In May 2011 Osama Bin Laden was killed at Abbotabad, just few hundred meters away from prestigious Kakul Military Academy, which is also not far away from Islamabad. The Pakistani commission which was constituted for its investigation has revealed many things which proved the allegation that OBL had a protection from the army. Just weeks before the killing of OBL, COAS General Pervez Asfaq Kayani was announcing from Kakul that we will eradicate terror but within 100 meters of the Academy, an army-protected safe haven was hosting OBL. It has also been revealed by the commission that OBL was in Pakistan since his ouster from Afghanistan. The billion dollar question arises that how was he living in Pakistan without the knowledge of intelligence agencies? Pakistan was protecting OBL merely to protect terror networks and used him to blackmail the United States.

Needless to say that it has soured Pakistan-United States relations. Pakistan feels that Afghanistan must be under the umbrella of her dominance and it is necessary for the strategic depth of Pakistan over India. The NATO presence in Afghanistan since last thirteen years has immensely benefited India. It has reduced the terror export to India in particular and rest of the world in general. Today if any terror act occurs in any corner of the globe the link goes to Pakistan and Afghanistan. It has also raised Afghanistan National Army (ANA) which is intended to defend the country after the withdrawal of the NATO forces. India has already contributed more than $ 2 billion into the reconstruction process of Afghanistan. India has also provided training to ANA personnel and slated to increase it due to prevailing circumstances in Afghanistan.

Afghanistan remains a hot spot not only between Pakistan and India or United States and Pakistan but entire globe has its genuine stakes in Afghanistan. It is producing over 80% of the global production of drugs. Drug trafficking has threatened the societies across the globe in general but adjoining to Afghanistan it has leased unprecedented harm to the younger generation. In the backdrop of NATO withdrawal Pakistan will try its level best to maximize its interests. It will wish that its pet Taliban must be in helm of affairs in Afghanistan. One must remember that whenever there was stability in Afghanistan, it had thorny relations with Pakistan. Afghanistan was the first country to oppose Pakistani demand of plebiscite in Kashmir in the United Nations. The issue of Pakhtunistan is raking high with the stability in Afghanistan. Pakistan feels worried in this situation therefore intended to keep Afghanistan as its satellite country. India, Iran and Russia oppose this possibility along with the like-minded countries of the western world. On Afghan front India and Pakistan must cooperate because Pakistan has witnessed the unprecedented violence at the domestic level, which has tarnished the developmental process. Peace in Afghanistan will be a push factor for the sustainable development of Pakistan.

Sustainability of Hobessian State of Nature in Afghanistan will be detrimental for Pakistan first.

Another issue is Kashmir. Since last 68 years it has been the core issue between India and Pakistan. Pakistan is claiming over Kashmir due to its religious and geographical proximities. It is also an open secret that despite many wars and cross-border terror in Kashmir, Pakistan has not been able to snatch Kashmir from India. This has helped the Pakistani military to remain most important and powerful institutions of the country. In May 2014, COAS, Raheel Sharif stated that Kashmir is jugular vein of Pakistan. Due to Kashmir the army will avail lion share within resource less Pakistani economy. This process has helped to militaries the country and thus negated fundamental freedom and human rights.

Kashmir, weak Afghanistan, nuclearisation and terror all are pet projects of the army. These projects are the lifeline of the army because it provides a kind of legitimacy to the illegitimate aspirations of the Pakistani army. For the promotion and protection of these projects hostility against India is a must, therefore army never allowed any civilian government to encroach this space and perhaps will not allow in foreseeable future too.

Aysha Siddika, an eminent military expert of Pakistan has opined in her famous book *Pakistan Military Inc* that even if India will hand over Kashmir to Pakistan in a silver plate, there is hardly any guarantee that animosity between both rivals will end. For the time being both countries must sustain the dialogue process on Kashmir till its final resolution and in the meanwhile cooperate on the areas where there are hardly any divergences like trade and commerce.

According to Munir Akram, Pakistan's former Ambassador to the UN, "The hostility between Pakistan and India has deep historical and popular roots in both countries. Despite cultural, linguistic and ethnic affinities, the mutual hostility between Hindus and Muslims of the sub-continent is real and endemic. It was the *raison d'être* for the creation of Pakistan. The history of last fifty years has, if anything, further intensified this hostility and gave a structural expression in the relationship between the two states. The Kashmir dispute, in essence, is but one expression of this divide and hostility, (Bangladesh relations with India displays the same dynamic). Thus, even if outside issues like Kashmir, are resolved, and some semblance of civility restored between Pakistan and India, their relationship will remain competitive for the foreseeable future. Those who argue that with goodwill and conflict resolution, peace and harmony can descend on the sub-continent are either ignorant or self-serving."[6]

Whenever the crisis of democracy/military regime started they are singing the saga of Kashmir to rescue themselves. The PPP led coalition (2008–13) did the same thing. President Asif Ali Zardari pledged to work for good relations with India earlier but in September 2012 while addressing United Nations General Assembly he raised six decade old Kashmir saga. PM Nawaz Sharif is known to promote trade with India but he also sings the raga of Kashmir in March 2014 when he met US President Barack Obama.[7]

The growing tentacles of terror have created an alarm well about the security of nuclear arsenals in Pakistan. In the aftermath of killing of OBL, many military instalments were attacked by the terror network. In June 2014, Karachi Jinnah International airport was attacked by suicide attackers, which resulted into the death of 38 people. It was also revealed by the investigations that there was insider information with the attackers. If such a kind of black sheep will exist in the security protection system of the nuclear devices then it could be dangerous for the human existence. Being the most targeted neighbour, India will be first casualty. Another aspect is nuclear weapons first use. There must be consensus between both countries in this issue. India must engage Pakistan in dialogue process and these pertinent issues will be solved mutually. It is in the interest of both the countries.

Cross-border terror in India has been supported by Pakistan. Pakistan has understood the reality that even after 3-1/2 war they could not gain the desired results therefore they have adopted the tactics of thousands cuts propelled first by Z.A. Bhutto. After Ajmal Kasab, another terrorist from Pakistan has been caught alive in July 2015 in Kashmir, which vindicates that Pakistan has tacit understanding with the terror groups based there and their terror attacks in India.

Till date the mastermind of Mumbai attack, Hafiz Saeed is enjoying full freedom and spreading hatred against India. Dawood Ibrahim is also in Pakistan. Pakistan must understand that sustainability of its support to the terror groups has been proved detrimental for the stability of the country. Comprehensive dialogue is on after 2009 Sharam-AL-Seikh (Egypt) Summit between both Prime Ministers. In August 2012 Prime Minister Dr. Manmohan Singh met President Asif Ali Zardari at Tehran during 16th NAM Summit. During September 2013 UN summit in New York both Prime Ministers met. It needs to be sustained.

There may be terror incidents in future to derail the process. Pakistani army will never like cordial relations with India. It could hamper its monopoly over the system which it has been availing since independence. According to Wilke Boris "The people in charge—bureaucrats on the one side, army officer on the other—were at great pains in protecting and dominating the state field against adversaries from in and outside the official borders. Internally, they had to confine their effort to some 'core' state; secular and most essential rules inside narrowly drawn boundaries, they had to prepare for war, since Pakistan's territorial status (if we include—as we must—following official ideology-Jammu & Kashmir) was not clearly determined. More importantly, external and internal matters were mixed right from the start, giving the army a key state building role."[8]

This is the reality but since we cannot remove neighbours therefore we have to make our region at least a place to live with peace and harmony. But we need to be alert and must promote gamut of people-to-people interactions to promote comprehensive dialogue process.

Economic cooperation on India–China module could be emulated by India and Pakistan also. India has already extended MFN status to Pakistan long back in 1995 but despite WTO requirements, Pakistan has not reciprocated it till date. By 2015 India and Pakistan bilateral trade projected to reach $10 billion but it has the capability to cross $20 if proper willpower will be applied. Prime Minister Nawaz Sharif persuaded Prime Minister A.B. Vajpayee for Lahore Bus Trip (1999) which culminated into Lahore Declaration, another consensual declaration by both countries after Shimla (1972) that they will resolve their bilateral problem on a bilateral level. The process was derailed by the Pakistani army by Kargil incursion. Now after 14 years, Nawaz Sharif has become Prime Minister. He has also promised for better ties with India. Let's hope that he will implement his promises. One has to understand the limitations of the electoral mandate in Pakistani context.

Army is all powerful in Pakistan. In the words of former army chief, General Jehangir Karamat, "Whenever there is a breakdown in …stability, as has happened frequently in Pakistan, the military translate its potential into the will to dominate, and we have military intervention flowed by military rule."[9] Since independence out of 69 years of history, Pakistani army has ruled 32 years and even when it is not ruling it is shaping the policies related to core issues of foreign policy like Kashmir, Afghanistan, United States, China and Nuclear, etc., when civilian regime is ruling over Pakistan our empirical experience vindicates that more anti-Indian megalomania prevails in the Pakistani system in comparison with the periods directly ruled by the army. The civilian regimes have no role to play in these matters.

Due to lopsided budgetary system where army is bound to utilize maximum national budget for its affairs a civilian government is bound to fail simply because it has no money on its disposal to meet with the aspirations of the common masses. It is happening in Pakistan since independence and even after the passage of CoD and famous 18th amendment of the constitution, army remains most powerful within Pakistani system. Many efforts were made to implement real notion of good governance. Given the fractured nature of politics, the growing power of the vested interests, and the greatly diminished ability of the civilian bureaucracy to function, these efforts, commendable as they are, may well be a case of too little too late, for they do not address the problem at its foundations. Pakistan needs a state strong enough to stand above primordial and religious pressures and deliver on promises or order and progress.[10]

These non-state actors are hell bent to radicalize bilateral relations between both rivals merely because it converges with their core interests. Mumbai (2008) was executed by the LET for this purpose.[11] They are trying to provoke incidents which could trigger extensive violence.

We need to be alert to safeguard our national interests in the given situation. We have to keep high arrangements to meet with any such urgent situation. But I will argue that at the same time, India should not break dialogue process, simply because through this response we will be serving the wishes of the Pakistani army and the terror network.

Pakistan has a long border with India which could have reached to all geographical areas of Pakistan. India is also an emerging global market. In a reciprocal way Pakistan is also crucial for ensuring energy security to India. India is presently the 5$^{th}$ global consumer of energy and slated to be on 3$^{rd}$ by 2020. Diversification of energy supply is must for energy security. Pakistan could be pivotal for this purpose because of its geo strategic position. Pakistan could take the benefits and must garner the benefits provided under the framework of SAARC. Lifting of sanctions from Iran could facilitate this process. Economic theory emphasizes the gains from trade. Sino-Indian module is an excellent example that despite thorny relations on strategic front they are cooperating on economic front and making an ambience to resolve outstanding issues. Sino-Japan, Sino-United States and Sino-ASEAN relations could also be invoked in this context. PPP government led by Asif Ali Zardari (2008–13) did ground work for emulation of India-China model but it did not work because Pakistani army did not allow due to mainly Afghan problem. Indian growing presence in the infrastructure building activities has been viewed by Pakistan detrimental to their strategic interests of strategic depth. It has not only blocked India-Pakistan economic relations but Afghanistan-India, India-Iran and India-Central Asia as well. Various gas pipeline projects like IPI, TAPI, etc., have become victims of this power struggle. According to an expert "while India and Pakistan fight each other for the expansion of their prospective influence in Central Asia, other states gain actual economic and political power in the region. More precisely, 'Thus, to consider the problem of lack of adequate transport corridors between Central and South Asia...will depend entirely on the fact whether these corridors reach India or not."[12] This process has been slowed down also due to non-reciprocal attitude of Pakistan on the issue of MFN and relevant trade issues. The positive aspect is that there is an influential section in Pakistan who is willing to expand economic relations with India. Again the billion dollar question remains unanswered that all powerful army will allow the civilian government to do this?

## Concluding Observations

Since its inception, Pakistan has perceived India as their immortal enemy. In recent years, Pakistan has witnessed killings of thousands of innocent citizens. This has triggered a smaller debate in Pakistan that its western border is more dangerous than its eastern border for national security. According to BBC, defence analyst Talat Masood "Pakistan army for the first time has admitted that the real threat is emanating internally and along the western borders and not from India, which was previously considered as number one enemy of the state."[13]

Through emulating China-India model, Pakistan could earn the financial leverage to eradicate its fundamental problems. But again all powerful army has prevented it to realize. There is a fear in Pakistan that due to huge in size India will be the ultimate beneficiary. But question remains that Pakistan has already accorded MFN status to China, which is superior economy than India. Pakistan can learn some lessons from this experience. It is an era of globalization and despite rhetoric it is clear that every country has to cooperate with another to sustain their developmental process. Pakistan could not ensure sustainable development without ensuring peace with India. As nuclear power both countries are aware about the consequences of conflict. As pointed out by E. Sridharan, "Explicit nuclearization with a demonstrated missile capability has assured Pakistan's security in a way that reduces the sensitivity to relative gains in the military sphere... Pakistan is more secure vis-à-vis a possible Indian military threat than ever before... Therefore, it has less to fear and much to gain from greater economic engagement with India."[14]

It is also true with lesser sense for India. It is well perceived by the Modi led BJP government. The fact remains that despite its hawkish posture, the BJP government has the capacity to deal with Pakistan properly. PM Modi gave this message to Nawaz Sharif during summit meeting in May 2014 at New Delhi and after that many meetings till Paris, December 2015. Nawaz has also reciprocated but the question remains unanswered that how long army will allow him to sustain the process. But Modi government must sustain its engagement policies with Pakistan. Resumption of NSA level talk (Bangkok December, 2015) followed by Foreign Minister Sushma Swaraj Islamabad visit again in December 2015 is a bold step towards engaging Pakistan.

India has emerged as an Asian power and aspiring for global power. India must shed its elder brother mentality within South Asia and must prove that it is a responsible and peace building country. Through this process India can not only sustain its developmental process but also convince the global community that despite all odds it is also abided by reconciliation and international norms in South Asia. This particular scenario will strengthen Indian space on global table of governance. Modi government has set the tone in its first year of power.

At this juncture the nature of international politics is shaky and for taking the benefits of this situation it is must for India to decentralize its focal attentions towards all directions of the globe. Still despite all-round diplomatic presence there are certain areas where our presence needs to be upgraded.

France and Germany fought many bitter wars and even fought from different poles in both World Wars. But they have learnt a good lesson from their bitter experience. The youth of France and Germany have played a vital role to bridge the gaps between the two countries. Both countries exchanged six million youth, who got education in each other's country. The Elysee Treaty of 1963 brought the two rivals closer for progress and prosperity. Both are cooperating in a massive way under the framework of the EU. India and Pakistan share not only common borders but common fate as well, therefore they must forget the past and cooperate with emulating France-Germany model.

Pakistan must understand Indian security needs in the context of the growing military might of China. Instead of making efforts to come parallel to India in terms of military might, Pakistan must focus of its socio-economic development. Buying peace with Pakistan will be a push factor in this direction of achieving bigger goals of Indian foreign policy as narrated by Kautilaya.

## NOTES

1. Iqbal, Rana Saleem, (ed) *The Quaid on Civil Servants; Speeches and Statements, October 1947 to August 1948,* National Documental Centre, Islamabad, 2007.
2. 2014 among deadliest years in AF with 10 k civilian casualties, *The Times of India,* New Delhi, August 9, 2015.
3. *Dawn,* Karachi, April 18, 2013.
4. Blame Game between India, Pak has to stop, *The Indian Express,* New Delhi, August 24, 2013.
5. Cohen, Stephen, *The Idea of Pakistan,* Oxford University Press, New Delhi, 2006, p. 278.
6. Munir Akram, Reversing Strategic Shrinkage in Maleeha Lodhi (eds) *Pakistan; Beyond the 'Crisis State',* Columbia University Press, New York, 2011, pp. 287–8.
7. *Dawn,* Karachi, March 29, 2014.
8. Boris, Wilke, 'State Formation and the Military in Pakistan; Reflections on the Armed Forces, their State and some of their Competitors, *Working Paper,* No-2, Research Unit of Wars, Armament and Development, University of Hamburg, 2001, p. 26.
9. Nawaz, Shuja, *Crossed Swords, Its Army, and the Wars Within,* Oxford University Press, Oxford, 2008, pp. xxvoii-xxviii.
10. Niaz, Ilhan, Identities and The State in Pakistan; A Study of Mentality, *Asian Affairs,* Vol. XLHI, No.111, November 2012, p. 469.
11. Burke, Jason, Pakistan Intelligence Services Aided Mumbai Terror Attacks, *The Guardian,* London, October, 18, 2010.
12. Rudenko, Yelena I (2013) 'Problem on the way to closer interaction between Central and South Asia' ' in Rashpal Malhotra, Sucha Singh Gill and Neetu Gaur (Eds), *Perspectives on bilateral and regional cooperation*; South and Central Asia, pp. 425,427, Chandigarh, CRRID.
13. *Dawn,* Karachi, January 9, 2013.
14. Sridharan E, 'Improving Indo-Pakistan relations; International Relations Theory, Nuclear Deterrence and possibilities for economic cooperation, *Contemporary South Asia,* Vol. 14, No. 3, September 2005, p. 322.

# 27

# India-Singapore Bilateral Relations

*S. Manivasakan and Rayeesunisa*

The year 2015 marks the 50th anniversary of the establishment of India-Singapore bilateral relations. India and Singapore established their bilateral relation when Singapore got Independence in the year 1965. India being distinguished as the rising power, she plays a major role in the platform of the South and Southeast Asian countries. The similarity between the two countries lies in the fact that both are democratic country whilst Singapore is a democratic authoritarian country. The difference is also projected through the fact that even though India is often praised as the world's largest democracy (population-wise)[1] it is a developing country while Singapore is already a developed country. The two countries have had experiences under the colonial rule because of which the friendliest of relations in forging a dynamic and multifaceted relationship could be seen.

Singapore first started as a trading settlement in the late 13th century during that time it was known as "Tamasek", people settled there were Malays, Chinese and Orang Laut[2] (early immigrants who inhabited along the coastline of Singapore Island during pre-colonial days).[3] This settlement grew in major importance in the 14th century, the opening of this settlement let to vistas of opportunities, and therefore attracted traders and people who began to settle in the island and thus population began to increase which in turn brought in wealth and development.

India and Singapore have a history of long-standing mutual relation, which is seen through the relations both countries maintain in the way people have contact with each other. Historically, India and Singapore link dates back to the period of the Cholas when they established a permanent settlement.[4] The modern day relationship between the two countries can be attributed to Sir Thomas Stamford Raffles who landed on the island State of Singapore in the year 1819, which was first established as a trading outpost. The British English East India Company eyeing the need of a base east of Bay of Bengal, the outpost played a major role in controlling the trade in the Malacca region. The camaraderie the two countries share is worth mentioning every time when India-Singapore relation is talked about.

The old and strong bond the two countries share were boosted further with the improvisation of India's "Look East Policy" under the leadership of Prime Minister Narasimha Rao in 1991. This strategic shift towards Asia led to the beginning of India-Singapore economic partnership. Since then, the relationships between the two countries have grown stronger and more vigorous. The Look East Policy also led Singapore to be a bridge connecting the rest of Asia with India, and India regard Singapore as a gateway to Southeast Asia and East Asia. The relationships or bilateral cooperation between the two countries has expanded since then and can be seen through the various MOUs signed and projects being undertaken be it in terms of Defence, Tourism, IT and other sectors.

## Political and Defence Relations

Politically the two countries' relation started when Singapore got her independence in the year 1965 after experiencing the rule by the British, Japanese, Dutch, Portuguese (in the case of India) and the French under whom India have had the same experience the only difference that India got her Independence earlier in 1947. The reason of the close friendship is because of the fact that since time immemorial there have been close contact between people because of the trade route which takes the people of India to Singapore. For centuries the two countries have maintained commercial, maritime and cultural exchanges as can be seen in the present days where many people of Indian origins are settled in Singapore. However, it must be noted that during the post-independence period the event of the cold war led to the fall in India-Singapore relations. But the inception of India's Look East Policy brought about various high level interactions between the heads of the two countries. Singapore took a major interest in the economic reforms of India in the 1990s when Prime Minister Goh Chok Tong visited India in 1994 as the Chief Guest at India's Republic Day celebration, which was followed by Prime Minister Narasimha Rao visit to Singapore in the same year.[5]

Singapore after her independence and separation from Malaysia was in mayhem and the government was left with a handful of things to do from building the nation from scratch to developing its infrastructure. By this time India had settled and had fought as many as three wars: 1947, 1962 and 1965 wars. For Singapore there was also the need to built its defence system and raise its own standing army. It was here that Singapore looked to India for training her army who have had experienced in fighting wars and who at that time had a well-developed standing army. It must also be noted that Singapore was the first country who came to support India in the war with Pakistan in 1965.[6] Moreover Singapore helped India in gaining the dialogue partnership in ASEAN in 1995.[7] Singapore also played a major role in bringing India and ASEAN countries together.[8] India has a close working relation with Singapore in the international platform and a number of regional mechanism bound these two countries together such as ASEAN, ASEAN Regional Forum (ARF), ASEAN-5+, East Asia Summit, and in the ASEAN Defence Ministers Meeting (ADMM)-Plus. The visitation to Singapore by the then External Affairs Minister in June 2007 saw the forming of the Joint Ministerial Committee (JMC) with the Foreign Ministers as heads and also the launch of CEO's Forum and the declaration of a Strategic Dialogue.[9]

The relation took a notch up with the signing of Defence Co-operation Agreement in 2003 since then there has been Defence related joint military exercises and training (Bold Kurukshetra exercise between the Indian Army and the Singapore Army, Anti-Submarine Warfare (ASW)-naval training operations) which includes naval and maritime exercises, taken up by both the countries or sometimes with some of the Southeast Asian countries like Indonesia, Malaysia, and Thailand (e.g. the SIMBEX series, the MILAN series). The Defence relation has expanded in the sphere of counter terrorism. Both the countries are affirmed to fight against terrorism of any kind. The two countries Defence Ministers have also renewed the bilateral agreement in 2013 on joint army training and exercises which will be valid for five more years.[10] It must be noted that Singapore is the only country to which India has offered its facilities for training and land exercises.[11] India ranks among the top 10 countries of the world with the highest military expenditure in 2013 (9$^{th}$ place). Singapore on the other hand has got the most advanced military in South East Asia, and the highest military spending in terms of GDP in the Asia-Pacific region.[12]

## Economic and Commercial Relation

Economic and trade relations play a major role in the two countries' bilateral relation. It was in this area of interest that the relation started off. India and Singapore signed the Comprehensive Economic Cooperation Agreement (CECA), which was the first of its kind for India and also the first for Singapore to have a bilateral economic agreement with a South Asia economy.[13] The CECA was signed in June of 2005, an agreement which covers on trade in investments, goods and services. This initiative took the relation to a whole new level. Since the implementation of this agreement it served as a gateway to more business initiations and avenues for the business communities. Hence, Indian business

## List of Bilateral Visits

**From Singapore to India**

| *Visiting Delegates* | *Date of Visit* |
|---|---|
| President Tony Tan Keng Yam | February 8-11, 2015 |
| Emeritus Senior Minister Goh Chok Tong along with Minister in the PMO and Second Minister for Trade and Industry and Home Affairs S Iswaran as well as Minister of State for National Development Desmond Lee | September 7-11, 2014 |
| Minister for Defence Dr. Ng. Eng Hen | August 18-20, 2014 |
| Minister for Foreign Affairs and Minister for Law K. Shanmugam | 30th June-4th July 2014 |
| Second Minister for Trade and Industry and Second Minister for Home Affairs S. Iswaran | January 27-29, 2014 |
| Emeritus Senior Minister Goh Chok Tong | December 3-6, 2013 |
| Minister for Defence Dr. Ng. Eng Hen | November 2012 |
| Prime Minister Lee Hsien Loong | July10-12, 2012 |
| Minister for Foreign Affairs and Minister for Law K. Shanmugam | May 7-10, 2012 |
| Prime Minister Goh Chok Tong | 2006 |
| Minister for Education Tharman Shanmugaratnam | September 2005 |
| Prime Minister Goh Chok Tong | July 8-11, 2004 |
| Deputy Prime Minister and Minister for Finance Lee Hsien Loong | January 10-19, 2004 |
| Prime Minister Goh Chok Tong | April 7-9, 2003 |
| President Sellapan Ramanathan | January 2003 |
| Prime Minister Goh Chok Tong | 17 January 2000 |
| Prime Minister Goh Chok Tong | 1994 |
| Prime Minister Lee Kuan Yew | 1966, 1970,1971 |

*Source:* Compiled from High Commission of India, Singapore; Ministry of Foreign Affairs, Government of Singapore; Ministry of External Affairs, Government of India. https://hcisingapore.gov.in, http://www.mfa.gov.sg/, http://www.mea.gov.in/.

**Visits from India to Singapore**

| *Visiting Delegates* | *Date of Visit* |
|---|---|
| Chief Minister of Telangana K. Chandrashekar Rao | August 20-22, 2014 |
| Chief Minister of West Bengal Mamta Banerjee | August 18-22, 2014 |
| External Affairs Minister, Sushma Swaraj | August 15-17, 2014 |
| Ministry of External Affairs Secretary (East) Anil Wadhwa | February 14-15, 2014 |
| Minister of Finance P. Chidambaram | November 21-22, 2013 |
| External Affairs Minister, Salman Khurshid | October 23-24, 2013 |
| External Affairs Minister, Salman Khurshid | July 3-4, 2013 |
| Defence Minister A.K. Antony | June 2013 |

| | |
|---|---|
| Minister of Civil Aviation Ajit Singh | April 2-4, 2013 |
| External Affairs Minister S. M. Krishna | March 8-11, 2012 |
| Prime Minister Dr. Manmohan Singh | November 19-20, 2011 |
| External Affairs Minister S.M. Krishna | May 5, 2011 |
| External Affairs Minister S.M. Krishna | March 2010 |
| Prime Minister Dr. Manmohan Singh visit to Singh to Singapore for 6th India-ASEAN Summit and 3rd East Asia Summit | November 20-21, 2007 |
| External Affairs Minister Pranab Mukherjee | June 19-22, 2007 |
| President Dr. A.P.J. Abdul Kalam | Jan 31st-3rd February 2006 |
| Prime Minister Atal Bihari Vajpayee | April 7-9, 2002 |
| Prime Minister Atal Bihari Vajpayee | October 2001 |
| President K.R. Narayanan | November 2000 |
| Prime Minister Narasimha Rao | September 1994 |
| President V.V. Giri | September 1971 |
| Deputy Prime Minister Moraji Desai | 1969 |
| Prime Minister Indira Gandhi | 1968 |

*Source:* Compiled from High Commission of India, Singapore; Ministry of Foreign Affairs, Government of Singapore; Ministry of External Affairs, Government of India. https://hcisingapore.gov.in, http://www.mfa.gov.sg/, http://www.mea.gov.in/.

community has emerged as the leading business community in Singapore. This later led to the signing of the Free Trade Agreement (FTA) between the two countries. Among the ASEAN countries Singapore is India's largest trade and investment partner and in the year 2013-2014, it is reported that Singapore is the 7th largest trade partner of India.[14] Because of the strong Indian presence and connectivity Singapore has become a favored destination for Indians to do business hence many Indian corporate offices and banks can be initiated there, such as Indian Overseas Bank, Indian Bank, ICICI, State Bank of India, Bank of India and Axis Bank and UCO Bank are some to mention.[15] The signing of the CECA in the later years led to the enhancement in cooperation related to education, science, technology, relaxation in visa regulations for Indians in the field of Information Technologies.

The recent news on Singapore's government appointing Ambassador-at-large Mr. Gopinath Pillai, as Special Envoy to assist Andhra Pradesh to render advice relating to the building of the new capital which included tourism and bringing in capital from foreign companies and also Singapore Companies is also a milestone achieved in the bilateral relations.[16]

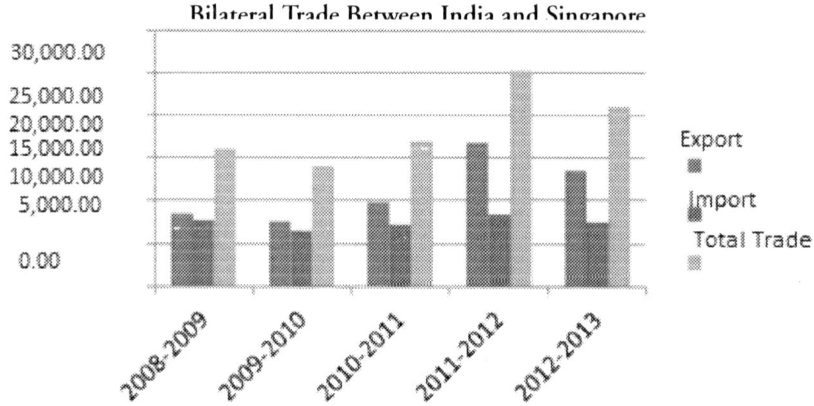


*Source:* Department of Commerce, Ministry of Commerce and Industry, GOI.

**Bilateral Agreement between India and Singapore**

| *Agreements* | *Year* |
|---|---|
| Bilateral Air Services Agreement | 1968 |
| Double Taxation Avoidance Agreement | 1994 |
| Memorandum of Understanding on Foreign Office Consultations | 1994 |
| Executive Programme on Cooperation in the Arts, Heritage, Archives and the Library | 2000 |
| Memorandum of Understanding Concerning a Third Country Training Programme | 2003 |
| Defence Cooperation Agreement | 2003 |
| Comprehensive Economic Cooperation Agreement (CECA) | 2005 |
| Protocol amending agreement on avoidance of double taxation and prevention of Fiscal Evasion | 2005 |
| Agreement on Mutual Legal Assistance Treaty | 2005 |
| Memorandum of Understanding for Army to Army Exercises | 2005 |
| Bilateral Agreement for the conduct Joint Military Training and Exercises | 2007 |
| Memorandum of Understanding on Cooperation in Vocational Education and Skills Development | 2011 |
| Memorandum of Understanding in Management Research and Education—Between the Singapore Management University (SMU) and Indian Institute of Management Bangalore (IIMB) | 2012 |
| Memorandum of Understanding on the establishment of the Nalanda University | 2013 |

Source: Compiled from Ministry of External Affairs Annual Reports, Government of India. http://mea.gov.in/annual-reports.htm?57/Annual_Reports

The recent visitation of President Tony Tan Keng Yam in the month of February 2015 which was a reciprocal visit to the External Affairs Minister, Sushma Swaraj's visit to Singapore in the month of August 2014, as a sign to commemorate 50 years of India-Singapore relation shows how close the leaders of these two countries feel about each other. The momentum of the relationship is gaining.

With the NDA government in the present scenario there have been many initiatives taken up by Mr. Narendra Modi, the Prime Minister of India such as the 'Make in India', 'Digital India' and 'Clean India' projects. The President of India, Pranab Mukherjee in the recent visitation by President Tony Tan Yam has invited them and has also shown interests in working together on such projects. He also stated that "Singapore's experience in skill development can also be valuable for India".[17]

In general, the large number of Indians settled in Singapore along with the initiatives of both the Governments plays a major role in connecting the two countries. So far the relationship has been on a smooth sail though there may be hiccups at times considering the international platform. India should always remember that even though Singapore is a small country it has proven itself to be a nation with whom countries like India need to engage with, as can be seen in Singapore's support to India becoming a permanent member in the UN Security Council.[18] Through Singapore, India can forge a deeper relation with the Southeast Asian countries.

## NOTES

1. Narlikar, Amrita. (2013). India Rising: Responsible to Whom?. *International Affairs*, 89(3),1.Retrieved from http://onlinelibrary.wiley.com/doi/10.1111/1468-2346.12035/pdf.
2. Lee, Edwin. (2008). *Singapore: The unexpected Nation*. Singapore: ISEAS.
3. Orang Laut, Singapore Infopedia, http://eresources.nlb.gov.sg/infopedia/articles/SIP_551_2005-01-09.html?s=People
4. High Commission of India, Singapore. https://hcisingapore.gov.in/pages.php?id=68
5. India-Singapore Relations. http://www.mea.gov.in/Portal/ForeignRelation/Singapore_Dec_2014.pdf
6. Mishra, Rahul. (2010) Locating Singapore in India's Strategic Radar. *Institute of Defence Studies and Analysis*.
7. V. Jayanth. (2000, November 9) Strengthening India-Singapore ties. *The Hindu*. Retrieved from http://www.thehindu.com/2000/11/09/stories/0209000b.htm
8. Ibid
9. India-Singapore Relations, Ministry of External Affairs, Government of India. http://www.mea.gov.in/
10. India, Singapore renew agreement on joint army traning. (2013, June 3). *The economic Times*. http://articles.economictimes.indiatimes.com/2013-06-03/news/39714637_1_indian-army-defence-minister-singapore-air-force.
11. External Affairs Minister's address at the Singapore India Chambers of Commerce and Industry (SICCI). Ministry of External Affairs, Government of India. July 4, 2013. http://www.mea.gov.in/bilateral-documents.htm?dtl/21908/

12. *SIPRI Yearbook 2014: Armaments, Disarmament and International Security*. (2014). Oxford University Press, United Kingdom.
13. http://www.fta.gov.sg/fta_ceca.asp?hl=6
14. Director General of Commercial Intelligence and Statistics. Ministry of Commerce and Industry, Government of India. http://www.dgciskol.nic.in/
15. Ministry of External Affairs. (2014). *India-Singapore Relations*. Government of India. http://mea.gov.in/portal/foreignrelation/singapore_july2014.pdf
16. Singapore names Special Envoy to Assist A.P. (2015, February 27). *The Hindu*, p.7.
17. High Commission of Inda. *India Looking Forward to Embarking Upon a Larger Role in Asia-Pacific, says President*. Singapore.https://www.hcisingapore.gov.in/slide.php?id=23
18. Shekhar, Vibhanshu. (2007). India-Singapore Relations: An Overview. *IPCS Special Report* No.41.

# 28

# Modi's 'Act East' Policy: Its Blueprint and the Future Promenade

*Tridib Chakraborti*

In the historical domain of Indian coalition politics, the Bharatiya Janata Party (BJP)—the largest partner of the National Democratic Alliance (NDA) led by other constituent partners—won 337 out of 543 parliamentary seats, emerging as a single majority party in the 16th Lok Sabha Elections of India held in April/ May 2014. In this election, the BJP won 282 seats in India's lower house of parliament (the Lok Sabha) and crushed the myth of coalition politics, gifting India its first single party government in three decades. Following this election, Narendra Modi became the Prime Minister of India by demolishing the BJP's old guard and has made his political clout much stronger than the past years within the BJP, particularly when compared to what Manmohan Singh had in the Congress, thereby trying to revitalize the Indian foreign policy's continuity rather than change, based on greater dynamism and acceleration. Before Modi became the Prime Minister of India, in several speeches he expressed his viewpoint of Indian foreign policy which remained quite steady and similar with our past foreign policy approach. However, the only departure from the past years had been his stress on making Indian foreign policy more geo-economic and commercial to the outside world in the context of the evolving processes of globalization and liberalization. He in a speech said: "I believe a strong economy is the driver of an effective foreign policy... we have to put our house in order so that the world is attracted to us." His foreign policy agenda remains to consolidate India's position as a responsible regional friend in South Asia and to attract the foreign direct investments (FDI) critical for India's growth through the concept of 'Make in India', aimed at attracting businesses from around the world to invest and manufacture in India. Moreover, he stresses a greater attention to long-term policy planning with a view to formulating a grand strategy in shaping India's national security and formulating doctrines where he emphasizes that the state governments which have shared borders, historical links, or cultural commonalities should have consulted and categorically emphasized the role of those Indian states in formulation and execution of framing foreign policy issues. Besides this, Narendra Modi's intonation is to refurbish India's 'ancient glory' to play a cilvilizational role on the basis of domestic strength. This outlook of Modi's foreign policy can be reflected in the Election Manifesto of the BJP published in the run up to the 16th Lok Sabha Elections of India held in April/May 2014. In the Manifesto, it was stated: "BJP believes a resurgent India must get its rightful place in the comity of nations and international institutions. The vision is to fundamentally reboot and reorient the foreign policy goals, content and process, in a manner that locates India's global strategic engagement in a new paradigm and on a wider canvass, that is not just limited to political diplomacy, but also includes our economic, scientific, cultural, political and security interests, both regional and global, on the principles of equality and mutuality, so that it leads to an economically stronger India, and its voice is heard in the international fora".[1] The Manifesto further stated: "We will build a strong, self-reliant and self-confident India, regaining its rightful place in the comity of nations...based on best National interests. We will create a web of allies to mutually further our interests. We will leverage all our resources and people to play a greater role on the international high table" and mentioned to revive "Brand India with the help of our strengths of 5T's: Tradition, Talent, Tourism, Trade and Technology".[2] Among the guiding principles as highlighted in the Election Manifesto, it was emphasized that BJP "will work towards strengthening Regional forums like SAARC and ASEAN"[3], and which appeared quite striking in its entirety. Even before he came in power, Modi had made his interest towards Southeast and East Asia prominent primarily on account of growing economic strength of this region and realized that India's brightest economic prospects lie towards East rather than in the West. The purpose of this article is to highlight the basic premises of Narendra Modi's 'Act East' policy in the context of the emerging security architecture of Asia-Pacific region.

After a landslide victory in the general election of 2015, the NDA government, under the leadership of Narendra Modi has initially focused on neighbouring countries and strategically located several Asian powers like Japan, Vietnam, and Australia without forging any formal security alliance in the Indo-Pacific region to avoid direct confrontation with China coupled with emphasizing on the two decades old 'Look East Policy' with a new name 'Act East' policy. Immediately after this new government came in power, the External Affairs Minister of India, Sushma Swaraj, paid her official visits to Southeast Asian countries and emphasized India's increasing thrust towards its Look East Policy, by re-defining and re-christening this policy as 'Act East' instead of simply 'Look East'. This statement was made by her on 24 August 2014, while addressing a gathering of the Indian community soon after her three-day visit to Vietnam. She also said that India had adopted a "Look East Policy" under the Atal Behari Vajpayee government and "now it is time to not just look but act. Under the Narendra Modi government, we will have an Act East Policy."[4] This concept of 'Act East' policy of the NDA government was further endorsed, when the Indian Prime Minister Narendra Modi in his address at the 9th East Asia Summit held in Nay Pyi Taw, Myanmar, on 13 November, 2014, said: "Since entering office six months ago, my government has moved with a great sense of priority and speed to turn our 'Look East Policy' into 'Act East Policy'. The East Asia Summit is an important pillar of this policy. No other forum brings together such a large collective weight of global population, youth, economy and military strength. Nor is any other forum so critical for peace, stability and prosperity in Asia-Pacific and the world".[5] Thus, through this new concept a fresh academic discourse has been evolved in the realm of Indian foreign policy

While analyzing Modi's 'Act East' policy, after his new assignment as the Prime Minister of India, certain pertinent questions have cropped in the sphere of Indian foreign policy. Is this 'Act East' policy a new term as has been coined by this NDA government or is it a continuation of India's early initiative, known as 'Look East' policy? Does it mean that India's overall 'Look East' policy in the past years lacked its proper direction? Does it mean that India's 'Look East' policy was simply to 'Look' and not to 'Act'? Does it mean that India's 'Look East' policy, since its inception, has achieved nothing in the last two decades? Does this statement mean that India wants to play a more positive leadership role in the emerging security architecture of the Asia-Pacific region through 'Engage and Act East' policy? Does this policy endeavour to keep a separate connotation and identity of the NDA government from its predecessors? As against such related questions, it is essential to evaluate the vision and achievements of NDA government's 'Act East' policy.

## India's 'Look East' Policy: A Prognosis

The policy of new regionalism towards Southeast Asia and beyond was evolved in reply to the prevailing global environment at the end of the Cold War. The sudden collapse of former Soviet Union in 1991 impelled the emergence of a new global political and economic scenario that led to the budge in India's strategic world view from its non-aligned posture and reliance on Soviet military hardware and the bilateral treaty commitments to an autonomous global outlook and pro-activeness. While keeping this changed global environment in the backdrop, in July 1991, India under the leadership of P.V. Narasimha Rao, announced its New Economic Policy, which was guided more by economic imperative and judiciousness and less by political rhetoric. Within a short span of time, after the Singapore Lecture in 1994 by the then Indian Prime Minister, P.V. Narasimha on India's policy towards Southeast Asia, known as 'Look East' policy, a new interaction is evolved with these countries. Gradually, this policy expands its wings from Southeast Asian region to East Asia and beyond since 2002 onwards. Before the NDA government came in power in 2015, India's 'Look East' policy had spanned a skill of more than two decades. During these twenty years of experience, India by executing this policy has achieved several economic, strategic and political advantages in the Asia-Pacific region. India, through its saga of relations with the countries of Southeast Asia and beyond, has been able to prove its genuine interests towards the region. Through its 'Look East' ASEAN policy, New Delhi clearly exhibited a progressive performance in its development of relations with these countries. In the last two decades, India's 'Look East' ASEAN policy has seen certain major achievements and they are as follows:

**First,** within a short span of time, India has been promoted from 'sectoral dialogue' partner in 1992 to summit level partner in 2002. In 1996, India also joined the security entity of the ASEAN, the ASEAN Regional Forum (ARF). Since 1998, the ASEAN"India Business Council was set up and where both the parties established three ASEAN"India working groups dealing with development cooperation, science and technology and trade and investment respectively.

The **second** achievement of India's 'Look East' policy has been its engagement with Southeast and East Asia, through East Asia Summit (EAS) consisting of 16 countries (ASEAN, China, Japan, Korea, India, Australia and New Zealand). The entry of this EAS initiative can be explained as the first step for establishing an East Asian Community on the lines of the European Economic Community, with the aim of promoting peace, stability and economic prosperity in East Asia and its surrounding areas. This entry of India in the ASEAN+1 and EAS are no doubt a good beginning for its ultimate integration with that region and led to the emergence of New Delhi as the largest trade partner, ahead of the EU and the US with reference to FTA of the entire region. In other words, in the context of emerging regionalism in Asia, India could emerge as a hub between East on the one hand, and South, West and Central Asian countries on the other, where Southeast Asia could act as a bridge. One of the important achievements that India has made through its EAS entry is that the leaders of the EAS have endorsed New Delhi's proposal to establish the Nalanda University as a centre of excellence in education and international understanding. While expressing this success, Manmohan Singh, described it as a "tremendous goodwill for India in South East and East Asia, and therefore the sky is the limit for our engagement with this region".[6] Thus, India's estimation of the EAS remains a compact move in the direction of realizing its long cherished dream of building the Asian community and its participation in the EAS is a real opportunity to broaden and deepen its engagement within the emerging Asian architecture.

The **third** success of India's 'Look East' policy remains its growing strategic and security cooperation in the Asia-Pacific region, with an outlook to activate a more prominent role in the emerging balance of power. Within these two decades India has evolved a deep-rooted maritime partnership with most of the countries in this region, where the Indian Navy has sent warships, tankers and submarines to Japan, South Korea, Thailand, New Zealand, Indonesia and Vietnam for joint exercises and thereby to generate regional confidence-building and cooperative mechanisms in various platforms, like in ARF, ADMM+8 meetings, etc. Moreover, New Delhi has actively synchronized its efforts to embark upon the regional sensitive issues like insurgency, trafficking of small arms and drugs, illegal migration, environmental pollution, terrorism and other security-related matters, including the safety of the sea-lanes-of-communication (SLOC), etc., which are indispensable for the maintenance of peace and security of the region. The signing of agreements like the Regional Cooperation Agreement on Combating Piracy and Armed Robbery against Ships in Asia (ReCAAP) remains a clear example in this juncture. Currently, the Indian naval activities in the Indian Ocean region, based on the Indian Maritime Doctrine of 2004, by displaying its latest designed missile destroyers, holding annual joint exercises in the Andaman Sea with the smaller littoral navies, exercising off-shore during extended "goodwill" tours with the host country's naval vessels, etc., have clearly exhibited its strategic existence. Moreover, India's naval presence in the South China Sea region is also another major achievement of New Delhi, which is supposed to guard against the growing Chinese influence, perceived by many countries that India is an ideal strategic partner to balance Beijing's overtures in the region. Moreover, India's enthusiasm to accede to the Treaty of Amity and Cooperation (TAC) in Southeast Asia and its endorsement of the Southeast Asia Nuclear Weapons Free Zone (SEANWFZ) has remained the best way to assure the region of its peaceful mindset towards the region.

The **fourth** achievement of India's 'Look East' policy remains the growing economic cooperation. Over the last two decades, India and ASEAN as regional trade partners, offer a huge and attractive interconnected, geographically contiguous market of more than 1.5 billion people. India's trade ties with ASEAN countries over the years have clearly revealed a sharp increase in trade figures. In the last five years, India's exports to ASEAN have increased by over 280% and India's imports from ASEAN countries have increased by around 220%. India's trade with the ASEAN members, during the year 2014-15 was US $76,738.90 million, which remained 20 times more than the year 1992-93. Similarly, India's total trade figure East Asia and beyond was US$1, 31,604.15 million in 2014-2015. This increase of trade figure has been mainly increase on account of signing of FTA and Comprehensive Economic Cooperation Agreement (CECA) with many of the countries of ASEAN on and before 2013. Therefore, though New Delhi has been a campaigner of multilateralism and acted as a responsible member of the WTO, regionalism as a reaction to the multilateral process has gained its ground in its foreign policy agenda in the present juncture, and this FTA remains a major step of India's 'Look East' policy in reducing its dependence on trade with U.S., E.U. and China and turning towards Southeast Asia, in order to strengthen its regional dynamics.[7]

The **fifth** achievement of India's 'Look East' policy has been its active participation in the Initiative for ASEAN Integration (IAI) programme, which is a regional framework for integration, aimed at narrowing the development gap within ASEAN and enhancing regional integration. This initiative had serious implications for ASEAN, which experienced the development gap when it achieved the ASEAN-10 by accepting the Indochina States (Vietnam, Cambodia and Laos) and Myanmar in the late 1990s. During that time, there was a serious gap in development between the old members and the newly joined CLMV (Cambodia, Laos, Myanmar and Vietnam) countries. To overcome this chasm, at the Fourth Informal Summit in November 2000, at Singapore, the Singapore Prime Minister, Goh Chok Tong proposed the IAI. Besides narrowing development divide between ASEAN's old and new members, the IAI aimed to promote equitable economic development, and help alleviate poverty of the new members. India being an active partner of ASEAN has currently playing a very constructive role in a number of projects with the CLMV countries. This energetic focus of New Delhi on the IAI has been looked upon by ASEAN countries as a sign of India's commitment to ASEAN and its processes. Therefore, India's 'Look East' policy in the 21st Century has truly become multi"dimensional and is clearly multi-pronged in character.[8]

The **sixth** achievement of India's' Look East' policy remains its connectivity policy (mainly in improving road, railway, sea and air linkages) initiated by both sides. Connectivity mainly with ASEAN-geographical, institutional or people-to-people—is a strategic priority for India. In December 2012, New Delhi hosted the India-ASEAN Commemorative Summit to mark 20 years of its connection with the grouping and 10-years of its summit level partnership. In this Commemorative meeting, germane mechanisms under the ASEAN-India framework to further support the connectivity policy were established. The key target of this connectivity policy is to promote ASEAN centrality in the regional architecture, facilitate the building of an ASEAN Community and pragmatically present it as a foundation for constructing enhanced connectivity outside the region and encouraging trade and investment. Currently, India has already involved in multiple connectivity projects with Southeast Asian countries and they are: India-Myanmar-Thailand Trilateral highway project, building bridges and upgrading 120 km road between Kalewa and Yargyi, land connectivity between Northeast India with Myanmar, the building of Mekong-India Economic Corridor, a Delhi-Hanoi road and railway link and also the transportation networks including the East-West Corridor project and the Trans-Asian highway, etc. These central proposals are viewed as the expansion of transport and infrastructure links, which would facilitate the cross-border movement of goods and services between India and ASEAN in the Mekong Basin, for further operation of the ASEAN-India FTA. The opening of 2$^{nd}$ Car rally (second time, which would traverse nearly 8,000 kms in 22 days) by Manmohan Singh on 21 December 2012 from New Delhi, in the presence of Heads of State and Governments of the ASEAN members has been another momentous event in recent times. The main aim of this programme is to acknowledge and reveal the geographical proximity between India and ASEAN members; stress on the need to develop efficient road links and seamless connectivity and to convey the driving message of augmenting people to people contacts.[9] While describing the India-ASEAN ties at an "exciting stage", Manmohan Singh in the inauguration programme of this car rally said: "Our future will be driven by the bonds of connectivity we build in the coming years. These physical bonds will be strengthened by digital links, which will help our younger generations to network better. Together, this web of linkages will help unleash the vast economic potential of our region, accelerate development and deepen our strategic partnership".[10] Another milestone event, which took place in the same year between India and ASEAN, was the establishment of an ASEAN-India Centre in New Delhi, followed by the ASEAN-India Strategic Partnership Agreement, representing an elevated echelon of a strategic understanding between them. In this December meeting, the leaders also adopted a Vision Statement or a blueprint for future India-ASEAN cooperation. The declared principles of this Vision Statement were that India and ASEAN are Strategic Partners; India agreed to support ASEAN community (to be setup in 2015); Work for ASEAN-India Partnership for Peace, Progress and Shared Prosperity (2010-2015); support and cooperate closely with ASEAN to realize the ASEAN Community in 2015, comprising three pillars, namely, the ASEAN Political Security Community, the ASEAN Economic Community and the ASEAN Socio-Cultural Community; to establish an

ASEAN-India Centre using existing capacities, and political and security, economic, socio-cultural and development cooperation in future.[11] Therefore, this Car Rally endeavour clearly discloses the indispensability of India-ASEAN connectivity for further integration, which remains one of the primary aims of India's 'Look East' policy.

The **seventh** achievement of India's 'Look East' policy remains the sub-regional forum initiatives in order to develop better connection with this region. In order to advance New Delhi's "Look East" policy, India propelled multilateralism as a primary means in its geo"strategic perception. In terms of geo-politics, the contiguous sea spaces of the Bay of Bengal"South China Sea could be regarded as hubs of geo-economic and geo-strategic advantages and opportunities for New Delhi. It was felt by the Indian government that poor trade ties with ASEAN countries during the Cold War years had largely reduced its idea of an extended neighbourhood policy and kept dormant the transport links with this region. However, this attitude was radically changed when New Delhi professed that the immediate neighbourhood policy would be of vital national interest in the context of India's emerging Asian economic profile. This pragmatic viewpoint resulted in that in the later part of its 'Look East' Phase I, India actively supported the formation of bilateral and sub"regional groupings, to set off its larger goal of enhancing India-ASEAN ties. The creation of the Bangladesh–China–India–Myanmar (BCIM) Forum for Regional Cooperation, established in 1999 and formerly known as the 'Kunming Initiative', a sub-regional initiative by India, as against the backdrop of its 'Look-East' Policy was fundamentally to encourage the long-term demand of India's North Eastern Region (NER) for the opening of trade, connectivity and people-to-people contacts with the neighbouring countries, which constitute nearly 98% of the region's borders. Besides this, the formation of BIMSTEC in 1997 and the Mekong-Ganga Cooperation (MGC) in 2000 has been instrumental in promoting cultural tourism as well as in defining regions in the new global economy and seeks to broaden and intensify joint efforts at economic cooperation between India and ASEAN in the Mekong region. Furthermore, these linkages between India and the countries of Indo-China States over land might accord New Delhi a chance to expedite economic development with the NER and its integration into the Eurasian land bridge system. Thus, the formation of BIMSTEC and MGC permits New Delhi to break out of the astringent confines of the subcontinent that it had long dented and be credited with the creation of geographical connectivity for the promotion of sustainable economic partnership between India and the Indochina States in the present century. The launching of India-ASEAN Car Rally in 2005—starting from Guwahati and ending in Indonesia—aimed to promote India-ASEAN relations, with reference to better scope for enhanced trade, road transport and connectivity, investment, tourism and people-to-people links, clearly confirmed a forward tread in this novel scheme.[12]

**The eighth** success of India's 'Look East' policy remains its benign image. Following China, India also cultivated its past cultural intercourses with the countries of Southeast Asia and beyond. It was the common cultural heritage of Buddhism and Hinduism, based on and the philosophy of compassion, tolerance, non-violence and peace had a past historical linkage laid India to accelerate its 'Look East' policy more and more vivacious through tourism. In recent times, India's 'open sky' policy and introduction of several low-cost international carriers (LCCs), like Air Asia and Tiger Airways, and multiple Indian airlines, including Kingfisher and Jet, apart from Air India; and the relaxation of visa process to many Southeast Asian countries and beyond, are ample examples of New Delhi's effective 'Look East' policy.

The **last,** but not the least achievement has been evident in the last few years through New Delhi's participation in a number of ARF meetings, ASEAN Defence Ministers Meet plus (ADMM+), ASEAN Maritime Forum and other strategic activities relating to confidence-building measures (CBMs), maritime search and rescue, peacekeeping, non-proliferation, preventive diplomacy and disaster management, which have been productive for the facilitation and introduction of appropriate CBMs among ASEAN members. Over these years, India has taken number of strategic decisions, in order to enhance her status not only among the ASEAN members, but also for developing a vibrant Asia in its entirety. The key strategic parameters shared between India and ASEAN in the last two decades are—Combating piracy; Intelligence sharing and counter terrorism; Maintenance of coastal security and protection of the legitimate sovereign use of International waters; Enforcement of International law; Disaster relief operations; Climate change; Conservation of environment, including marine; Comprehensive economic development; Re-establishing hearty cultural relations; Cooperation in education, science and technology and other multifarious areas, promoting people to people contact, etc. Summarily then, India's participation through these multiple activities, via its 'Look East' policy has carved a very favourable situation for New Delhi's overall 'Look East' policy in the last two decades.[13]

## Prime Vision of NDA Government's 'Act East' Policy

As against such achievements of India's 'Look East' policy, the next part of the article will deal with the prime vision and achievements of NDA government's 'Act East' policy. It is a fact that India's past performance of 'Look East' policy has elevated and accelerated the current NDA government's 'Act East' policy. The main vision of this 'Act East' policy is primarily as follows:

**First**, this policy envisages more hearty and constructive engagement with the countries of Southeast and beyond. While delivering a speech at Thailand on 28 June, 2015, the External Affairs Minister, Sushma Swaraj said: "Our Government came with the slogan of Minimum Government, Maximum Governance. We have strived to offer a stable, predictable and transparent policy regime, making the country an attractive destination for investors. The last one year of the new government has contributed to economic good governance and all-round development and to design policies and laws to promote growth and offering foreign investors 'red carpet' instead of 'red tape'."[14] In the same speech, she also mentioned that the Modi government in its 'Act East' policy is working on 3C mantra and they are "Commerce, Culture and Connectivity".[15]

**Secondly**, in the same speech Sushma Swaraj said: "The hallmark of the Government through 'Act East' policy has been to facilitate infrastructure development and manufacturing",[16] in order to make India a global manufacturing hub and rejuvenate the economic growth.

**Thirdly**, to execute and accomplish all pending projects by the NDA government through 'Act East' policy, which 'Look East' policy failed to implement. Moreover, this policy aims to move past these errors and establish a comprehensive and result-driven policy.

**Fourthly**, to accelerate the existing connectivity policy and to provide adequate recourses on a faster way both in the overland connectivity and in maritime domain, in order to craft India as a maritime power in the Indo-Pacific region and follow the overland option with much superior dynamism. This policy emphasizes more momentum for the establishment of the railway links between the regions of South and Southeast Asia for better connectivity through the Bangladesh, China, India and Myanmar (BCIM) Economic Corridor and where Kolkata to Kunming Highway (K2K) constitutes an important element of the corridor. If this project will finish as early as possible, then this corridor proposal will not only contain the exiting ethnic insurgency, terrorism, smuggling, and cross-border human trafficking, but also aim to form a thriving economic belt, focusing on cross-border transport, energy and telecommunication networks as well as the Trans-Asian Railway which will offer the Delhi-Hanoi rail link with these countries. This is probably realized by NDA government through its 'Act East' policy.

**Fifthly**, to make the Northeast region an integral part of India's foreign policy and to utilize this region as a base in order to develop better connectivity with the other nations through the land route. Through this policy, the significance of infrastructure development, connecting markets and increasing trade is highlighted. Moreover, this policy tacitly signalled that the North eastern states must have more say and importance for better implementation through this policy.

**Sixthly,** this policy is about injecting new vitality and rationale into India's Asia policy and where the government of India needs access to capital, technology, resources, energy, markets and skills, a secure environment, a peaceful neighbourhood as well as a stable global trading system".

**Seventhly,** the 'Act East' policy has been an upgraded version of India's 'Look East' policy, aimed to propel the Modi government's slogan of 'Making outside India'.

**Eighthly** by rechristening it 'Act East' policy, a more vigorous role as desired by the NDA government, is born out of her strategic capability with China in the neighbourhood that has huge potential in trade, defence, tourism, education and cultural ties. Moreover, as China initiated to play a greater role in maritime Silk Route, India, through its 'Act East' policy felt necessity to bond with the countries of Southeast Asia more strongly, since it will not only increase the trade, economic and cultural ties, but also counter the increasing influence of the Chinese in South Asian region and Indian Ocean region: in other words, to avoid any power vacuum, on account of growing Chinese strategic and political influence in the Southeast Asia and beyond.

**Ninthly,** during the visit of the Bangladesh President, Mohammad Abdul Hamid from 18-23 December 2014 to New Delhi, the Indian Prime Minister, Narendra Modi in a speech said that "India's Act East starts with Bangladesh", firmly indicating that Bangladesh will be integrated with the Act East policy. Here through this statement, the Indian Prime Minister clearly included and emphasized that the role of Bangladesh is intrinsic to the success of India's 'Act East' policy.

**Tenthly**, through 'Act East' policy, India wants to re-activate and thereby generate the leading Asian economies, like Japan, Koreas, Thailand, Indonesia, Malaysia, Australia, Singapore, etc., for competitive impulses to involve more projects and stronger engagement with these countries to balance China's rapid rise in this Asia-Pacific region. Through this mindset, India's 'Act East' policy has to be woven by the twin strands of economic engagement and strong security ties.

**Finally,** on account of emerging global geo-strategic security, India through its 'Act East' policy could play a more effective and rightful role as an emerging great player in the field of international relations. Thus, 'Act East' policy incorporates greater action and dynamism than the 'Look East' policy.

## Some Admirable Initiative of 'Act East' Policy

It is really difficult to assess the achievements of India's 'Act East' policy within this short tenure. Following the exceptional mandate which took place in the last three decades, the Government of India under the leadership of Narendra Modi, got an excellent chance to convert India into a more prominent strategic player in the emerging global order. Modi's past achievements of economic miracles in his home state of Gujarat made him assemble his past experience to re-activate India's development process in a more dynamic way. In fact, this new government led by Prime Minister Modi has sought to change and radically alter the past legacies and to bring out Indian foreign policy on a more solid and mutually beneficial and supportive foundation. After his assignment as a Prime Minister of India, he initiated a more dynamic and determined foreign policy agenda for a greater comprehensive role. His method of conducting foreign policy can be branded by the effort of profound personal rapport with foreign leaders. Within a short span of time, Prime Minister Narendra Modi, through his 'Act East' policy has tried to develop ties with emerging economic countries of Southeast, East Asian countries and beyond, like, Japan, Vietnam, Australia, ASEAN, and Indonesia, South Korea, United States, China, etc. for better economic cooperation. Strategically, these countries are also important for her "Act East" policy, on account of growing Chinese presence in the Indian Ocean region, as well as motivated by India's desire for more economic and diplomatic engagement in the whole Asia-Pacific for a greater global role on account of its rise as an emerging trading nation. During this short tenure, Prime Minister Modi has visited number of countries and highlighted his idea of 'Make in India'. There are numerous diplomatic means that the present NDA government initiated to make India's 'Act East' policy more effective and they are:

**First** to establish a vibrant and dynamic economy, putting more focus on economic growth in order to create a much better space for the foreign investors and to set up an affable environment instead of 'red tapism'.

**Secondly**, during his visit to Japan, USA, Australia, Bangladesh, Nepal, Bhutan, China, etc, Modi agreed to set up smart cities, improving infrastructure, producing bullet trains, promoting green energy, strengthening manufacturing capacity, favourable economic environment, etc. Besides this, he has signed number of agreements with these countries. Moreover, Modi through his 'Make in India' doctrine drawing his government's commitments to attract foreign investments to the tune of billions of dollars from Japan, China, Russia, Australia and American big business through this policy. Furthermore, during his visit to Australia, the Prime Minister Modi, through his personal skill convinced and finally it was agreed by the Australian leadership to sell uranium, which has hitherto been dilly-dally in nature. With Japan, during his visit short, the Prime Minister Shinzo Abe, promised to mobilize nearly $35 billion dollars of aid and investment into India in the next five years. Similarly, the Chinese President Xi Jinping during his visit to India set an investment target of about $ 20 billion in the coming years. Besides this, the Modi government also, partially resolved the major knots of the existing nuclear deal with the United States during Obama's India visit to New Delhi from 25-27 January 2015, as a chief Guest at India's 66th Republic Day celebrations. The two countries in order to strengthen global non-proliferation and export control regimes, agreed to work towards India's phased entry into the Nuclear Suppliers Group (NSG), the Missile Technology Control Regime (MTCR), the Wassenaar Arrangement, and the Australia Group. The President reaffirmed the United States' position that India meets MTCR requirements and is ready for NSG membership and it supports India's early application and eventual membership in all four regimes and also reaffirmed his support for a reformed UN Security Council of India as a permanent member. Moreover, in the Joint Statement titled ''Shared Effort; Progress for All" issued during the US President's visit, both the countries evoked: "Noting that India's 'Act East Policy' and the United States' rebalance to Asia provide opportunities for India, the United States, and other Asia-Pacific countries to work closely to strengthen regional ties, the Leaders announced a Joint Strategic Vision to guide their engagement in the region".[17]

**Thirdly,** attempts have been made to use soft power pro-actively and effectively to strengthen its existing bilateral ties with shared civilizational bonds as well as multilateral relations with its partners as a prime means, in order to attract India as a big market and its rise and growth as a major and influential strategic, political, economic international player in emerging global scenario.

**Fourthly,** processed to attract, harness and utilize the energy and economic potency of the Indian Diaspora, who are spread all over the globe for the economic development of India. This attempt of the Prime Minister Narendra Modi with the overseas Indians would remain an important attempt from the perspective of 'Act East' policy.

**Fifthly,** the NDA government is also fully engaged with the emerging political challenges in Southeast and East Asia. The Indian Prime Minister has reaffirmed the centrality of ASEAN in building a stable and prosperous order in Southeast, East Asia and in the Pacific region. He firmly reiterated that the region, where territorial disputes are threatening peace, against the expansionist concepts of the 19th century and sustained the focus on development. On the territorial disputes in the South China Sea, Modi was firm in stating India's deep interests in the freedom of navigation in sea and air. He underlined the importance of all parties abiding by the principles of the United Nations Convention on the Law of the Seas.

6 **Finally,** one of the major achievements of the Modi government is its economic performance with reference to 'Act East' policy. The Average Index Values of CNX NIFTY was 7,083.2 in May 2014, and rose to 8,664.1 in March 2015.The most important indicator of investor confidence is FDI. Ever since Prime Minister Modi shifted focus to 'Make in India', the FDI inflow has shown a remarkable increase of 56 percent.[18] So far as trade figure is concerned with reference to 'Act East' policy, the bilateral trade ties with the countries of Southeast, East Asia and beyond increase very sharply during the year 2014-2015, compared to 2013-2014.

## Major Challenges of 'Act East' Policy

The **first** challenge of NDA government's 'Act East' policy remains the connectivity between Northeast states with other Indian states on the one hand and North East states with India's immediate neighbours, mainly Myanmar and Bangladesh, on the other. In the Northeast region, there are four Indian states namely Arunachal Pradesh, Mizoram, Manipur and Nagaland, have borders with Bangladesh and Myanmar and they are strategically important on account of a number of reasons and they are: First, to develop better linkages with these countries in order to prevent the promotion of cross-border anti-national activities; Secondly, improvement of the economic condition of NER will be essential since this region solely determines the connectivity point from Northeast to Myanmar and beyond; Thirdly, the energy issue is an important factor as Myanmar and Bangladesh are well connected, and also since it is a prime means to addressing the exponentially growing demands for energy consumption at the domestic level. India's energy demands and its connectivity policy, would be essential for cross border communication networks including air, roads, railways and waterways promoting free trade and transit facilities as well as development of trans-national oil and energy transmitting pipelines.

However, the major hurdles with reference to this region are the weak communication link between the Central government and the North Eastern states, which resulted in the existence of lack of 'we feeling'. Besides this, there are important hurdles that the North Eastern States feel and they are: Difficult regional geography (mountains, jungles, waterways); No harmonization of railway networks; No standardization of all-weather paved roads; Inefficient and underdeveloped land border customs stations; Absence of enabling software such as smooth transit procedures; Inadequate use of security personal; Cumbersome trade documentation requirements; Illegal immigration tensions between India,

Bangladesh, and Myanmar; Poor Health policy and weak health infrastructure; Rule of Law and Anti-Corruption; Other Non-traditional Security Threats; Human, Narcotics, and Arms Trafficking and Food Insecurity etc. So, improved governance, increased trade with neighbours, increased agricultural productivity and improve infrastructure, intra-regional connectivity between Northern states and mainland of India as well as to generate a congenial environment to produce goods, which can be exported to the neighbouring countries are the core essential points for the region to re-activate the current government's 'Act East' policy.

The **Second** would be the existence of the Armed Forces Special Powers Act (AFSPA) in the Northeast states of India which could act as a prime hurdle in connecting the region to the Southeast Asian countries. The NDA government must review this AFPSA Act[19] more logically, in order to make its 'Act East' policy more effective in its entirety.

The **Third** challenge will be the lack of infrastructure facilities for the promotion of more foreign investments. To promote this facility, opening and building of more roads, railway lines as well as sea ports will be essential. Already some projects are underway like, India-Myanmar-Thailand trilateral highway, Chennai-Dawei Sea Port Project, Kaladan Multi-Modal Transit Transport Project etc, but besides these projects, more projects with special reference to Air connectivity between North Eastern states with mainland and outside India must be initiated in order to make Modi's 'Act East' policy more dynamic.

The **Fourth** hurdle, which is now directly connected with India's 'Act East' policy, is the development of better ties of India with some South Asian neighbours (mainly Bhutan, Nepal and Bangladesh). This has been evidently clear when Narendra Modi, during the visit of the Bangladesh President Mohammad Abdul Hamid from 18-23 December 2014 at New Delhi, in a speech categorically mentioned that "India's Act East starts with Bangladesh", firmly indicating that Bangladesh will be integrated with the Act East policy and thereby amply signalled that the role of Bangladesh is intrinsic to the success of India's 'Act East' policy. Moreover, his visits to Bhutan and Nepal within six months after his assignment as Prime Minister thoroughly exhibit his clear cut foreign policy orientation. This attempt on India's part would be also essential as a means to persuade the neighbouring countries to halt the various insurgents groups, who are operating and captivating sanctuary in these countries.

**Fifthly,** India's Look East policy of engagement with the region has not been sensible; more often, it appears hesitant rather than lacking in long-term strategy and proper planning. In fact, New Delhi has failed to spell out its interests, concerns and strategic ventures rationally, which often results in substantial bewilderment, especially in Southeast Asian region and beyond. The NDA government through its 'Act East' policy probably attempts to erase these hurdles.

**Sixthly**, a new phenomenon that the present policy makers of India are facing is the emergence of Coalition politics, where on a number of occasions the regional political parties, may or may not be a Coalition partner, often play a very significant role in influencing our various foreign policy issues. This has become particularly evident with respect to the position of political parties in West Bengal regarding our relations with Bangladesh, attitude of parties in Tamil Nadu regarding relations with Sri Lanka and of parties in J&K in the context of our relations with Pakistan. In recent years, political strength of these governments in these States has tended to create road blocks in implementation of policies being pursued by the Central Government with our neighbours. Although, the Modi government, finds itself in a much more authoritative and comfortable position as it commands a majority in the Lok Sabha and does not depend for its survival on support of any of the small, regional parties in these or other states. Since 'Act East' policy remains a long term and not at all a short term policy, what will happens in coming years if this government is not in power, how to overcome these occasional hurdles are very difficult to predict. Therefore, growing federalization of formulation of India's foreign policy particularly with respect to our neighbouring countries remains a vital component of India's 'Act East' policy.

**Finally,** China remains an important hurdle of India's 'Act East' policy. China does not favour a strong Indian presence and influence in Southeast Asia and beyond. China is aware of the various cultural and spiritual ties that India shares with Southeast Asia, which could naturally attract the two regions to come closer. Knowing well that India is the only country that could possibly challenge its ascendancy and potential hegemony in Asia, Beijing tries hard to keep India under pressure. Traditionally, China has been very dismissive of India, treating it as a mere South Asian player. However, over the last two decade or so, the Chinese have been somewhat puzzled and intrigued by the steady rate of India's economic growth and its political stability. So, they have no option but consider India more seriously in the regional calculus. Besides this, China expansion of wings and diversified strategies at multilateral and bilateral levels in the Southeast Asian region through aid and assistance to the ASEAN countries during the East Asian financial crisis and the global meltdown in 2008, thereby earning an enormous confidence from the ASEAN end, which India missed towards this region. China has pragmatically resolved land territorial disputes with most of its neighbours and generated a favourable environment for enhancing its position and economic development process with most of the countries of Southeast Asia. Furthermore, China's continuous political tensions with the claimant countries in the South China Sea have been a great cause of concern for India. China has provided military support to most of India's neighbours and significant assistance to

Pakistan for its nuclear programme, thus becoming a serious destabilizing factor for India. Despite occasional irritants on a number of issues between New Delhi and Beijing, presently China considers India a power in the security architecture of the Asian region, to be reckoned with. Currently, India, through its 'Act East' policy primarily aims at significantly increasing its regional profile. Smaller states in the region are now looking to India to act as a balancer in view of China's growing influence, while larger states also see it as an attractive engine for regional economic growth.

## Conclusion

Having examined in retrospective the 'Act East' policy of the NDA government under the leadership of Prime Minister Narendra Modi, it is quite difficult to assess its achievements since this NDA government has been in power for just more than a year now. However, within this short span of time, NDA government's communications and actions with the United States, China, Japan, South Korea, Australia, Vietnam, Indonesia and the other ASEAN members, novel cooperation with Mongolia and the South Pacific Island nations give the impression that India would like to act as an autonomous pillar in Asian affairs through its 'Act East' policy. In the present scenario, India holds for the future of Asia and other countries of the globe, a template for democracy, inter-faith coexistence, secularism, gender equality and a dynamic, expanding middle-path economy that can become a model for a large number of nations to follow. Right now, it is a key player in the ongoing multilateral negotiations on major global issues, namely trade, climate change, energy security and global security issues, particularly international terrorism and proliferation of weapons of mass destruction. Today, with no political uncertainty on account of acquiring a massive mandate to rule, this NDA government has acquired a safe mode role to re-activate its current 'Act East' policy more dynamically than the past governments and it is generally expected that by creating an image of a responsible major power, a benign power of consequence, systematic and comprehensive engagement with the region, it could play a more vibrant international role in the emerging global order, commensurate with its power and strength as reflected through this policy.

## NOTES

1. *BJP Election Manifesto 2014*, Bharatiya Janata Party, New Delhi, 2014, p. 39.
2. *Ibid*, p. 40.
3. *Ibid.*
4. See http://news4u.co.in/2014/08/time-for-act-east-policy-and-not-just-look-east-swaraj/ (accessed on 26 September 2014).
5. http://mea.gov.in/Speeches-Statements.htm?dtl/24238/Prime_Ministers_ remarks_ at_ the_ 9th_East_Asia_Summit_Nay_Pyi_Taw_Myanmar ( accessed on 22 February 2015).

6. For details see http://mea.gov.in/outoging-visit-detail.htm?5094/PMs+Press+ Conference + following+7th+IndiaASEAN+and+4th+East+Asia+Summit (accessed on 22 June 2014).
7. Tridib Chakraborti, "India's Rendezvous with ASEAN in the New Global Order: Achievements and Pitfalls", *POLITICO,* Vol.2, No.2, 2014, p. 148.
8. *Ibid*, p. 151.
9. *Ibid*, p. 152.
10. For details see http://www.tehelka.com/india-asean-relations-at-exciting-stage-manmohan-singh/(accessed on 21 June 2014).
11. For details see http://mea.gov.in/bilateral-documents.htm?dtl/20982/Vision+ Statement ASEANIndia+Commemorative+Summit (accessed on 21 June 2014).
12. Tridib Chakraborti, n.7, pp.153–4.
13. *Ibid*, p.154.
14. For detailed speech as delivered by External Affairs Minister during interaction with Indian Business Leaders Group in Bangkok on 28 June, 2015, see http://www.mea.gov.in/Speeches-Statements.htm?dtl/25410/Remarks_by_External_ Affairs_ Minister_ during_ interaction_ with_Indian_Business_Leaders_Group_in_Bangkok (accessed on 30 July, 2015); see also *The Economic Times*, 28 June, 2015.
15. *Ibid.*
16. *The Economic Times*, 28 June 2015.
17. http://pmindia.gov.in/en/news_updates/joint-statement-during-the-visit-of-president-of-usa-to-india-shared-effort-progress-for-all/ (accessed on 24 June, 2015)
18. http://www.elections.in/government/one-year-achievement-of-modi-sarkar.html (accessed on 22 August 2015).
19. *The Financial Express*, 27 March, 2015.

# 29

# Sustainable India-Australia Partnership Calls for Rationalization of their Expectations vis-à-vis Preferences

*Y. Yagama Reddy*

## Premise of Expectations

The students of geology, geography, history and international relations, who are specialized in their respective fields concerning the Indian Ocean region, generally entertain fond hopes over the potentials of partnership, simply the prospects of sustained bilateral relations. It is the geological history, in the first instance, unraveling the semblance between the Indian peninsula and the Australian continent in their geological formations and mineral wealth owing to super-continent connection. Geography and history have also bestowed on these nations many complementary features of mutual advantage. India and Australia, thanks to their historical legacy as the British colonies and geographical proximity as the Indian Ocean littorals, have certain shared values and linkages as, for instance, democratic system of governance, English language, accountancy and jurisprudence as well as climatic pattern and crop structure. As logical corollary, there are discernible advantages on a win-win situation basis for both these Indian Ocean littoral states. Evidently, the set of commonalties and complementarities had become conducive to promoting the bilateral relations particularly, the trade, from the beginning of 19th century. But, historiography amply portrays the India-Australia relations as having witnessed longer periods of estrangement intercepted by accidental and brief spells of cordiality. The common denominators between them and their complementary features were found to be no consequence in steering on good stead the bilateral partnership. Thus, India-Australia bilateral relationship is replete with the envisioned prospects and failure of expectations testifying to invidious preferences.

## Unequivocal Contribution of Indians to the Australian Economy in 19th Century

Aboriginal Australia had never evolved any economic system based on agriculture, livestock and mineral wealth; as a logical corollary the newly settled Britishers endured food shortages coupled with famine conditions that forced the British Australia depend on the food supplies from India. Rice was imported from Calcutta by sending 'Sydney Cove' in 1792, a few years after the colonization of Australia in 1788 (Asia Link and University of Melbourne 2008). As the farming undertaken by the convicts deported from Britain was proved to be a futile exercise, Australia's farming became virtually dependent on the itinerant Indians from the early 19th century. Besides largely engaged as labourers in pastoral and sugar industries as well as household servants, the Indian indentured labourers especially the camel drivers, were instrumental for keeping the transport and communication lines open from the coastal cities to the interior parts in early 18th century and later on for developing the telegraph (1870-72) and other construction projects like Central Australian Railway (1870-1929) and Transcontinental Railway from Augusta to Kolgoorlie (1912-1917) (*Australian Encyclopedia* 1958: 156). Having gained thorough exposure to different facets of India during his extensive travel in India much before he became the Prime Minister of Australia (1903-04, 1905-08, 1909-10), Deakin had reportedly observed in his book, *Irrigated India* (1893) that "the future relations of India and Australia possess immeasurable potencies. Their geographical proximity cannot but exercise a very real and reciprocal influence upon the forces of national life in each" (ASSCFADT 1990).

## Australia's White Policy Aberrations

But, the observations of Blainey and Deakin were proved to be a myth in the context of discrimination against Indians who, although declared as the British subjects, were victimized on account of the restrictions on the immigrants all through the period of 19th century. Australians who were proud of being identified as the European 'cultural outpost' at the tail-end of Asia, had a very thin memory of the remarkable contribution of the Indian community to the economic development in Australia in the 19th century. The newly formed Federated State of Australia (1901) had only reinforced the restrictions through its White Policy of 1901. India's wartime help so impressed Australia as to reward Indians through the Hughes' Reciprocity Resolution of 1918 and the four Imperial Conferences between 1917 and 1923. Nonetheless, the privileges became obliterated; and the State legislations discriminated against Indians, who, for practical purposes, remained victims of the White Policy weirdness (Palfreeman 1967: 19- 42). The Indian population had thus hardly witnessed any growth during the period from 1901 (7760) to 1947 (7500), and this does not even qualify for comparison of its growth over a period of 40 years since 1861 (2500) (Hugo 2004, pp. 229-298). Though the Indian Prime Minister Jawaharlal Nehru strongly felt that the demographic composition was essentially a policy of the nation concerned, Indians became critical of the offensive White Australia Policy and its aberrations, despite the Commonwealth connection between India and Australia.

## Envisioned Prospects of Australia-India Partnership

In the midst of Indian misconceptions and resentment over the Australian White Policy, there were well-expressed intentions for strengthening the future relations as, for instance, by Betram Stevens, the Premier of New South Wales and H.V. Evatt, the Australian External Affairs Minister and instances of indicative of the spirit of cooperation at regional and global levels, besides keeping up close and cordial relations. On the eve of opening of the official mission in New Delhi in 1944, Stevens favoured "*close commercial links with India in view of the implicit benefits of trade (for Australia) and of employment opportunities that would improve the living standards of life in India*" (ASSCFADT 1990: 10). Evatt in his message on the eve of independence to India emphasized "*the mutuality of interests and a sense of belonging to a shared region*" based on their "*geographical proximity and common interests in the affairs of Indian Ocean and Southeast Asia...*" (Gurry 1996: 5). His successors, Spercy Spender (1949-51) and R G Casey (1951-63) too envisioned fruitful Australia-India partnership. Newly independent India led by Nehru enjoyed close and sympathetic relations with Australia under the Labour Government of Prime Minister, Joseph Benedict Chiefly. Besides developing a good perception of India's non-aligned policy, Australia also collaborated with India on the issue of Indonesia's independence (1947-49).

## Ideological Divergence eclipsed Benevolence and Support

It was a great incongruity that these colonial cousins began drifting apart along the Cold War ideological equations. The repulsive behaviour in their bilateral relationship was perpetuated due in large part to their differential estimates of security risks and differential methods of ensuring security in the context of Cold War. While India was wedded to the policy of Non-alignment, Australia's responses were determined by its alliance with the Western bloc. To Nehru,

SEATO was an anti-thesis of Panch Sheel; on the other, the Australian Prime Minister Menzies considered security in the area as a collective concept that called for Australia's participation in SEATO, ANZUS and ANZAM (Greenwood and Harper 1963: 342-345). Their arguments were much "deeper than the differences" to the extent of enduring divergence on matters of no relevance to their bilateral relationship and eclipsing the Australian gesture towards India in the form of food-aid in 1950s and 1960s under the Colombo Plan, benevolent assistance on the eve of 1962 Chinese aggression on India and refusal to concede the Pakistan's demand for military assistance during the Indo-Pak war 1965. The proposal of Australian Prime Minister John Gorton that India was to evince real interest in playing a role in Southeast Asia received only lukewarm response from the visiting Indian Prime Minister Indira Gandhi in May 1968 (*AR* 1968: 834-837). India, having wedded to non-aligned policy, was neither mindful of Australia's negligence of India, nor mainly interested to promote relations with Australia. Yet, there was mismatch between the importance attached to India by Australia and the insignificant view of Australia in India's global interests (Neale 1968: 67). All said and done, Australia was the first Western bloc country to recognize the newly liberated Bangladesh through the Indo-Pak War of 1971 (*AR* 1972: 10645-46).

## Poverty of Knowledge-Indifference-Nonchalance

The lackluster relationship, due in large part to 'lack of knowledge of Australia' in India and an 'ignorance or neglect of India' in Australia, made the peoples of both the countries develop exotic impressions of each other. Deplorably, Indians were ignorant of Australia's geographical location and the human geography of the Aborigines, leave alone that of the linkages between India and Australia. On their part, Australians have gained a scanty knowledge of India that it was once a British domain. This was nothing but 'the poverty of communication links', as commented by the Indian Minister for Information & Broadcasting, I.K. Gujral, on 7 November 1972 at the meeting of the Consultative Committee of the Colombo Plan (*IFR* 1972: 7-9). The former Australian Prime Minister, Gough Whitlam, during his visit to India in June 1973, lamented "the inability of India and Australia in forging the much expected 'very close relationship' is as an anomalous... though shared common values in democracy and democratic institutions, links in the commonwealth and their belonging to the geographical region of the Indian Ocean" (*AR* 1973: 11392). Bruce Grant who was then the Australian High Commissioner recollected Whitlam's observation that "India, a great democracy, had been neglected by previous Australian Prime Ministers because of its 'neutrality' in the Cold War" (Grant 2014).

The Labour government of Gough Whitlam attached much importance to improving the relations with India even at the cost of its traditional alliance with the US; and its official reaction was pretty mild in the face of the Conservative Party's intense opposition to India's nuclear tests of May 1974. The succeeding Malcolm Fraser's government got the Whitlam's Asia-oriented policy reverted to the old dictum of alliance with the US and favoured the continuation of the US bases in the Indian Ocean by subscribing to the 'concept of balance' as opposed to the 'Indian Ocean Zone of Peace' championed by India and other Indian Ocean littoral states. The US withdrawal from Southeast Asia and India's enhanced naval capabilities had further widened the gulf for over two decades until late 1980s. Australia was used to look at India as 'a key player' in South Asian politics, a 'champion' of non-aligned movement, and a 'critic' of the US and a 'proxy' or simply an 'ally' of the Soviet Union during the Cold War period. That "Australia has mostly been the suitor and India the reluctant bride" bears testimony to their nonchalant attitude (Gordon 2007).

## Post-Cold War New Economic Order and Bonhomie

The much needed rapprochement between the Indian Ocean littorals was facilitated by the initiatives of the Indian Prime Minister Rajiv Gandhi and his Australian counterpart Bob Hawke. The post-Cold War imperatives of globalization propelled the oft-demurred nations to embark on strategies for reinforcing the bilateral relationship through a series of initiatives like India's Look East Policy (1992) complemented by Australia's Look West Strategy (1994), establishment of Australia-India Council (1992), India Today Festival (1994), DFAT's study of India's Economy at the Mid-night Hour (*EAAU* 1994), and launching of Australia-India New Horizons Campaign (*DFAT* 1996) that had won the bipartisan support. Australia, probably taking India's eventual response for granted, has repeatedly exemplified the commonalities (based on geology, mineral wealth, geography and climate) and the essential complementarities in their economies in pursuit of promoting "developmental cooperation with India on a sounder basis" and identifying the avenues of cooperation in commerce and trade, transfer of scientific and technical know-how, and investment. It was most probably the Cold War political adrift between these two nations that over-shadowed the unequivocal scientific fact all through the four decades until the recession of Cold War. Post-Cold War-related security issues and bilateral trade prospects, has brought these two Indian Ocean littorals closer through certain common denominators. In pursuit of "expanding the awareness and understanding" of each other country *(IDSA NR* 1991: 566), it was Australia that had taken the lead to rediscover the basic linkages (cricket, Commonwealth, accountancy, legal system and English language owing to British colonial legacy), while India was found lagging far behind Australia.

Of much relevance to the present context is the observation of Australia India

Institute (n.d.) in its Submission to the *White Paper on Australia in the Asian Century,* that "strategically, both countries need to work to develop stable and co-operative security architecture for the Asia-Pacific region, and there is a greater urgency for Canberra and New Delhi to coordinate their policies on critical global issues". India has been looked upon to provide security to the sea lanes of communications (SLOCs), particularly to the commercial ships from non-conventional threats like sea piracy, in the corridor spanning the Indian Ocean-Malacca Strait-South China Sea. In retrospect, the Dibbs Report (1987) and the Senate Standing Committee Report (1990) dispelled the apprehensions over India's blue water capabilities. India and Australia have "common security interests" linked with Southeast Asia and "immense potentials for building strong economic and defence ties". ASEAN looks upon India to work closely with ASEAN in combating international terrorism and other forms of trans-national crime.

## Australia's Reaction to India's Nuclear Tests incompatible to Claims of Shared Values

That the Australian mindset had for long been Pacific-oriented was well evident: For instance, the former Prime Minister Paul Keating was opposed to India's inclusion in APEC; the famous 1989 Garnaut Report as well as the 1997 *White Paper* had no mention of India in them. Further, Aus-tralia and India have for long adopted an approach of "rubbing each other up the wrong way on prac-ti-cally every issue on which their in-ter-ests touched" (Wesley 2012). For all the eloquent appreciation of India's economic reforms and self-reliant security mechanism, Australia scorned the India's nuclear tests of May 1998 in the form of a series of sanctions, besides its unsuccessful diplomatic maneuvers at the ARF meeting in Manila (July 1998) towards the end of indicting India. The diplomatic chill between these two nations manifested in a setback to the burgeoning bilateral relationship after decades of stagnation. Unlike the short-sighted official policy, Australian public, nonetheless, showed a better grasp of India's nuclear imperatives (*The Hindu* 1998: 12). While quoting this statement in his *Foreword* to *AII's submission to the White Paper on "Australia in the Asian Century"*, Professor Amitabh Mattoo, Director of Australia India Institute (AII) remarked that:

> ...while New Delhi and Canberra may know each other, they still do not have a nuanced understanding of each other. This needs to change if the two countries are to work with each other and in the interests of the region. Australia cannot afford to have a purely mercantilist approach towards India. Indeed, the Australia-India relationship cannot realize its full potential without a more comprehensive Australian knowledge of India (Mattoo, n.d.).

This gets an oblique support from the statement of the then Deputy Prime Minister and Minister for Education, Julia Gillard in September 2009 that the Australian Government "is committed to building a greater understanding between our two peoples and Australians' understanding of India, its culture, its history and place in the world." In the context of India's role being increasingly sought after by all the regional powers in this region and the Indo-US blossoming relationship, Australia didn't like to find itself lagging behind in forging security and strategic partnership with India. The India-Australia relationship was aptly described by Peter Varghese, Australian High Commissioner to India, in his lecture at the Observer Research Foundation, New Delhi, on 3 May 2012 that "ours was a friendly yet largely undeveloped relationship, punctuated by phases, usually short-lived, when we rediscovered each other" (Varghese 2012). Varghese further observed that India with high moral tone of its foreign policy and Australia being strategically an anxious nation inhabited different universes. While underscoring the need for Australians to come to terms with a dynamic and resurgent India, Kama Maclean, Editor of Journal of South Asian Studies, was critical of the Australians' hypothesis that 'English is enough' to get by in India and their failure to appreciate India's glorious historical, political and social complexities (Maclean 2012).

## India's Expectations and Impediments

Australia expects India's significant role in the emerg-ing power balance in the region, but with an element of doubt over the latter's capacity. Australia's attachment to the mechanics of multilateralism and unilateral assumption of middle power role is something like a loath to India. Democratic India, Wesley (2012) laments, "will almost certainly disappoint such expectations....India has a sense of status that is not matched by its capacity to shape events beyond South Asia; its influence will be rhetorical and potential rather than actual". Even as Australia's unilateral assumption of custodian of Southeast Asia's security concerns and its military engagement in East Timor had incurred the wrath of ASEAN, India expected Australia to accept India's greater role in ASEAN and cooperate with India.

For all its eloquent appreciation of India and its economic reforms, Australia abhorred bureaucratic hassles which remained a major hurdle in the flow of Australian investments into India and the growth of trade; and hence Australians showed nothing but a profound concern for the snail pace of India-Australia relations. The much expected closer Indo-Australian relationship has always faced confrontation between an impatient Australia and a non-committal India. Indians' belated decisions in the eleventh hour have always frustrated the impatience of

Australians who have been used to the line of thinking up initiatives and executing them in short order (Wesley 2012).

But, there was perceptible change noticed in the Australia's *2003 White Paper* and the Foreign Minister Alexander Downer considered the emerging India vitally important to Australia's national interest. For all his China's inclination, Kevin Rudd belatedly include India along with the US, China, Japan and Indonesia. If his foreign minister Stephen Smith strongly supported India's bid to join APEC, so did his Indian counterpart Pranab Mukherjee favour the inclusion of Australia as an observer in SAARC. Considerable improvement in the political and security relationship over a decade no doubt reflects a convergence of strategic perspectives; and this would have been a prelude for the visiting Australian Prime Minister Kevin Rudd in 2009 to share with the audience in New Delhi that India and Australia were "natural partners" destined to become "strategic partners"; and his visit paved the way to take the relationship to the level of a strategic partnership. They are also "natural maritime partners" to attain an increased level of naval cooperation (Bishop 2011) as well as to become "active participants in the provision of maritime security through the entire Indo-Pacific littoral" (Sheridan 2013).

But, Australia is neither a major power that is inherently important to India nor a small and useful "gateway" state, such as Singapore (Brewster 2014). Appreciably, having realized the importance of India to Australia's national prosperity and regional security, Howard had restored the post-Pokhran mired bilateral relations and renewed sense of purpose into the strategic relationship through bold decision of selling Australian uranium to India for its civilian nuclear power needs and Australia entering into a security arrangement—the Quadrilateral Initiative—with India, the United States and Japan. But, what was diplomatically unpalatable was the reversal of decision to sell uranium to India by his successor Kevin Rudd. The ban on uranium sales, as per the joint research paper by the Lowy Institute (Australia), the Observer Research Foundation (India) and the Heritage Foundation (USA), was identified as a key impediment to a closer security relationship between Australia and India. Furthermore unforgivable snub to India was Rudd's announcement of Australia's withdrawal from the Quadrilateral Initiative in the presence of the visiting Chinese Foreign Minister. Equally surprised all was Rudd's unilateral decision to withdraw from the four-power naval exercises which had Australia, Japan, Indonesia and India participating without any prior consultation with India or any others. A series of violent attacks on Indian students in Australia in 2009-10 triggered diplomatic discomfort to India; and a research by Lowy Institute for International Policy observed that 61 per cent of the respondents viewed the attacks on Indian students as a reminiscent of the continuation of the White Australia policy (Sugden 2013).

In fact, Australian disdain over nuclear testing, violence against the Indian students and uranium ban set the Indian minds against Australia.

Being distrustful of rising China, both these Indian Ocean littorals have a common focus convergence in their strategic concerns: India needs to build stronger diplomatic, military and commercial linkages with the countries to its southeast, while Australia realizes a new the strategic importance of the Indian Ocean. Though both are apprehensive of China's insatiable interests and hefty actions, both have differential expectations and preferences. For all his explicit inclination to China, Prime Minister Rudd expected India and Australia to provide a bridge to the Asia-Pacific Community idea and lobbied successfully to have India included in the G20 meeting held in Pittsburgh in September 2009 (Drysdale 2008). "Through shared membership of multilateral institutions including the G20 and the East Asia Summit", Bishop and Medcalf justifiably argued, "Australia and India (are) natural partners to work together to resolve the issues facing the region" (Bishop 2011; Medcalf 2013).

Australia has of late pursued a skillful diplomacy as evident from the announcement of its Prime Minister Julia Gillard that India would be ranked in the same category of strategic importance for Australia as the United States, Japan, China, South Korea and Indonesia (Jain 2012). It was in 2011 that Gillard's Labour Party government tipped over the hoary ban on uranium sale to India for its use in peaceful nuclear programmes, besides the decision to conclude a civilian nuclear-energy cooperation agreement on the eve of Gillard's visit to India on 15-17 October 2012.

In pursuit of understanding the imbalance between these oft-demurred nations, a comprehensive survey of Indian public opinion on key foreign policy issues and critical challenges of governance was conducted in 2012 by the Lowy Institute for International Policy and the Australia-India Institute with 1233 adults across the length and breadth of India representing different strata of society. Interestingly, the Indians ranked Australia in the top four nations, next to the US, Japan and Singapore, besides being appreciative of Australian values. Even as being critical of attacks on Indian students, a strong positive perception of Australia among Indians was discernible: Australia a safe country and a good place to live and to get work (50%) and a country with welcoming people (51-71%); Australia a good supplier of energy and other resources (60%), agricultural produce (57%); Australia well-disposed to India (50%); both countries having similar national security interests (59%) and qualified to be good security partners in the Indian Ocean (56%); and Australia known for excellence in science (61%) and in tertiary education, besides being considered as a preferred tourist destination. All said and done, according to the *Anholt-GfK Roper Nations Brands Index* (2010), Australia's reputation in India as a welcoming country fell dramatically from fifth place in 2008 to 49th in 2010 (Bishop 2011). Similarly, according to the study carried out by Australian Council for Educational Research, there was a decline of 71 per cent (2012) in Indian students in Australia from 120,000 (2009) as against a meager of 20,512 in 2004. Of much significance is the rapidly growing Indian community of nearly 450,000 in Australia (India World Forum 2011).

For all the tall claims and rhetoric of commonalities, there is a lack of complementarity between the two economies (Gurry 1996: 75) manifesting in weak trading relationship. Yet, there has been phenomenal growth in the bilateral trade from $3.3 billion in 2000 to over $20 billion in 2011. Australia is India's sixth largest trading partner and India is Australia's fifth largest. India has its rank among the Australia's export destinations improved from twelfth to fourth over a short span (2003-04 to 2009-10); and the Indian investment in Australia has witnessed impressive growth and vice versa (http://www.dfat.gov.au/fta/aifta).

## Modi's Visit transcending India's Sluggish Attitude

The need of the hour is to develop mutual un-der-stand-ing and adapt-abil-ity in pursuit of obliterating the troubled history due, in large part, to mismatched personalities and lack of commitment. The divergence was persisted on account of lack of reciprocity in the visits of heads of state or heads of government of India. Every Australian Prime Ministers starting with Robert G Menzies— save Harold Holt, John McEwen, John Gorton, William McMahon and Paul Keating—visited India, while only four Indian Prime Ministers (Indira Gandhi, Morarji Desai, Rajiv Gandhi and Narendra Modi) did visit Australia, including the visits on the occasions of Commonwealth Heads of Government Meetings (CHOGM). Glaringly, none of the seven Indian Prime Ministers paid a state visit to the Down Under in the last 28 years, since the Rajiv Gandhi's visit in October 1986; while seven Australian Prime Ministers paid official visits to India since the government of Bob Hawke in 1989. Never in the past had the Indian Prime Minister missed participating in CHOGM. Contrary to this tradition, the Indian Vice-President attended the last CHOGM in September 2011 at Perth; and this simply speaks of India's symbolic importance attached to Australia and India's apathy towards Australia as well. Remarkably, close on the heels of the visit of Australia Prime Minister Abbott in September 2014 Modi reciprocated the visit in just couple of months; furthermore he became the first ever Indian Prime Minister to address the Australian parliament. Unlike the Congress party's rhetorical attachment to nonalignment, the Modi Government is likely to have greater ideological freedom to develop closer security relationships with Australia and other middle powers in the Indian Ocean and Asia-Pacific regions. Accordingly, Modi in Canberra avowed that "Australia will not be at the periphery of our vision, but at the center of our thoughts"; and thus, Modi's visit has paved the way for a new chapter in bilateral ties. Certainly, it was for the first time that Australian and Indian Prime Ministers underscored the growing depth of the Australia-India strategic partnership and building on converging interests, shared values and common democratic institutions as well as harnessing the potential of the economic relationship, especially in priority areas such as resources, education, skills, agriculture, infrastructure, investments, financial services and health (Gupta 2014). Modi's visit has set the tone for the future of the relationship through strengthening people-to-people links to enhance mutual understanding and thereby to improve the relationship to the level of strategic partnership. In pursuit of enhancing India's global diplomacy, Modi strongly believed that subnational governments have a pivotal role in the foreign affairs. Modi has during his visit to Australia in last November called upon' the India Community to contribute to his vision of a 'new India' and for his Make in India' initiative (Jain and Maini 2014). India-Australia relations need to transcend the three 'Cs' and embark on the strategies for deepening trade, security, cultural, educational, and services ties that together provide considerable ballast to the bilateral relationship. Both India and Australia are members of the G-20, Commonwealth, IOR-ARC, ARF, EAS, Asia-Pacific Partnership on Climate and Clean Development, and the Five Interested Parties (FIP) in the WTO context, besides Australia's Observer status in SAARC; and their membership in a gamut of multilateral bodies is not diplomatic tactic, instead it provides a critical platform for strategic economic cooperation between India, China, Japan, Southeast Asia and Australia.

## Conclusion

Despite its two-millennium-long contacts with the Southeast Asian region abutting on the Australian continent, it is ironical that until and after the British colonization of Australia in late 18th century, India was totally ignorant of the geography of the vast continent inhabited far and wide by the Aborigines who have a degree of ethno-linguistic semblance with some tribal communities in the peninsular India. The great distance between Australia and England, as Blainey interpreted in his "Tyranny of Distance" (1966) made Australia to become an economic satellite of India in the late eighteenth century, besides being a colony of England (Blainey 1966, 2001). Similarly, Alfred Deakin was fully convinced of the prospects of Australia-India bilateral relationship. But, the infirmities of White policy had further impeded people-to-contacts; and as a consequence Australia and India were swayed by the exotic impressions that had only perpetuated their ignorance and the state of hibernation.

It is a great paradox that Australia and India which forged partnership during both the World Wars could not share a uniform vision during the peace time thereafter. There was apparent India's reluctance towards the Australian-proposed Five Power Defence Arrangements in the context of India's penchant for the Soviet Union through the Treaty of Friendship and Cooperation (1971) and contempt for Australia's alliance with the US. Australia found no enthusiasm in the expansion of relations with India which too regarded Australia as an ally of the US thereby considered it irrelevant to its interests. It was simply the attitude of 'indifference' that eventually manifested in 'drift and discord' attitude exemplifying the state of impercipience and nonchalance.

Though 'commonalities and complementarities' have become the catchphrase for Canberra, in fact, there had been such efforts made long back by the Australian Prime Ministers (Deakin, Hughes, Chiefley and Whitlam) and the External Affairs Ministers (Evatt, Spender and Casey) who had envisioned the potential prospects of India-Australia cooperation and partnership. The climatic semblance was identified as early as 1879 during the interaction between Sir Henry Blandford (Director of Indian Meteorological Service) and Charles Todd (South Australian meteorologist), and so was the super-continent connection between India, Australia and Antarctica brought to light by Dubey (Director General of Geological Survey of India) in 1953. In the face of disengagement, all that 'extraordinary potential based on so many commonalities', the 'mantra' of shared experiences and 'English is enough' to get by in India would be of no consequence, simply unproductive. These basic linkages have scarcely served to bring them closer, at the most to bring transient reconciliation of omissions and commissions.

India needs to remind itself of its indifference to Australia's proposal in 1968 for India's active role in the Southeast Asian affairs and its refusal to join the Australia's proposed FPDA in 1971 as well as its predicament of having remained as mute spectator of the 1998 financial crisis that worst-hit the ASEAN economies. India's 'betwixt and between' position on account of its implicit inclination to the Soviet Union almost shattered the well-spirited age-old contacts with Southeast Asia. It was simply India's longing for identity contrary to the past. Both these Commonwealth nations have a troubled history of relations; both are termed as being hypocritical in their interests and priorities with scant regard to the other. Both have bitterness of discontented objectives: India's Look East Policy is yet to build up significant economic linkages and power-projections in the Pacific, including its unfulfilled ambition of becoming a member of APEC; and Australia has been equally worried of its feeble grip over the affairs of Indian Ocean.

Certainly, India has been unfortunately displaying a nonchalant attitude in matters of deriving benefit out of Australia's forthcoming fascination for India.

India's has been critical of Australia's inclination to China, but unable to reconcile to the need of adopting action-oriented approach. This speaks of "less about acts of commission than about acts of omission and avoidance of decision-making", laments the former Indian Foreign Secretary Shyam Saran who further points out, "there is a continuing reluctance to acknowledge that the post-Independence framework can no longer meet the domestic and external challenges that confront India today" (Saran 2012).

Despite their abiding interest in the maintenance of a stable strategic balance in the Indo-Pacific, Australia and India suffer from lack of symmetry in the modus operandi due to exigencies of geography and geo-strategy. If India is obsessed with the disgruntled neighbours in South Asia, Australia is relatively secure in its southern ocean. Further, it is highly uncertain of their alignment: India's position in the event of a confrontation of China with the US and its allies in the Pacific as much as Australia's ambivalence in the context of a Sino-Indian confrontation. Australia is equally worried of a predicament in the event of a confrontation between its economic partner (China) and strategic ally (the US). Further, as pointed out by Frederic Grare, Director of South Asia Program at the Washington-based Carnegie Endowment for International Peace, these two Indian Ocean littorals "want to prevent the emergence of a China-dominated regional order. (But) neither country views the other as a potential security provider in the face of China's rise; (as) India and Australia enjoy strong ties to Washington, they have few incentives to look for alternative partnerships" (Grare 2014). As a corollary, Australia is figured in the calculus of India's foreign policy priorities as a third-tier partner among a large group of nations of limited strategic significance to India. Implicitly, the observation of Bonnor that "neither country is central to the other's strategic planning, yet both are influential in regions about which the other wants a deeper understanding" (Bonnor 2001, p.17), is an attestation of "little understanding that each is a crucial element in the other's security" (Brewster 2014) testifying to old rhythm their impercipience stemmed from mutual ignorance and negligence.

It is largely believed that the upsurge in the Indians' settlement would continue; and this trend would have its impact on the spread of social networks which in turn would facilitate the pursuit of strengthening India-Australia partnership. Furthermore, the spirit of bonhomie in their bilateral relationship depends more on the political will than on any other parameter for the integration of these two communities in the spirit of accommodating the interests and appreciating the attitudes of each other. Australia-India relations hold great promise: rapidly growing trade, major economic complementarities, shared democratic values, common security concerns such as terrorism, and potentially convergent attitudes on how to address uncertainties in their shared wider region, the most profound of which is China's rise. The deep complementarity between our two economies serves as stimulant in shaping the future of the Australian and Indian partnership in Asia. India and Australia are on the cusp of an historic opportunity for sharing a new, much more important relationship in the future than they have shared in the past.

## REFERENCES

Asia Link and University of Melbourne (16 July 2008), "High Commissioner's Address at Asia Link", (Accessed 26 August 2009).

*AR (Asian Recorder)* (1968), 14(30), 22-28 July.

*AR* (1972), 18 (10), 4-10 March.

*AR* (1973), 9(17), 16-22 July.

ASSCFADT (Australian Senate Standing Committee of Foreign Affairs, Defence and Trade) (1990), *Australia-India Relations: Trade and Security,* Canberra, Australia Government Publishing Service.

Australia-India Institute (n. d.), Submission to White Paper on *Australia in the Asian Century,* Australia-India Institute, Victoria, The University of Melbourne, *Australian Encyclopedia* (1958), vol. 3: 156.

Bishop, Julie (2011), "Charting the future of Australia-India relations", *Australian Polity,* Vol. 2, No.3. <http://australianpolity.com/australian-polity/ charting-the-future-of-australia-india -relations> (Accessed 22 December 2012).

Blainey, Geoffrey (1966), *The Tyranny of Distance: How Distance Shaped Australia's History,* Melbourne, Sun Books.

Blainey, Geoffrey (2001), *The Tyranny of Distance: How Distance Shaped Australia's History,* Melbourne, Pan Macmillan: 413 p.

Bonnor, J (2001), *Australia–India Security Relations: Common Interests or Common Disinterests?* Working Paper no. 67, Canberra, Australian Defence Studies Centre.

Brewster, David (2014), "Australia-India Strategic Relations: The Odd Couple of the Indian Ocean?" *Future Directions International,* Dalkeith (Australia).

*DFAT* (Department of Foreign Affairs and Trade) (1996), *Australia-India New Horizons: Towards a Strengthened Partnership;* at *http:// www. dfat. gov. au/ media/ Speeches/ foreign/ 1996/ india_ci.html*

Drysdale, Peter (5 June 2008), "Where does Australia really want regional architecture to go?" *East Asia Forum,* http://www.eastasiaforum.org/ 2008/ 06/ 05/where-does-australia-really-want-regional-architecture-to-go/ (Accessed 12 August 2013).

*EAAU* (East Asia Analytical Unit) (1994), *India's Economy at the Mid-night Hour: Australia's India Strategy,* Canberra, Department of Foreign Affairs and Trade.

Gordon, S (2007), *Widening Horizons: Australia's New Relationship with India,* Canberra, The Australian Strategic Policy Institute Ltd.

Grant, Bruce (28 October 2014), "He imagined a different Australia", *Indian Express,* at http:// indianexpress.com/article/opinion/columns/he-imagined-a-different-australia/

Grare, Frederic (2014), *The India-Australia Strategic Relationship: Defining Realistic Expectations,* Washington, Carnegie Endowment for International Peace.

Greenwood, Gardon and Harper, Norman (eds.) (1963), *Australia in World Affairs, 1950-1960* (Vol.2), Melbourne.

Gupta, Sourabh (24 November 2014), "A new vision for Australia-India relations", *East Asia Forum,* at http://www.eastasiaforum.org/2014/11/24/a-new-vision-for-australia -india-relations/ (Accessed 26 November 2014).

Gurry, Meg (1993), "A Tale of Missed Opportunities: Australia's Relations with India since 1947," Marika Vicziany (ed.), *Australia-India Economic Relations: Past, Present and Future*, Nedlands, Indian Ocean Centre for Peace Studies, the University of Western Australia.

Gurry, Meg (1996), *India: Australia's Neglected Neighbour? 1947-1996*, Centre for the Study of Australia-Asia Relations, Brisbane, Griffith University: 105 p.

Hugo, Graeme (2004), "Recent Population Movements between India and Australia: Trends and Implications", D. Gopal and Dennis Rumley (eds.), *India and Australia: Issues and Opportunities*, New Delhi, Author Press.

*IDSA NR (IDSA News Review on Southeast Asia)* (1991), 23 (10), October.

*IFR (Indian & Foreign Review)* (1972), 10 (3), 15 November.

India World Forum (July 2011), "India Australia Relations and Strategic Partnership", *foreign relationsofindia.blogspot.in*, http: // foreign relationsofindia.blogspot. in/ 2011/07/ india-australia-relations-and-strategic.html (Acc. 13 August 2013).

Jain, Purnendra (23 October 2012), "Australia plays catch up in India", *eastasiaforum.org*, http://www.eastasiaforum.org/2012/10/23/australia-plays-catch-up-in-india/ (Accessed 26 July 2013).

Jain, Purnendra and Maini, Tridivesh Singh (8 December 2014), "Modi's new Diplomatic Instruments for a New India", *eastasiaforum.org*, http:/www. eastasiaforum. org/2014/ 12/ 08/modi's-new-diplomatic-instruments-for-a-new-india/ (Accessed 13 December 2014).

Maclean, Kama (9 March 2012), "Australia–India relations and the Economy of Ideas", *eastasiaforum.org*,http://www.eastasiaforum.org/2012/03/09/australia-india-relations-and-the-economy-of-ideas/ (Accessed 17 August 2013).

Mattoo, Amitabh (*n.d.*), "Foreword to AII's submission to the White Paper on Australia in the Asian Century", *Australia-India Institute*, Victoria, The University of Melbourne.

Medcalf, Rory (25 January 2013), "Australia and India: Common Goals, Budding Partnership", *thediplomat.com*, http://thediplomat.com/flashpoints-blog/2013/ 01/ 25/ australia-and -india-common-goals-budding-partnership/ (Accessed 17 August 2014).

Neale, R.G. (1968), "Australia's Changing Relations with India", Millar, J.D.B. (ed.), *India, Japan, Australia:Partners in Asia?*, Canberra, Australian National University.

Palfreeman, A.C. (1967), *The Administration of the White Australia Policy*, Melbourne, Melbourne University Press.

Saran, Shyam (20 June 2012), "A Season of Missed Opportunities", *Business Standard*, http://www.business-standard.com/.../shyam-saranseasonmissed opportunities/ 4... %E2%80% 8E (Accessed 26 July 2013).

Saran, Shyam (15 August 2012), "India's next tryst with Destiny", *Business Standard*.

Sheridan, Greg (20 March 2013), "Australia and India 'could lead region'," *theaustralian.com.au*; at http://www.theaustralian.com.au/national-affairs/ policy/ australia-and-india- could-lead-region/story-fn59nm2j-1226601040340# (Consulted 18 June 2013).

Sugden, Joanna (17 April 2013), "Australia's Reputation Still Poor in India", *Indiarealtime*, http://blogs.wsj.com/indiarealtime/2013/04/17/australias-reputation-still-poor-in-india/ (Accessed 26 August 2013).

*The Hindu* (1998), 30 September.

Varghese, Peter (2012), "Australia-India Strategic Partnership in an Asian Century", *Observer Research Foundation (ORF) Discourse*, Vol. 5, Issue 16.

Wesley, Michael (February 2012), "The Elephant in the Room: Australia–India Relations", *themonthly.com.au*, No. 75, http://www.themonthly.com.au/australia-india-relations-elephant-room-michael-wesley-4522 (13 August 2012).

# 30

# Contemporary Indo-Bhutanese Relations: Challenges for the Modi Government

*Unnikrishnan G.*

## Introduction

The bilateral relations between the Himalayan Kingdom of Bhutan and the Republic of India have been traditionally close. The basis for the bilateral relations between India and Bhutan is formed by the Indo-Bhutan Treaty of 1949, which provides for, among others, "perpetual peace and friendship, free trade and commerce and equal justice to each other's citizens".[1] The Article 2 in this Treaty, in principle, calls for Bhutan to seek India's advice in external matters, while India pledges non-interference in Bhutan's internal affairs.[2] This treaty was updated and signed in 2007 during the visit of His Majesty Jigme Khesar Wangchuk of Bhutan to India and in it the provision requiring Thimbu to seek New Delhi's guidance in foreign policy was replaced with a broader sense of sovereignty for Bhutan.[3] Moreover, India is Bhutan's largest trading partner and India's economy significantly relies on Bhutan for hydroelectric power besides other socio-political and economic overlaps. Recently, Indo–Bhutan relations got a further momentum with the Prime Minister of India, Narendra Modi's maiden foreign visit to Bhutan. Although there are no big agreements concluded, but the Modi's short visit marked his high regard for the South Asian neighbourhood over the extended international community.

## Historical Background

The geo-political scene in the entire Himalayan region and in the Indian subcontinent underwent great change following the formation of the People's Republic of China in 1949 and the takeover of Tibet by People's Liberation Army in 1950. These events, plus the presence of Chinese troops near Bhutan's border, the annexation of Bhutanese enclaves in Tibet and the Chinese claims all led Bhutan to re-evaluate its traditional policy of isolation and the need to develop its lines of communications with India became an urgent necessity (Kohli 1993: 63-64). Consequently, Bhutan was more inclined to develop relations with India and the process of socio-economic development began thereafter with Indian assistance. For India's own security too, the stability of Himalayan states falling with its strategic interest was a crucial factor to consider (Hasrat 1980: 112). With border tensions between India and China escalating into military conflict in 1962, India could not afford Bhutan to be a weak buffer state.

Based on this backdrop, Indo-Bhutan relations began to take on a concrete form following the state visit made by the third King of Bhutan, His Majesty Wang Chuk to India, and by Prime Minister Jawaharlal Nehru of India to Bhutan between 1954 and 1961 (Kohli 1993:88-90). Besides emphasizing India's recognition of Bhutan's independence and sovereignty in his public statement in Paro, Nehru's visit in 1958 was also significant with discussions initiated for development co-operation between the two countries. Formal bilateral relations between Bhutan and India were established in January 1968 with the appointment of a Special Officer of the Government of India to Bhutan (Verma 1988: 78-80). The India House (Embassy of India in Bhutan) was inaugurated on May 14, 1968, and Resident Representatives were exchanged in 1971. Ambassadorial level relations began with the upgrading of residents to embassies in 1978. In addition to this, India is Bhutan's most important economic and trading partner, accounting for nearly 60 percent of Bhutan's exports and 75 percent of its imports, as well as being a vital donor of economic aid to the country.

## Geo-political Importance of Bhutan

The kingdom of Bhutan is often described as being physically small with limited economic scope and military might. In spite of these limitations Bhutan has earned the reputation of being a peaceful country where the development of threats from militancy, terrorism and economic disparity within itself has virtually been absent. In this sense, Bhutan has been more fortunate than many of its neighbours in the South Asian region. Moreover, at first glance, the Kingdom of Bhutan would not seem to be a country that would factor heavily in the calculus of regional powers. But this landlocked Himalayan country has now become increasingly important strategically to both New Delhi and Beijing, and the main reason for this importance is, Bhutan's geographical location (Parmanand 1998: 125–8). Recently it finds itself caught up in a discreet but high stake diplomatic battle between India and China and the main factor which induces this diplomatic battle is the issue of territory (ibid. 130).

The three main territorial areas of Bhutan are the Jakarlung and Pasamlung valleys on the Bhutan-Chinese north-central border, and the Doklam Plateau in Eastern Bhutan. While the first two territories of the north are of interest to China due to their proximity to Tibet, Doklam Plateau is strategically significant to India (Yadav 1996: 148). The Doklam Plateau lies immediately east of Indian defences in Sikkim. The Chinese occupation of Doklam would turn the flank of Indian defences completely and it gave Chinese the commanding view of the Chumbi Valley and the Silguri Corridor. The Silguri Corridor (described by some analysts as a 'Chickens Neck') is a narrow stretch of land that connects India's North Eastern states to the rest of India. If the Chinese were to gain possession of the Doklam Plateau, in the event of hostilities, it would have the ability to essentially 'cut-off' India's land access to 40 million citizens in its north-east territories (ibid. 168). Moreover, there are reports of grave concern to India, like the activities of insurgent groups from north-eastern India which have taken sanctuary along Bhutan's treacherous border with the Indian state of Assam and also the Chinese army's activities in north and north-west Bhutan (Rizal 2013: 12). Apart from the above factors, Bhutan also plays a significant role in ensuring energy security to the region through the provision of hydroelectric power.

## Issues for the Modi Government

While India and Bhutan share an extraordinary warm friendship, issues such as the growing Chinese influence in Bhutan, the liberalization policies in India and its implications for Bhutan and the illegal presence of militants using Bhutan as a base against India are the most important issues that demand greater attention from the Modi Government.

### *The China Factor*

The anxieties about China's intentions is a factor in India's relations with its neighbours now, the same is the case of Indo-Bhutanese relations also. Though neighbours Bhutan and China have not yet established diplomatic relations, and Bhutan is China's only neighbour which does not have diplomatic relations with the People's Republic of China (Kumar 2010: 243–2). Even trade and economic contacts between the two countries are very small and their common border remains closed. This fact must be understood in the larger context of Chinese suzerainty claims on Bhutan till the recent past, border conflicts ranging from cartographic to geographical intrusion, integration of Tibet to the 'mother land' and the China-India relation factor (Bisht 2012: 14–18). The two countries have long- standing differences on the delineation of their common border, which follows the watershed of the Chumbi Valley in the north-west and the crest of the Great Himalayan range in the north.

But the situation is changing since 1970s and thereafter China–Bhutan relation entered a period of normalisation (Mathou 2003: 174–88). In 1971, Bhutan joined the United Nations and voted in favour of giving to the People Republic of China the Chinese seat in the UN. In 1974, China, along with few other countries, was invited to the coronation of King Jigme wangchuk.[4] It was a unique opportunity for Bhutan to assert its personality on the international scene. The Chinese delegation's visit to Thimbu was described by Bhutanese News Agency as a 'new page in the friendly contacts between the two countries' (Ying 2012: 8–10). The Chinese congratulatory message emphasised the 'desire of the Bhutanese government in developing its economy and safeguarding its national independence'. The invitation of a Chinese delegation in Thimbu was a clear message showing that Bhutan was ready to normalise its relations with China. Also Bhutanese table tennis teams visited China in 1977 and 1979.

Furthermore, Bhutan has shown support to China in defeating anti-China drafts at the UNCHR conference, maintaining the 'One China' policy, voting against the drafts on Taiwan's participations in the United Nations and opposing Taiwan's bid to host the 2002 Asian Games (ibid 10). The surprise meeting of the then Prime Ministers of Bhutan and China, Jigme Thinley and Wen Jiabao respectively, on the side-lines of an international summit in Brazil in 2012, regarding border dispute is another remarkable event. Bhutan's Prime Minister described the visit as of great historic significance, as it marks the first meeting between the heads of the two governments. He further asserted that Bhutan must firmly stick to the 'One China Policy' and has strong desire to strengthen understanding and friendship with China (Gopilal 2012: 22–4).

In short, China's pragmatic foreign policy in contemporary times with the smaller South Asian countries indicates that China fully takes into account the geographical and economic importance of Bhutan. China fully knows that Bhutan could hold the key to China's legitimacy claims regarding Tibet and act as the last milestone in discrediting and demoralising India in its own backyard (Singh 2013: 19–22). Moreover, China's continued motivation in engaging Bhutan relates to the strategic benefits its geography can deliver. So like Nepal, China will employ a mix of persuasion and coercion with Bhutan as well as reminding the repercussions of siding with India. With Pakistan, Nepal, Sri Lanka, and even Bangladesh offering China more leverage in South Asia now against India than ever before, Bhutan also could play a critical role for China—firstly in furthering its strategic depth against India's north eastern periphery; secondly in restraining its Tibetan dilemma from spilling over into Bhutan; and lastly in stopping Bhutan from being guided by Indian concerns alone (ibid. 26–8).

This does not mean that China expects a lean from Bhutan to the Chinese side overnight. But it aims at neutralising Bhutan in the wake of any political or military conflict with India and use it as a base to further trade and commerce in Tibet and rest of South Asia. China also induces Bhutan to look up to her as an effective and reliable counterbalance to contain the inevitable Indian domination. Moreover, Bhutan's transition from monarchy to parliamentary democracy saw the revision of the 1949 treaty with India in 2007 and this is a welcome sign for China. The next would be the Indian military presence there. As recent developments suggest, it could be a matter of time that Bhutan moves to balance its tilt towards India (Bisht 2012: 26–7).

## *India's Liberalization Policies and its Impact on Bhutan*

The second important issue of grave concern to Modi government is the issue of India's growing liberalization policies and its impact on Bhutan. Until 1990s, Bhutan has enjoyed more or less protected status in its trade relations with India. With the economic liberalization on the rise in India, Bhutan is facing a gradual loss of this earlier status, and unless Bhutanese industries are able to remain competitive they could lose their market share in the increasingly open market in India. Bhutan has already felt the impact of the reform in India's subsidy policies that has resulted in a gradual phasing out of subsidies and a decrease in India's budget assistance to Bhutan (Yadav 1996: 210–2). Bhutan will also have to face the effects that would be brought on by India gradually moving towards privatizing its power, petroleum and other traditional public sectors. At the same time China looks for more economic, tourism, hydroelectricity and infrastructure related co-operation and resource exploitation within Bhutan; areas where it has a decisive edge. China probably believes that with the rise of economic and other related interaction involving financial stakes, other benefits will naturally occur (Krishnan 2012).

## *Anti-India elements and Bhutan*

The third issue for the Modi government is the illicit establishment of camps by the United Liberation Front of Assam (ULFA), National Democratic Front of Bodos (NDFB) and the Kamtapuri Liberation Organization (KLO) in the dense jungles of South-East Bhutan.[5] The unwanted but continued presence of the above militants on the Bhutanese soil has not only posed potential threat to the friendly relations between Bhutan and India but also created problems for commercial activities of the business sector and affected implementation of development programmes in the country.[6]

The militants started infiltrating into Bhutanese forest after the Indian Army launched operations against the ULFA militants in 1990–1. It was easy for the militants to take advantage of the 266 Kilo meter porous and open Assam-Bhutan border since military posts at that time were mainly concentrated along the north bordering China and the Bhutanese government was largely occupied with the rise of the problems in the southern Bhutan. The presence of the militants inside the country came to the government's attention only in the mid-90s and since then Bhutanese government repeatedly urged the militants to leave the country peacefully. In spite of the Bhutanese government's effort, militants had no real intention of leaving Bhutan until their own objectives had been fulfilled.

## Conclusion and Recommendations

In short, India still maintains an advantage over China in Bhutan case as it has a deep and long-standing relationship with Bhutan. This naturally gives India a wide array of diplomatic options. Firstly, and most importantly, India must ensure that Bhutan will not go the Nepal way, where the perceived creation of dependency on New Delhi and interference by it had caused resentment against India. It pushed Kathmandu closer to China, which is now the biggest foreign investor in Nepal overtaking India.[7] The action by Modi to select Bhutan as the first country for his foreign trip is a welcome sign and he must continue this momentum. It also shows his high concern for the immediate neighbourhood and its geographical and strategic significance.

As Bhutan is on its way to democratization, the number and variety of stakeholders in that country are increasing and India must prop up its foreign policy with consultations across the sectors, particularly the emerging business community. Trust factor is another element which has been an area of strength between both the countries. Efforts should specifically be made from the Indian side to sustain it. There is also a need to focus on technological up gradation. Given that 50 per cent of the Bhutanese population is young and economically Bhutan seems to be opening up and a new generation of Bhutanese youth also seem to be emerging. Thus the key to contemporary Indo-Bhutan relations would depend on the engagement and experiences of this age group.

Finally, the public diplomacy or keeping people at the centre of the bilateral relations is another option for India. Since India–Bhutan share a 699-km long border, interaction across borders should be institutionalised, through frequent border haats. Even while patrolling the area, good contacts with the locals is important. Further, a lot of Bhutanese students are now coming to India for education and more scholarships should be given to them. New Delhi should also make an effort to reach out to the people of Bhutan. A lackadaisical attitude on the part of New Delhi could be detrimental to the relations of both the countries in the long run.

## NOTES

1. As quoted on the website of the Indian Embassy in Bhutan at http: www.eoithimpu.org (last viewed on 15 November 2014).
2. Ibid.
3. India-Bhutan Friendship Treaty 2007, Ministry of External Affairs, Government of India. http:/mea.gov.in/images/pdf/india-bhutan-treaty-07.pdf (viewed on 18 November 2014)
4. The only representatives allowed to attend the crowning ceremony were those of Bangladesh, China, India, Sikkim, the Soviet Union and the United States.
5. The ULFA, Fighting for the independence of Assam; NDFB, fighting for an independent State of Bodoland; and KLO; fighting for an independent State of Kamtapur.
6. Trade routes of at least twelve of twenty districts in Bhutan have to pass through the Indian Territory in Assam.
7. China is the largest FDI source for Nepal, overtakes India now, The Hindu, 26 January 2014.

## REFERENCES

Bisht, Medha (2010): "Sino- Bhutan Boundary Negotiations: Complexities of the 'Package Deal'." IDSA Comment: 19 January 2010. http://www. Idsa.in/idsacomments/sino-bhutan boundary negotiations- mbisht-190110 (Viewed on 30 November 2014)

Bisht, Medha (2012): "Chinese Inroads in to Bhutan: Diplomatic Gimmick or Strategic Reality?". IDSA Strategic Comment: 14 August 2012. http//www.idsa.in /idsa comments/Chinese inroads in to Bhutan- mbisht-140812 (Viewed on 2 December 2014).

Gopilal, Acharya (2012): "When the small Dragon meets the Big One". *IPA Journal*: 30 July 2012. http:/ipa journal. Com /2012/07/30/ when-the-small-dragon-met-the-big-one (Viewed on 8 December 2014)

Hasrat, B.J. (1980): History of Bhutan: Land of Peaceful Dragon (Thimpu: Education Department, Royal Government of Bhutan)

Kohli, Manorama (1993): From Dependency to Interdependence- A Study of Indo- Bhutan Relations (New Delhi: Vikas Publishing House).

Krishnan, Ananth (2012): "China's rail network to touch India's border". *The Hindu*, 18 January 2012.

Kumar, Pranav (2010): Sino-Bhutanese Relations- Under the Shadow of India- Bhutan Friendship (New Delhi: Pragati Publications).

Mathou, Thierry (2003): "Bhutan-China Relations: Towards a New Step in Himalayan Politics". Paper presented at the International seminar on Bhutanese studies, Thimphu, Centre for Bhutan studies, 20-23 August 2003.

Parmanand (1998): *The Politics of Bhutan* (New Delhi: Pragati Publications).

Rizal, Govinda (2013): "China sets up Three Camps; PLA's Patrol inside Bhutan", 29 June, Bhutan News Service, http://www. Bhutannewsservice.com/main-news/china-sets-up-three-camps-plas-petrol-inside-bhutan (Viewed on 12 November 2014).

Sing, Teshu (2013): "India, China and the Nathula understanding Beijing's Larger Strategy towards the Region". IPCS Issue Brief: 9 August 2013. http://www.ipcs.org/pd.f-file/ issue/ IB204-CRP- Teshu-Nathula- pdf (Viewed on 18 December 2014).

Verma, Ravi (1988): *India's Role in the Emergence of Contemporary Bhutan* (New Delhi: Capital Publishing House).

Yadav, Lal (1996): *Indo- Bhutan Relations and China intervention* (New Delhi: An-mol Publications).

Ying, Fu (2012): "It is time for China and Bhutan to Develop bridges of Friendship and Cooperation". Kuensel online: 9 August 2012. http:/www. Kuensel online. Com/2011/ ?p=35042 (Viewed on 5 December 2014).

# Index